# ship

**A History in Art & Photography**

# ship

## A History in Art & Photography

Edited by Andrew Lambert

CONWAY

# Contents

# Contributors

**Andrew Lambert** is Laughton Professor of Naval History in the Department of War Studies at King's College, London. He is a Fellow of the Royal Historical Society and also Director of the Laughton Naval History Unit housed in the Department. His recent books include *Franklin: Tragic Hero of Polar Navigation* (2009), *Admirals* (2008) and *Nelson: Britannia's God of War* (2004).

**Alessio Patalano** is a lecturer at the Department of War Studies, King's College London, specializing in East Asian security and naval history. Alessio is deputy director of the Asian Security and Warfare Research Group and visiting lecturer in Naval Strategy and East Asian Security at the Italian Naval War College, Venice.

**Bruce Peter** is an architecture and design historian working in the Glasgow School of Art's Department of Historical & Critical Studies. His research interests address the Modern Movement in architecture and design and its relationship with popular culture, mass leisure and transport environments. Widely published, Bruce has recently completed *Ship Style*, with Philip Dawson, a book on the Modern Movement at sea. He is also a design journalist, critic and media consultant.

**Colin Jones** is a naval historian and a contributor to Conway's *Warship* annual. He formerly worked in Australian government administration while maintaining a lively interest in other matters. He has written books on a number of subjects apart from the navy, including radio, trams and ferry boats.

**David Cordingly** is one of the UK's leading naval historians. Formerly Keeper of Pictures and Head of Exhibitions at the National Maritime Museum, Greenwich, he is a noted authority on piracy, Thomas Cochrane and the sailing navy. His publications include *Cochrane the Dauntless* (2007), *Billy Ruffian* (2003) and *Under the Black Flag* (1996).

**Geoff Hunt** is one of the world's foremost marine artists. A former President of the Royal Society of Marine Artists, he is well-known as the illustrator of Patrick O'Brian's Jack Aubrey novels although he paints a wide range of subjects both historical and modern. Geoff's books include *The Frigate Surprise* (Conway, 2008) and *The Marine Art of Geoff Hunt* (Conway, 2004).

**Howard Fuller** is Senior Lecturer in War Studies at the University of Wolverhampton. He specializes in nineteenth-century Anglo-American history. Howard is a former Fellow in US Naval History through the US Naval Historical Center and a West Point Fellow in Military History. He is a regular contributor to conferences and journals on both sides of the Atlantic and Associate Editor for the International Journal of Naval History.

**Huw Lewis-Jones** is a historian, media and broadcasting consultant and an expert in maritime and polar exploration history. Formerly a Curator of Art at the Scott Polar Research Institute, University of Cambridge; Visiting Fellow at Harvard University, and Curator of Imperial and Maritime History at the National Maritime Museum, Huw is now editorial director of Polarworld Publishing. His books for Conway include two volumes in the acclaimed Face to Face series; *Polar Portraits* (2009) and *Ocean Portraits* (2010).

**Jean Hood** is an acclaimed maritime and naval author. A former Information Officer at Lloyd's Register of Shipping, her books for Conway include *Marked For Misfortune* (2003) and *Come Hell and High Water* (2006). Jean has also edited two anthologies of first-hand accounts of naval service; *Submarine* (2007) and *Carrier* (2010).

**James Taylor** was an auctioneer with Phillips Fine Art Auctioneers, Head of Victorian Paintings, and former curator of art, exhibition organiser and Corporate Membership Manager at the National Maritime Museum, Greenwich. James is an expert on maritime art, and lectures regularly to a wide of range of societies, including NADFAS around the world. He is the author of Conway's *Yachts on Canvas* (1998), *The Voyage of the Beagle* (2008) and a new work on the art of Fougasse, *Careless Talk Costs Lives* (2010).

**John Blake** spent twelve years in the Royal Navy, leaving the service as a Lieutenant-Commander. He subsequently initiated the licensing of the archives of maritime cartography in the UK Hydrographic Office. John is a Fellow of the Royal Institute of Navigation and the author of the celebrated *The Sea Chart* (Conway, 2003) and *Sea Charts of the British Isles* (Conway, 2005).

**John Jordan** has been the Editor of Conway's *Warship* annual since 2005. He is an acknowledged expert on many aspects of naval history, in particular the French and Russian navies. His Editorship is renowned for its detail and clarity, and he has written or contributed to many books, articles, journals and papers.

**Kate Eberwein** has a BA in History and Astronomy from Vassar College, New York and an MA in Victorian Studies from Royal Holloway, University of London. She is currently completing a PhD dissertation on Salon Culture in Regency London while working at the Royal College of Music.

**Marcus Faulkner** is currently a Visiting Lecturer at the Department of War Studies, King's College London, teaching intelligence and naval history. The focus of his research work is on the development of military intelligence organizations in the early 20th century with particular emphasis on British, American and German naval intelligence and the use of signals intelligence.

**Martin Robson** is a military, naval and maritime historian. He has written a number of books for Conway including *The Battle of Trafalgar* (2005) and *Not Enough Room to Swing a Cat* (2008). Martin has lectured at The Royal United Services Institute, The Institute of Historical Research, The National Maritime Museum, The Joint Services Command and Staff College and the Institute of Romance Studies.

**Mingi Hyun** completed an MA and BA(Hons) at the Department of War Studies, King's College London. He is now Naval Expert & Research Fellow at the Korea Institute for Maritime Strategy (KIMS).

**Paul Brown** is senior lecturer at the University of Northampton and an established shipping, maritime heritage and naval history author. His books include *Britain's Historic Ships* (Conway, 2009) and *Maritime Portsmouth – A History and Guide* (2005).

**Philip Dawson** is an author and journalist specializing in shipping, transport and design-related subjects. His book *The Liner: Retrospective and Renaissance* (Conway, 2006) won broad acclaim. His earlier work includes the authoritative *Cruise Ships: An Evolution in Design* (Conway, 1999) and the best-selling *Canberra: In the Wake of a Legend* (Conway, 1997).

**Richard Endsor** is a seventeenth-century shipbuilding historian and author of *The Restoration Warship* (Conway, 2009). Richard is a trustee of the Nautical Museums Trust, Chairman of The Warship *Anne* Trust, and a member of the Society for Nautical Research and the Samuel Pepys Club. He has written numerous research articles for a range of publications. Richard has also exhibited his own paintings at the Royal Society of Marine Artists.

**Seppo Laurell** is a Finnish sea captain, author and lighthouse historian. He is also Honorary Chairman of the Finnish Maritime Historical Society. In 2001 his children's book *Tervatassuisten*, the story of a ship's cat, was nominated for the Finlandia Junior Prize, and in 2009 his book *Valo Merellä* (Light at Sea) was nominated for the Information Finlandia prize.

**Simon Stephens** is Curator of Ship Models at the National Maritime Museum, Greenwich, overseeing the museum's world-class collection of over 3000 models. He has recently been instrumental in cataloguing and re-photographing much of this important national collection.

**John Lee**, **Alison Moss** and **Matthew Jones** are members of the in-house editorial team at Conway Publishing.

# Introduction

This is a book of ships, but not the best 360 ships, the worst, or even a typical sample. These 360 represent a wide spectrum of ships and vessels, taking care to address form, function, meaning and image, nationality, success and failure, fame and notoriety – in fact and fiction, history, art and film.

Throughout recorded history ships have been the largest moving structures created by man, the pinnacle of technology, the expression of human invention, and the ultimate physical manifestation of the human aspiration to reduce the natural world to order. The ability to build a ship, especially the largest, and most prestigious types, has been a symbol of national might for centuries; a demonstration of technological prowess, national wealth and political power. Little wonder these potent totems have been works of art, conscious attempts to convey messages of power and speed, majesty and elegance, comfort and convenience. The carefully contrived style of such disparate icons as the Athenian trireme, Nelson's *Victory*, the *Cutty Sark*, HMS *Hood* and the *Normandie* reflect different concepts of what is aesthetically pleasing; but all achieve their object, they are unforgettable, emblematic representations of the people who created them and the purposes they were designed to serve. But this is more than a celebration of ship style, of art at sea; it is about what ships mean. With access to the right 'language' and adequate information a ship can be read as easily as a book, it can give up the secrets of its design, function, and purpose.

## What is a ship?

The ship is the single most important artefact created by the human intellect. Ships transformed a world in which humans lived in isolated communities, largely self-sufficient, and often unaware of others into a modern global society, one where events on the other side of the planet have an immediate impact. Ships allowed men to travel for trade, settlement, war and pleasure, they facilitated successive intellectual revolutions, beginning with the essential requirement for navigational knowledge, which kick-started the advanced study of astronomy, meteorology and magnetic variation. Contact with other civilizations made men aware of themselves, of their history, customs and beliefs – of the comparisons that could be drawn across time and space, and how these could be integrated into ever more sophisticated approaches to life, politics and religion. The ship lifted the shackles of parochialism from the minds of mankind, it made us free in time and space. Little wonder they excite a reverence that veers between blind passion and religious awe.

The ship has been an effective symbol of power, progress and prosperity since men have gone to sea to fish and trade long before the dawn of recorded history. In the Aegean, archaeology suggests ships were in use 12,000 years ago, fairly simple craft propelled by oars. It took another 7000 years before sails appear on Egyptian wall paintings. Primitive log boats, rafts and sewn plank constructions had one dominating feature; they could only be built and operated by social groups, extended families, tribes or communities, with a food surplus and accepted methods of apportioning labour between tasks. The ship was, from the outset, a social construction. Building and operating ships required a more consensual society than one dependent upon military conquest, and this may explain the emergence of more democratic political institutions in seafaring communities. In ancient Greece only the Athenians would have called a ship *Demokratika*.

Other seafaring communities, from Phoenicia and Carthage to Venice, Holland and Great Britain have also been at the forefront of political development. In essence, states that acknowledged the value of seafaring by giving ship owners and merchants a stake in society, access to political power, rank and recognition through democratic means, have prospered – while state-controlled maritime activity has generally failed. It is no accident that the modern western tax-raising bureaucratic state was developed in Holland, and carried to an advanced level in Britain, both pre-eminent maritime powers of the seventeenth and eighteenth centuries. Their mixed constitutions, republican or royal, gave merchants real political power. By contrast the maritime empires of France and Spain faltered under the centralized direction of absolute rulers.

Ships have reflected those ideologies. Monarchical power inspired prestige flagships, or in the case of Bourbon France, an entire navy named for King Louis XIV, from the *Soleil Royale* through a host of impressive adjectives. The Dutch preferred more prosaic flagships, *De Zeven Provinciën*, or *Groot Hollandia*, the British employed *Britannia* and *Royal Sovereign* to symbolize the intimate connection between royal and national power at sea. After the 1688 Revolution it remained the King's Navy, but it was paid for and controlled by Parliament.

As the world expanded, societies that avoided going to sea, or artificially limited their interest to coastal fishing soon became victims of more ambitious and dynamic nations. While advanced in many areas the pre-Columbian American societies of Mexico and Peru, the Aztec and Inca, demonstrated no interest in ships, and paid the ultimate price. Others tried to reverse the course of progress. Five hundred years ago the East Asian nations of China, Japan and Korea banned the construction of sea-going ships, only to be forced to reverse that decision in the face of rampant Western imperialism.

Ships, and the ability to use them, have decided the destinies of empire from ancient Athens to the global conflicts of the twentieth century. Ships like the *Santa Maria* of Christopher Columbus explain why south and central American countries are mostly Spanish speaking and Catholic; while the Pilgrim Fathers' *Mayflower* established a slave-free origin for Anglophone North America – in contrast to the earlier English settlement at Jamestown in Virginia. In either case the willingness of the English to cross the ocean to a new continent explains why North Americans speak English. Other ships, such as HMS *Victory*, represent the process that made English the global language of the modern world, and explain why so many people play cricket.

For all our dependence on cars, computers and commercial flight, the ship remains the central transport system of the modern world. Ships are the most economical and ecologically sound option, what they lack in speed they compensate in cost. Without ships we could not afford either cars or aircraft, let alone the fuel they require, and how many computers would withstand overland transport from China is hard to guess. Quite simply ships keep the global economy at work, linking materials, manufacturers and markets. And yet, with a few exceptions, the world has lost sight of ships. As long as the goods keep arriving on our shelves no one needs to think about the ships which carry them, or the business of going to sea.

The military use of the sea is almost as old as the commercial, and has a vast history. However, the tendency among historians of the sea is to divide the spheres: to study wars, and economic activity as if the two were not aspects of one and the same thing – the human will to conquer and control. In classic strategic theory warships are used to secure control of the sea, or sea power; the basis for a strategy that exploits the advantages of the sea against land-bound rivals. Sea power is the ability to use the sea for military and economic activity, while denying the enemy the same opportunity. The obvious advantages lie in applying power from the sea to the land. In the first half of the twentieth century the raids and petty invasions of the distant past were replaced by massive combined operations and aircraft carrier strikes that produced strategic, even decisive effects in global conflict. The arrival of the atomic bomb transformed the strategic role of the sea. Sea-based strategic weapons, initially carrier-based bomber aircraft, and then submarine-launched ballistic missiles, mean that four of the world's five major nuclear powers have a significant part of their strategic deterrent constantly at sea – out of sight, but never out of mind.

Because so many countries depend on sea-based economic activity, the blockade – using naval forces to control shipping – became a significant strategic instrument. The ability to cripple a country's economy, or its food supply, provided navies with a serious alternative to military occupation. This option, suitably re-named an 'embargo', is now the United Nations' preferred method of using non-lethal force to resolve diplomatic difficulties. Like the blockades of the past it remains a slow, deeply flawed weapon, more useful against some nations than others, and likely to inflict suffering on those least able to respond.

In periods when command of the sea is in question, sea powers have used ships designed to acquire and sustain command, ultimately by defeating any hostile force in battle. The ships of the line, or modern battleships, are the classic vessels built for this type of warfare – and normally operated in fleets or squadrons. While naval history used to focus on rare, but climactic battles such as the Salamis, Actium, Lepanto, the Armada, Trafalgar and Midway, modern scholars have emphasized the longer-term issues of sustaining and exploiting command, of the dockyards and bases that maintain ships, and of alternative strategies.

For all their drama, serious contests for command of the sea between approximately equal powers have been rare. More common is the situation where one power has command, and the weaker rival tries to deny them the full benefits of that command. The options were to keep a smaller battle fleet 'in being' to deter action, by deploying a coast-defence navy, or a commerce-destroying force. This last option, using privateers in the sailing-ship era, or submarines in the two world wars of the twentieth century, sparked a range of ship developments. Coast-defence warships using conventional weapons usually sacrificed range and speed to obtain the critical advantage of shallow draught. Others relied on new technology or new weapons – the torpedo boats, motor torpedo boats and, more recently, missile boats.

The submarine, in fact and fiction, was always the great leveller. Jules Verne employed the *Nautilus* to enforce world peace, Irish-American John Philip Holland built his submarine to sink the hated Royal Navy, with help from the Irish Republican movement. Ironically the British were the first international customers for the Holland Boat. Their object was to understand the threat, and counter it. In two world wars they would face a determined and efficient German *unterseeboot* force, and on both occasions would win a grinding battle of attrition that inspired the development of specialist anti-submarine warships, sloops, corvettes and frigates. The sinister allure of the submarine – dark, silent and unseen – forms a powerful alternative to the pomp and parade of surface craft.

Like any economic agents seafarers have been subject to crime. Piracy was a problem before history; it remains a threat today. Once divested of the *Black Pearl*'s Hollywood glamour, piracy is no more than armed robbery at sea. It is often linked to economic hardship, unemployment and opportunity. The definitive sea monster Edward Teach, better known as Blackbeard, emerged in circumstances that repay study. After almost 30 years of warfare between maritime empires in the West Indies, a large number of men had become professional privateers, licensed predators. When the war ended their careers, most turned to legitimate employment, but a hard core abandoned their allegiance to states and turned pirate. The weakness of local authority and the easy money made the option attractive. But once the national authorities were forced to recognize the economic damage caused by piracy, they were quick to react. Warships and professional warriors made short work of the pirates – even the ferocious Blackbeard. Ships like the recently re-discovered *Queen Anne's Revenge* occupied the world stage for a brief moment, but the problem they symbolize will endure for as long as men live on a planet with oceans.

But for all the drama of piracy and war, the greatest danger to ships and seafarers is the sea itself. The sea has always been a dangerous place, investing any ocean passage with a heightened emotional meaning. Any ship can sink, but some are more dangerous than others. The ocean-going square-rigged sailing ship was one of the most lethal means of transport ever devised. The combination of large amounts of canvas spread to catch the wind, limited or non-existent meteorological forecasting and the changeable nature of the weather, placed a premium on the experience of the mariners. Only long experience could equip captains with the knowledge needed to anticipate the weather and take in sail before the wind changed. To learn those skills boys went to sea very young, and preferred practical experience to book learning.

The disasters of sea, combining elemental force and human suffering on a large scale, have turned some ships into household names, famous only for the manner of their end, and the human cost it entailed. Like any man-made object, ships are flawed, products of the human condition, as like to be good as bad. The *Mary Rose*, *Vasa*, *Medusa*, *Captain* and *Titanic* have made the transition from ship to icons of disaster, hubristic emblems of human frailty in the face of the natural world.

## Meanings

While the uninitiated might assume that the craft used to exercise such disparate functions as fishing, fighting, trade and travel would be prosaic and, of themselves, quite insignificant, this would be a serious mistake. In all seafaring cultures, but only in such cultures, ships have been invested with a striking range of meanings and characteristics.

Ships have excited the imagination since men first used log rafts. The ability to float, move and face the mighty ocean has invested them with rich and strange meanings. Little wonder that ships have inspired the highest tributes that the human condition can achieve – in words, wood, steel, aluminium and composite materials. They have been recorded in oil and ink, words and print; photographed; carved, painted and decorated; worshipped, burnt and deified. Throughout recorded history, men of genius – scientists, mathematicians and engineers – have applied their talents to the business of going to sea. The history of the ship is the history of man as a creative animal, of the desire to exploit the waters, to travel and discover, conquer and plunder.

In 1856 poet, philosopher and artist John Ruskin put the ship into a cultural context, one that dovetailed perfectly with his hatred of industrial production, his love of craft design and social aesthetic:

> Take it all in all, a Ship of the Line is the most honourable thing that man, as a gregarious animal, has ever produced. By himself, un-helped, he can do better things than ships of the line; he can make poems and pictures, and other such concentrations of what is best in him. But as a being living in flocks, and hammering out, with alternate strokes and mutual agreement, what is necessary for him in those flocks, to get or produce, the ship of the line is his first work. Into that he has put as much of his human patience, common sense, forethought, experimental philosophy, self-control, habits of order and obedience, thoroughly wrought handwork, defiance of brute elements, careless courage, careful patriotism, and calm expectation of the judgement of God, as can well be put into a space of 300 feet long by 80 broad. And I am thankful to have lived in an age when I could see this thing so done. (Ruskin, J. *Harbours of England* p.25)

For this achievement, and this alone, he considered his own century was worthy of reverence. Fascinated by the relationship between the ship and the sea Ruskin believed the evolution of the ship, from primitive raft to modern ship bore witness to something innate and wonderful:

> …through all these changes, it gained continually in grace, strength, audacity, and beauty, until at last it has reached such a pitch of all these, that there is not, except the very loveliest creatures of the living world, anything in nature so absolutely notably, bewitching, and, according to its means and measure, heart-occupying, as a well handled ship under sail in a stormy day. Any ship, from lowest to proudest, has due place in that architecture of the sea; beautiful, not so much in this or that piece of it, as in the unity of all.
> (ibid. p.18)

If it required a poet of genius to find the sublime in a ship, and enable others to see the same, his legacy is that every modern ship reflects a conscious design process; it possesses a meaning that can be read by those who know the language. While ships are works of art, and some reach the level of Ruskin's sublime, a picture of a ship is a secondary thing, if it be an honest attempt to represent the work of man.

4

By contrast artists have used ships to tell stories, illuminate the drama of the sea and link man with the ship, from Attic painted vases to Turner's 'Fighting Temeraire'. Ship portraits, battle scenes, harbours, docks and broad oceans offer an endless range of options, from factory-fresh icon to Clarkson Stanfield's 'The Abandoned', a terrifying examination of human despair that caught Ruskin's eye in the Royal Academy exhibition of 1856 – a 'very beautiful picture' that led men 'to meditate upon fate' [Ibid.p.27]. Little wonder he worshipped Turner, and considered the Temeraire his last great picture.

## History

The lives of ships offer another point of entry. Some ships begin life as icons; others become iconic through design or performance; yet others, the majority, achieve fame in use. Some of these ships stand out from the crowd because they represent larger processes: Nicholas Monsarrat's Flower class corvette HMS *Compass Rose*, the war-winning American Liberty Ship the *Jeremiah O'Brien*, and the *U-99*, protagonists in the Battle of the Atlantic, the greatest naval campaign of them all. These vessels represent vast fleets of escorts and transports built to wage the last great struggle between land and sea, mass-produced twentieth-century hardware, created on a heroic scale, and yet each with a unique tale to tell.

Then there is the tragic *Captain*. Named for Nelson's flagship at Cape St Vincent, this flawed Victorian wonder weapon was driven under the waves by her own sails, taking her inventor, and all but a handful of her crew to their doom. The *Vasa*, flagship of a Swedish Empire, named for the royal dynasty, and created to represent the might of a monarch, was a disaster. It turned over and sank within minutes of setting sail. Because it survived almost intact it has become our gateway to the world of the seventeenth-century ship, and because it was the prestige flagship it combined art, power and the ultimate argument of kings, a mighty battery of bronze artillery.

The ship has always been a compound of many requirements. It must float, move under power, carry men and cargo, support activities at sea – from fishing to fighting – and do so for an economically useful period of time. To meet these requisites ships quickly evolved from the first simple water craft into increasingly specialized types. While they were built of wood and powered by sails or oars, there were significant limits on what could be achieved; indeed the eighteenth century witnessed something approaching technological stasis, only for the science of design to emerge, and lay the foundations for new developments.

The size and design of ships reflects the limits of material technology. Wood limited the size of ships, while the limits of metal technologies decided how that wood could be processed. Ancient Greek and Roman ships were built with advanced carpentry methods that were only possible with high-quality saws. By contrast the Vikings lacked steel saws, and had to cut their plank with axes, and used simpler joint techniques. The Venetian Arsenale developed a system based on the use of written treatises and plans, in part inspired by ancient technology, which it used to mass produce war galleys in times of crisis. Northern Europeans built ships as unique craft products, each one differing from the last, even when the same plans were employed. While scientists tried to improve the theory of the ship, as a structure and moving object in a resistant medium, they found the imprecise, uneven and impermanent nature of the basic material limited the application of their results. Only when wood was finally replaced by iron and steel could the naval architect escape the ivory tower of advanced mathematics, and come down to the shipyard.

That said, the wooden ship reached its zenith after the Industrial Revolution. Driven by the pressures of war, timber shortage and structural weakness, the British naval architect Sir Robert Seppings developed a new wooden ship, one that could be doubled in size and carrying capacity, and met the new demands placed on the ship by crude, heavy, rumbling steam engines – monsters that stressed the need for new materials. The same Industrial Revolution produced economical iron and then steel plates, welding, aluminium and other exotic materials; a process that began with Isambard Kingdom Brunel's epochal SS *Great Britain* and culminated in the titanium-hulled Soviet Alpha class submarines, before moving on to make extensive use of carbon fibre and other laminates. The history of this process has often been told, but the meaning all too often escapes understanding amid a welter of detail. The ship is the inspiration for progress, for new ideas, new solutions, new technologies and new packages. Ultimately it is a complex machine, one that requires a balance of experience and innovation. Because men think faster than they build, progress has been pushed by ideas and ambition, and technology has usually been the answer, not the opportunity.

For Brunel the ship was the ultimate template on which to hammer out the meaning of genius, to prove himself the worthy son of an illustrious father, and to make his mark on the world as 'the engineer'. He built ships that changed the course of history, the paddle-wheel Atlantic liner *Great Western* and the iron screw liner *Great Britain*. That his last ship, the *Great Eastern*, was a monster, a true Leviathan, three times larger than any other ship of the age, was only one way in which his achievement surpassed that of all other creative men.

As a mighty technological solution to a problem that did not exist the *Great Eastern* said more about the state of the British Empire in the mid nineteenth century than any other artefact. At the same time single-minded perfectionists drove the development of specific ship types or systems to their ultimate expression in such perfect packages as Hercules Linton's *Cutty Sark*.

While their complex construction has a fascination all of its own it should not obscure the meaning of the artefact. Ships convey a range of potential meanings. Rarely has this mix of advanced technology and iconic power been more obvious than in 1906. After fifteen years of design stability a new British battleship changed the standard of naval power. The revolutionary *Dreadnought* gave her name as the generic descriptor for every battleship that followed, but it was an ancient name, richly encrusted with three hundred years of accumulated glory, the mythic power of the Armada and Trafalgar. The Elizabethan love of compound words created an inspired, poetic embodiment of the purpose of the ship. The name has remained in use for more than 400 years, surpassing every other warship name to become a noun forever linked with the genius of Admiral Lord John Fisher, and one that retains a strongly naval flavour in the latest version of the *Oxford English Dictionary* (2nd edn, 1989).

While she represented a quantum leap in fighting power *Dreadnought* was not built to fight. The British had no reason to expect a major war in 1906, and no desire to start one. Britain had secured the 'lions' share' of the world, dominating the capital, finance and shipping services that exploited her unquestioned naval mastery. Britain's national interests lay in preventing a major conflict, and so she used her wealth, advanced technology and shipbuilding industry to send a signal to her imperial competitors. *Dreadnought*, the ultimate technology demonstrator of the Edwardian era, was built to sustain the century old British strategy of avoiding war through the possession of overwhelming naval force. The British Empire secured peace and expansion with arms races and deterrence. This was why *Dreadnought* was built, why she was given such a potent name, and why the design was consciously styled to achieve maximum visual effect. Germany accepted the challenge, beginning a 'Dreadnought' arms race, only to find the British possessed deeper pockets, more shipyards, and were willing to raise the technical stakes. By 1912 the race was over; the British had won, without firing a shot.

## The purpose of ships

Ships are not random or accidental creations. With few exceptions they have been made by rational men, for obvious reasons – reasons that should be revealed by a careful study of their design. To take the famous clipper ship – the sharp hull and massive spread of canvas reflected the commercial premium that could be made carrying low-bulk, high-value cargoes on oceanic routes before economic compound steam engines. Emigrants to California or tea from China warranted the reduced carrying capacity, extra crew and the higher running costs. More modern craft are equally simple to deconstruct. A warship's draught of water, fuel supply and freeboard normally indicate the intended operational environment, while the weapons and sensors fitted quickly differentiate between roles. Commercial ships are even more task specific than warships; commercial logic determines they will achieve greater mission specialization, and require less flexibility. The faster pace at which merchant ships adopted steam propulsion in the 1820s and 1830s was often held up as an example of naval conservatism. The simple fact is that primitive steam engines were far more useful for commercial shipping on pre-determined routes, running at regular speeds. Unreliable, inefficient and uneconomic engines remained an auxiliary power for navies for another two decades, because they were incapable of providing long distance cruising and reliable performance.

## The impact of technology

The opportunities and dangers of the sea have ensured that sane men try to make their ships as safe as technically possible. But technology has always lagged behind the human imagination – imagination that has inspired the endless process of development. The emergence of iron and steel as shipbuilding materials merely increased the options open to innovative designers. Iron hulls improved the ability of ships to carry heavy loads, be they cargo, engines, guns or armour. The first armoured warships, the Crimean war batteries, used 4 inch (10cm) thick wrought iron plates to keep out exploding shells. They were tested on battle at Kinburn on 17 October 1855. They proved the concept.

By 1860 the iron ship allowed nations to design warships that met their specific strategic needs. The British built ocean-going capital ships to control the seas, and coast-attack craft to carry that control on to the enemy's coast and into his harbours. The epochal iron-hulled armour-plated frigate HMS *Warrior*, completed in 1861, used the new materials to enhance the design of the last wooden-hulled frigate. While aspects of her design – the knee bow, figurehead and elegant above-water lines – belonged to an earlier age, others – the armoured battery and breech-loading rifled guns – were entirely new.

Across the Channel, the famous *Gloire* had a fatal flaw; her wooden hull was rotten within a decade. French industry simply could not produce the quantity of metal needed to build an all-iron battlefleet.

During the American Civil War (1861–1865) both sides built shallow-draught ironclads – the south for defence, the north to fend off the British, and then to attack the south. John Ericsson's Federal *Monitor* provided the smaller European navies with a model that met their coast-defence mission to perfection.

But for every new technology of war there is an obvious answer. Armour plate, initially 4 inches (10cm) of wrought iron, promoted ever larger guns. *Warrior* fired 110lb shells, by 1873 HMS *Devastation*'s 12 inch (30cm) rifles fired 700 pound projectiles. In 1915 the new *Warspite*'s 15 inch (38cm) guns fired projectiles of 1920 pounds, and could fire over the horizon. These guns forced the pace of armour development: wrought iron soon gave way to iron-steel compounds, and complex steel alloys. The cost of armour was astronomical, but no one wanted a ship without protection.

The relative invulnerability of ironclads to artillery emphasized the importance of underwater weapons. Although attempts had been made to sink wooden sailing ships by underwater attack there was little need – big warships rarely approached the coast. Between 1855–1865 steam engines and iron armour decisively changed the balance of power between ships and forts, prompting the rapid development of mines and then torpedoes to counter the enhanced strategic power of ships by preventing them from operating on the coasts of weaker powers. The minesweeper, the torpedo net and the torpedo boat destroyer soon followed.

When detection equipment entered the electronic age with sonar and radar, the response was predictable – current 'stealth' technology mirroring the desperate efforts of the U-boat arm to cloak their boats in non-reflective rubber in the Second World War. In both cases the object is to avoid being detected by non-visual means – to avoid being hit. Modern warships are not designed to absorb damage: the old armoured strength of the battleship has given way to an electronic defence system.

## Changing roles

For much of recorded history warships were little more than armed merchant ships. Only when the ability to use the sea, and deny it to others, was worth the cost did nations construct purpose-built warships. The ancients knew that victory at sea could change the course of history, as the battles of Salamis and Actium demonstrated. This is why the advanced civilizations of the ancient world built oared galleys with a single-function weapon system that represented a massive investment of manpower and materials – the massive bronze ram. Little wonder the major wars were won by the richest powers.

The end of the ancient world witnessed the abandonment of the specialist warship. Pirates and raiders like the Vikings, seafarers who resorted to violence on land, rarely needed to fight at sea. Their open-decked oared 'long ships' were ideal raiding craft, to supplement more seaworthy 'round ships' used for trade and settlement. When the Vikings fought at sea they lashed their long ships together, to form a fighting platform. The English King Alfred the Great is credited with meeting the Vikings at sea, with larger and more heavily manned versions of their ships, but the details remain obscure. The Vikings used tough, seaworthy ships to spread trade and political power, from Scandinavia to the New World, colonizing Iceland and Greenland, securing colonies in Ireland, Normandy and Eastern England, founding Russia and linking the Baltic with the Black Sea by river.

Early medieval Europe used very different ship types in the North Sea, Atlantic and Mediterranean. Ocean-going clinker-built Viking types evolved into larger vessels, the Bremen Cog being a good example of the merchant ships used to move cargo around this area. A few high-value oared craft remained for prestige purposes. In the Mediterranean larger ships and oared craft evolved along very different lines. The Venetians made a conscious effort to recover the design and construction technologies of the ancients; knowledge they put to good use in their massive arsenal, the basis of Venetian power and profit. That the very word arsenal is of Arabic derivation (*dar sena* or workshop), reveals the conduit by which Greek and Roman ideas reached Western Europe. Admiral is also an Arabic word (*amir al bahr*), adopted by the Spanish. Both powers were in constant contact with the Muslim world of the Near East and North Africa.

By the fifteenth century Northern European powers were building very large sailing ships, primarily for war. Large Gascon wine traders were developed by the English into massive infantry combat platforms to control the English Channel. King Henry V's *Henri Grace á Dieu* represented something of a dead end: too expensive to man and use, it was laid up after Henry's death. Big ships only made economic sense if they possessed overwhelming advantages.

In the following century the introduction of Mediterranean hull construction methods, sophisticated rig and heavy cannon transformed the military value of the warship. When Henry VIII's *Mary Rose* went into battle in 1545 she carried enough heavy guns to inflict serious damage on another ship, as well as archers and musketeers. Over the next century the warships and the merchant ship began to diverge. In 1588 many of the English ships that defeated the Armada were armed merchantmen, but they did not take a prominent part in the fighting, until Drake used some of them as fireships.

The increasing availability of heavy iron cannon pushed warship design along a very specific route. The need to carry up to 100 guns, each weighing up to 6 tons, placed a premium on structural strength. This strength was equally important to resisting the savage, attritional bombardment of projectiles that characterized the sea fighting between 1650 and 1815. Cannon crippled ships, and killed their crew, but they did not inflict mortal blows. Ships were lost when the crew lacked the manpower, or the will to fight on.

However, the purpose of the warship has never been restricted to war. Throughout recorded history warships have been the most potent representatives of a naval power. Prestige ships, iconic embodiments of royal or national power have been a commonplace. From Gustavus Adolphus's ill-fated *Vasa*, and Charles Stuart's *Sovereign of the Seas*, to the Imperial Japanese Navy's *Yamato*, monster battleships have been an obvious symbol – a floating demonstration of power, technology and wealth, one that could be deployed to support diplomacy, or threaten war. Every megalomaniac with a coast either possessed such a symbol, or lusted after one. Even Stalin could not resist, but his flagships were still-born, victims first of Operation Barbarossa, and then his own death. In the language of warships deterrence is an important word.

In the twentieth century the emergence of wholly new ways of fighting, under the sea, and then in the air, created new warships. The submarine, the dream of Cornelis Drebbel and Robert Fulton, became a useful weapon when John Holland's craft was powered by diesel engines and rechargeable batteries, and armed with heater torpedoes. In September 1914 *U-9* proved the technology in a single afternoon, only a month after the First World War began. But thereafter they were not so effective in their designed role of sinking warships. Instead the submarine became the ideal commerce raider, the perfect replacement for privateers and corsairs. It spawned new warships, anti-submarine escorts, the modern sloop, frigate and corvette, and new technologies, sonar and magnetic anomaly, to locate the unseen. Post 1945 nuclear power released the submarine from dependence on the atmosphere for power and ventilation, while the ballistic missile gave it a new role, upholding peace through deterrence. In that role it has replaced the mighty battleships of Nelson and Lord Fisher; little wonder the British ballistic missile submarines carry names made famous in countless battles, from the Armada to Jutland. These are the capital ships of the modern age.

Another twentieth century technology, the aeroplane, prompted the development of the aircraft carrier. In the First World War increasingly radical conversions of existing warships and merchant ships provided the capability to take wheeled aircraft to sea, initially just to launch, then to recover. The Washington Treaty of 1922 halted a new round of capital ship construction, leaving Japan and the USA with unwanted half-built battlecruisers and battleships. Four were reconstructed as gigantic aircraft carriers, *Akagi* and *Kaga*, *Lexington* and *Saratoga*. From these ships important lessons were learned, and by 1939 Britain, Japan and the USA had new, purpose-built carriers. When HMS *Ark Royal* crippled the German battleship *Bismarck* in May 1941 it was clear that the age of the battleship was drawing to a close. This reflected a more complex process than is often acknowledged. The battleship remained the strongest, and the most powerful fighting ship, but it lacked the range and flexibility of the carrier. The reach of a battleship was little more than the horizon, that of the carrier was limited only by the range of her aircraft. After 1945 the carrier made more sense because only three nations had modern battleships, the USA, Britain and France, and they were allies. With no hostile battleships to fear such ships were too costly to operate in peace time, given their inflexibility. The revival of the American *Iowa* class battleships in 1950, 1967, and 1982–91, however, reflected their key advantages; namely the ability to project power ashore cheaply and accurately, without risking pilots.

At the Battle of Midway in June 1942 a massive Japanese fleet was defeated when three American carriers, *Yorktown*, *Enterprise* and *Hornet* sank all four Japanese carriers. Without his carriers Admiral Yamamoto's armada of battleships and cruisers, troop transports and destroyers simply turned round and went home. Naval air power was the key to victory in the Pacific, and a major contribution to the final defeat of the Atlantic U-boat campaign. In both cases mass production became the norm. U-boats, merchant ships, escorts and aircraft were mass produced, built in sections, often miles from the sea. Industrial age warfare had industrialized shipbuilding to an unprecedented degree, and laid the foundations for modern ship technology.

Postwar the American carrier fleet survived the attempts by the United States Air Force to cancel new construction, proving in a series of wars from Korea to the Gulf that the mobility and sustainability of well-handled carrier task forces is the key to effective overseas deployment. Even the British, who had abandoned the carrier, were saved from humiliation in 1982 by innovative vertical/short take off and landing Sea Harriers, an old ex-carrier, and a new ship that had been masquerading as a helicopter cruiser. The decision taken in 2007 to build two new 65,000- ton carriers marks a radical reversal of policy, and a recognition that the future of the large deck carrier is assured, for half a century at least. Quite simply Britain cannot act as an international player without the ability to deploy aircraft, men and helicopters across the globe, and the large deck carrier is the only option. The *Queen Elizabeth* and the *Prince of Wales* will represent the country for decades to come, statements of power that can be deployed across the globe.

In wartime, navies were always desperate for more ships. The old tradition of making extemporized warships out of commercial ships carried on long after the sailing ship era. For Drake and Nelson merchant ships were used as privateers, fireships, makeshift fighting ships and troop transports. In the world wars armed merchant ships, liners and tramps, replaced scarce cruisers as raiders, or escorts. No better example of the type could be found than the armed merchant cruiser HMS *Jervis Bay*, which was lost in a hopeless, one-sided battle with a powerful German warship, and saved her convoy in the process.

## Merchant Ships

As soon as ships were used for commerce specific design functions began to evolve – designs that maximized profit. The Dutch *fluyt* or fly boat provided low cost carriage in Northern European waters, once the threat of war and piracy had passed. Lightly built, with shallow draught and a small crew, they sustained an exchange of fish, grain, timber and other goods between Holland and the Baltic. Once piracy had been crushed merchant ships did not need their own defences.

Such exceptions aside, the development of vessels to support fishing and trade followed an obvious path; larger, more efficient or more economical types gradually replacing older designs, new technologies being adopted when they offered real advantages, while the sea provided the ideal medium for the exchange of ideas by contact across national boundaries. Regional craft evolved to suit local conditions; the dhow, the junk and Inuit Umiak might not fit into European ideas of ship design, but they evolved over centuries into craft that served local needs with local resources.

Among the many commercial ship types some, like Atlantic liners, clippers and East Indiamen have achieved particular status, their style and purpose elevating them above the common herd, while others, often more significant, lack their iconic presence.

In the nineteenth century the severely practical approach to commercial shipping that had driven design for centuries was interrupted by the growth of nationalism and aggressive imperial states. In 1837 the British Government privatized the carriage of mail overseas, offering subsidy contracts for all the main routes, to ensure the regular, reliable delivery of strategic, commercial and political intelligence across the globe. The speed with which intelligence was moved would be the key to national security, and national wealth. Suitably bolstered by government funds, British companies were able to undercut their rivals, not least Isambard Kingdom Brunel's Great Western Steamship Company, and foreign competition. Other states took up the challenge by subsidizing their own liners, much as they erected tariff barriers against British trade. The American Collins Line was funded to compete with the British Cunard Line on the North Atlantic route, only to suffer a run of tragedies and collapse.

By the end of the nineteenth century a new player had entered the Atlantic arena: Imperial Germany. The Germans saw their liners as potential warships, building them with the speed and power required for a cruiser. Only a hefty subsidy, and the massive emigrant traffic that filled their holds, could keep such costly ships running. The British Government finally gave in to the pressure for similar ships in 1906, with the *Mauritania* and *Lusitania*, the first turbine-powered ocean greyhounds, designed to carry a cruiser's armament, and counter the German super-liners, just as the new turbine-powered battlecruisers provided a better answer. White Star went for size and luxury, but their titanic trio came to curious ends. The middle ship, the eponymous *Titanic*, sank on her maiden voyage, with terrible loss of life, shattering the complacent Edwardian illusion of endless progress. Although *Olympic* sank a cruiser and a lightship by accident, and a U-boat by design, she managed to serve out a long career. The *Britannic* never carried fare-paying passengers; completed as a hospital ship she was torpedoed by a U-boat in the Aegean, en route to the Gallipoli beachhead.

In 1917 the US Government took over German liners that had been interned at New York, and used them to carry American soldiers to fight the German army in France. After the war Britain and American took some of these massive liners as war booty, the American *Leviathan* and British *Majestic* remaining the largest liners afloat for more than a decade. In the 1930s a renewed wave of liner construction, sparked by Italy and Germany, resulted in two design icons; the beautiful, ultra-modern French *Normandie*, and her conservative sister the British *Queen Mary*, which proved both the better ship, and the more fortunate. If *Normandie* declared French ambition in art deco style, flair and fashion, *Queen Mary* was an Arts and Crafts monument to British power rendered in metal. *Normandie* was lost soon after the collapse of the French state that built her: *Queen Mary* survived war, the end of Empire and the last days of Atlantic passenger traffic to become a moored attraction and film set at Long Beach. Her half-sister, the *Queen Elizabeth*, was saved from a similar fate by a fire in Hong Kong Harbour.

The prestige passenger ships of the twenty-first century are cruise liners, remarkable only for their size – they dwarf the Atlantic Greyhounds of the inter-war era, which were themselves the largest ships afloat – and the desperate attempt they embody to ensure that passengers can see the sea, but are not otherwise inconvenienced by it.

In the nineteenth century the development of steam-powered cooling plant allowed the development of new trades, in chilled meat from South American and Australasia, and bananas from the West Indies. The ships quickly adopted specialized designs to make the most effective use of the technology. While these single-use ships have their modern equivalents, the key event in the modern history of commercial shipping was the introduction of the shipping container in the 1950s. By standardizing the load and linking it to lorry transport by increasingly automated handling systems, the container ended the long history of dock labour, and prompted the development of new deep water terminals; large, soulless truck parks served by high cranes. The system is economic, accountable and efficient, but no one goes to see the ships: hideous, slab-sided monsters, festooned with close-packed tins, the contents of which are unknown, and infinitely variable, a fact revealed to an unsuspecting Britain by the wreck of the *Napoli* in Branscombe Bay in January 2007.

The romance of the sea was never very strong among those who had no choice but to endure the life, but the last fifty years have destroyed the last vestiges of such feelings among the general population. The *Napoli* prompted a sudden resurgence of shore side plundering as the cargo came ashore, leaving the police to consult their history books, and the British people to reflect on the baser side of human nature.

Similar changes have affected other commercial ship types. While most oil was moved from the Middle East to Europe via the Suez Canal the size of oil tankers was necessarily circumscribed, 30,000 tons being the upper limit. The 1967 Arab-Israeli war changed all that. Scuttled ships blocked the Canal until 1975, and tanker fleets responded by building larger ships for the Cape route, helping to keep the cost of oil within economic bounds for another four decades.

By the early 1970s Mitsubishi in Nagasaki had built a dock capable of constructing an Ultra Large Crude Carrier (ULCC) of 1 million tons deadweight, but the order never came. Ships of over 300,000 tons were the limit, and with the recession of the 1980s and the development of North Sea oil and pipelines these became uneconomic. The major operating problem with monster ships has been the need for monster harbours, docks and jetties to service them, but the main concern of the public has been the inevitable accident, and ecological disaster that would follow. If the *Torrey Canyon* and the *Exxon Valdez* have achieved the greatest prominence, rarely a year passes without a major spillage of crude oil. Modern tankers are built with double-skinned hulls, to reduce the risks, but the sea is no place for those who think that accidents can be avoided.

Other, far smaller tankers, carry refined petroleum products, or liquefied natural gas, a major growth area in modern shipping. By super-cooling gas at source, in the Middle East or Siberia, it can be massively reduced in bulk for transport in special cold storage ships, and returned to normal temperature in controlled environments at the user end of the voyage. The dangers inherent in this system mean that new terminals are built away from population centres, and the ships are closely monitored, possessing as they do an earth-shattering explosive potential in the wrong hands.

Equally revealing of the way in which the sea is essential to all life on the planet is the tanker traffic between south eastern Turkey and Israel. The tankers deliver water to an expanding population in an arid land. The exponential growth of the world economy, the same growth that has seen massive shipments of oil to Europe, America, Japan, China and India, has also generated global demands for other raw materials, notably metallic ores, timber and foodstuffs, has seen bulk carriers reach monstrous proportions. For decades the economic logic of globalization has shifted manufacturing industry from the developed to the underdeveloped world, constantly making more work for shipping. Sub-assemblies criss-cross the globe in search of cheap labour to connect up the parts, and every few years the market moves on to yet cheaper markets.

Monster transporters are built to carry increasingly specific cargoes, be they cars, engines or the sheet steel chassis stamping. The ecological impact of basing world economic development on consumer driven spending has reached levels that seem positively insane to most people. In 2007 a Grimsby based company selling processed fish products admitted that it sent crayfish harvested off the north of Scotland all the way to Thailand by sea, simply to have them peeled by hand, before returning them to Grimsby for final processing. Just when everyone had concluded this was insane a high-powered investigation concluded that the process was less damaging to the environment than using machinery to peel the crayfish in Britain!

Shipping has never been cheaper, or more economical. The vast scale of modern ships, the use of containers, chilling and other techniques have shrunk the world. If the British want to eat hand-peeled scampi, but refuse to pay fellow Britons to peel it, then a Thai plant will be happy to oblige. As the world population grows the range of raw materials that will carry the cost of bulk shipment by sea will grow, and the poorest countries will end up selling everything but the air they breathe to the richer nations. If we need to find a moral for all this from the sea we need only look at the fishing industry. In the late nineteenth century industrial technology created the steam-powered bottom trawler, which hoovered up fish stocks without discrimination, the harpoon gun that annihilated whale populations, the freezer factory that could preserve fish catches and thereby exploit the distant quarters of the globe. Sonar removed the element of chance, and before too long fishing quotas followed. Industrial whaling is still banned, despite the efforts of Japan and a few others to resume the barbaric business. Canada has effectively stopped Atlantic fishing, and found a new use for her navy in the process, the European Union is trying, in its inconsistent, unbalanced way, to make a difference. Other areas will soon follow. The sea is not limitless, it cannot absorb all our pollution and it cannot provide all our food. Just because we can does not mean we should.

The growth of monster ships has not been without human cost. The loss of the British built bulk carrier *Derbyshire* with all her crew in the Far East led to a long enquiry, which demonstrated that the lethal combination of design flaws and a typhoon had been responsible for the disaster. The sea is no more kind today than it ever was, just because man has made his ships more seaworthy than they were does not mean they are any more 'unsinkable' than the *Titanic*.

## Exploration and Scientific vessels

The same enquiring minds that first led men to put to sea has sustained human interest in the ocean world, from charting the seas, finding new worlds to exploit, mastering the pattern of winds, currents and tides and improving scientific knowledge of the ocean depths. Until recently the ships used for exploration and science were borrowed from other activities, Columbus and Magellan used merchant ships, Cook's *Endeavour* was a humble collier, John Franklin's *Erebus* was an old bomb-vessel, built to fire heavy shells into coastal cities, and HMS *Challenger* a naval corvette. While the ships themselves were unremarkable, their achievements became the stuff of legend, none more so than Franklin's *Erebus*. Taking a ship named for the portal of Hades to transit the North West Passage was an act of hubris, the tragedy that ensued was as predictable as it was gruesome. In the twentieth century oceanographic research required specialist craft, including bathyscapes for deep ocean research, adding new and often bizarre vessels to the list of ship types.

## Specialist shipbuilding

Although the great majority of ships are built for commercial or security purposes, the exceptions can be revealing. The lifeboat began life as a buoyant rowing boat, before the addition of engines, pumps, and improved design created the modern self-righting boat used around the world. Despite the latest technology the nature of lifeboat work, often required to operate close to the coast when all other ships have left the area, meeting the most extreme conditions of sea and storm, tragedies still occur. The loss of the Penlee lifeboat off the coast of Cornwall in 1981 was one such modern tragedy. The crew put to sea in conditions that kept the rescue helicopters grounded: they paid the ultimate price for their courage and commitment. While seagoing ships have always carried small boats that could be used for lifesaving, it took the *Titanic* tragedy to link the scale of lifeboat provision on merchant ships with the number of passengers and crew. The demand for space quickly prompted the development of collapsible, and later inflatable safety types, which made a massive contribution to lifesaving in the world wars of the twentieth century. For centuries light ships provided a less dynamic contribution to maritime safety, anchored over dangerous offshore shoals, but improved automated equipment, increased labour coasts, and the thankless nature of the work has seen most replaced by unmanned buoys.

The twentieth-century development of the ship gradually restricted the number of usable harbours for ocean-going merchant shipping and major warships. The process of concentration has been reinforced by the high cost of modern dockyard infrastructure and inland communications. The ability to use harbours and rivers has also been challenged by the natural process of sedimentation. The coasts of the world are littered with old ports, no longer economically viable, but often turned over to leisure pursuits. However, the main reason for abandoning ports has been lack of scope for expansion. Others have been developed from small beginnings into superports. The Belgian port of Antwerp, initially a river frontage, has been developed, by excavating the low lying land to the north of the city, to become the largest in Europe.

The need to keep ports open prompted the development of dredgers and other seabed-cutting ships, which shift mud and rock down to a fixed depth, and transfer the spoil into barges for removal. For all their prosaic function the first English ship with a steam engine was a bucket dredger, a reflection of the limits of steam technology, and the value of dredging.

Equally prosaic, if rather more 'ship-like', the specialist cable laying ship was developed soon after the introduction of the submarine telegraph cable in the 1850s. Initially oceanic cables were laid by large warships, or the unique *Great Eastern*, but Siemens Brothers' purpose-built *Faraday* of 1874 reflected the economic attraction of a specialized ship for the function. After a hiatus in the late twentieth century trans-oceanic cable-laying is back in vogue, with fibre optics replacing insulated wire as the medium.

## Fiction

Inspired by the ocean, by their own sea lives, or by a lost past, poets and writers have created their own imaginary sea worlds from Homer to O'Brian, always using a telling detail, a careful analogy, and passages of richly coloured narrative to lure the unsuspecting landsman into their snare. However, there is a major distinction to be made. Where some set their story on a ship, simply to isolate the characters from outside interference, others see the ship as critical to the story. Reality and imagination soon unravel in the minds of men like Herman Melville, who used his fictional ships as setting and character in rich, allusive narratives of life in a sailing man of war or a Yankee Whaler. His was a unique genius, one that grows with every reading, creating this wooden world, from the inside, to see the dynamics of the ship as a living entity, more ants' nest than inert box. Melville's *Neversink* and *Pequod* are the heroes of *White Jacket* and *Moby Dick*. Another sailor novelist, Joseph Conrad, found inspiration in a more successful seagoing career, but lacked the same engagement with the ship as an entity. This line was more powerful in the work of William Golding, in *Rites of Passage*, where a passage to Australia under sail gave the ship time to influence the lives of all on board. These ships come to life, they affect and alter the narrative, they show the fickle side of their nature, they are home; they have character, they intervene, imposing their spirit, for good or ill, on puny humans. In the modern imagination the malign spirit of a wooden ship has been replaced by artificial intelligence: Arthur C. Clarke's *2001: A Space Odyssey* has the 'ship' controlled by a rogue computer, because modern technology is incapable of random evil.

Modern visual media has found the ship problematic. No director could ignore the visual power and intellectual meaning of such a large, free moving structure, be it at war, or on the edge of the unknown. But ships are costly items, and hard to film. Sergei Eisenstein was able to use a suitable ship for his 'Battleship Potemkin' because the Soviet state was anxious to create the propaganda, little expecting a cinematic masterpiece. Elsewhere, keeping the cost of the ship on a more manageable scale has influenced story telling. Hollywood has made 'The Mutiny on the Bounty' three times, in part because the ship is small, and the story simple, and in part because it serves as an allegory of the American Revolution. Peter Weir's film of the Patrick O'Brian series, 'Master and Commander', a striking visual recreation of an older world, failed to find the audience to warrant a follow on. Perhaps such attempts to recreate reality have outlived their usefulness, with CGI (computer generated images) opening limitless possibilities, although the use of this medium is arguably still in its infancy when it comes to creating sea-scapes. When the *Titanic* disaster attracted the attention of Hollywood, as the setting for a fairly prosaic story of love and loss, with good and evil suitably highlighted by the dramatic sinking of the ship, the scale of the ship made this the biggest film of all time – a box-office record eclipsed only by James Cameron's next feature-film; 2009's 'Avatar'.

## The Modern World

In the 1980s ships returned to the centre of the international stage. As the Cold War entered the final phase, President Reagan used a naval build-up – a '600 ships navy' – as part of his economic/technological assault on the crumbling Soviet regime. The 'New Maritime Strategy' of 1986 used new weapons and sensors, AEGIS cruisers, Tomahawk land attack missiles, nuclear submarines and carrier battle groups to pose a threat to the Soviet ballistic missile submarines, calling into question the security of the deterrent. It may have been no more than rhetoric, but in the fevered atmosphere it played a significant role in winning the war, and breaking the Soviet Union.

The end of the Cold War prompted a dramatic return to the sea as a strategic medium, as Western Europe, freed from the incubus of massive Warsaw Pact armies on the inner German border, slowly recovered the ability to see the world as a blue globe. The Gulf War of 1990–91, for all the technological wizardry of air-launched precision guided munitions, was entirely dependent upon a massive sea-based logistics effort to bring vehicles, munitions and consumables into theatre. Only the men arrived by air. A naval blockade severely degraded Iraq's military capability. The threat of a major amphibious operation pinned key Iraqi forces to the coast, allowing the coalition army to swing through the desert, while carrier aviation, naval cruise missiles and naval electronic warfare assets knocked out the Iraqi air defence system. The American nuclear-powered aircraft carriers were the key instrument of war. They arrived in theatre within hours of the invasion of Kuwait, stabilizing the situation until troops and ground-based aircraft could be deployed. Naval strategic instruments developed to meet the Soviet Union proved highly capable against a lesser state. The lesson was widely read by those with reason to fear similar treatment. However, naval might, with all its reach and precision, has been less successful in meeting the new threat. Post 9/11 naval forces played a critical role in defeating the Taliban regime in Afghanistan, but as yet they have not been able to deal with Al Qaeda, whose operatives struck the USS *Cole* at Aden, and a tanker off the Arabian coast.

The new strategic environment has prompted a major run-down of conventional surface warships in the destroyer/frigate categories. Naval warfare, in any meaningful sense, is an unlikely eventuality. The new warships are larger, amphibious platforms, helicopter or aircraft carriers, or small, stealthy coastal assets, like the troubled

American Littoral Combat Ship programme. The stakes are high, and the hopes riding on these ships are immense. Little wonder the Americans have called the new ships *Liberty* and *Freedom*.

American dominance at sea, unquestioned since the end of the Cold War, needed a rival, if only for the budget battle on Capitol Hill. For over a decade the Chinese People's Liberation Army Navy (PLAN), a large, if unremarkable force with few pretensions to ocean-going capability, has been built up as the 'threat'. The curious history of the former Soviet carrier *Varyag*, the most interesting part of the PLAN story, suggests there may be long term sea power ambitions in Beijing. Meanwhile oil-rich Russia is rapidly returning to sea, the sure sign that Moscow is ready to take a leading role in world affairs. Since the days of Peter the Great a big navy has been the obvious symbol of Russian ambition, and it is no coincidence that the current Russian flagship bears his name. However, the tragic loss of the submarine *Kursk* in 2000 revealed another side of the Russian naval image, the lack of skilled and experienced manpower. For the next half century it is highly likely that naval power will remain in the hands of a Western consortium, led by the United States, Europe and Japan. The reason is simple: these states depend upon the sea to a far greater extent than any other group of countries.

## The Future

The ship has been the ultimate cultural artefact for three millennia, a mobile symbol, on the largest scale. It can carry national, commercial, or individual brands, it can shout, or whisper. And yet as we enter the twenty-first century the age of the ship as a unique creative product may be at an end. No longer do men make ships by hand, now every piece is cut by computer, welded by robots and built in sections. Computer design has deprived them of their idiosyncrasy, and their unique character, while economies of scale have turned them into mass-produced inventory items. Science and precision have replaced the human spirit, and in the process we have lost a great deal: beauty, truth and that unique inspiration that shows how man can inspire to the sublime, the divine and the magical. Corporate convenience and economic necessity have turned passenger ships from style icons to misshapen monstrosities, a tower block wrapped around a shopping mall. If anyone doubts this truth they need only compare the timeless elegance of the *QE2* with the truly grotesque pastiche that is the *Queen Mary 2*; a boxy, ill-proportioned confession of the failure of the human imagination. Dressing a cruise liner up like an Atlantic greyhound was never going to work, cramming in ever more high rental balconied sea-view cabins only emphasized the point. Not only have we lost sight of the ships that make our global lives possible, but when they do appear they lack the visual power to excite the imagination – becoming just one more mass market artefact, with converging, drab designs dictated by concerns that have nothing to do with the ocean.

**Andrew Lambert**
**Laughton Professor of Naval History**
**Department of War Studies**
**King's College, London**

# Noah's Ark   Biblical ship c. 4990 B.C.

The fifteenth-century parish church of St Neot in Cornwall is fortunate in still having more than half of its original early sixteenth-century stained glass, including a window in the south aisle filled with panels narrating the biblical story of Noah's Ark, a story common to several faiths, primarily Judaism, Christianity and Islam. In this particular panel, in which Noah reaches out towards the dove returning with the olive branch in her beak, the artist departs slightly from the biblical story because the ark should by now have grounded rather than be still afloat. The vessel is shown as a contemporary, three-masted Hanseatic type of late cog or holk. A door to the left and two closed and shuttered windows to the right of Noah suggest a superstructure, but the artist appears more interested in showing his knowledge of shipbuilding: the carefully delineated shrouds, the furled sails and the treenails that fastened the overlapping planking to the frames of the hull.

There is no attempt at a realistic scale: Noah takes centre stage on the ship — the length of which appears hardly more than twice that of Noah.

Creationist historians have attempted to calculate the size and seaworthiness of the Ark from the dimensions given in cubits in Genesis. The cubit was based upon the distance between the point of the elbow and the tip of the index finger, but its precise measurement differed between cultures and could vary between 17.5in and 21.5in (0.45m–0.55m). Given the biblical dimensions, the Ark could have ranged from 463ft to 515ft (133–157m) in length, in all cases making it both the largest vessel constructed before the nineteenth century and, with three decks, theoretically adequate to carry every creature that needed to be brought inside for survival. *JH*

515.8ft x 86ft x 51.6ft (157.2m x 26.2m x 15.7m) [dimensions based on the Royal Egyptian cubit of 524mm] • 15,000+ tons [B] • Hull wood ('gopher wood', which has not been identified with any known wood) • Complement 8 (Noah, his wife, three sons and daughters-in-law) • Built c. 4990 B.C.

# Khufu (Cheops) Ship Solar barge c. 2500 B.C.

The Khufu ship, now housed in The Khufu Boat Museum next to the Great Pyramid at Giza, Egypt, is the world's oldest intact surviving ship. The location is appropriate for it was probably constructed for the Great Pharaoh Khufu (Cheops in Greek) who most people agree built the Great Pyramid at Giza sometime around the middle of the third millennia B.C.

The Khufu ship was built of cedar sourced from Lebanon and is described by Egyptologists as a Solar Barge — a special ship with religious and or ceremonial significance. The Khufu ship was probably built to carry Pharaoh Khufu across the heavens in the afterlife. The fact that the entire ship, consisting of 1224 individual pieces, had been disassembled and laid out like an enormous model kit seems to support this theory. The Egyptians were masters of organisation and this would seem the logical way to plan for the ship's use in the next world. Moreover, there is much evidence of the Egyptians building ships in kit form at Alexandria, carrying them overland for use on the Red Sea, then breaking them back down for storage back at Alexandria.

Yet the Khufu ship does seem to have had some practical use during the Pharoah's lifetime as it carries evidence of being immersed in water at some point, perhaps for religious duties or even as the funeral barge for Khufu. Perhaps we will never know for certain, but it is a unique piece of maritime history and compelling proof for the extraordinary craftsmanship and organization of the Ancient Egyptians. *MR*

*Khufu (Cheops) ship, Giza, Egypt (photograph). Alison Moss, 2002, Conway Picture Library*

143ft x 19.5ft (43.6m x 5.9m) • Hull wood (Lebanese cedar) • Built Egypt, c. 2500 B.C.

# Argo   Jason and the Argonauts' ship c. 1300 B.C.

Except for those with a passion for Greek mythology the *Argo* is probably familiar to most people thanks to the 1963 film 'Jason and the Argonauts'; the Argonauts being, of course, those who sail in the *Argo*. The *Argo* was built so that Jason could sail to Colchis and obtain a golden ram's fleece, ostensibly in order to free the country of Iolcan from a curse bedevilling the King, Pelias. Of course, Jason had a legitimate claim to the throne himself and the mission was very much to get him out of the way. Undaunted, Jason had a shipwright called Argus build him a ship with 50 oars – a pentaconter; in return the ship was named after her creator. Constructed from seasoned timber from Mount Pelion, Jason received a fine gift from the goddess Athene: a piece of timber for the prow which was blessed with prophetic power. According to the myth

the whole build took only three months; certainly swifter than the three years taken to construct the 2008 replica. The Argonauts included legendary heroes such as Orpheus, Herecles (Hercules), Peleus (the father of Achilles) and the twins Castor and Pollux, who were later transformed into the Gemini constellation.

Many today will remember the film adaptation for the glorious stop-motion of the legendary film animator Ray Harryhausen, in particular fighting the huge bronze statue of Talos or crossing swords with armed skeletons. The *Argo* herself is often overlooked in all this, yet the ship sits at the heart of the myth – her story, and that of the Argonauts, is testament to the skill of Greek shipbuilders and seafarers. *MR*

THE LAVNCHING OF THE ARGO

**The Launching of the *Argo*** *(colour lithograph), after Henry Matthew Brock, Private Collection / The Bridgeman Art Library*

# Jonah and the Whale   Biblical ship c. 765 B.C.

In the biblical story, Jonah tried to evade God's orders by fleeing to Joppa and taking a ship bound for Tarshish, a port that scholars have never definitively identified and which may be a catch-all term for a distant destination. A vicious storm sprang up and, at his suggestion, the terrified crew threw Jonah into the sea as a sacrifice, whereupon the sea grew calm. Jonah was swallowed by a whale and spent 72 hours in its belly before asking God for aid and being regurgitated on dry land.

Although the Genoese artist Carlo Antonio Tavella was primarily a landscape painter, he captures the violence of the storm that has ripped the flag at the stern and is tearing loose the foresail. The helmsman is clutching the tiller unable to steer the ship, and Jonah stands with outspread arms as the sailors prepare to throw him. However, the realism of sky, sea and onboard drama is in contrast to the depiction of the whale as a sea monster with rows of teeth and spouting water in two vertical jets from its nose. Tavella may have gleaned his erroneous concept of whales from old travellers' tales or he may deliberately have chosen to portray this specimen as a ferocious creature of fantasy in order to emphasize human helplessness in the face of the alien elements.

The ship is a typical Mediterranean type: a two-masted 'settee' with lateen yards. *JH*

**Jonah and the Whale** *(oil on canvas), Carlo Antonio Tavella, mid seventeenth century, Palmer Collection, National Maritime Museum, London (BHC0881)*

No data available

# Athenian Triremes Galleys c. 480 B.C.

By the fifth century B.C. Athens held a pre-eminent position among the Greek city-states. The wealth, power and influence of the *polis* derived in large part from its access to the sea – the port of Piraeus was an important trading base, and Athenian merchants imported corn, copper, iron, pitch and timber in exchange for domestic produce like olives, wine and silver.

Such commercial interests demanded protection, and accordingly Athens maintained a fleet of triremes – light and narrow wooden warships with a low draught, primarily oar-powered, although fitted with one or two single-sail masts, which could be raised and lowered. The trireme took its name from the three banks of oars it carried on each side, with one rower (*eretai*) per oar. Although fast and agile, such vessels demanded considerable skill and discipline to manoeuvre effectively. This meant that the crews were rarely slaves; instead they were principally drawn from the *thetes*, the lowest rank of Athenian society. Triremes were prestige ships; decorated accordingly – the painted eye on the prow symbolising that the ship would find its way.

Triremes also carried a complement of sailors, commanding officers and a detachment of hoplites, whose role was largely defensive, protecting the unarmed crew from boarding actions. As such the principal weapon of the Athenian trireme was the ram – the ship's strong cypress wood keel tapered to a point at the prow of the ship, on or just below the waterline. This was tipped with bronze, designed to rake the hulls of enemy ships.

The Athenians were proficient seamen and developed effective battle tactics in their use of trireme fleets, the ultimate example of which occurred at the Battle of Salamis in 480 B.C. Although heavily outnumbered by the Persians, the Greek fleet, led by the Athenian general Themistocles, used the narrow straits of Salamis to divide and compress the great Persian navy, scoring a decisive victory after a bloody battle. The triumph was a key turning-point in the Greco-Persian wars, and arguably paved the way for the development of the Greek Mediterranean Empire; the first great thalassocracy and the cradle of modern Western civilisation. *MJ*

**Athenian galleys in action in the fifth century B.C.** *Mark Myers, 1994*

[Typical data] 121.1ft x 18.1ft x 4.1ft (36.9m x 5.5m x 1.3m) • 70 tons [D] • Hull wood (pine and fir) • Armament bow ram, missile weapons – spears, stone slings, arrows • Complement approx. 200 • Built Piraeus, Athens, Greece, c. 480 B.C.

# Roman Galleys  Battle of Actium c. 31 B.C.

The most famous galley battle fought by the Romans took place off Actium at the entrance to the Ambracian Gulf on the western coast of Greece in 31 B.C. when the forces of Octavian met those of his bitter rival and former fellow consul, Marcus Antonius, whose fleet was reinforced by vessels from Queen Cleopatra's Egyptian navy.

Led by Agrippa, Octavian's galleys were mainly light, highly manoeuvrable liburnians, with two banks of oars, while the majority of Antonius's fleet comprised heavy quinquiremes, also known as 'Fives'. These were not, as was once thought, galleys with five banks of oars, but very probably triremes, with one man per oar on the bottom row and two men per oar on the middle and upper rows, and they were armoured with bronze plates and square timbers that the rams of the lightweight liburnians had little chance of holing. However, Antonius's crews were too depleted by sickness to be able to provide the propulsion needed to overwhelm the enemy.

Historians still speculate as to whether Antonius knew he could not defeat Octavian. What is certain is that, having sailed out of his base in the Gulf and into the open sea, he concentrated his attack on Octavian's centre, broke through and, in company with Cleopatra and her Egyptian squadron, abandoned most of his fleet to its fate. Demoralized by the departure of their leader and incapable of moving or turning at sufficient speed, the quinquiremes fell victim to the rocks and blazing torches hurled into them by the ballistae mounted on Octavian's liburnians.

When Octavian caught up with Antonius and Cleopatra in Egypt they committed suicide, and Octavian was proclaimed Emperor under the name Augustus. *JH*

**The Battle of Actium, 2 September 31 B.C.** *(oil on canvas) Lorenzo A. Castro, 1672, Palmer Collection, National Maritime Museum, London (BHC0251)*

# Sutton Hoo   Anglo-Saxon ship c. 624 A.D.

In 1939 archaeologists were invited to investigate a series of burial mounds at Sutton Hoo, Suffolk. Beneath a thousand tons of earth they discovered a complete ship burial dating back to the seventh century A.D., almost certainly the grave of the Anglo-Saxon king Rædwald who ruled from c. 617 until his death in c. 625. The treasure was stunning in its quality, from the fragments of the iconic helmet to the cloisonné mountings of the scabbard and sword belt, and from the huge, solid gold buckle of the money belt to the gold and silver frame of the purse lid with its intricate decoration of glass, garnet and millefiori work.

The acid sand of the area had destroyed any organic material so no trace remains of clothing, body tissues or ship's timbers. Nevertheless, by looking at the stained sand and iron rivets, archaeologists were able to build up a very clear picture of this royal boat. Each side of her hull was constructed from nine overlapping longitudinal planks of 1in (2.5cm) thick oak, riveted together, and 26 internal ribs. Built some 600 years before the hinged stern rudder, the ship was steered by a steering board attached toward the stern of the starboard side; in fact the term 'starboard' derives directly from 'steer board'. There is no evidence of a 'step' to indicate that the ship had a mast, leading some experts to assume she was a purely oared craft. However, an amidships mast could well have been removed before the king's body was laid out down the centre of the boat. A modern half-size replica, the *Sæ Wylfing*, fitted with a mast and square sail has demonstrated that the Sutton Hoo ship would have had fine sailing qualities. *JH*

**Sutton Hoo Ship during excavation** *(photograph), The Trustees of the British Museum*

approx. 89ft x 14ft (27m x 3.9m) • Hull wood • Built England, c. 625 A.D.

# Oseberg Ship Viking ship c. 800 A.D.

Excavated in 1904 after some 1200 years beneath a burial mound at Slagen in Norway, the Oseberg ship remains the earliest clinker-built, masted ship discovered in Scandinavia. Although classed as a karv, a coastal vessel, it had limited sailing qualities – as experiments with a replica proved in 1987; it may have served as a ceremonial vessel before becoming the burial ship of two women in A.D. 834, one of high rank, the other perhaps a servant. The weight of the mound had crushed the ship, the stern of which rotted, but archaeologists were able to reconstruct the hull and reveal the unequalled quality of the intricate, flowing carving. The stem had been completed not as a dragon's head but in another traditional design: a snake's head spiral. The stern terminated in the snake's tail.

The original builders of the ship began by joining two pieces of straight timber to create a 46ft (14m) keel to which they attached the high, curving stem and stern posts. Twelve overlapping oak planks – strakes – fastened to one another by iron rivets and caulked to keep out water, formed each of the sides, and the hull was then strengthened internally with cross beams. Fifteen holes for oars were cut into each side of the uppermost strake, and a mast carrying a square sail set forward. The ship was steered by an oar attached to the starboard side at the stern, as with the Sutton Hoo ship.

The Oseberg ship and associated material is on display at Oslo's Kulturhistorisk Museum. Although the site had been looted of any treasure, it yielded a wealth of rare artefacts including textiles. *JH*

**Oseberg Viking ship** *(photograph). The Art Archive / Viking Ship Museum Oslo / Alfredo Dagli Orti*

72.3ft x 16.4ft (22m x 5m) • 11 tons [B] • Hull wood (oak) • Complement approx. 32 • Built South Western Norway, c. 800 A.D.

# Gokstad Ship  Viking ship c. 890 A.D.

Considered by some to be a longship and by others to be a karv like the Oseberg ship, the Gokstad ship dates from around A.D. 890 and is larger, far more seaworthy and stunningly elegant, despite being less ornate. The keel measures almost 58ft (17.3m) and was cut from a single piece of straight oak, giving the vessel great strength; an increased freeboard was obtained by cutting the ports for the 64 oars along the third strake rather than the gunwhale. These ports could be closed with hatches whenever the vessel proceeded under sail alone, to stop water coming in. The mast, which was firmly held by a long keelson and stout step, may have been as tall as 40ft (12m). As with the Oseberg ship, no thwarts for the rowers were found. The assumption is that they sat on chests. Thirteen years after the initial discovery, the success of the design was proved when a replica of the Gokstad crossed the Atlantic to the Chicago World Fair of 1893 in 40 days.

The burial mound that preserved the Gokstad ship in blue clay and with less damage than was done to the Oseberg ship, was that of a nobleman or king aged around 60. His remains were found in a bed in a wooden chamber, and his grave goods included a sledge, three small boats built to a design that can still be found in Norway, a peacock and a rucksack.

Among other surprising finds were remnants of the woollen sail cloth and the remains of 64 shields – half of them black, the rest yellow – which were hung ceremonially on the outside of the hull, overlapping one another and with the colours alternating.

The Gokstad ship is preserved at Oslo's Kulturhistorisk Museum. *JH*

**Gokstad ship, Sandefjord, Vestfold, Norway** *(photograph), Eirik Irgens Johnsen, Museum of Cultural History, University of Oslo*

78.7ft x 16.4ft x 6.2ft (24m x 5m x 1.9m) • approx. 20 tons [B] • Hull wood (oak) • Complement approx. 33 • Built Norway, c. 890 A.D.

# Acheron Ferry  Boat from Dante's *Inferno* c. 1308

Guided by the poet Virgil, Canto III of the *Inferno* sees Dante on the banks of the Acheron, 'the joyless', the first of the great Rivers of Hell. Here he encounters Charon the boatman, who ferries an endless procession of the souls of the dead across the river to the First Circle of Hell. Classical sources envisage him as a swarthy mariner, with unkempt beard and flashing eyes, spewing foul language. Dante sees him as a white-haired boatman, with oar in hand, ready to beat those who linger on the shore. His craft is a simple wooden boat, of generic type, but Charon is reluctant to receive Dante, recognising him to be both a living being and a soul in grace, stating that 'a lighter skiff must bear thy load'. Virgil commands him to take them across, however, since Dante's journey is of divine purpose.

In both a textual and a physical sense the passage marks the entrance to Hell proper; an important event, and one acknowledged by the French illustrator Gustave Doré in his self-financed 1861 French edition of the *Inferno*, who depicts Charon and his boat accordingly. He captures the essence of the figure vividly in a Michelangelesque nude surrounded by ominous skies, towering cliffs and turbulent waters, although here Charon looks to be equipped with a long pole for punting rather than an oar.

Doré's Dante illustrations are considered among his crowning achievements – a perfect marriage of artistic skill and poetic imagination. Still published today in numerous editions, they were also widely copied and reproduced throughout the late nineteenth and early twentieth centuries, as in this example by Stephane Pannemaker, a renowned Belgian wood-engraver who worked extensively in Paris until his death in 1930. *MJ*

**Charon, the Ferryman of Hell, from Dante's** *Inferno* (engraving), Stephane Pannemaker after Gustave Doré, c.1868, Private Collection / The Bridgeman Art Library

No data available

# Bremen Cog  Hanseatic trading vessel 1380

In October 1962 the remains of what became known as the Bremen Cog (or Kogge) were uncovered during dredging work on the River Weser for the building of a new dock. Until then there had been no archaeological evidence for one of the most distinct types of vessels in maritime history. The simple, round, flat-bottomed single-masted vessels were the backbone of seaborne trade in the Baltic and North Seas during the medieval era. It is likely that the cogs, first mentioned in records in the tenth century, evolved from the small Friesian coasters and the Norse Knarr, a combined oar-and-sail powered general-purpose vessel. By contrast the cog relied on a single square-rigged sail and, while this did not allow the vessel to sail into the wind, it only required a small crew.

Initially cogs were steered by means of a steering oar although later stern rudders were used to improve handling. Cogs were also more robust than coastal-going vessels, allowing voyages of longer duration across open waters. They were more spacious than other contemporary vessels and thus could carry far greater cargoes, making them valuable for the Hanseatic League's expanding seaborne trade. Utilizing the abundant supply of oak in the Baltic meant they were relatively inexpensive to construct and maintain. While all cogs shared the basic design, their displacement could vary considerably, from very small 10-ton to larger 150-ton vessels. The Bremen cog was salvaged and restored over a 19-year period and is now housed in the German Maritime Museum in Bremerhaven. *MF*

**Bremen Cog** *(photograph), Deutsche Schiffahrtsmuseum, Bremerhaven, Germany*

78.7ft x 26.2ft x 11.5ft (24m x 8m x 3.5m) • approx. 80 tons [B] • Hull wood • Built Baltic region, Europe, c. 1380

# Alexander the Great's Diving Bell Diving bell 1445

During the Medieval and Early Renaissance period, the life of Alexander the Great (356–323 B.C.) and the legends that sprang up around him, were popular subjects for writers and illustrators in Europe. This exquisite miniature, taken from the *The Romance of Alexander*, an old French manuscript produced in Rouen in 1445 and now in the British Library, is just one of several depicting Alexander being lowered into the sea in a glass barrel in order to observe the wonders of the deep. Sometimes he is shown alone, sometimes with companions, human or animal. According to one version, Alexander's favourite mistress was given charge of the chain attached to the barrel, but she let go of it in order to run off with her lover. Although there is no historical foundation for any of the stories, the technique of lowering an inverted bucket into the sea, so that divers could extend their time underwater by breathing the trapped air, was known in Alexander's day and described by his teacher, Aristotle.

Alexander and his assistants are portrayed wearing the courtly French fashions of the 1440s, and their ship is a cog. This ubiquitous single-masted, square-rigged vessel, which first developed as a cargo carrier in the twelfth century, had a flat bottom that made it ideal for use in the shallow coastal waters of Northern Europe and its small raised forecastle and poop could be used as platforms for armament. The image gives an excellent view of the straight sternpost and hinged rudder, a technical advance which not only made the earlier steering oar obsolete but allowed much bigger ships to be built. The clear glass barrel is delightful fantasy: such glassmaking technology did not exist either in Alexander's time or in the fifteenth century. *JH*

**Emperor Alexander the Great, exploring the sea in a diving bell** *(illuminated French manuscript), from 'The Romance of Alexander', 1445.* *The Art Archive / British Library, London*

# Ship of Fools   Allegorical ship c. 1495

'The Ship of Fools', part of a dismembered altarpiece by Hieronymus Bosch and now in the Louvre gallery, Paris, was painted at the end of the fifteenth century, satirizing human vices by subverting the popular medieval metaphor of the Church as the ship that brings the faithful safely to heaven. Bosch's audience would have also recognized an element of reality in his visual metaphor. At a time when people were scared of, but fascinated by, madness, and medical science had no understanding of mental health problems, those designated mad were sometimes expelled from their communities and given into the care of sailors who could confine them on board seagoing ships.

The Ship of Fools is drifting towards hell: the passengers on their voyage through life have abandoned virtuous behaviour in favour of self-indulgence: a drunken woman makes advances to a man; a Franciscan monk and a nun lead the other passengers in a bawdy song, while simultaneously trying to eat a pancake suspended from the mast; a glutton vomits over the stern; and the oarsman has swapped his oar for a ladle. The Tree of Life has been dug up from the Garden of Eden to serve as both a mast and a maypole, and Madness, symbolized by the crescent moon at the hoist of the long pennant, rules over everyone.

In astrology the moon was associated with madness, folly and sin: the word 'lunatic' derives from the Latin *luna*. A number of interpreters see the crescent as a symbol of Islam, believing that the painting castigates the Church for corruption, and failed leadership. The ship is without a sail; it has no proper rudder and no captain: it drifts helplessly through the allegorical landscape. *JH*

**The Ship of Fools** *(oil on canvas), Hieronymus Bosch, c. 1495, The Art Archive / Louvre, Paris / Alfredo Dagli Orti*

# Santa María  Merchant ship 1492

If one had to choose a ship whose voyage may be reckoned the most important in the history of seafaring, then the *Santa María* may claim the prize. As the flagship of Christopher Columbus's first voyage across the Atlantic Ocean in 1492, the *Santa María* rightly deserves her place as a tribute to man's ambition, ingenuity and courage to seek out the unknown.

The ship was originally named *La Gallega* (the Galician), built in Pontevedra, Galicia, northwest Spain, as a three-masted merchant ship for use in overseas trade. Her owner Juan de la Cosa would join Columbus on the voyage as the pilot. She was accompanied by the caravels *Santa Clara* (remembered as the *Niña*) and *Pinta*. Though Columbus found her a dull sailer, she performed well during the crossing and their investigations of islands and coastlines of the modern-day Bahamas, Cuba and Haiti. While working their way eastward, on Christmas Eve tragedy struck. With the master and helmsman both asleep, and probably drunk, shortly after midnight *Santa María* grounded on a coral reef. Beyond repair, Columbus ordered his men to salvage all they could, stripping the timbers to fashion an emergency fort in which a number of men volunteered to stay as there was not enough room in the other ships to make a safe passage back across the Atlantic. As fate would have it, none would survive to greet Columbus on his return there later that year.

Since the 400th anniversary of her pioneering voyage, a number of replicas of *Santa María* have been built. As neither detailed plans nor descriptions survive, the dimensions and quality of these ships have varied hugely. In the years since, a few replicas have taken to the open seas, some have navigated carnivals as elaborate festival floats, while another currently sits in a man-made lake in a Canadian shopping mall. An icon of maritime exploration, *Santa María* has now featured on coins and stamps the world over; there is even a cliff on the planet Mercury named in her honour. *HLJ*

**The *Santa Maria* at Anchor** *(oil on panel/frame), Andries van Eertvelt, c. 1628, Palmer Collection, National Maritime Museum, London (BHC0753)*

58-86ft x 19-26ft x 10-11ft (18-26m x 6-8m x 3m) • 108-239 tons [B] • Hull wood • Armament 9cm Lombard, 4.5cm falconets • Complement 40 • Built Galicia, Spain, 1492.

# Turkish Galleys  Battle of Zonchio 1499

This striking woodcut impression is one of the earliest examples of a print documenting an actual naval battle. It was produced by an unknown Venetian artist shortly after the event depicted; a critical stage during the Battle of Zonchio, which took place in August 1499.

Three large ships are identifiable along with numerous smaller, oared craft. The main combatants are an Ottoman vessel and two Venetian carracks. All three are locked together as the Venetians have attempted to board the Ottoman ship; in an act of desperate retaliation the Ottomans have set all three on fire. Flames lick around the base of the masts and on the high fore- and stern castles. It was a crucial moment in the battle – the sight of the great ships burning together destroyed Venetian morale, resulting in a victory for the Ottoman Empire. Antonio Loredan, one of the Venetian captains, was killed when his ship burned, while the Ottoman commander Ahmed Kemaleddin ('Cemali', seen on the deck of the Ottoman ship),

captured the second Venetian captain, Albano d'Armer. He was taken back to Constantinople as a prisoner, where the Ottoman Sultan, Bayezid II, reputedly had him cut to pieces.

The print has been the subject of extensive interpretation among medieval historians – Susan Rose has highlighted the tubes that seem to be projecting flaming material onto the oared Turkish ships harassing the *Pandora* and the *Nave del Armer*, while Giovanni Santi-Mazzini identifies a feature in the topcastle of the *Nave Turchesca* as being a *trombe del fuoco*, a type of firework mentioned by seventeenth-century Italian authors. It thus constitutes an important piece of evidence as to the methods and weapons used in naval warfare of the period, when boarding actions at close quarters were still dominant, although early ballistic weapons are evident, as is the very real threat of fire to wooden ships, which would induce terror among seamen for centuries to come. *MJ*

A **near-contemporary illustration of the Battle of Zonchio** (*woodcut*), *by an unknown Venetian artist, c. 1499, Conway Picture Library*

# Venetian Ships  Carracks and barges c. 1500

'The Meeting of the Betrothed Couple and the Departure of the Pilgrims' is the fourth painting of Venetian artist Vittore Carpaccio's cycle now in Venice's Accademia. Nine canvases relate the fifth-century legend of St Ursula, a British princess who agreed to marry Hereus of Brittany provided he delay the wedding for three years while she made a pilgimage to Rome with her 11,000 virgin followers. On the way home, the party was attacked by Huns at Cologne and all were massacred, Ursula because she refused to marry a Hun leader.

Carpaccio translates the story to contemporary Italianate settings, revelling in the detail of fashion, architecture, carpets, pageantry, working life and ships, with Venice assuming the role of Ursula's Breton city. Partitioned by the flagstaff but unified by sky and water, the huge canvas narrates several episodes, starting on the left in Britain where Hereus takes leave of his father. Outside the fortified city walls of the British capital a large carrack has been careened for repairs, its hull held fast by wooden shafts, a timber balk supporting the mainmast. Now Hereus's carrack heads out to sea, its lateen sail furled, its square mainsail revealing the ominous word *malo*, warning that there will be no happy ending.

Immediately right of the flagstaff, Hereus steps ashore in Brittany and Ursula meets him for the first time. The couple are then blessed in the city by her father before she and her followers board the barge to be rowed out to the carracks that will take them on their pilgrimage. The eye is drawn again to the carrack bearing that word *malo*, which now becomes Ursula's ship and closes this chapter of the cycle. *JH*

**The Meeting of Etherius and Ursula and the Departure of the Pilgrims, from the St. Ursula Cycle** *(oil on canvas), originally in the Scuola di Sant'Orsola, Venice, Vittorio Carpaccio, 1498, Galleria dell' Accademia, Venice, Italy / The Bridgeman Art Library*

70.8ft x 16.7ft x 5.2ft (21.6m x 5.1m x 1.6m) • 11 tons [B] • Hull wood • Complement 35 • Built Mediterranean, c. 1500

# Mary Rose   Tudor warship 1511

Notorious for sinking in 1545 with huge loss of life, the *Mary Rose* would have been little more than an obscure footnote in naval history had it not been for the discovery and raising of her hull in 1982 just off the coast of Portsmouth. A major part of the hull survived, and it also proved to contain, in an extraordinarily well-preserved condition, thousands of objects, ranging from shoes to longbows, which constitute a complete time-capsule of the period.

*Mary Rose*, one of the largest vessels of her time, was originally built in 1509 as a carrack, her military capability supplied by a crew of hundreds of soldiers armed with handguns, bows, iron darts and stones. In this configuration she fought in a number of actions, and was so well-regarded that she was described as the king's 'Noblest Shippe'.

In the 1530s, as part of Henry VIII's naval re-armament programme, *Mary Rose* was partly rebuilt. Many more gunports were cut along two decks and she was armed with 39 carriage cannon of various sizes and types, some made of iron and some of bronze, some firing stone cannonballs and some iron. However, it appears that the high fore- and stern-castles, characteristic of the carrack type, were not much reduced in height, if at all. Stability and freeboard may have been serious problems when she sailed out from Portsmouth to meet the enemy, a large French fleet which had arrived off the eastern end of the Isle of Wight, on 18 July 1545. It is unclear exactly what went wrong, but what is certain is that the ship sank with the loss of at least 400 crew, including her vice-admiral Sir George Carew, under the eyes of Henry VIII himself, who was watching from Southsea Castle. *GH*

The ***Mary Rose*** *(oil on canvas), Geoff Hunt, 2008, courtesy of the Mary Rose Trust*

106ft x 39.33ft (32.3m x 11.9m) • 600–800 tons [BM] • Hull wood • Armament 39 carriage cannon, 52 lighter guns, longbows, iron darts • Complement approx. 500 • Built Portsmouth, England, 1509

# Henry Grace à Dieu Tudor warship 1514

Two years after the Anglo-French treaty of 1518, the 29-year-old King of England, Henry VIII met King Francis I of France at Calais in an event that subsequently became known as the Field of the Cloth of Gold. It was an expensive festival of pageantry as both kings tried to impress each other with brilliance rather than substance. The event was recorded in two 12ft (3.7m) long paintings that are now at Hampton Court Palace as part of the Royal Collection. One painting records the Field of the Cloth of Gold and the other the embarkation of Henry VIII at Dover. It is not known who the original artist was although many names have been suggested. Both figures of Henry are based on the famous 1537 painting by Holbein indicating they were produced many years after the event. The picture was designed to hang in the Royal Palace at Westminster to impress visiting ambassadors with the naval might of England. It has been copied in numerous paintings and prints ever since, most notably by the Society of Antiquaries. This copy by Friedrich Bouterwek is particularly colourful and accurate.

Dover Castle can be seen to the left of the picture and the two towers in the foreground are the Archcliff Bulwark and the Black Bulwark. King Henry can be seen standing on his flagship, which would almost certainly have been the *Henry Grace à Dieu*. Other large ships in the fleet are present and the one nearest the viewer with four masts may be the *Mary Rose*. *RE*

**Embarkation of Henry VIII (1491-1547) on Board the *Henry Grace à Dieu* in 1520** *(oil on canvas), Friedrich Bouterwek, 1806-67, Musée de la Marine, Paris / Giraudon / The Bridgeman Art Library*

175-200ft x 50ft (53.3-61m x 15.2m) • 1500 tons [BM] • Hull wood • Armament: 43 heavy guns, 141 light guns • Complement 700–1000 • Built Woolwich Dockyard, London, England, 1514

# Victoria  Ferdinand Magellan's ship 1519

The Flemish cartographer Abraham Oertel published the first atlas of the world, *Theatrum Orbis Terrarum* in 1570. Among all the exquisite embellishment of the 1599 edition is this depiction of the *Victoria*, a small Portuguese carrack, or nao, firing her guns off the Pacific coast of South America. Beneath it, a Latin inscription reads:

> Prima ego velivolus ambivi cursibus Orbem
> Magellane novo te duce ducta freto.
> Ambivi, meritoque vocor VICTORIA: sunt mî
> Vela, alæ; precium, gloria; pugna, mare.

> (With sails flying, I was the first to circle the globe,
> I led you, Magellan, to your newly discovered strait.
> I have the right to be called VICTORIA.
> The sails and the wings, the prize and the glory, the struggle
> and the sea: these are mine.)

In 1519 the navigator Ferdinand Magellan was out of favour in his native Portugal, so offered his services to the Spanish and was appointed to lead a five-ship expedition to the Spice Islands of Indonesia. During the voyage down the South Atlantic, mutiny took its toll of men and ships, but in October 1520 the expedition reached Cape Virgines and Magellan led them through a long and spectacular strait that he named for himself. Emerging into calm waters on 28 November 1520, Magellan named the new sea the Pacific Ocean and pressed on to the Philippines only to be killed at Cebu by local forces. Juan Sebastián Elcano became the expedition leader, eventually transferring from the unseaworthy flagship, *Trinidad*, to the *Victoria*, by then the only other surviving ship. Instead of retracing the route home, he continued westwards, and three years after sailing, he brought the *Victoria* home to Spain, the first ship to achieve the circumnavigation of the globe. *JH*

*Maris Pacifici* [detail], an early map of the Pacific basin *(coloured engraving), Abraham Ortelius, 1589, Private Collection / The Bridgeman Art Library*

# Carrack  Trading ship c. 1521

The carrack, which developed in the fourteenth century and could still be seen three hundred years later, was something of a cross between the north European cog and the Mediterranean caravel, but larger than both. Early carracks had two masts, but as they increased in size – later Spanish and Portuguese carracks could measure as much as 2000 tons – three and four masts became the norm. They were square rigged on the foremast and mainmast, and lateen rigged on the mizzen and bonaventure masts. The projecting forecastle and raised poop of the cog were built up much higher, into huge sterncastles and forecastles, that in turn required higher masts and the addition first of topsails and later of topgallant sails. Extra lengths of canvas, called bonnets, could be attached to increase the sail area. Broad in the beam and primarily designed to carry cargo, carracks were typically cumbersome craft and difficult to manoeuvre.

The anonymous painting known as 'Portuguese Carracks off a Rocky Coast' is generally thought to have been painted after 1521 to commemorate the arrival of the Portuguese princess Beatriz at Villefranche to marry the Duke of Savoy. The carracks in the foreground fly the Portuguese flag, while the two galleys display the colours of Savoy, and several salutes are being fired. Yet none of the carracks suggests any of the well-documented pomp of the Infanta's voyage: no canopies or royally dressed people; nor is the largest carrack an accurate depiction of the Infanta's flagship, the Bombay-built Indiaman, *Santa Maria de Monte Sinai,* because the specially fitted stern-galleries are not in evidence. Nevertheless, the work was probably inspired by the occasion and is remarkable both as a fine example of maritime painting and as one of the very first of the genre. *JH*

**Portuguese Carracks off a Rocky Coast** *(oil on panel), circle of Joachim Patinir, c. 1540, Caird Collection, National Maritime Museum, London (BHC0705)*

No data available

# Galleass Galley 1571

When the Turks invaded Cyprus and threatened a westwards advance in 1570, Don John of Austria, persuaded a number of the Mediterranean Christians, including Spain, Venice, Genoa and the Knights of Malta, to set aside their rivalries for long enough to oppose the Ottoman fleet at sea. The Holy League assembled a fleet of more than two hundred galleys and at the Battle of Lepanto, fought in the Gulf of Patra on 7 October 1751, decisively defeated a slightly larger fleet under Ali Pasha.

Don John's inspired tactics aside, a significant factor in the Holy League's victory was its superior fire power – much of it concentrated in six Venetian galleasses. These huge galleys, three-masted, lateen-rigged, and converted from laid-up merchantmen, acted as mobile gun-platforms. Don John ordered two to be stationed half a mile in front of each of his three first-line squadrons, while the Genoese Admiral, Giandrea Doria, replaced his

swordsmen and pikemen with hundreds of harquebusiers who fired hails of musket balls into the enemy from the higher galleass decks.

The panoramic view clearly shows the confusion of a large scale galley battle in which ships become almost locked together and boarding parties race across the oars. The artist was evidently unaware that the galleys of the Holy League removed their rams before the battle because they encouraged the gunners on the forecastle to aim high and hit the rigging, instead of firing down into the enemy hulls below the waterline. The Venetian galleys fly white masthead pennants displaying the Lion of St Mark, and the galleasses are differentiated from them by the gunports encircling their decks, above the benches where the oarsmen sat.

Although war galleys saw action for a further century in the Mediterranean, Lepanto was the last full-scale galley battle. *JH*

**The Battle of Lepanto, 7 October 1571** *(oil on canvas), H. Letter, late sixteenth century, National Maritime Museum, London (BHC0261)*

168.5ft x 58.57ft x 10.1ft (51.36m x 8.71m x 3.1m) • Hull wood • Armament c. 40+ guns; lower deck 13kg (28.6 lbs); upper deck 23kg (50lbs) • Complement (including soldiers) approx. 1000 • Built Venice, Italy, c. 1570

# La Real  Galley 1571

Flagship of young Don John of Austria, the Spanish galley *La Real* fired the first shot for the heterogeneous fleet of the Holy League against the Turks during the Battle of Lepanto on 7 October 1751. With the wind suddenly in their favour, and the crucifix banner flying at *Real*'s masthead, the League's galleys had advanced on the Turkish line without returning fire until that signal from *Real* unleashed their superior firepower. Don John ordered his captain, Juan Vasqez Coronado, to steer for the *Sultana*, flagship of Ali Pasha himself, and as the two galleys closed, he allegedly danced a galliard on the poop gun-platform while his 300 crack Sardinian harquebusiers waited. The two ships crashed together, but boarding nets repelled two Turkish attacks. Then, with a female harquebusier, Maria la Bailadora, among the first, the Sardinians poured over the bow. In the fighting Ali was decapitated, his head paraded aboard the *Real*. By 4 p.m. the combined forces of Spain, Genoa,

Venice, Sicily, the Papal States and the Knights of Malta had won a bloody but major victory, long to be remembered.

Commemorating the quarto-centenary of Lepanto, the reconstruction of *La Real* is housed in Barcelona's Maritime Museum, inside the former Royal Dockyard where her predecessor was built three years before the battle. The foremast and mainmast stand 49ft (15m) and 72ft (22m) tall, and carry two lateen sails totalling 7437.8ft$^2$ (691m$^3$) and 24,402.8ft (7438m) of canvas. Although Don John's *Real* was a war galley, she had, nevertheless, been palatially decorated with gilded carvings and painted panels depicting Christian and mythological themes designed by Juan de Mallara. His detailed descriptions allowed modern artists to recreate these on the reproduction. The three great stern lamps that figure prominently in the photograph below symbolize the virtues of Faith, Hope and Charity. *JH*

196.8ft x 20.5ft (60m x 6.2m) • Hull wood • Armament 5 guns, bow ram • Complement 236 oarsmen, approx. 300 soldiers • Built Barcelona, Spain, c. 1571

# Golden Hinde   Francis Drake's galleon 1577

The Elizabethan adventurer Francis Drake circumnavigated the globe during his epic voyage of 1577–80 aboard the galleon *Pelican*, which he renamed *Golden Hinde* as he approached the Straits of Magellan. This name honoured his patron, Sir Christopher Hatton, whose heraldic crest featured a golden hind (a female deer). Drake, encouraged by Queen Elizabeth I, planned to loot treasure from Spain's empire. He successfully raided ports and captured Spanish ships off the west coast of South America, accumulating large amounts of gold and silver. Drake sailed on to the west coast of North America, claiming land for England as Nova Albion. The extent of this territory and the exact point of Drake's landing have been debated by historians for many years, but the coast of northern California has been tentatively identified as being the most likely location.

Thence he headed west to the East Indies and continued homeward via the Cape of Good Hope, becoming the first Englishman to complete a circumnavigation. In September 1580 the triumphant Drake arrived at Plymouth, England, and was later knighted by Elizabeth aboard his ship at Deptford, London.

The illustration shows a full-size *Golden Hinde* replica displayed on London's South Bank. She was built in 1973 and has sailed more than 140,000 miles under sail, including a circumnavigation of the globe. She is open to the public and also caters for educational visits and sleepovers by groups of schoolchildren, who can dress up as Tudor sailors and receive living history lessons on 'Drake and the Age of Exploration'. Another replica of the ship is at Brixham in Devon. *PB*

Golden Hind *(photograph), Paul Brown, 2008*

120ft x 18ft x 9ft (36.6 m x 5.5m x 2.7m) • 300 tons [BM] • Hull wood • Complement approx. 80 • Armament 22 guns • Built Appledore, Devon, England, 1577

# The Ship of State Allegorical ship c. 1580

For thousands of years the nautical environment has provided the world with metaphors, verbal and visual, particularly when it comes to politics: the very word 'government' derives from the Latin for 'to steer'; politicians pay attention to the 'groundswell' of public opinion; and the economy heads into 'uncharted waters'. A late sixteenth-century Spaniard would take a very uncomfortable message from the curious allegory known as 'The Ship of State' by the Flemish artist Frans Francken the Elder (1542–1616). It was painted at a time when the Netherlands were in revolt against their Catholic Spanish masters and when Protestantism was gaining importance.

The Catholic Church is represented as the Ship of Peter, and the Pope himself stands at the stern above his cardinals, bishops and monks. In front of him is a figure in scarlet and ermine who is probably King Philip of Spain, thus showing the unity of Church and State. At first glance, the ship glides through the treacherous waters with a favourable wind, contemptuous of the dangers: wolves in the cave, a blazing meteorite striking a rock, smoke spurting from the rock in the foreground. Wild giants threaten with clubs, mermaids preen themselves – symbols of lust, vanity and transience. A closer look at the occupants tells a different story. The galleon is oddly equipped with oars, but the oarsmen seem passive; nobody is in obvious command of the vessel or providing a lookout. Some passengers seem oblivious to their peril; others, like the king, are clearly alarmed. Spanish power in the Netherlands is heading for the rocks. *JH*

Allegory: The Ship of State *(oil on panel), Frans Franken the Elder, late sixteenth century, National Maritime Museum, London (BHC0708)*

# Ark Royal   Galleon 1588

Five Royal Navy ships have carried the name *Ark Royal*, four of them twentieth-century aircraft carriers. The name had first been bestowed on a warship in 1587 when, at a cost of £5000 Queen Elizabeth purchased a new four-masted galleon built for one of her favourite courtiers, Sir Walter Raleigh. The ship had been launched as *Ark Raleigh*; she entered naval service as *Ark Royal* and became the flagship of Admiral Lord Howard of Effingham during the 1588 campaign to defeat the Spanish Armada.

In this detail from a painting of the main action off Gravelines on 8 August, executed by an unknown artist of the period, *Ark Royal* is seen stern on, firing into the bows of a large Spanish galleass. She flies the English Royal Ensign from her maintop and also the Cross of St George. Although the stern castle appears high, almost obscuring the fourth mast, the forecastles and stern castles of the English galleons were now much lower than those of the Spanish, making the ships lighter, faster and more stable than their enemy's and at the same time increasing the number of cannon. It gave them a significant advantage in the battle and afterwards when, unable to escape westwards down the Channel, the Spanish were pursued into the North Sea. Bad weather and navigational limitations then completed the Spanish defeat.

*Ark Royal* participated in other operations against the Spanish and after Elizabeth's death she was renamed *Anne Royal* in honour of James I's queen, rebuilt and enlarged. Her career continued into the reign of Charles 1; she was Lord Wimbledon's ship in the bungled 1625 attack on Cadiz. In 1636 she was accidentally sunk in the River Medway and despite being raised at great cost, broken up. *JH*

**English Ships and the Spanish Armada, August 1588** *(oil on poplar panel), English School, sixteenth century, National Maritime Museum, London* (BHC0262)

103ft x 37ft x 16ft (31m x 11m x 4.9m) • 800 tons [BM] • Hull wood • Armament 42 guns of various weights of shot • Complement approx. 400 • Built R. Chapman, Deptford, England, 1587

# Geobukseon  Turtle ship c. 1592

Between the fourteenth and sixteenth centuries, Korea suffered from a continuous barrage of Japanese pirate attacks, many of which penetrated deep inland, resulting in rampant vandalism and murder. At one point, debates arose concerning the possibility of moving Goryeo, Korea's capital. When Korean forces began to confront the pirates at sea, they found themselves grossly outnumbered, as Japanese armadas often involved several hundred ships. In an act of desperation in 1380, the Goryeo Navy led by Admiral Shim Deok-Bu and the forefather of Korean firearms, Choi Mu-Seon, sailed to sea with cannon installed aboard their decks. The ensuing seabourne encounter, later known as the Jinpo Naval Battle, would become the first naval battle in world history to involve anti-ship naval gunnery.

The Goryeo Dynasty would soon fall, and the Joseon Dynasty took over. Yet naval developments continued under the personal direction of each monarch. The range and lethality of naval gunnery improved, and various ship designs were attempted, with a number of them commissioned into service. During the latter half of the sixteenth century, nearly two centuries of development culminated in the birth of the two most lethal 'ship-killers' East Asia would see until the birth of the Imperial Japanese Navy (IJN) in the nineteenth century: the Panokseon and the Geobukseon or turtle ship.

First launched in 1555, the ships proved their value during the Imjin Waeran (1592–98), a seven-year war between Korea, China and Japan. Though assisted by Ming China on land, Joseon Korea saw no Chinese naval assistance until the war's very last naval battle. Under the direction of Admiral Yi Sun-Shin, the Joseon Navy never lost a sea battle throughout the seven years, including 12 major engagements which included the Battle of Myeongryang, when the Joseon Navy's 13 Panokseons defeated 133 Japanese ships. In the war's final battle, the Battle of Noryang, Admiral Yi led a unified Ming-Joseon fleet, and a mix of Chinese and Korean vessels, to destroy more than 200 Japanese ships. In total, more than 700 Japanese warships were destroyed throughout the seven years, the vast majority of them by the Panokseon and the turtle ship.

The Joseon Navy's victories at sea and their successful severance of the logistics chain between Japan and the Asian continent resulted in Japan's inability to continue the war effort. The war ended in 1598, and the Japanese retreat forced by the Joseon Navy would last almost 300 years until the Meiji era rejuvenated Japan's desires for power projection. *MH*

**Yi Sun-Shin's Turtle Ship, National War Memorial, Korea** (photograph) *War Memorial of Korea, Yongsan-dong, Yongsan-gu, Seoul, South Korea*

No data available

# Amsterdam  Merchant ship 1597

This arresting painting has come to be known as 'The Wreck of the Amsterdam' because the coat of arms of Amsterdam is clearly visible on the stern of the principal ship, but the name of that vessel, along with the name and nationality of the artist, the date and the event commemorated, remains an intriguing puzzle. It is easier to exclude artists than to attribute the work to any one, though the style is that of a Flemish or Flemish-trained painter and the design of the ship points towards the early seventeenth century.

The bold, dynamic composition with its dramatic lighting brings alive the savage weather. The remnants of a vessel wrecked on the rocks on the left are going down; the carving of the Virgin Mary on her stern – in a pose close to that on a flag in Adam Willaerts's 'Dutch squadron attacking a Spanish fortress' – suggests she is a Spanish ship. Central to the painting is the Dutch ship, intact but on her beam ends, with crewmen climbing the rigging and a claw-like wave threatening to drag her down. As hellish lightning picks out the spars and rigging of a third ship, two more vessels can be discerned heading towards brighter skies.

Shipwreck paintings were frequently allegories – religious, moral or political. During the sixteenth century, Dutch provinces banded together to wrest independence from Spain.

Until 1578, however, Amsterdam had sided with Spain. If the painting is a warning to the city not to tie her fate to that of Spain, that would date it to pre-1578, which is unfeasible. Almost certainly executed during the 80-year conflict the painting could be an illustration of the devastation of war and the sacrifices that the people of Amsterdam were willing to make to gain their freedom. JH

The Wreck of the *Amsterdam* (oil on canvas), Anonymous, c. 1630, Palmer Collection, National Maritime Museum, London (BHC0724)

# Duyfken  Barque 1606

On 18 November 1605 a small three-masted yacht belonging to the Vereenigde Oost-Indische Compagnie (VOC) sailed from Bantam, a trading station in the Dutch East Indies, to explore beyond the Spice Islands. The vessel was the *Duyfken* – 'Little Dove' – commanded by an excellent seaman and navigator, Captain Willem Janszoon. She called at the Kei group, and the New Guinea coast – where several of her crew were killed by local people – and eventually reached the Cape York peninsula of northern Australia.

Janszoon charted the coastline for some 300 miles as far as Cape Keerweer, before returning to Bantam, making this the first European expedition not only to have reached the fabled *Terra Australis* but also to have made contact with Aborigines. Yet the Dutch achievement never gained the same fame as Captain Cook's much later voyage. *Duyfken* paid the price of years of active service in eastern waters: built in the Netherlands in 1595, by 1608 the teredo worm had taken such a toll on her hull that she was condemned at Ternate.

In 2000 a new *Duyfken* sailed from Fremantle. Constructed using sixteenth century techniques and authentic materials sourced from around the world, from plans based on three sketches and the few known details of the original, *Dufken* surprised everyone by being fast, stable and easy to handle. Although she had a shallow draught which made her ancestor ideal for surveying and coastal exploration, no problems were experienced in re-enacting Janszoon's epic voyage. In 2002, following the same route that the first *Duyfken* had taken in her trading voyages for the VOC, she made a return voyage to Texel in the Netherlands as part of the 400th anniversary celebrations that commemorated the founding of the VOC in 1602. *JH*

**Duyfken** *(photograph). The Duyfken 1606 Replica foundation Inc. (www.duyfken.com)*

[Replica specifications, unless otherwise stated] 72ft x 19.7ft x 9.5ft (21.9m x 6m x 2.9m ) • Hull wood • Armament (original ship) 4 'murderers' (small anti-personnel cannon), 12 x 3 pdr • Complement 16 • Built Fremantle, Australia, 1999

# De Halve Maen Henry Hudson's ship 1609

For centuries North European explorers searched for a navigable northern passage linking the Atlantic and the Pacific oceans, offering an alternative to the route to China and the Indies that was controlled by the Spanish and Portuguese. For the Englishman Henry Hudson it became a fatal obsession that would cost him his life. His first attempt ended when stopped by polar ice in the Svalbard Islands; a second venture failed the following year. In 1609 he was hired by VOC (the Dutch East India Company) to command the *Halve Maen* (*Half Moon*), a three-masted, square-sterned yacht to pursue the search. Thwarted by ice at Norway's North Cape, he decided on a radically different approach, sailing to the east coast of America and, from 12 September, investigating the river that now bears his name. He passed the island known as Manna-hatta and sailed as far as Albany, after which the river became un-navigable, and on 23 September *Halve Maen* began her return voyage. Contact was made with Native Americans, with whom Hudson traded on a generally friendly basis. On the basis of Hudson's glowing report, the Dutch went on to establish a settlement named New Amsterdam – later New York.

In 1610 Hudson made a fourth and final voyage, to what is now Hudson's Bay, Canada, for English interests. When, after a winter ashore, Hudson refused the crew's demand to return, he was set adrift with those loyal to him and left to perish.

'The Landing of Henry Hudson' was painted in 1838 by Robert Walter Weir (1803-1889). Weir belonged the Hudson River School which celebrated the landscape of the Hudson in dramatic romanticism, often through the use of light effects known as Luminism.

Two replicas of *Halve Maen* have been built: one in 1909, the second in 1989 at Albany. *JH*

*The Landing of Henry Hudson* (oil on canvas), Robert Walter Weir, 1838, David David Gallery, Philadelphia, Pennsylvania, USA / SuperStock

No data available

# Prince Royal  55-gun ship of the line 1613

King James I's decision to commission Phineas Pett to build a full-size version of the model warship that the inexperienced shipwright had presented to the Lord Admiral Howard provoked jealousy and scepticism. The result, however, was the largest ship built in England at the time, the sumptuously decorated, four-masted, 55-gun *Prince Royal*, named for young Prince Henry (1594–1612) who officiated at her launch in 1610. Technically the first three-decker, only after 1621 did she have three continuous gun decks; by the outbreak of the English Civil War in 1642 she mounted 70 guns.

The war ended with the execution of Charles I, and *Prince Royal*, now part of the Commonwealth Navy, was renamed *Resolution*, becoming the flagship of Generals-at-Sea Monck, Deane and Ayscue during the First Anglo-Dutch War. At the Restoration she reverted to her old name and was again enlarged. As a 90-gun First Rate she fought in the Second Anglo-Dutch War but grounded at the battle of Scheveningen and was captured and burnt by the Dutch. Ayscue was the last English Admiral to be captured in battle.

Adam Willaert's painting depicts *Prince Royal* as built. The canvas commemorates the departure from Margate in 1613 of James I's daughter Elizabeth and her bridegroom, Frederick, the Elector Palatine. Despite the busy-ness and detail there is a sadness in the picture: the returning small boat, the distance from shore, the white cliffs, and the crowds beginning to lose interest. The princess was not happy. The young couple briefly held the throne of Bohemia as Europe plunged into the Thirty Years War. Widowed in 1632, Elizabeth continued in hand-to-mouth exile, returning to England a year before her death in 1662. She was the mother of the royalist commander, later Admiral, Prince Rupert, and grandmother of George I. *JH*

**Embarkation of the Elector Palatine in the *Prince Royal* at Dover, 25 April 1613** *(oil on wood panel), Adam Willaerts, 1622, National Maritime Museum, London (BHC0266)*

[As built] 115ft x 43.6ft x 18ft (35m x 13.3m x 5.5m; [after 1663] 132ft x 45.2ft x 18.10ft (40m x 13.8m x 5.74 metres) • [As built] 1200 tons, [after 1663] 1432 tons [BM] • Hull wood • Armament 55 guns, after 1663 92 guns • Complement 500 • Built Woolwich, England, 1610

# Mayflower   Merchant ship 1620

A distinctly seventeenth-century ship approaches an iconic twentieth-century skyline on the most important day in the US calendar: 4 July.

*Mayflower II* was the realization of Warwick Chorlton's 1950 dream to create a gift symbolizing all the links that bound Britain and the USA: a 'replica' of the *Mayflower*, the ship that brought the Pilgrim Fathers to the coast of Massachusetts in 1620. All that was known of the original was that she was old, carried topsails, and measured about 180 tons. The three-masted barque that emerged from Stuart Upham's Brixham yard in 1957 was based on similar-sized merchant ships of the early seventeeth century. Her hull was constructed of English oak, with Oregon pine for the masts and spars. Her sails were made from flax canvas and hemp was used for the 400 individual ropes. Althought fitted with a wheel, she could also be steered authentically from the deck by means of a whipstaff, a vertical timber connected via a pivot to the end of the tiller below deck.

Captained by Alan Villiers, who had been a Master Mariner in the last days of merchant sailing ships, and with a crew that included a descendant of the Pilgrim Fathers, the ship's builder, and Chorlton himself, *Mayflower II* departed Britain from Plymouth on 20 April. Shaping a 5000-mile southerly course to avoid any ice, and greeted effusively by passenger liners and naval ships, she reached Plymouth Massachusetts 55 days later. After visiting East Coast ports, including New York, *Mayflower II* returned to Massachusetts to be presented to the Plimoth Plantation, a living history museum commemorating the colony founded by the Pilgrim Fathers, at which she can be visited today, still in seaworthy condition. *JH*

*Mayflower II* **entering New York Harbour** *(photograph), Conway Picture Library*

[Replica specifications] 106ft x 25ft x 12.6ft (32.3m x 7.62m x 3.84m) • 180 tons [D] • Hull wood (oak) • Complement 21 • Built J W & A Upham Ltd, Brixham, Devon, England, 1957

# Vasa  Flagship 1628

As the ship billed as the heaviest and most splendid of the Swedish navy, the career of the *Vasa* was an ignominious disaster. Having sailed for less than a nautical mile during her maiden voyage on 10 August 1628, she heeled over and sank. Top-heavy and perilously unstable, even in still waters in port, her ballast was insufficient in anything other than a breeze and her open lower gun ports were quickly flooded with water. She sank in full view of a crowd of hundreds, if not thousands, of well-wishers. As many as 50 members of the crew drowned that day. The flags and the tops of the main mast were still visible above the surface.

She was intended to be a statement of imperial pride and expansionist ambition for Sweden, and the glory of King Gustavus Adolphus, but instead became a national embarrassment. Though her bronze cannon were salvaged in the seventeenth century, she remained largely forgotten until she was located again in the late 1950s, in a busy shipping lane just outside Stockholm harbour. Amazingly, when salvaged in 1961, the hull was relatively intact and by 1990 she was preserved and housed in a special museum in the city. One of Sweden's most popular tourist attractions, *Vasa* has now attracted almost 30 million visitors and has become a precious work of art. *HLJ*

**Stern of the warship *Vasa*, built 1628** *(photograph). Ken Welsh, Vasa Museum, Stockholm, Sweden / Ken Welsh / The Bridgeman Art Library*

226ft x 38ft x 16ft (69m x 11.7m x 4.8m) • 1200 tons [BM] • Hull wood • Armament 48 x 24 pdr, 8 x 3 pdr, 2 x 1 pdr, 6 x howitzers • Complement 145 sailors, 300 soldiers • Built Henrik Hybertsson and Henrik Jacobsson, Stockholm, Sweden, 1626-1628

# Batavia  Dutch East Indiaman 1629

One of the most savage mutinies on record took place in 1629 involving the Dutch East Indiaman, *Batavia*, bound for modern-day Jakarta. Longstanding differences between the ship's captain, Adriaen Jacobz, and the cargo superintendent, Francisco Pelsaert, who was in overall command of the voyage, led to Jacobz planning a mutiny. He intended to seize control of both ship and treasure and then turn pirate, but on 4 June the *Batavia* ran onto a reef in the Abrolhos Islands, off the coast of Western Australia, with 294 crew and soldiers and 38 passengers on board.

Most of the complement were ferried in the boats to nearby islands, where there was little water, and Jacobz and Pelsaert set off in the boats to bring help from Jakarta, 1600 miles away. With them went the ship's officers, leaving Pelsaert's deputy, Jeronimus Cornelisz, as the senior officer. Unbeknown to Pelsaert, Cornelisz had been heavily involved in the mutiny

plot. He rapidly took control on his island, gathering around him a band of thugs to impose his will through a sadistic regime of rape, murder and torture. The only opposition came from 20 soldiers under Wiebbe Hayes who had been left on another island in a vain search for water, or so Cornelisz erroneously hoped.

Cornelisz was determined to wipe them out, and even after he was captured his mutineers carried on. In the middle of the final battle, on 17 September, the rescue ship was sighted, and the mutineers went to meet and seize it. Hayes, however, got there first. The mutineers were tried, and a number executed. Two were marooned on the mainland, the first Europeans to settle in Australia.

An ocean-going replica of the *Batavia* was launched in the Netherlands in 1995 and is on display at Lelystad. *JH*

**The replica of the *Batavia* on the Markermeer** *(photograph), 15 March 2007, ADZee / Public Domain*

[Replica specifications unless otherwise stated] 185.6ft x 35.4ft x 16.7ft (56.6m x 10.5m x 5.10m) • 1200 tons [BM] • Armament 24 guns • Complement (original ship) 294 • Built (original) VOC, Amsterdam, Holland, 1628; (replica) Batavia Yard, Lelystad, Netherlands, 1995

# Dutch Racing Yachts Early yachts 1630

The Antwerp-born artist Andries van Eertvelt (1590–1652) depicts a dramatic scene of what is traditionally believed to be Dutch yachts and working boats racing off a northern European coast, in a large-scale oil painted in the 1630s. The boats are shown in a stiff breeze and the crews are frantically working the sails to harness the wind to full advantage.

The specific course of the yachts is not clear and that has led some scholars to question the subject of the picture. However, the sunlight streaming in from the left under the dark rain clouds, the highlighted hulls and taut sails confirm the sense of vigour and competition evident in this vivid painting. It is arguably the earliest recorded oil painting of racing yachts and is painted in a stylized theatrical Flemish method traditionally known as 'Flemish Mannerism'. Two boats to the right fly the flag of the United Provinces, while in the centre the yachts fly the Dutch flag. To the far left the vessel flies the arms (three silver crosses below a crown) of the City of Amsterdam.

Andries van Eertvelt joined the Guild of St Luke as a Master in either 1609 or 1610. His painting style derives in part from Pieter Bruegel the Elder; later in his career, however, he demonstrates a greater degree of 'naturalism' and this may be through association with, or the influence of, Hendrik Vroom and also Jan van Goyen. *JT*

1501-1650

**Dutch Yachts Racing** *(oil on canvas), Andries van Eertvelt, c. 1630, National Maritime Museum, London (BHC0741)*

No data available

# Barbary Ships   Corsairs' raiding ships c. 1640

From the age of the crusades right up to the 1830s the Barbary corsairs were the scourge of the Mediterranean and Atlantic trade. The Battle of Lepanto may have halted Muslim expansion in the Mediterranean, but the pirates continued to raid the coasts of Italy and Spain and to prey on merchant ships, not only stealing the cargoes but enslaving or holding for ransom hundreds of thousands of men, women and children. The term 'Barbary' referred to the North African coast which had come under the control of the Ottoman Empire in the sixteenth century, and the pirate 'capital' of the Mediterranean was Algiers. The corsairs were privateers, working for the empire rather than for themselves.

'Spanish engagement with Barbary pirates', by the Flemish painter Andries van Eertvelt was executed in the early seventeenth century, the period when the raiding power of the corsairs was at its height. At this time they were extending their range into the Atlantic as far as Iceland, frequently snatching and enslaving inhabitants from Ireland and the south-west of England. Van Eertvelt depicts a savage encounter with the Spanish, showing the large scale on which the pirates operated. Their light galleys, similar to xebecs, with fine lines, banks of oars and lateen sails, were fast and more manoeuvrable than the ships they attacked. They carried huge crews for boarding, and in the painting two of them are attempting to surround the large Spanish galleon, despite a hail of fire from the soldiers. The dismasted, sinking galley on the left, however, suggests that perhaps on this occasion the pirates have met their match.

Over the centuries the navies of various states, from Venice to Spain and the USA, attempted to stamp out the piracy but it ended only around 1830 when the French captured Algiers. *JH*

**Spanish engagement with Barbary pirates** *(oil on panel), Andries van Eertvelt, seventeenth century, National Maritime Museum, London (BHC0747)*

# Sovereign of the Seas First Rate ship of the line c. 1645

*Sovereign of the Seas* was built as a prestige warship after a meeting in 1634 at Woolwich Dockyard between King Charles I and the Master Shipwright, Phineas Pett. Her epic proportions and huge cost appalled just about everyone from Trinity House to the ordinary citizen who would have to pay for her with a special Ship Money Tax. Her carvings and decorations were designed by Sir Anthony van Dyke and finished in real gilt rather than paint. She also had an expensive new set of 104 lightweight bronze guns of revolutionary design, which quickly wore out and proved unsuccessful. Not only that but she was an anomaly in the fleet, her deep draught precluded her from sailing in shallow waters where smaller, more nimble ships could

operate. In spite of these ominous beginnings her mighty presence in battle established the English practice of having three-decker First and Second Rates at the heart of their battle squadrons.

The ship was completed by Phineas Pett's son Peter, who was painted by the famous portrait artist Sir Peter Lely, with the ship to his right. Unlike a contemporary print of the ship, which shows her with main, topmast, topgallant and royals, this portrait shows her with main and topmasts only. The artist also appears to have made a mistake in showing a square tuck rather than a round. *RE*

1501-1650

Peter Pett and the *Sovereign of the Seas* (oil on canvas), Sir Peter Lely, c. 1645-50, Caird Collection, National Maritime Museum, London (BHC2949)

232ft x 48ft (70.7m x 14.6m) • 1141 tons [BM] • Hull wood • Armament 102 guns • Complement approx. 800 • Built Woolwich, London, England, 1637

# Galliot  Ships of the Anglo-Dutch War 1653

Fought between 1652 and 1654 to settle conflicts over trade, the First Anglo-Dutch War culminated in the Battle of Scheveningen in August 1653 when the 100-strong Dutch fleet of Lieutenant-Admiral Tromp lifted the blockade of Vice-Admiral de With's fleet at Texel. The English fleet, commanded by General-at-Sea George Monck in *Resolution*, brought the Dutch to battle on the 10 August but, despite destroying many of their ships, was too badly mauled to capitalize on its success. The major casualties included Tromp and Rear Admiral Robert Graves.

In the grisaille drawing by Willem van de Velde the Elder, events are compressed. The two fleets are closely engaged as they pass, the Dutch on the starboard tack, the English on the port. While the Dutch fly their tricolour flag, the English ships fly that of the Commonwealth of England.

The main focus on the battle is found in the right foreground where the Dutch fire ship, the *Fortune*, has attacked the 66-gun *Andrew*, setting it ablaze and forcing the crew to abandon ship. The billowing smoke and flames hide all but the topmasts of the *Jong Prins te Pard*. However, identification of many of the ships is made possible by the detailed depiction of their carved sterns; for example, the figure of *Fortune*, the star on the *Ster* and the greyhound on the *Winhond*.

At this time van de Velde was the Dutch Navy's official artist and the work suggests the Dutch have the upper hand. An eye-witness of the battle, he can be seen calmly sketching in the small galliot in the foreground. A galliot was a bluff, barge-like craft with a shallow draught, lee-boards and fore-and-aft rigged sail on a single mast. It was primarily a coastal trader. *JH*

**The Battle of Scheveningen, 10 August 1653** *(oil on panel with pen and brush), Willem van de Velde the Elder, 1655, Caird Collection, National Maritime Museum, London (BHC0277)*

# Royal Escape Royal yacht c. 1660

At eight o'clock on the morning of Wednesday, 15 October 1651 Francis Mansell's collier brig *Surprise*, captained by Nicholas Tettersall, weighed anchor at Shoreham, ostensibly bound for Poole.

Two hours later, Parliamentarian soldiers arrived at Shoreham in search of a 6ft 2in man with dark hair and a swarthy complexion. They were too late: Charles II, a fugitive since his defeat at the Battle of Worcester on 3 September, was safely aboard the collier which, that afternoon, changed course for France and landed him at Fécamp the following morning. Captain Tettersall reached Poole quickly enough to allay any suspicions about his activities. He had earned himself £60, £940 less than Parliament would have paid him for betraying his King.

At the Restoration in 1660, Tettersall sailed the *Surprise* up the Thames for the public to view and the King to notice. Charles, who had enjoyed messing about in boats during his exile in Holland, purchased her, renamed her *Royal Escape*, and had her rigged as a smack-rigged yacht with the royal coat of arms on her stern and gilding around her companionways and ports.

'The Royal Escape Close-Hauled in a Breeze' is one of two paintings of the yacht commissioned by Charles from Willem van de Velde the Younger, whose marine paintings were frequently produced from his father's superb drawings and who does not attempt to flatter the squat former collier. The *Royal Escape* was given to the navy for general service in 1673, just after the two artists settled in London, but it is very tempting to look at the costume worn by the small figures emerging from the stern cabin and speculate on the identity of the wearers. *JH*

**The *Royal Escape* Close-Hauled in a Breeze** *(oil), Willem van de Velde the Younger, date unknown, National Maritime Museum, London (BHC3600)*

No data available

# De Zeven Provinciën First Rate ship of the line 1666

Named for the seven provinces comprising the Dutch Republic, the 80-gun ship of the line *De Zeven Provinciën* saw early action against the English as the flagship of Admiral de Ruyter at the Four Days Battle, 1666, part of the Second Anglo-Dutch War. The battle ended in a costly Dutch victory, and the English took revenge in August in the St. James's Day Battle, during which *De Zeven Provinciën* lost her topmast to a broadside from the *Royal Charles*.

The following year, *De Zeven Provinciën* blockaded the Thames while other ships of the Dutch fleet sailed up the Medway, destroyed several ships of the line and triumphantly towed away the *Royal Charles*. A brief anti-French Anglo-Swedish-Dutch alliance was followed by the Third Dutch War which now pitted the Dutch against the combined Anglo-French Fleet. *De Zeven Provinciën* fought in all four of the naval battles, once again as de Ruyter's

flagship. At the last, the Battle of the Texel, de Ruyter again proved his tactical brilliance. Reduced to 76 guns, and no longer a flagship, she fought for the last time at the Battles of Barfleur and La Hogue in 1692, when the Anglo-Dutch fleet commanded by Admiral Edward Russell defeated the French. She sustained serious damage in the engagement and was later broken up. Hers had been a remarkable fighting career, one in which she had rarely been on the losing side. A replica is currently under construction at Lelystad.

In his highly detailed painting 'Royal Prince and other Vessels at the Four Days Battle, 1–4 June 1666' Abraham Storck gives her great prominence in a stern view that displays the arms of the Republic and her year of launch, exchanging fire with the grounded English flagship *Royal Prince*, which was later captured and burnt. *JH*

The *Royal Prince* and other Vessels at the Four Days Battle, 1–4 June 1666 *(oil on canvas), Abraham Storck, c. 1670, National Maritime Museum, London* (BHC0286)

151ft x 40ft x 15ft (47m x 12m x 4.6 m) • 1522 tons [BM] • Hull wood • Armament [as built] 12 x 36 pdr, 16 x 24 pdr, 14 x 18 pdr, 12 x 12 pdr, 26 x 6 pdr • Complement 500 • Built Salomon Jansz van den Tempel, Rotterdam, Holland, 1665

# Royal Charles  First Rate ship of the line 1667

Among the exhibits on display in Amsterdam's Rijksmuseum is the counter of the English First Rate *Royal Charles*, emblazoned with the sovereign's coat of arms. In 1667 the Dutch Navy under their brilliant admiral Michiel de Ruyter, executed an audacious plan by sailing into the River Medway, attacking the Royal Dockyard at Chatham, and returning in triumph to Hellevoetsluis with two ships including the *Royal Charles*. The ship drew too much water to be of use to the Dutch so they broke it up, keeping the counter as a trophy.

Even larger than the *Sovereign of The Seas*, the *Royal Charles* had been built in 1655 as the *Naseby*, with a figurehead modelled on Oliver Cromwell and seen action during the First Anglo-Dutch War. Five years later, renamed and minus the figurehead, she brought the restored monarch, Charles II, home from exile in the Dutch Republic. Given all the circumstances, her loss was a national humiliation for England but commemorated gleefully for the Dutch by various artists.

'Dutch attack on the Medway: The Royal Charles carried into Dutch Waters, 12 June 1667' was painted by Ludolf Bakhuizen the same year. Meticulous about the technical accuracy of the ships he painted, he also understood drama and public relations. The stern of the *Royal Charles* is prominent in the three-quarter view, as is the Dutch tricolour, and, on the left, a richly decorated Admiralty yacht has come out from the naval base at Hellevoetsluis to view the prize. The yacht is a typical Dutch galliot with a large leeboard visible on her starboard. Two well-dressed men watch from the shelter of the canopy. Their identity is speculative, possibly Bakhuizen's client, maybe a senior naval figure, or even the Grand Pensionary Johan de Witt whose brother, Cornelis sailed with de Ruyter. *JH*

**Dutch attack on the Medway: the *Royal Charles* carried into Dutch Waters, 12 June 1667** *(oil on canvas), Ludolf Bakhuizen, 1667, National Maritime Museum, London (BHC0292)*

162ft x 42.5ft x 11ft (49.4m x 13m x 3.4m) • 1230 tons [BM] • Hull wood • Armament 80 guns • Complement 500–650 • Built Woolwich, London, England, 1655

# St Michael  First Rate ship of the line 1669

The construction of scale ship models originates from the mid-seventeenth century when members of the Navy Board, the body responsible for the design and building of the full-sized warships, used them as a 'three dimensional plan' for deciding upon the proposed designs of the Navy's warships. The models were generally built to a standard scale of ¼in to the foot (1:48), the same scale as the ship's plans, using fruitwoods and employing a plank-on-frame method. Their primary purpose was to show the shape and layout of the hull, the arrangements of the guns and the carved decoration. The model of the *St Michael* is thought to be the oldest contemporary example which can be positively identified. This has been verified by comparing known dimensions of the actual ship together with the drawings of the ship and decoration by the Dutch marine artist Willem

Van de Velde the Younger. The most noticeable features of the 'Navy Board' models are the stylized open hull frames below the waterline. It is thought that the contrast of the wooden frames alongside the dark shadow of the spaces between highlights the complex curves around the bow and stern, a detail that would be difficult to interpret from the two dimensional ship's plan. The omission of some of the deck planking also allowed light into the model to show the layout of the accommodation and internal features such as the cooking galley, riding bitts and capstans used for working the rigging and anchors. Most models of this period were not fully rigged as there was very little innovation in this area until the early eighteenth century. The masts, spars and some of the standing rigging are original, with repairs to the running rigging made in the 1930s. *SS*

*St Michael*, **1:48 scale Navy Board style model** (wood, cotton, brass, mica, paint, gilt, varnish), c. 1672, Caird Collection, National Maritime Museum, London (F9219-003)

125 ft x 40.9ft x 17.5ft (38m x 12.4m x 5.31m) • 1118 tons [BM] • Hull wood • Armament 90 guns • Built John Tippetts, Portsmouth, England, 1669

# Gouden Leeuw First Rate ship of the line 1673

In 1672 Charles II abandoned his alliance with Holland and Sweden and concluded another with France. The following year, after a French advance by land into Holland had stalled, the English fleet under Prince Rupert joined with the French in an attempt to destroy the Dutch fleet and thus permit a supporting seaborne invasion. The ensuing Battle of the Texel proved inconclusive, but Admiral de Ruyter's brilliant strategy allowed his outnumbered fleet to thwart Anglo-French ambitions, leading to the end of the Third Anglo-Dutch War.

In 'The Battle of the Texel, 11-21 August 1673', Willem van de Velde the Younger shows the *Gouden Leeuw* or Golden Lion, Admiral Tromp's flagship firing her port guns at a distant HMS *Charles* and bringing down her mizzen topmast. The large ship to starboard is HMS *Royal Prince*, and on the horizon between them is Prince Rupert's flagship HMS *Royal Sovereign*. At the time of

the battle, the Dutch artist had just settled permanently in London under the patronage of Charles II. He continued to execute Dutch commissions, however, and it is possible that this painting, completed in 1687, was for Tromp himself. Significantly, perhaps, *Gouden Leeuw* had been withdrawn from service in 1686.

Van de Velde's genius is not just in the accurate depiction of ships in battle but – for the second time in two years – in creating an iconic image of this particular Dutch ship. He places the *Gouden Leeuw* at the centre of the composition and takes a low viewpoint, requiring the viewer to look up at the ship proudly flying her national flag. From outside the painting a shaft of brilliant sunlight cuts through the bruised sky and smoke, transfiguring the sails and stern gilding. *JH*

**The Battle of the Texel, 11-21 August 1673** *(oil on canvas), Willem van de Velde the Younger, 1687, National Maritime Museum, London (BHC0315)*

165ft x 40ft x 15ft (50.3m x 12m x 4.6m) • Hull wood • Armament lower deck, 28 guns; upper deck, 28 guns; forecastle, quarterdeck and poop, 26 guns • Complement approx. 490 • Built Amsterdam, Holland, 1666

# Britannia  First Rate ship of the line 1682

In the winter of 1672-3 the famous marine artists, Willem van de Velde the Elder and his son Willem van de Velde the Younger emigrated from the Dutch Republic to England and became marine artists to Charles II on a yearly retainer of £100 each. The King set them up in a studio at the Queen's House, Greenwich, with the Elder acting primarily as draughtsman while the Younger produced oil paintings. They and their studio artists produced masterly works on an almost industrial scale. The Elder produced more drawings of ships that were built or laid up near his studio but did make excursions further afield, often to record the King's travels along the Thames and Medway. On one such excursion to Chatham in about 1684 he made a number of drawings recording the fleet laid up and out of commission in ordinary. Among them was this drawing of the *Britannia* showing the port side and bows with the figurehead of the King on horseback riding over a winged dragon.

*Britannia* was the only 100-gun First Rate ship of the thirty ship building programme of 1677. She was built by Sir Phineas Pett at Chatham, probably the best Master Shipwright of his age and was only slightly smaller than the mighty *Sovereign* of 1637. After first going to sea in 1690 she was found to need an increase of breadth but proved herself in battle as Admiral Russell's flagship at the Battle of Barfleur during which she fought a bloody duel with the French flagship, *Soleil Royal. RE*

**Portrait of the *Britannia*** *(isometric drawing; graphite; grey wash on paper), Willem van de Velde the Elder, c. 1684, National Maritime Museum, Greenwich, London (PZ7581)*

136ft x 47.4ft x 24ft (41.5m x 14.4m x 7.3m) • 1620 tons [BM] • Hull wood • Armament 100 guns of various weights of shot • Complement 780 • Built Chatham, England, 1682

# Siamese Parade Boat Royal barge c. 1688

'It is a light parade boat, very long and extremely narrow, no more than seven feet across. There are oarsmen on both sides who are only half a foot above the water and whose oars are a sort of wooden stick that they called Pagaye. Some of these types of boat have 120 oarsmen, others less, which gives them extraordinary speed. In the centre is some kind of throne…'.

This description, like the image, is taken from *Voyage de Siam des Peres Jesuit,* an account by a French priest, Father Trenchard, published in 1688. Trenchard had accompanied the new French ambassador to the Court of Siam and witnessed the lavish welcome provided by King Narai the Great: 'Four enormous barges came to welcome us, each manned by 80 oarsmen. I have never seen such a sight. The first two were in the shape of sea-horses and entirely gilded, looking extremely realistic as they sailed up from afar.' Later,

he was present at a much larger event: 'The long Royal Barge procession that moved in an orderly fashion consisted of over 150 barges. Together with other boats, they covered the river as far as the eye could see. It was a breathtaking sight. The sound of traditional chanting reverberated along both banks of the river which were crowded with people who were waiting to see the spectacular event'.

Thailand's barge processions date back to at least the fouteenth century and had both secular and religious significance. The barges were river warships, and the Royal Kathin Ceremony, involving 300 boats, acted as a form of peacetime naval exercise to keep the sailors in training. The traditions lapsed during the first half of the twentieth century, but were successfully revived on a smaller scale by King Bhumibol Adulyadej in 1959. *JH*

**A Siamese Parade Boat from an account of the Jesuits in Siam, 1688** *(w/c on paper), French School, seventeenth century, Bibliotheque Nationale, Paris / Archives Charmet / The Bridgeman Art Library*

# First Rate  Ship of the line c.1690

After the launch of the new First Rate *Britannia* in 1682 a number of drawings and prints appeared showing the longitudinal section of a similar-sized First Rate. Edmund Dummer, a junior to the Surveyor of the Navy produced delicate drawings for Samuel Pepys, Secretary to the Admiralty. A print was published, rather surprisingly by a Venetian monk, Vincenzo Coronelli while Thomas Phillips, an engineer, produced a large print at 0.25in to the foot (0.6cm to 30cm). The painting below is very closely associated with the Phillips print and, being in reverse, may be based on an offset rubbing, and may even be by Phillips himself.

The colours in the painting not only add interest but clarify contemporary works contracts which say cabins must be painted in veined stone. The great cabin is painted like this and in accordance with contemporary records there are no hanging 'knees' in the officers' cabins, while a smooth ceiling is added under the beams above so that the cabins appear like the inside of a stately home. The arms, navigation instruments and seascapes in the senior officers' cabins, the cookroom and the construction of junior officers' cabins between the gunports are also convincing and accurate. The artist was not so interested in the technical side of the ship and shows simplified construction details. Unfortunately, and in common with the other sectional drawings of the period, no attempt is made to show the powder and filling rooms. Surprisingly the sheaves through the side of the ship for the fore sheet are strangely placed at right angles to their correct angle. *RE*

**Section through a First Rate, around 1690** *(oil on canvas), Thomas Phillips [attributed], c. 1701, National Maritime Museum, London (BHC0872)*

# Soleil Royal  First Rate ship of the line 1692

Richard Paton was a Londoner who became one of the leading marine artists of the eighteenth century, producing a large series of contemporary sea battles. As a child he was reputedly sent out by his family to beg but rose through the navy before becoming an Assistant Accountant at the Excise Office. He came to prominence as an artist late in life when he was at least 40 years old but his mastery of light and dramatic action in works such as 'The Battle of Quiberon Bay' of 1759 puts him amongst the best of marine artists. However, his portrayal of the Battle of Barfleur, which looked back to the seventeenth century and thus portrayed ships with which he was unfamiliar, is, at least in terms of historical accuracy, not among his best.

Why he chose this unfamiliar subject is easier to understand, as it was at that time England's greatest naval victory over the French, a triumph which would not be surpassed until Trafalgar. The painting does not seem to show any known stage of the battle although Admiral Russell's flagship, *Britannia*, can be identified by the union flag at the main and a red flag at the foremast head, the signal to engage the enemy. The following private three-decker ship is probably the *St Andrew* under the command of George Churchill. Both ships are drawn too narrow towards the top of the stern. Opposite the *Britannia* is the French flagship *Soleil Royal* under the command of the Comte de Tourville. *RE*

*The Battle of Barfleur, 19 May 1692 (oil on canvas), Richard Paton, eighteenth century, Greenwich Hospital Collection, National Maritime Museum, London (BHC0332)*

200.1ft x 51.2ft x 24.9ft (61m x 15.6m x 7.6m) • 1630 tons [BM] • Hull wood • Armament 104 guns • Built Brest, France, 1669

# Quedagh Merchant Captain Kidd's ship 1698

This striking illustration, which appeared in *Harper's New Monthly Magazine* for December 1902, is by US illustrator Howard Pyle and shows the privateer captain William Kidd burying his treasure. Riding at anchor on the horizon is Kidd's ship, the *Quedagh Merchant*, which he had captured on 30 January 1698 off Cochin, India. At the time, it was Indian-owned, with an English captain, but it flew the flag of Armenia as it had been chartered by Armenian merchants based in India who had trade agreements with the Honourable East India Company. Because it was making a voyage under French protection, Kidd deemed it legitimate prey and renamed it the *Adventure Prize*. Leaving it in the Caribbean, he went to New York in a less contentious vessel to clear his name of accusations of piracy, but he was arrested, sent to England and hanged in 1701.

Kidd had concealed his ship in a lagoon on Santa Catalina, a small island off the Dominican Republic, but those entrusted with looking after it until his return proved untrustworthy, and a report reached New York that it had been stripped of all valuables and then burned. Notwithstanding this, legends grew up about the hiding place of Kidd's treasure. By entitling his work 'Pirate William Kidd burying his treasure on Oak Island', Pyle opted for Oak Island in Mahone Bay off Nova Scotia, where the discovery of a strange pit had given rise to stories of buried treasure.

In December 2007 archaeologists from Indiana University discovered the remains of a ship close to the coast of Santa Catalina. Twenty-six cannon and what appears to be part of the keel have been identified and there is cautious optimism that this vessel will prove to be the *Quedagh Merchant*. JH

**Pirate William Kidd burying treasure on Oak Island** *(colour lithograph), Howard Pyle, Private Collection / Peter Newark Pictures / The Bridgeman Art Library*

No data available

# Amsterdam Ships Yachts and merchant vessels 1700

It is traditionally believed that this painting is related to, or derives from, a series of paintings by Storck commemorating the arrival of Peter the Great (1672–1725) Tsar of Russia in the City of Amsterdam in 1697. This was part of an extensive two-year tour of Western Europe in 1697 during which he studied many industrial techniques, including shipbuilding and brought craftsmen back to work in Russia. He was responsible for founding the modern Russian navy.

The City of Amsterdam laid on spectacular fireworks, festivities and maritime displays and reviews. The Tsar participated in mock sea battles involving Dutch yachts and merchant vessels staged on what is now the Ijssel Meer. However, although Peter the Great is evident in other Storck paintings (see 'Review of Dutch yachts before Peter the Great'), he is not obviously present in this picture and there are no Russian flags flying, although there is a figure standing centre right in a yacht, which is traditionally believed to be Peter surveying the numerous vessels that may be preparing for a mock battle.

Abraham Storck was a superlative painter of marine subjects, usually set in his native city of Amsterdam. He had trained and worked with his father and became a member of the Guild of St Luke in Amsterdam. Storck was influenced by Ludolf Bakhuizen and Jan Abrahamsz Beerstraten, and he excelled at lively quayside and beach scenes with diverse shipping and craft and people. He also painted fanciful Mediterranean views and accurate sea fights. Like the two Willem van de Veldes, he demonstrated considerable aptitude in the accurate portrayal of ships' rigging and technical details. *JT*

**Peter the Great inspecting a ship at Amsterdam** *(oil on canvas), style of Abraham Storck, c. 1700, National Maritime Museum, London (BHC0704)*

No data available

# Paramour 6-gun pink 1702

In 1698 the astronomer Edmond Halley set a precedent in becoming the first and last civilian to be given command of a Royal Navy ship. Despite having no sea-going experience he captained the *Paramour* pink – a small, square-rigged and flat-bottomed vessel with a narrow, overhanging stern – on two scientific voyages to plot the variation in the Earth's magnetic field in order to improve navigation. The *Paramour* initially sailed from Deptford on 20 October 1698, returning on 22 June 1699, before setting sail again in the September to return a year later. The chart shows the lines of magnetic variation Halley measured in the Western Atlantic.

Problems arose with the crew during the first voyage to the point where the First Lieutenant and some crewmembers were replaced before the second. From then on naval ships commissioned on scientific voyages were always commanded by a Royal Navy officer.

Halley made a third voyage in the *Paramour* in 1701 to observe the tidal currents in the English Channel. Thereafter HMS *Paramour* was fitted as a bomb-ketch and sailed in Sir George Rooke's Mediterranean squadron in the war against France in 1702.

Edmond Halley returned to his work in astronomy and in 1705 published *A Synopsis of the Astronomy of Comets*. He successfully predicted the return in 1758 of the comet that would take his name. In 1720 he became Astronomer Royal at the age of 64. *AM*

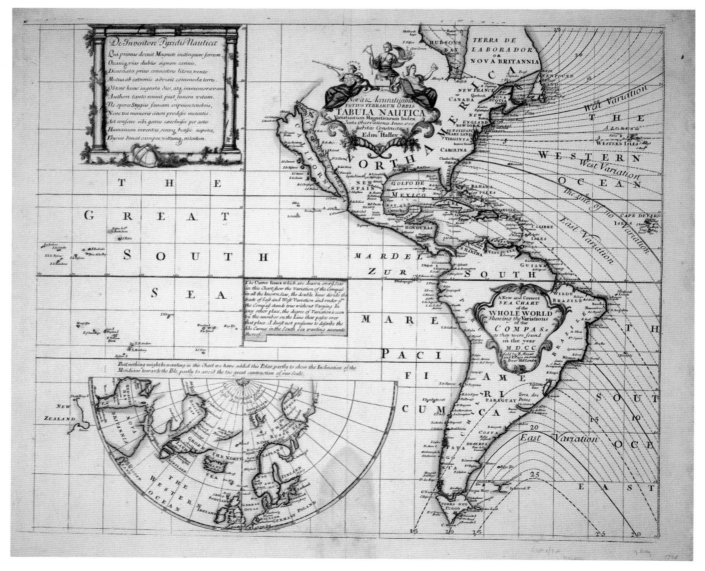

*A new and correct sea chart of the whole world showing the variations of the compass as they were found in the year M.D.CC (coloured engraving), Edmond Halley, 1702, National Maritime Museum, London (F1965)*

64.8ft x 18ft x 9.6ft (19.7m x 5.5m x 2.90 m) • 89 tons [BM] • Armament 6 guns • Complement approx. 20 • Built Fisher Harding, Deptford, England, 1694

# Royal Sovereign  First Rate ship of the line 1703

Willem van de Velde the Younger depicts the First Rate ship *Royal Sovereign*, presumably at anchor. She is identified by the horse and rider on the tafferel. Built in 1701 at Woolwich Dockyard she carried 100 guns and is shown here with the royal standard at the main, the Admiralty flag at the fore and the Union flag at the mizzen. The ship is firing a salute to port and in the left foreground an admiral's barge is shown approaching her stern. The vessel to the right of the picture is the ketch-built yacht *Isabella*.

An entry in the *Royal Sovereign*'s log (5 June 1702) reveals that the painting is likely to be linked to a specific event at Spithead on 4 June 1702 when Prince George of Denmark dined on board with James Butler, 2nd Duke of Ormonde: '…at 1 yesterday afternoon Prince George ye Duke of Ormond and severall Lords din'd on board, we hoisted ye standard at ye main.' On 21 May 1702 Prince George had been appointed Lord High Admiral.

This monumental composition was painted when the artist was 70 years of age. The younger son of Willem van de Velde the Elder, he was born in Leiden and studied under Simon de Vlieger, and also with his father before moving with him to England in the early 1670s at the behest of King Charles II, who provided them with studio space in Inigo Jones's Queen's House at Greenwich. The van de Veldes worked independently, but also collaborated on pictures of sea-battles for the King and his brother James, Duke of York. They were instrumental in establishing a school of maritime art in Britain. Their enduring popularity perhaps lies in their ability to create accurate, animated and harmonious compositions with expert handling of naturalistic and atmospheric effects. *JT*

**Calm: the English ship *Royal Sovereign* with a royal yacht in a light air** *(oil on canvas), Willem van de Velde the Younger, 1703, National Maritime Museum, London (BHC3614)*

174.6ft x 141.7ft x 50.3ft (53.2m x 43.2m x 15.3m) • 1883 tons [BM] • Armament; gun deck 28 x 32 pdr, main deck 28 x 18 pdr, upper deck 28 x 9 pdr, quarterdeck 12 x 6 pdr, forecastle 4 x 6 pdr, RH 2 x 6 pdr • Complement 780 • Built Woolwich, London, England, 1701

# Association Second Rate ship of the line 1707

In 1697, the *Association* (in the foreground, below), was launched at Portsmouth Dockyard as a 90-gun ship of the line. She served as the flagship of Admiral Sir Cloudesley Shovell (1650–1707) in the Mediterranean during the War of Spanish Succession (1701–14), and played a prominent part in the capture of Gibraltar on 21 July 1704 and the Battle of Toulon in summer 1707. Although not a successful action, the French were forced to scuttle the larger part of their squadron to prevent the British burning them. With his squadron of 21 ships Shovell then headed home to England.

During the homeward journey disaster struck on the night of 22 October 1707, when *Association* and several other ships including *Eagle*, *Romney* and *Firebrand* were driven onto rocks off the Isles of Scilly. The *Association* struck the Outer Gilstone Rock, and was wrecked with the loss of her entire crew

of around 800 men. The loss of the other ships brought the death toll to almost 2000. This appalling maritime disaster occurred as a result of navigational errors and prompted the Admiralty and the British Government to create a competition with substantial prize money to discover a more precise method to determine longitude. The prize was eventually awarded to the clock-maker John Harrison, after much stalling from the Board of Longitude, in a series of instalments from 1665-1773.

Shovell was born in Cockthorpe, Norfolk. As a teenager he served as a cabin-boy and at 17 he was a midshipman on the *Royal Prince*, the flagship of the Duke of York, the future James II. Well liked and highly capable, he rose to become an admiral and a knight and was described by a contemporary writer as 'a very large, fat, fair Man'. *JT*

**Sir Cloudisly Shovel [sic] in the *Association* with the *Eagle, Rumney* [sic] and the *Firebrand*, Lost on the Rocks of Scilly, October 22, 1707** *(engraving with etching), after an unidentified artist and engraver, c. 1707-8, National Maritime Museum, London (1034)*

165ft x 45.3ft x 18.2ft (50.3m x 13.8m x 5.6m) • 1459 tons [BM] • Hull wood • Armament 26 x 32 pdr, 26 x 18 pdr, 26 x 9 pdr, 18 x 6 pdr • Complement 680 • Built Portsmouth, England, 1699

# Peregrine  Royal yacht c.1710

The yacht *Peregrine* was built by and named after her original owner, Vice-Admiral Peregrine Osborne, Marquis of Carmarthen, later Duke of Leeds, a keen yachtsman and innovative ship designer. Osborne also enjoyed a wild social life – so much so that when a kindred spirit in the form of Tsar Peter the Great visited England in 1698, he was given the task of looking after him. By day the pair went sailing; at night they got drunk, and the royal visit was a great success. The Tsar returned home with a ship designed by Osborne and much technical knowledge.

In 1711, the *Peregrine* became Queen Anne's royal yacht. Following her death in 1714, it was sent to bring George I, the first of the Hanoverian kings, to England. The captain, William Sanderson, was knighted before the monarch disembarked at Greenwich on 27 September 1714, and the yacht's name was afterwards changed to *Carolina* in honour of the King's daughter-in-law. 'The *Peregrine* and Other Royal Yachts off Greenwich circa 1710', by the Dutch artist Jan Griffier, the Elder, shows *Peregrine* broadside on, revealing much of the activity on deck: one sailor climbs up the topgallant mast shrouds; another has just caught the rope thrown from the small shallop bringing an aristocratically dressed couple to the yacht; a second lady has already embarked and looks over the rail. Royal yachts were used for pleasure and diplomatic work; George I used them for his journeys to Hanover where he retained responsibilities.

The identity of the other two yachts is unknown, but the location off Greenwich, where royal yachts were usually stationed, is easily recognizable: behind the *Peregrine* is the unfinished Royal Hospital with the Observatory just to the left of the *Peregrine*'s red ensign. *JH*

The *Peregrine* **and other Royal yachts off Greenwich circa 1710** *(oil on canvas), Jan Griffier the Elder, c. 1710-1715, National Maritime Museum, London (BHC1821)*

86.6ft x 71ft x 22.10ft (26.4m x 21.6m x 6.7m) • 196 tons [BM] • Hull wood • Armament 16 x 6 pdr, 4 x 3 pdr • Complement 50 • Built Sheerness, Kent, England, 1700

# Centurion Fourth Rate ship of the line 1737

In the years 1740 to 1744 Commodore George Anson took this most aptly named of 60-gun line-of-battle ships around the world, losing the rest of his squadron, most of his men, and all of his teeth to scurvy. In the process he captured the ultimate prize, the Manila galleon *Nuestra Senora de Cavadonga*, on 30 June 1743 and returned home rich and famous. He married the Lord Chancellor's daughter, and ran the Navy for the next two decades.

On the surface there was nothing unusual about his 1000 ton ship, built at Portsmouth between 1729 and 1733, one of many tough, durable units that formed the backbone of global power. But her deeds lived up to her name, and turned her into an icon for a nation that saw itself as the new Rome — solid, reliable, virtuous and free. Anson's flagship embodied the desires of a political class equally anxious for new heroes, Spanish gold and the maintenance of the protestant succession. Her voyage saved a beleaguered ministry, funded their war, and began the process of destroying the Spanish grip on the Pacific. After her return the ship was rebuilt and fought in a major fleet action. Her final campaign, the capture of Havana in 1762, had been planned by Anson, completing the ruin of Spanish power that began the day *Centurion* entered the Pacific. Although the ship was broken up in 1769 her name had already been established in the pantheon of British glory, and there would be many more *Centurions* to fight the nation's battles — the last sacrificed as a breakwater for the D-Day landings. *ADL*

The capture of *Nuestra Senora de Cavadonga* (oil on canvas), Samuel Scott, c. 1743, National Maritime Museum, London (BHC0360)

177.7ft x 40ft x 16.5ft (54.2m x 12.2m x 5m) • 951 tons [BM] • Hull wood • Armament: gun deck 24 x 24 pdr, upper deck 26 x 9 pdr, quarterdeck 8 x 6 pdr, fore-castle 2 x 6 pdr • Complement 400 • Built Portsmouth, England, 1733

# Victory First Rate ship of the line 1744

This very fine model of the *Victory* is thought to have been made during the 1740s, either for the Royal Naval Academy in Portsmouth Dockyard or the Admiralty Boardroom, London. It is arguably one of the finest examples of eighteenth-century modelmaking and depicts this impressive 100-gun warship in every detail. It is noticeably different from the earlier 'Navy Board' models in that the hull is fully planked and finished in a style that is closer to the actual ship. The increased use of English boxwood during this period enabled the craftsmen to produce models with much cleaner and sharper lines as well as being able to undertake the complex carved decoration, as illustrated by the figurehead. The reason for using native hardwoods such as box- and fruitwoods was that they were slow growing.

This produced wood with very little noticeable grain; being more acceptable visually as well as hard enough to work at a small scale. In addition to wood, other materials such as bone, ivory, and glass were used, in some cases to highlight certain features of the ship. This is more apparent on this model around the stern galleries where the modelmaker clearly wants to attract the attention of the Navy Board or senior naval officers to their living accommodation on board. The model is also fully rigged, most of which has been laid up from silk and then stained. It also shows the transitional development of the sailing rig with the inclusion of the older sprit-topmast and newly introduced jiboom, both of which are set on the bowsprit above the figurehead. *SS*

*Victory*, **starboard broadside, full-hull model** *(boxwood, cotton, brass, mica, paint, varnish), Greenwich Hospital Collection, National Maritime Musem, London (D3816_3)*

141.7ft x 50.6ft x 20.6ft (43.2m x 15.4m x 6.28m) • 1869 tons [BM] • Hull wood • Armament; gun deck 28 x 32 pdr, main deck 28 x 24 pdr, upper deck 28 x 12 pdr, quarterdeck 12 x 6 pdr, forecastle 4 x 6 pdr • Complement 850 • Built Portsmouth, England, 1738

# Geldermalsen Dutch East Indiaman 1752

For 333 years the East Indiaman, *Geldermalsen,* lay quietly disintegrating on the bed of the South China Sea. She had belonged to the Vereenigde Oostindische Compagnie ( Dutch East India Company), one of eight virtual monopolies established during the seventeenth and eighteenth centuries by leading mercantile powers (including Britain and France) to gain their share of the lucrative trade with the East. Their ships, the largest merchantmen in the world, were heavily armed for defence against pirates, privateers and, on occasion, enemy warships.

*Geldermalsen* sailed on her maiden voyage on 16 August 1748 and spent the next 29 months trading between India, China, Japan and Batavia (Jakarta). In the calm afternoon of 23 January 1752, 15 days out from Canton and homeward bound with a cargo of tea, gold, silk and porcelain worth 800,000 guilders, she ran onto the infamous Admiral Stellingwerf Reef. Despite coming off, she foundered during the ensuing night, and just 32 men reached Batavia, where the VOC authorities wondered aloud whether there was more to the loss of the ship than met the eye: could the survivors have saved and hidden the gold?

In May 1985 the remains of the *Geldermalsen* were found by Mike Hatcher and Max de Rham. The silks had rotted, but the gold remained (thus refuting the suspicions of VOC officials in Batavia). Buried beneath a thick mattress of tea was the porcelain: whole dinner services, plates, bowls, cups, saucers, butter dishes, spitting dishes: more than 150,000 pieces, most of them intact, and the least valuable part of the cargo as far as the VOC was concerned. The following year, in an auction arousing international enthusiasm, and vastly exceeding all estimates, the porcelain and 126 gold ingots fetched 37 million guilders. *JH*

**Porcelain bowl from the wreck of the *Geldermalsen*** *(photograph), Jean Hood Collection*

# Cambridge Third Rate ship of the line 1755

At first sight this painting appears to be a faithful scene of shipping and craft at the Royal Dockyard of Deptford. However, it is a composite of two events, combining the launch of the *Cambridge*, on 21 October 1755 (the ship shown adorned with five flags), with a view of the *Royal George*, 100 guns, which was in reality launched a year later at Woolwich Dockyard. In fact her draught would have prevented her from reaching this far up the Thames. Whoever commissioned the painting – perhaps a senior naval or dockyard official or the master shipwright – must have been someone who was personally involved with both ships and therefore wanted them painted together.

To the far left is the master shipwright's house built in 1708, and to the right, is the great storehouse. The *Cambridge* was one of the improved 80-gun three-decker Third Rates and is shown here being floated out from the double dry dock where she was built. The *Royal George*, launched in 1756, lies at anchor to the right. She sank at Spithead, Portsmouth on 29 August 1782 with the loss of more than 800 lives.

Born in Southwark, John Cleveley was the head of a remarkable family of English marine artists. Cleveley excelled at dockyard scenes and ship launches. He was apprenticed to a carpenter in Deptford Dockyard, but later became a full-time marine painter, perhaps encouraged by the economies being implemented in the dockyards. By 1704 the cost of carving decorations on ships was so high that it was severely restricted and replaced with painted decoration.

The architectural details, the inclusion of figures on board the various ships and smaller craft, and the quayside strollers, show Cleveley was familiar with the work of Canaletto and Vernet. To the left the artist has included a Dutch coastal vessel flying the Dutch flag and there is a gaff-rigged royal yacht moored in the centre. A ceremonial barge with trumpeters moves in front of the stern of the *Royal George* and a Thames lighter, laden with kegs, can be seen to the right, propelled by two watermen standing up and dragging long sweeps (oars) through the water. *JT*

The *Royal George* at Deptford showing the launch of the *Cambridge* (oil on canvas), John Cleveley the Elder, 1757, National Maritime Museum, London (BHC3602)

139.3ft x 47ft x 20ft (42.4m x 14.3m x 6.1m) • 1636 tons [BM] • Hull wood • Armament; gun deck 26 x 32 pdr, main deck 26 x 18 pdr, upper deck 24 x 9 pdr, quartedeck 4 x 6 pdr • Complement 650 • Built Deptford, England, 1755

# Monarch   Third Rate ship of the line 1757

'At 12 Mr Byng was shot dead by 6 Marines and put into his coffin'.
So reads the blunt entry for 14 March 1757 in the master's log of HMS *Monarch*, a 74-gun Third Rate then anchored at Portsmouth.

Admiral John Byng had been sentenced to death by court martial for breach of the Articles of War, arising from his actions whilst commanding a British squadron at the Battle of Minorca eight months previously. Although acquitted of the charges of personal cowardice and disaffection, he was convicted of not having done his utmost, a capital offence.

The last admiral to be executed in this fashion, history seems to have judged Byng harshly; initially public outcry at the British failure to defend Minorca from French invasion, despite the heroic stand of a British garrison

at Fort St Philip, led to his arrest, and the Admiralty were quick to blame Byng for the loss of a key strategic Mediterranean anchorage. The battle itself, in numerical terms an equal encounter, was brief and indecisive, although the leading British ships sustained considerable damage. But Byng was unable to relieve the island garrison and did not pursue the French ships, taking the decision to return to Gibraltar and apparently abandoning Minorca to the Duke de Richelieu's invasion force, perhaps sealing his fate. It duly came at the hands of a firing squad on the quarterdeck of *Monarch*, as depicted here in a sombre, valedictory painting that captures one of the significant but perhaps less distinguished moments in the long history of the Royal Navy. *MJ*

1651-1860

*The Execution of Admiral Byng, 14 March 1757 (oil on canvas), British school, c. 1760, National Maritime Museum, London (BHC0380)*

149.10ft x 47.3ft x 20.2ft • 1775 tons [BM] • Armament; gun deck 28 x 32 pdr, upper deck 30 x 18 pdr, quarterdeck 10 x 9 pdr, forecastle 6 x 9 pdr • Complement 650 • Built Brest, France, 1747

# Fire Ships Combustible vessels 1759

For hundreds of years, fire ships exploited the ability of fire to spread panic and devastation. Old ships were packed with combustible materials such as tar and allowed to drift with a favourable wind towards the enemy fleet. Alternatively, a skeleton crew sailed the vessel, abandoning ship at the last minute, leaving the fuse to burn down and start the blaze. Additional ports cut in the planking encouraged the fire to blaze upwards, creating terror among an enemy fleet with hulls full of powder kegs, particularly one blockaded in port with no escape. Fire ships were used by the Tyrians against Alexander the Great in 332 B.C. at Tyre and by Sir Francis Drake against the Spanish Armada in 1588.

In June 1759, during the Seven Years War fought between France and Britain, the British fleet was at anchor in the St Lawrence below the French-held city of Quebec when, at midnight on the 28th, the French despatched fire ships. Unfortunately, they lit the fuses too early, giving Admiral Saunders time to send in heavily manned ships' boats to throw grappling irons and tow the fire ships away from the fleet. Dominic Serres's painting 'French Fireships attacking English Fleet off Quebec, 28 June 1759' conveys the intensity of the fire and the closeness of the British ships to one another, and it leaves the viewer in no doubt of the disaster that was so narrowly averted.

The British troops under Major-General Wolfe were able to land, their campaign proceeded through the summer, not always smoothly, and within a year of the fall of Quebec on 18 September the whole of Canada had become British. Both Wolfe and the French general, the Marquis de Montcalm, were killed in the battle for the city. *JH*

French Fireships Attacking the English Fleet off Quebec, 28 June 1759 *(oil on canvas), Dominic Serres the Elder, date unknown, Greenwich Hospital Collection, National Maritime Museum, London (BHC0394)*

# Royal George   First Rate ship of the line 1759

Named for the monarch George II, at over 2000 tons *Royal George* was the largest warship in the world when she was launched in 1756. This year also marked the beginning of the Seven Years War, a global conflict fought across four continents that involved all of the major colonial powers. *Royal George* would prove her worth in this tumultuous period, notably at the Battle of Quiberon Bay, the most decisive naval encounter of the war.

In 1759 Admiral Hawke's Western Squadron had blockaded the French fleet at Brest to prevent the escort of a large fleet of transport craft, which had been built to invade England. In early November the desperate French ships, under Admiral de Conflans, took advantage of a gale that had driven Hawke's ships off station to put to sea. Hawke, commanding *Royal George* as his flagship, soon returned, sighting the French ships on the 20th and

ordering a general chase. De Conflans' ships crowded on sail and sought refuge in the dangerous shoal waters of Quiberon Bay, hoping that Hawke would halt the pursuit. He followed, however, and in the ensuing battle, which took place largely in the dark and close to the shore, Hawke's squadron destroyed the French fleet as an effective fighting force.

This painting by Nicholas Pocock, executed around 1812, commemorates the decisive victory. It is partly based on an earlier work by Dominic Serres and shows *Royal George* with Hawke's blue admiral's ensign at the main, in action with de Conflans' *Soleil Royal*. To the left the French 74-gun *Thésée* sinks by the bows. Hawke's triumph vindicated British naval strategy and finished the French navy; they made no further efforts at sea for the remainder of the war and France's colonial empire soon fell to the British. *MJ*

**The Battle of Quiberon Bay, 20 November 1759** *(oil on canvas)*, Nicholas Pocock, 1812, National Maritime Museum, London (BHC0399)

144.7ft x 51.10ft x 21.6ft (44.1m x 15.8m x 6.6m) • 2065 tons [BM] • Armament; gun deck 28 x 42 pdr, main deck 28 x 24 pdr, upper deck 28 x 12 pdr, quarterdeck 12 x 6 pdr, forecastle 4 x 6 pdr • Complement 850 • Built Woolwich, England, 1756

# Bucintoro  State galley of the Doges of Venice 1768

In 1798 Napoleon underlined his conquest of Venice by deliberately destroying the Doge's ceremonial barge. It effectively ended the city-state's 800-year-old custom of the Festa della Sensa in which, on Ascension day, the Doge travelled by galley from the San Marco Basin out into the Lido. Initially the ritual was held to beg God's protection for Venetian seafarers. From 1177, however, it took the form of a wedding ceremony in which the Doge cast a ring into the Adriatic to symbolize Venice's marriage with the sea from which her power and prosperity derived.

In the fourteenth century the Senate authorized the construction of a special vessel for the Doge to use on state occasions: the first documented Bucintoro. This vessel was replaced in 1526, 1606 and 1729, each galley more lavishly decorated than its predecessor. Francesco Guardi's 'Le Départ du Bucentaure vers le Lido de Venise, le jour de l'Ascension', circa 1780, preserves the blinding brightness of the carved and gilded panels, the golden figurehead of Justice and the rich red paint of what was to be the last Bucintoro; soft Venetian light gleams on the curtained glass windows that illuminate the canopied upper deck inside which the Doge sits. The San Marco Basin is filled with gondolas, many of them sumptuously gilded, ready to accompany the procession. Venice understood pageantry and even the crew of the Bucintoro was decorative: the forty-two 36ft (11m) oars were pulled by 168 young men chosen for their strength and good looks.

Guardi's lyrical painting propagates the illusion of Venetian glory while mourning its decline. The viewer barely notices the faded palazzi constructed when Venice was a world power, concentrating instead on the dazzling barge, itself an anachronism. Less than 20 years later the last Doge would abdicate and Napoleon's men would burn the gilded panels to recover the gold. *JH*

Le départ du *Bucentaure* vers le Lido de Venise, le jour de l'Ascension *(oil on canvas), Francesco Guardi, c. 1768, The Art Archive / Louvre, Paris / Gianni Dagli Orti*

110ft x 24.5ft x 26ft (35m x 7.5m x 8m) • Hull wood • Complement 211 • Built Arsenale, Venice, Italy, 1729

# Endeavour  Expedition barque 1768

In 1768 the naval explorer James Cook was given command of HM Barque *Endeavour* on what was to be his first Pacific Voyage of nearly three years. She was a 368-ton Whitby 'cat' or collier, a type in widespread use in northern Europe until the nineteenth century, launched in 1764 as the *Earl of Pembroke*. Built to a Norwegian model with a canoe stern, projecting quarters and a deep waist, she was of shallow draught, with a wide 30ft (8.9m) beam to a length of 106ft (32.3m).

Her design was invaluable for surveying inshore waters. Although her best speed was seven knots, her sturdy build gave her remarkable sea-keeping qualities and a large capacity, which she needed carrying some 98 crew, including the scientific party appointed by the Royal Society, and stores and equipment for a two-year exploration. *Endeavour* was armed with ten 4 pdr carriage guns and 12 swivel guns and had an additional lower deck added along with an extra skin of planking to help protect against woodworm.

The scientific party included botanists such as Joseph Banks, artists and an astronomer to assist Cook in the ostensible purpose of the voyage, to observe the transit of Venus across the sun from Tahiti in the Society Islands. The other secret purpose was to identify and survey the enormous land mass thought to exist towards the South Pole.

*Endeavour* left Plymouth on 26 August 1768 and from the Society Islands headed south to latitude 400°. Cook found no land and headed west, discovering and carrying out an extraordinary six-month running survey of the coastline of New Zealand. Heading west he discovered Australia at Botany Bay, and surveyed the coast north to the indeterminate Torres Straits. After charting 5,000 miles of unknown coastline and without losing any crew to scurvy, Cook brought *Endeavour* home to England on 13 July 1771 after a voyage of 2 years and 11 months. Such an achievement was as great as those of Vasco da Gama, Columbus and Magellan, and ultimately Cook charted more of this planet than any other man before or since. *JB*

**Triumph of the Navigators – *Endeavour* in the Dover Straits, July 13th 1771** *(oil on canvas), Robin Brooks, courtesy of the Artist / Black Dog Studios*

106 ft x 29.3ft (32 m x 8.92 m) • 368 tons [BM] • Hull wood • Armament 10 x 4 pdr, 12 x swivel guns • Complement 94 • Built Thomas Fishburn, Whitby, England, 1764

# Santisima Trinidad First Rate ship of the line 1769

Famous throughout her career as the largest ship in the world, and the only one to mount four complete decks of artillery, the Spanish *Nuestra Senora de la Santisima Trinidad* was originally built as a 120-gun ship. Later in her career other ships appeared, French and Spanish, which mounted fewer guns but were in fact larger. She was nevertheless an unforgettable sight, particularly in the striking colour scheme she wore at the Battle of Trafalgar, and deserved her celebrity status. Having participated in an action off Cape Spartel in October 1782, her first large-scale battle was off Cape St. Vincent, 14 February 1797. Here she was under fire for five hours, at one time sighting four British ships at once, and was very severely damaged, with an appalling casualty list. But she escaped capture, was repaired, and reconstructed with the extra gunports that brought her total armament to 136 guns. In this guise, wearing the flag of Rear-Admiral de Cisneros, she was again very heavily engaged in the Battle of Trafalgar. More than one British observer remarked on her colouring, bright red sides with white stripes. At 5.30 p.m. she finally struck her colours to HMS *Prince*, who took her in tow. But in her already damaged condition, with 5ft (1.5m) of water in the hold, the great storm after the battle sealed her fate. Her British captors, after taking off every living thing on board, including a cat, were forced to abandon her, and the greatest ship in the world sank. *GH*

**The First Rate 136-Gun Ship** *Santisima Trinidad (oil on canvas), Geoff Hunt, 2006*

220.6ft x 58ft x 28.9ft (63.4m x 16.7m x 8.3m) • 2475 tons [BM] • Hull wood (Cuban mahogany and cedar) • Armament 32 x 36 pdr, 34 x 24 pdr, 36 x 12 pdr, 18 x 8 pdr, 6 x 4 pdr, 10 x 24 pdr carronades • Complement 1110 • Built Artillero Real, Havana, Cuba, 1769

# Resolution Expedition sloop 1773

Having returned to England from his first major voyage of discovery, Commander James Cook was commissioned by the Royal Society to determine the existence of a great southern continent. His flagship was the newly acquired HMS *Resolution*, originally a barque-rigged North Sea collier refitted and rerigged as a naval sloop for the pioneering scientific voyage. She joined HMS *Adventure* at Plymouth, and the two ships left English waters in July 1772. After a stay at Cape Town, they sailed south to become the first ships known to have crossed the Antarctic Circle, on 17 January 1773.

Further remarkable discoveries in the Pacific followed. No less impressive than their contribution to geographical knowledge is the fact that, thanks to Cook's strict regimen of keeping the ship clean and well-ventilated and sticking to an anti-scorbutic diet to avoid scurvy, over the course of the three-year, 70,000-mile voyage, only four of *Resolution*'s crew died, with only one lost to sickness. Cook's care for his crews should be as highly regarded as his cartographic excellence.

Cook was soon off on a third voyage, this time to find the fabled Northwest Passage and *Resolution* was again commissioned. 'The ship of my choice', he called her, 'the fittest for service of any I have seen'. After Cook's death in Hawaii, *Resolution* would penetrate the Arctic Circle, before returning to Britain in 1780. She was later converted into an armed transport and sailed for the East Indies. On 10 June 1782 she was captured by the French ships *Annibal* and *Sphinx*, northwest of Sri Lanka. She made for Manila, to take on French stores and to press any seamen found there. She sailed on 22 July and was never seen again. Either lost, sunk in action, or recaptured, it is hard to believe so famous a ship should have so mysterious an end. *HLJ*

**A View of Cape Stephens in Cook's Straits with Waterspout** *(oil on canvas), William Hodges, 1776, Ministry of Defence Art Collection, National Maritime Museum, London (BHC1906)*

110.8ft x 30.6ft x 13.1ft (33.7m x 9.3m x 4m) • 462 tons [BM] • Hull wood • Armament 12 x 6 pdr, 12 x ½ pdr swivels • Complement 110 • Built Whitby, England, 1770

# Carcass  Arctic survey vessel 1773

Designed by Thomas Slade, the Infernal class bomb vessel *Carcass* was first commissioned as a sloop for action in the English Channel. She was present at the bombardment of Le Havre in 1759 and the following year captured the 10-gun *Mercury* off La Rochelle. Converted to a bomb vessel, she also served in Jamaica and the Irish Sea. In 1773 she was refitted once more in preparation for Constantine Phipps' expedition to the Arctic. The young Horatio Nelson was assigned to the *Carcass* as midshipman, under the command of Skeffington Lutwidge. *Carcass* joined HMS *Racehorse* at the Little Nore, and both ships headed north on 3 June.

In the challenging waters to the north of Spitzbergen, the ships navigated to within 10° of the North Pole, but were forced back by an impenetrable field of pack ice. Both ships managed to free themselves from the floes and reached Britain in September 1773. By 1800, Lutwidge began to circulate a story that while the *Carcass* had been trapped in the ice, the young Nelson has absconded in pursuit of a polar bear. His later version, told to biographers after Nelson's death at the Battle of Trafalgar, was that the gallant midshipman had fought the beast with the butt of his musket before it had been scared off by the *Carcass*'s guns. On being questioned by Lutwidge, the future hero had apparently said: 'I wished, Sir, to get the skin for my father.' The anecdote of Nelson's youthful bravery soon ascended into myth, repeated by each new generation both in juvenile books and more learned histories.

After the Arctic, *Carcass* eventually found commissions for service on the African coast and in the West Indies before being sold off in 1784. An anonymous end, perhaps, but the ship would forever be remembered for that fanciful battle between a boy and a bear. *HLJ*

**Nelson and the Bear** *(oil on oak panel), Richard Westall, c. 1806, Greenwich Hospital Collection, National Maritime Museum, London (BHC2907)*

92ft x 28ft x 9ft (27.9m x 8.5m x 2.7m) • 309 tons [BM] • Hull wood • Armament 8 x 6 pdr, 14 x swivels, 1 x 13in mortar, 1 x 10in mortar (14 x 6 pdr as sloop) • Complement 60 (110 as sloop) • Built Rotherhithe, England, 1759

# Dartmouth  Merchant ship 1773

When the British East India Company ships *Dartmouth*, *Eleanor* and *Beaver* sailed into Boston harbour in late November 1773, they sparked an incident that became a potent revolutionary symbol and proved to be a catalyst in the American War of Independence, crystallizing colonial opposition to British authoritarianism in North America.

The ships carried some 342 chests of tea for import into the colony of Massachusetts, a contentious cargo due to the new Tea Act, which had been passed earlier in 1773. The legislation imposed a duty on imported tea, which colonists believed unlawful since, as the famous rallying cry had it, there could be 'no taxation without representation', and the American colonies had no elected Parliamentary interest.

A stand-off resulted. British law required the *Dartmouth*, as first ship into the harbour, to unload and pay the duties within twenty days. A group of colonists, led by a core of Whigs known as the Sons of Liberty, organized a mass meeting in which a resolution was passed to urge the captain of the *Dartmouth* to send his ship back without paying the import duty. They also prevented the tea chests from being unloaded. However, Thomas Hutchinson, the British Governor, refused to permit the ship to leave without delivering her cargo and paying the import duty.

On the evening of 16 December, direct action was taken by the colonists. 30 to 130 men, some disguised as Mohawk Indians, boarded the ship and, over the course of three hours, dumped all the tea into the harbour. Whether an act of principled protest or frenzied outrage, the British reaction was swift and severe. The Government responded by closing the port of Boston until the British East India Company had been repaid for the loss of the cargo, part of a series of measures collectively termed the Coercive Acts, known in the USA as the 'Intolerable Acts', and directly responsible for the uprisings that became the War of Independence. *MJ*

## THE DESTRUCTION OF TEA AT BOSTON HARBOR

The Destruction of Tea at Boston Harbour *(lithograph), Nathaniel Currier, 1846, Mary Evans / Glasshouse Images*

79ft x 9.8ft (24m x 3m) • Hull wood • Built Bedford Village, New York, North America, 1767

# Tahitian war boat Wooden canoe 1776

William Hodges dramatic painting of 'The war boats of the island of Otaheite' (Tahiti) was as much an exotic vision of the Pacific islanders as it was an expression of British overseas endeavour. These were among the first images of these craft shown to the Western world. Hodges had been appointed by the Admiralty to record the places discovered on James Cook's second voyage of 1772–5. He made hundreds of drawings during the voyage on *Resolution* and *Adventure*, and later worked up many of these sketches into larger oil canvases. Developed from a number of studies, this painting was perhaps the largest from the voyage and was, according to Hodges, 'one of the most magnificent sights in the South Seas'.

Part of the Tahitian fleet was preparing for a punitive expedition against the neighbouring island of Moorea. The reasons for this engagement, part of a long-lasting dispute based upon tribal ambitions, are obscure. Cook took great interest in these war preparations and described them in detail. He estimated that the expedition involved upwards of 4000 warriors, raised from the four districts of Tahiti. It is said that one of the Tahitian chieftains, Te-ari'i-fa, suggested that Hodges might make some drawings of their fleet as it gathered on 30 April 1774. The painting is a romantic composite, both the setting and the figures are contrived, but it nonetheless gives us some idea of the nature and detailing of these remarkable canoes as they ready for battle. A tropical squall approaches, so too the storm of war. *HLJ*

**The war boats of the island of Otaheite [Tahiti]** *(oil on canvas), William Hodges, 1776, Ministry of Defence Art Collection, National Maritime Museum, London (BHC2374)*

No data available

# Turtle Submersible 1776

Designed by David Bushnell of Connecticut in 1775, the world's first submersible craft employed in combat was a naval revolution conceived during the War of Independence. Resembling more of a pod than a cylinder, the one-man vessel nevertheless incorporated ballast for controlling depth and hand-driven screw propellers for locomotion. The critical flaw of the *Turtle* was her weaponry: a keg of gunpowder which had to be fixed against the underwater hull of an enemy warship after manually boring a hole (all but impossible given the movement of water).

As British forces closed in on New York City in September 1776, Bushnell's 'infernal machine', bravely piloted by Ezra Lee, closed with the Third Rate ship of the line, HMS *Eagle* – the imperial flagship. The *Turtle*, however, was unable to drill through the thick hull, and abandoned the attempt. Further sorties were impractical and she was sunk at dock in New Jersey when the British occupied Fort Lee in November. *Turtle*'s place in the history of the War of Independence is at best a footnote; but she epitomized a bold new tradition of asymmetric naval warfare whereby radical technology was desperately employed to offset vastly superior numbers. A successful attack against the *Eagle* might have hazarded the British anchorage and complicated further combined operations against the Americans; yet the effects for both sides would be largely psychological. *HF*

The *Turtle* submersible; model, showing interior *(photograph), 1998, Science & Society Picture Library / Getty Images*

10ft x 6ft x 3ft (3m x 1.8m x 0.9m) • Hull wood reinforced with tar and steel bands • Armament 130lb (59kg) gunpowder keg • Complement 1 • Built Thomas Bushnell, Old Saybrook, Connecticut, North America, 1775

# Bonhomme Richard Frigate 1779

Perhaps the most energetic captain serving in the 'Continental Navy', as the precursor of the United States Navy was named during the American War of Independence, John Paul Jones was determined to carry the struggle against King George back across the Atlantic into British waters. In his first foray in 1777, while in command of the 18-gun sloop *Ranger*, he reached the Irish Sea and captured a Royal Navy sloop, the *Drake*, of a similar size to his own. In 1779 he was given command of a Franco-American squadron consisting of the American frigate *Alliance*, the French frigate *Pallas*, and some smaller vessels, while the *Bonhomme Richard* was his flagship.

This ship had a curious history. It had been built in France in 1765 as an East Indies merchantman, the *Duc de Duras*, and made two voyages to the Far East in that role. Jones had her converted to a warship mounting 40 guns. The name is equally unusual; it derives from the French version of Benjamin Franklin's *Poor Richard's Almanac*. In this ship, with more obstruction than help from both the *Alliance* and the *Pallas*, Jones fought an epic battle by moonlight, on 23 September 1779, off Flamborough Head in Yorkshire. His opponent was HMS *Serapis*, 44 guns, commanded by Captain Pearson, which also had a smaller warship in company. Called upon to surrender, Jones allegedly shouted back, 'I have not yet begun to fight!' then promptly boarded and captured the British ship. The *Bonhomme Richard* herself was so badly damaged that she sank the following day. Though not appreciated by his contemporaries, today John Paul Jones is honoured for this action and revered as the father of the United States Navy. *GH*

The *Bonhomme Richard*: John Paul Jones' flagship *(oil on canvas)*, Geoff Hunt, 2000

154.5ft x 39ft x 18.7ft (47m x 11.9m x 5.69m) • 900 tons [BM] • Hull wood • Armament 6 x 18 pdr, 28 x 12 pdr, 6 x 8 pdr • Complement 380 • Built Segondat-Duvernet, L'Orient, France, 1765

# Supply Brig 1789

A group of 11 ships known as the First Fleet sailed from Portsmouth on 13 May 1787 to establish the first European colony in New South Wales, where they arrived in January 1788. Carrying convicts, and led by Captain Arthur Philip, they established the first penal settlement at a place Philip named Sydney Cove. This was part of a plan by the Home Secretary, Lord Sydney, to transport thousands of prisoners to Australia. The illustrations, by George Raper, show the fleet's two naval escorts – HMS *Sirius* and HMS *Supply* – at Sydney Cove in 1789. These two ships stayed in the colony, while the commercially chartered transports returned to Britain.

*Supply* was a brig-rigged armed storeship that was built in 1759 for the Admiralty. *Sirius*, a 22-gun Sixth Rate, was wrecked on Norfolk Island in March 1790, leaving *Supply* as the only means of obtaining supplies and communicating with the outside world. In April 1790 she made a trip to Batavia (in the Dutch East Indies) to obtain much-needed provisions. In November 1791 she left for England and, on her return, was sold and renamed *Thomas and Nancy* to become a collier on the Thames. In 1962 the Royal Australian Navy named its first fleet replenishment ship *Supply* in recognition of the pioneering work of her namesake. *PB*

His Majesty's Brig SUPPLY 1790
off Lord Howe Island – Disc.d Feb.y 1788

His Majesty's Ship SIRIUS in Sidney Cove 1789

**H.M. Brigs *Sirius* and *Supply*, ships in the First Fleet, Sydney Cove, Australia, 1789** *George Raper, late eighteenth century, The Art Archive / British Museum, London*

79.4ft x 22.6ft x 11.7ft (24.2m x 6.9m x 3.6m) • 388 tons [BM] • Hull wood • Complement 55 • Armament 8 guns • Built Rotherhithe, England, 1759

# Brooks  Liverpool slaver 1789

Immediately following the government's 'reforms' that tied the maximum number of slaves that could be carried on any one voyage to the size of the particular ship carrying them, British anti-slavery campaigners ordered the construction of a scale model of the Liverpool-registered slaver *Brooks* in 1789. Pasted on the decks were simple images of prone human figures, as passive as bags of grain, showing exactly how little space was allotted to individual slaves. The men, who were chained in pairs, had just 6ft (1.8m) by 16in (40cm) each; boys, 5ft (1.5m) by 14in (35cm); women, 5.8ft (1.8m) by 16in (45cm); girls 4ft (1.2m) by 12in (30cm). This meant that the *Brooks* could hold 600 slaves, in a ship originally designed to carry no more than 451. The owner had simply erected staging between the decks, dramatically reducing headroom which, in the case of the 147-ton *Venus*, amounted to just 21in (53cm).

The Member of Parliament for Hull, William Wilberforce, a committed abolitionist since 1787, took the model into the House of Commons to disabuse fellow members – many of whom had vested interests in slavery – of the idea that there could be anything humane about a trade that treated human beings like cargo. At the same time, a poster based on the same deck plans as the model was widely circulated among abolitionists up and down the country. The poster misspells the ship's name as *Brookes*.

The model, now in the Museum of Slavery in Hull, did not end the slave trade on its own, much less slavery, but it added significant weight to other rational arguments, secular and religious outrage, graphic descriptions of the foetid and brutal conditions, testimonies of sailors, first-hand accounts by freed slaves and agitation by existing slaves. The slave trade was finally abolished in 1807. *JH*

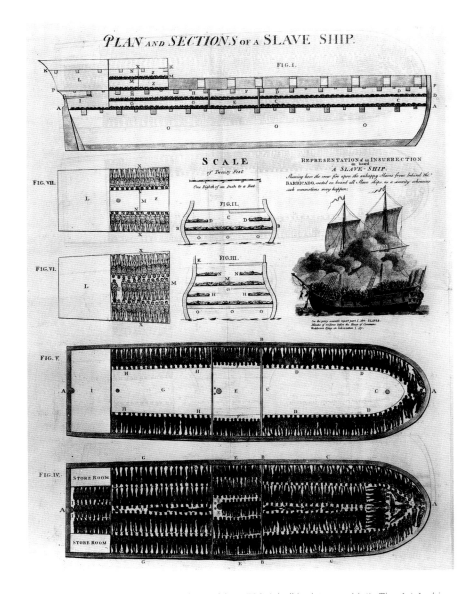

**Plan and cross sections of the *Brookes* [sic], Liverpool-based slave ship, 1789** *(abolitionist pamphlet), The Art Archive*

100ft x 24.3ft (30.5m x 7.4m) • 297 tons [B] • Hull wood • Built Liverpool, England, 1781

# Bounty Expedition ship 1789

Built as the three-masted collier *Bethia* and purchased by the Admiralty in May 1787, *Bounty* was a relatively small and unremarkable ship of the Royal Navy, but she rose to prominence as the setting for one of the most infamous mutinies in the history of the service.

She was refitted at Deptford before sailing from Spithead on 23 December 1787. The mutiny itself took place on 28 April 1789 during a voyage of the ship to the Pacific to collect breadfruit plants which were destined for plantations in the West Indies. The mutiny was popularised in a 1935 Hollywood film starring Charles Laughton as Lt Bligh (captain of the ship) and Clark Gable as Fletcher Christian (the master's mate and acting lieutenant, who led the mutiny); in all, five films of the incident have been made, including that of 1984 — which starred Anthony Hopkins as Bligh and Mel Gibson as Christian. Some members of the crew had been allowed to live ashore in Tahiti to care for the potted breadfruit plants, but this led to breaches in discipline and concomitant punishments: the disaffection this engendered was to help precipitate the mutiny. Bligh and eighteen of the ship's company were set adrift in the ship's 23 ft (7 m) launch without charts and only meagre rations. All but one survived a 41 day voyage to safety in Timor, Dutch East Indies, though five died soon afterwards. *Bounty* was burnt and sunk by the mutineers in 1791 to avoid detection. The mutineers eventually settled on Pitcairn Island. *PB*

*Mutiny on Board the Bounty.*

**Mutiny aboard the *Bounty*** *(engraving), artist unknown, nineteenth century, National Maritime Museum, London (D4759)*

69.11ft x 24.4ft x 11.4ft (21.1m x 7.4m x 3.5m) • 220 tons [BM] • Hull wood • Armament 4 x short 4 pdr, 10 swivels • Complement 45 • Built Hull, England, 1784

# Pandora Sixth Rate post-ship 1790

The frigate *Pandora*, commanded by Captain Edward Edwards was sent by the Admiralty to search for the mutineers from HMS *Bounty* in the south Pacific, and sailed from Portsmouth on 7 November 1790. She carried extra crew members so that *Bounty*, when found, could be manned for a return voyage. *Pandora* arrived in Tahiti on 23 March 1791 and fourteen members of the *Bounty*'s crew either came on board voluntarily or were arrested by armed search parties there. On 8 May 1791 the ship left Tahiti and spent three months searching various Pacific islands for the other mutineers and for the *Bounty*. They had no luck and headed west, but ran aground on the Great Barrier Reef, where the ship sank with the loss of 31 crew and four prisoners

on 30 August 1791. In echoes of Bligh's voyage the remaining 99 men took to the four ship's boats and sailed for Timor, where the survivors arrived on 16 September 1791. Ten prisoners were later court-martialled - five were found guilty, of whom three were hanged whilst two were pardoned.

*Pandora* was a Porcupine class Sixth Rate. She had seen service in the English Channel and North America. Her wreck was discovered in 1977 and many artefacts have been recovered; they are now on display at the Queensland Museum, Australia. This 1835 etching of *Pandora*'s sinking is from a sketch by Peter Heywood, a midshipman in *Bounty*. *PB*

**H.M.** *Pandora* **foundering, from John Barrow's** *The Eventful History of the Munity and Piratical Seizure of H.M.S. Bounty* (etching), Robert Batty, 1835. *Bibliotheque Nationale, Paris, France / Archives Charmet / The Bridgeman Art Library*

114.3ft x 32ft x 10.3ft (34.8m x 9.8m x 3.1m) • 513 tons [BM] • Hull wood • Armament: upper deck 22 x 9 pdr, quarterdeck 2 x 6 pdr • Complement 160 • Built Deptford, England, 1779

# Winterton East Indiaman 1792

By the end of the eighteenth century the Honourable East India Company (HEIC) had become the most powerful company the world had yet seen, and, in addition to its traditional trade in tea, spice and fabrics from India and China, it had begun the military conquest of India, where it maintained its own administration, regiments and a small navy, and collected taxes. It owned few ships; instead it chartered them, at uncompetitive rates, from privileged consortia of wealthy individuals who benefited considerably from this cosy arrangement.

Capacious and flush-decked, *Winterton* was a typical regular Indiaman of her day. Thomas Luny painted her off the Downs, around 1782, when she was new, showing three different views within the one picture. In May 1792 she sailed for Madras and Bengal with a hundred crew, 30 passengers, 124 soldiers and a cargo that included 8 tons of silver. At 3 a.m. on 20 August she hit a reef off Madagascar's southwest coast, and two days later went to pieces. Miraculously 200 people reached land and eventually gained the protection of a local potentate. Third Mate John Dale took a party of volunteers in the ship's yawl to seek Portuguese help in Mozambique. Six months later he returned with a ship to collect the rest of the survivors, only to find half the people dead of fever.

Ignorant that Britain was now at war with France, the survivors continued towards India, only to be captured by a French privateer. But following a sharp engagement with the Dutch East India Company's *Ceylon*, the privateer surrendered and released her prisoners. Dale was sent home from Madras on an HEIC sloop, only to be swept up by a French squadron bound for Norfolk, Virginia. He finally reached England in July 1794. *JH*

HEICS *Winterton* (oil on canvas), Thomas Luny, c. 1783, courtesy of Colin Denny

143ft x 35ft x 23ft (43.6m x 7.6m x 7m) • 900 tons [BM] • Hull wood • Armament: 26 guns • Complement: approx. 115 • Built Dudman, London, England, 1782

# Agamemnon   Third Rate ship of the line 1795

Built at Bucklers Hard on the Beaulieu River, the Third Rate line of battle ship *Agamemnon* enjoyed an active career and is famous for her association with Nelson, who referred to her as his favourite ship. She was one of those ships that always seemed to be in the middle of the action, appearing at the Battle of the Saintes in 1782; Toulon in 1793; Hotham's action of 1795; the Nore Mutiny of 1797; Copenhagen in 1801; Calder's action of 1805; and at the Battle of Trafalgar.

In January 1793 Captain Nelson, a little-known officer who had not been employed at sea for five years, was appointed to command of the Agamemnon. It was an opportunity which he was to seize with great energy, and it launched the brilliant later part of his career. Typical both of the ship and Nelson was the engagement with the *Ça Ira*, in which Nelson, sailing ahead of the main British fleet, intercepted a much larger French 80-gun ship (with not untypical exaggeration, Nelson said that this ship was 'absolutely large enough to have taken the *Agamemnon* in her hold'). The *Ça Ira* was captured the following day. But however heroic *Agamemnon's* career, nothing could disguise the fact that she was a 64-gun ship at a time when the standard battleship of the day mounted 74 or even 80 guns firing a heavier shot; and when in 1809 she was damaged running aground in Maldonado Bay, Uruguay, being worn out by years of service, it was not thought worthwhile saving her. *GH*

**HMS *Agamemnon* opens fire on the *Ça Ira*, 13 March 1795** *(oil on canvas), Geoff Hunt, 1998*

160ft x 44.4ft x 18ft (48.6m x 13.5m x 4.9m) • 1376 tons [BM] • Hull wood • Armament 26 x 24 pdr, 26 x 18 pdr, 12 x 9 pdr • Complement 500 • Built Buckler's Hard, Beaulieu, England, 1781

# Surprise Frigate 1796

The *Surprise* was a French-built frigate, rather small for her day, approximating to the French category of corvette or the British Sixth Rate. She began life as *L'Unité*, but in 1796 she was captured in the Mediterranean by Captain Fremantle's HMS *Inconstant*, and re-named. It was not unusual for French ships of this size to be captured. What makes the *Surprise* so special is not that she had two careers, serving in both the French Revolutionary Navy and then the Royal Navy, but that she had three – her third career being a fictional one.

Her first Royal Navy commission was in the Adriatic, as the first command of Captain Ralph Miller. In 1797 she passed into the hands of Captain Edward Hamilton, who took her out to the West Indies and to her most celebrated action, the cutting-out and recovery of the lost British frigate *Hermione*. But the *Surprise* has become well-known to a much wider audience than naval historians since the writer Patrick O'Brian decided to make her the favourite command of his redoubtable naval hero, Captain Jack Aubrey – not to mention his voyaging companion, Stephen Maturin. *Surprise* appears in no fewer than 11 of those novels, and is the setting for Peter Weir's 2003 film, *Master and Commander*. The ship that appeared in the film is actually the 'HMS *Rose*' (sic), a 1970 American-built replica of a British Sixth Rate of 1757, which is very close in size and general appearance to the *Surprise*. Currently in the care of the San Diego Maritime Museum, this vessel is a fascinating glimpse of what a Sixth Rate was like – considerably smaller than heavy frigates like the USS *Constitution* or even standard frigates such as the surviving HMS *Trincomalee*. GH

**HMS *Surprise* on the far side of the world** *(oil on canvas), Geoff Hunt, 2003*

126ft x 31.8ft x 10ft (38.3m x 9.6m x 3m) • 578 tons [BM] • Hull wood • Armament (in 1798) 24 x 32 pdr carronades, 16 x 18 pdr carronades, 2 x chase guns • Complement 200 • Built Le Havre, France, 1794

# Constitution Heavy frigate 1797

America's iconic warship was built in Boston and commissioned in 1798, one of three 44-gun American super-frigates, significantly larger and more heavily armed than contemporary European vessels of the same rate. After a decade of peace time service she went to war in July 1812, narrowly escaping from a superior British force off New Jersey, before capturing the British ships *Guerriere* and *Java*. Both actions were strikingly one-sided, *Constitution* being one third larger, more heavily armed and manned than her opponents, but America desperately needed victories of any sort, as the army invasion of Canada had become a humiliating debacle. Consequently the ship and her captains became national heroes. In the *Guerriere* action astonished British sailors noted that their cannon balls seemed to bounce off her stout hull and she acquired the nickname 'Old Ironsides', a sobriquet which has endured to this day. The smaller British ships *Cyane* and *Levant* were captured off the Cape Verde Islands in 1815. After extensive post-war service she became a training ship for the Naval Academy during the Civil War, and then a museum. She remains afloat today in Boston Navy Yard, a national treasure that is turned around every year, and was last at sea under her own sails in 1997. *ADL*

*Constitution* **off the Barbary coast** *(oil on canvas), Geoff Hunt, 2000*

1651-1860

175ft x 43.5ft x 22.5ft (53.3m x 13.3m x 6.9m) • 2200 tons [BM] • Hull wood • Armament 32 x 24 pdr, 20 x 32 pdr, 2 x 24 pdr • Complement 450 • Built Boston, Massachusetts, North America, 1797

# Hermione Fifth Rate frigate 1797

The most famous mutiny in the Royal Navy's history was that aboard the *Bounty* in 1789, but it was a model of civilized behaviour compared with the *Hermione* mutiny of 1797; and the much-maligned Captain Bligh a saint compared with the *Hermione*'s monstrous Captain Pigot. Under his command HMS *Hermione* was a hell-ship. The final crisis came on 21 September 1797, in the Caribbean. Pigot's brutality had caused the deaths of three sailors on the 20th, and on the 21st he had had 12 men flogged. That night the crew rose up and slaughtered all the officers except one, throwing them overboard to the sharks. They sailed the ship 500 miles to La Guaira, in Venezuela, and surrendered it to Spain. The Spanish were puzzled to know what to do with the mutineers, not wishing to encourage mutiny themselves, but they kept the ship; and two years later she was at Puerto Cabello when another British frigate, HMS *Surprise* arrived in the area. This ship was commanded by Captain Edward Hamilton, who was determined to recapture the *Hermione*. Now re-named the *Santa Cecilia*, she had been re-armed with 44 guns, carried 390 crew, and lay in a defended harbour under the cover of 200 fortress guns. But on the night of 14 October 1799, Captain Hamilton led his ship's boats, carrying 108 men, into the harbour and in a desperate action captured and brought out the lost frigate. Hamilton, seriously wounded, was knighted for his action; the *Santa Cecilia* was re-named HMS *Retribution*. As for the mutineers, 33 were eventually captured and tried, and 24 of those were hanged. Of the others, more than one hundred men, nothing more is known. *GH*

**Illustration for Dudley Pope's *The Black Ship*** (oil on panel), Geoff Hunt, 1997

129ft x 35.4ft x 12.8ft (39.2m x 10.8m x 3.8m) • 710 tons [BM] • Hull wood • Armament 26 x 12 pdr, 6 x 6 pdr, 12 swivels • Complement 220 • Built Teast, Tombs & Blaming, Bristol, England, 1782

# L'Orient  First Rate ship of the line 1798

The destruction of the mighty French flagship *L'Orient* at the battle of the Nile quickly became the defining image of war at sea in the age of Nelson. Many artists painted the scene, perhaps the most dramatic moment in an age of high drama. The 120-gun three decker, the largest ship afloat at the time, had been built as the *Dauphin Royale*, renamed *Sans Culotte* by the Jacobins, and then once again to reflect Bonaparte's ambition to follow in the footsteps of Alexander the Great. Under Admiral Francois Brueys she led the French invasions of Malta and Egypt, only to be caught at anchor, at the heart of a powerful French fleet, in Aboukir Bay by Nelson and his 'band of brothers' late on the afternoon of 1 August 1798. During the battle *L'Orient*'s guns shattered and dismasted the *Bellerophon*, but then her luck ran out. Arriving

after dark Alexander Ball, commanding HMS *Alexander*, and Ben Hallowell, commanding HMS *Swiftsure*, manoeuvred their ships onto the French flagship's bow and quarter, where few guns would bear. When the oil-based paint caught fire *L'Orient* was doomed. The detonation of her powder magazines turned night into day, and deafened everyone: the fighting stopped for several minutes. After the battle Hallowell used part of *L'Orient*'s main mast to make a coffin, which he presented to Nelson as a reminder of his mortality. Nelson would be buried in it eight years later. Through his anxiety to annihilate the enemy Nelson transformed the art of war at sea, the explosion of *L'Orient* provided the sublime, apocalyptic embodiment of his genius. *ADL*

**The destruction of *L'Orient* at the Battle of the Nile, 1 August 1798** *(oil on canvas), George Arnauld, 1825-1827, Greenwich Hospital Collection, National Maritime Museum (BHC0509)*

209.5ft x 53.3ft x 26.6ft (65.2m x 16.3m x 8.1m) • 5095 tons [BM] • Hull wood • Armament 120 guns • Complement 1079 • Built Toulon, France, 1791

# Sutherland  Third Rate ship of the line c. 1798

The fictional HMS *Sutherland* is the setting for C.S. Forester's novel *A Ship of the Line*, published in 1938. Forester describes *Sutherland* as a captured Dutch ship, formerly the *Eendracht* (the name of a famous Dutch flagship from the Anglo-Dutch wars) now 'the ugliest and least desirable two-decker in the Navy List', having a shallow draught, a lower-deck armament of 24 pdr cannon, and a round bow. Apparently Forester takes this to mean lacking a beakhead, but this is surely either a misprint or a misunderstanding. In large ships a 'round bow' simply meant that the upper deck was rounded, lacking the usual square bulkhead. During the 1790s the British had captured three Dutch 74-gun ships, the *Washington*, *Jupiter*, and *Vryheid*, none significantly smaller than their British contemporaries, and none of them mounting 24

pdrs as their heaviest battery, while it is unlikely that any of them lacked a beakhead. Whatever her appearance, under the command of the enterprising Captain Horatio Hornblower, *Sutherland* is sent out to the western Mediterranean under Admiral Leighton. *A Ship of the Line* chronicles her adventures en route and then off the Catalan coast – beating off an attack on her convoy, storming a battery, cutting-out a ship, saving the dismasted flagship in a storm, landing forces on the mainland and so on – before the final dramatic scene in which the ship is thrown against an overwhelming force of four heavier French warships, including a three-decker flagship and an 80-gun ship, in a doomed bid to delay them while British reinforcements arrive. *GH*

**HMS *Sutherland*** (oil on canvas), Geoff Hunt, 2004

1651-1860

# Lutine Frigate 1799

This 18in (46cm) diameter brass bell weighing 106lb (48kg) hangs in the Underwriting Room of Lloyd's of London. Although engraved St. Jean 1779, it is the bell of the French Navy's *La Lutine*, a Magicienne class frigate which was handed over to the British by French Royalists at Toulon in 1793, re-commissioned as the Fifth Rate HMS *Lutine* and wrecked on 9 October 1799 off the Dutch island of Terschelling with the loss of some 270 lives and up to £1,200,000 of gold and silver.

*Lutine*'s cargo had been intended to prop up the economy of Hamburg, which had suffered dramatically during the years of blockade that followed the outbreak of the Revolutionary Wars. Captain Lancelot Skinner was familiar with the treacherous waters off the Dutch coast but whether through negligent navigation or bad weather, the ship went aground and was broken up by the savage surf. The Admiralty hastily blamed the disaster on natural causes, Lloyd's dutifully paid out the huge insurance claim, and several salvage attempts took place with varying degrees of success, including an 1858 operation that recovered the bell and presented it to Lloyd's.

For almost 150 years the Lutine bell was rung at Lloyd's when reliable news of an overdue ship was received: once for bad, twice for good. For as long as a ship was overdue, her underwriters would try to reinsure some of their risk, in case the ship proved to be a total loss. The ringing of the bell allowed the new information to reach everyone at the same time. The bell has also been rung as an air-raid warning, and to mark events as diverse as the sinking of the *Bismarck*, the safe return of the Apollo 8 astronauts and the 9/11 terrorist attack. *JH*

The *Lutine* Bell, on the Underwriters' floor of the Lloyd's Building, London *(photograph), Bruno Vincent, 2005, Getty Images*

143.3ft x 38.8ft x 12.6ft (44.1m x 11.8m x 3.7m) • 950 tons [BM] • Hull wood • Armament 26 x 12 pdr; 8 x 6 pdr; 4 x 24 pdr • Complement 240 • Built Toulon, France, 1779

# Elephant   Third Rate ship of the line 1801

Built to the lines of the Sir Thomas Slade's Arrogant class, *Elephant* was at that time the largest ship ever constructed at Bursledon, on the river Hamble; after launching she was towed to Portsmouth for fitting-out and completion. The early part of this ship's career was very undistinguished but she suddenly jumped into the public glare when Vice-Admiral Lord Nelson selected her as his flagship for the attack on Copenhagen, on 2 April 1801, transferring from the 98-gun *St George* because *Elephant* had a shallower draught. In the ensuing battle, *Elephant* avoided the fate of several British ships which ran aground, and took her place in the line of battle. Following this day in the spotlight,

*Elephant* served a further three commissions with much less excitement, two of them in the West Indies, where she fought an inconclusive action with the subsequently famous French 74 *Duguay-Trouin*.

In her final commission, while in home waters, her captain was Francis William Austen, one of Jane Austen's two naval brothers. In 1818 *Elephant*, as a well-built ship that had had little hard use, was selected together with her sister-ship *Saturn* to be cut down and re-modelled as a powerful double-banked frigate of 58 guns. However she never served a commission in this guise, and *Elephant* was eventually broken up in 1830. *GH*

**The Battle of Copenhagen, 2 April 1801** *(oil on canvas), Nicholas Pocock, 1809, National Maritime Museum (BHC0529), London*

168ft x 46.9ft x 19.9ft (51.2m x 14.3m x 6m) • 1604 tons [BM] • Hull wood • Armament 28 x 32 pdr, 28 x 18 pdr, 18 x 9 pdr (in 1801; 2 x 9 pdr, 16 x 32 pdr carronades) • Complement 550 • Built Bursledon, England, 1786

# Speedy Brig 1801

Lord Cochrane was 24 years old when he took command of the *Speedy* in the harbour of Port Mahon, Minorca, in April 1800. During the next 15 months he carried out a devastating series of raids on French and Spanish shipping in the western Mediterranean. His success was largely due to his bold tactics and seamanship, but also owed much to his crew who had been highly trained by the *Speedy*'s previous commander, Jahleel Brenton. On 6 May 1801 the *Speedy* was intercepted off Barcelona by the 32-gun xebec frigate *Gamo* and the resulting battle is generally regarded as one of the most remarkable single-ship actions in the Royal Navy's history. The *Gamo* had a crew of 319 and could fire a broadside seven times the weight of the *Speedy*'s fourteen 4

pdrs. With a crew of only 54 men and boys Cochrane manoeuvred his ship alongside the Spanish vessel, boarded her and forced her surrender. The Spanish lost 15 killed and 41 wounded, the *Speedy* had three men killed and eight wounded. Lord Vincent described it as a 'very brilliant and spirited action'. Five weeks later the *Speedy* was captured off Gibraltar by a powerful French squadron but Cochrane was acquitted at the courts martial which followed and in due course he was promoted to post-captain. Patrick O'Brian used the exploits of the *Speedy* as the basis for *Master and Commander*, the first of his much-admired novels featuring Jack Aubrey and Stephen Maturin. *DC*

**Lord Cochrane's *Speedy* tackles the *Gamo*** *(oil on canvas), Geoff Hunt, 1998*

78.3ft x 25.8ft x 10.10ft (23.9m x 7.9m x 3.3m) • 287 tons [BM] • Hull wood • Armament 14 x 4 pdr, 12 swivels • Complement 90 • Built Dover, England, 1782

# Essex   Whale ship 1802

On 18 February 1821, the British brig *Indian* came upon an open boat in the South Pacific containing three exhausted, starving men who had been 90 days adrift, and for the last 10 they had existed on the flesh of a dead shipmate. They were the First Mate, Owen Chase and two other members of the American whaler *Essex*.

The *Essex* had been attacked on 20 November the previous year by an aggressive 85ft (25.9m) sperm whale while most of her crew were off hunting in the whaleboats. Nobody was killed, and before she sank the crew managed to take off enough provisions to allow themselves limited rations for what they thought would be a 56-day journey to the South American coast. The ill-luck that had dogged them since leaving Nantucket in August 1819 continued as food and strength ran critically low. After Christmas three men decided to take their chance on what proved to be the Henderson Islands in the Pitcairns, and during January the boats became separated; one would never be found. The deaths began that same month. Captain Pollard and his men resorted to eating the dead, and when that supply of food ran out they drew lots to decide who should be killed for food. Pollard's young cousin drew the short straw and was shot by one of the survivors. Five days after the first boat was spotted by the *Indian*, Pollard's whaleboat was sighted by another Nantucket ship, by which time only Pollard and one other man remained alive, and in April the men on Henderson island were found.

Several of the survivors wrote accounts of the disaster, one of which was shown to Herman Melville. It became the inspiration for his most enduring novel: *Moby Dick*. JH

**Title page to the *Account of the Loss of the Essex*, 1824** *(woodcut), American School, nineteenth century, American Antiquarian Society, Worcester, Massachusetts, USA / The Bridgeman Art Library*

87.7ft x 25ft x 12.6ft (26.7m x 7.6m x 3.8m) • 238 tons [B] • Complement 21 • Built Amesbury, Massachusetts, North America, 1799; converted to whaler not later than 1804

# Truelove  Whale ship 1804

Built in Philadelphia in 1764, *Truelove* fell into English hands during the War of Independence when she was captured as a privateer. She was subsequently sold to a Hull wine merchant and later converted into a whaling ship. Over a long career, she made more than 80 voyages to the Arctic, dispatching an estimated 500 whales. In 1835 she was part of the fleet trapped in ice in Melville Bay, when some 20 ships were crushed, but she came out unscathed. The captain described her as being 'handy as a cutter, safe as a lifeboat, and tight as a bottle'.

Most ports in the northeast of England and Scotland began whaling in the early 1750s and the trade thrived to become a successful industry. Whale blubber was made into oil that was, long into the nineteenth century, used to light the streets of Britain's rapidly expanding cities. By the 1890s, Dundee was the only port still operating whalers and in 1892 company owners turned their attention south and sent a whaling expedition to the Antarctic.

The *Truelove* was the last of the Hull whalers. Though she sailed alongside many of the steam-powered vessels in the 1860s she could not compete with this new technology. In 1873 she travelled to Philadelphia and was presented with a flag in honour of her 'birth' there 109 years earlier. Although there were calls for her to be made into a floating museum, she ended her days as a hulk on the Thames, before being broken up sometime in the 1890s. *HLJ*

The *Truelove* of Hull *(aquatint), print by William Ward, 1804, Hull Museums*

110ft x 30ft x 16ft (30m x 9.1m x 4.9m) • 400 tons [D] • Hull wood • Built Philadelphia, Pennsylvania, North America, 1764

# Invasion raft Napoleonic invasion ship 1805

This is one of many prints produced in England responding to the French invasion scare of 1803-1805, when Napoleon built a huge 'National Flotilla' of invasion barges, stationed in Channel ports from Flushing in Holland to Etaples in France, to carry over an 'Army of England' of over 100,000 men. The main invasion port was to be Boulogne, which was massively developed for the purpose, despite its tidal unsuitability.

During this period rumours were rife that the French were developing a wide range of what appear to modern eyes to be Heath-Robinsonesque floating machines. None of them were viable, although they provided a rich source of inspiration for the caricaturists of the day. In this image the artist has visualized an enormous raft that the French were supposedly constructing on the Channel coast in order to land vast numbers of troops. Powered by the dual principles of wind and water mills, this fearsome vessel purportedly carries '60,000 men' and '600 cannons'.

It is almost certainly by the popular and multi-talented caricaturist Robert Dighton who also worked as an actor, print-seller and drawing master. He was born in London and his father was a tradesman. Robert studied at the Royal Academy of Arts (RA) schools in 1772 and exhibited his first watercolours at the RA in 1774. In addition to painting and printmaking he also acted and sung at Sadler's Wells and other theatres. *JT*

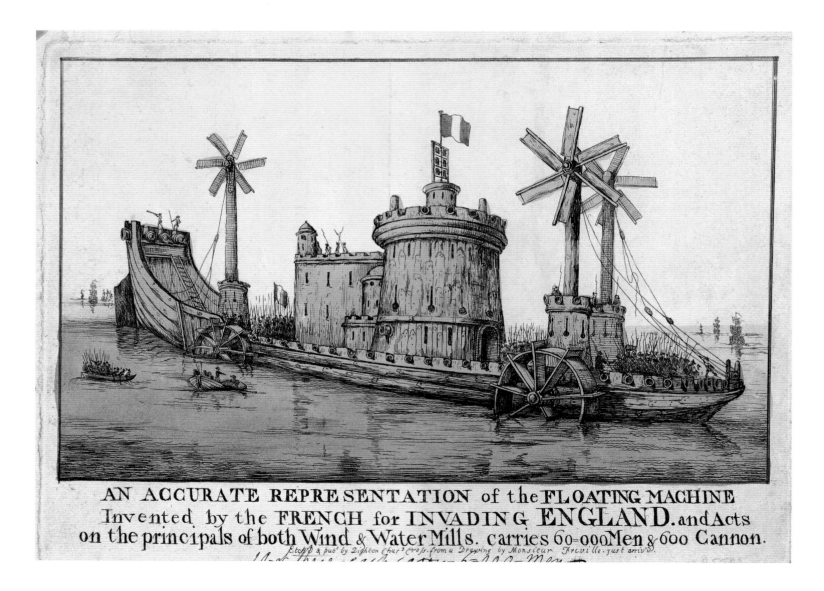

**An Accurate Representation of the Floating Machine Invented by the French for Invading England** *(hand-coloured etching), c.1805, National Maritime Museum, London (A5505)*

# Victory   Nelson's First Rate ship of the line 1805

The most famous ship in the world found a worthy artist in Joseph William Mallord Turner. For Turner HMS *Victory* was always far more than a mere ship, however famous. She was the icon of a nation at war, the badge of hope in dark times, and the shrine of the national warrior god. In his only Royal Commission Turner captured a sublime moment in the history of the sea. Nelson's flagship, signals flying, occupies centre stage, at the very moment the hero had been mortally wounded, a detail that can be glimpsed between the main mast and the shrouds. The foreground is filled with men struggling in the water, an apocalyptic reference to the Biblical Flood. The monumental canvas was widely criticised by naval officers, not least William Duke of Clarence, Nelson's old friend, for obvious factual inaccuracies. George IV soon lost interest in naval glory, and sent the only masterpiece he ever commissioned down to the Royal Hospital at Greenwich. No-one has ever captured the ship as hero, icon and emblem with the grandeur and power of Turner. Once misunderstood and maligned, his Trafalgar remains the ultimate expression of ship, man and moment in modern art. *ADL*

**The Battle of Trafalgar, 21 October 1805** *(oil on canvas), Joseph Mallord William Turner, 1822-24, Greenwich Hospital Collection, National Maritime Museum, London (BHC0565)*

186ft x 51.10ft x 21.6ft (56.7m x 15.8m x 8.7m) • 2162 tons [BM] • Hull wood • Armament; gun deck 30 x 42 pdr, main deck 28 x 24 pdr, upper deck 30 x 12 pdr, quarterdeck 10 x 6 pdr, forecastle 2 x 6 pdr • Complement 850 • Built Chatham, England, 1765

# San Ildefonso 74-gun ship of the line 1805

In the days of sail all naval ships, of whatever nation, carried several large ensigns in order to aid recognition, particularly in battle; the largest was usually hoisted from the stern. The Spanish ensign captured from the ship *San Ildefonso* at the Battle of Trafalgar by HMS *Defence* is huge, measuring 9.8m by 14.4m (32.2ft x 47.2ft). With all the shot flying around quite often the ensign would be shot away. This was important as lowering the ensign was the usual signal of surrender, hence if a ship intended to keep fighting it was essential to keep the ensign flying. In such cases it was often nailed to the mizzen mast, a practice which is the origin of the phrase to 'nail one's colours to the mast'.

Although numerous enemy ships were taken or destroyed at Trafalgar, many were lost in the storm following the battle and the *San Ildefonso* was one of only four ships that remained in British possession. As this ensign hung solemnly in St Paul's Cathedral at Nelson's funeral on 9 January, the ensign served as a visible symbol of the immense victory gained by the Royal Navy and the irreplaceable loss of Nelson. Kept in storage at St Paul's for a century it was presented to the Royal Naval College, Greenwich, in 1907 and is currently in the possession of the National Maritime Museum. In February 2005, in preparation for the Trafalgar bicentennial, the ensign was carefully photographed, thereby allowing for its reproduction here. *MR*

**Captured Spanish naval ensign** *(hand-sewn, painted wool and linen), c. 1805, Greenwich Hospital Collection, National Maritime Museum, London (F4077)*

No data available

# Pickle   Armed tender 1805

Like many ships of the French Revolutionary and Napoleonic Wars, the name of the schooner HMS *Pickle* would probably have been forgotten. It has not for one very good reason – *Pickle* was a fast vessel and hence was the ship tasked by Admiral Cuthbert Collingwood on 26 October to take his dispatches relating to the Battle of Trafalgar back to England. They contained the immortal line, 'The ever to be lamented death of Vice Admiral Lord Viscount Nelson, who, in the late conflict with the enemy, fell in the hour of victory…'. It was, therefore, the *Pickle*, and her commander Lieutenant John Lapenotière, who brought to England the news of this great victory and the loss of Nelson. *Pickle* and Lapenotière justified Collingwood's faith in them, arriving at Falmouth on 4 November making the passage in just nine days.

Here *Pickle*'s role in the tale ended; for Lapenotière there was the journey up to the Admiralty in London – a journey that usually took a week. Changing the horses pulling his post chaise 19 times Lapenotière made it in just 37 hours and presented himself at the Admiralty at 1 a.m. on 6 November.

*Pickle* herself was wrecked off Cadiz in 1808 though a modern-day replica, built in 1995, took part in the Trafalgar 200 celebrations in 2005. The memory of the *Pickle* lives on in the Royal Navy for while commissioned officers traditionally celebrate Trafalgar Night on 21 October, it is the Warrant Officers who have their own celebration on 5 November, very appropriately called 'Pickle Night'. *MR*

The 6-gun schooner *Pickle* (oil on canvas), Geoff Hunt, 1999

73ft x 20.7ft x 9.6ft (22.3m x 6.3m x 2.9m) • 127 tons [BM] • Hull wood • Armament 6 x 18 pdr carronades or 6 x 12 pdr carronades • Complement 30/35 •
Purchased as the mercantile topsail schooner *Sting*, 1800

# Príncipe Real First Rate ship of the line 1807

In 1807, following Napoleon's invasion of Portugal, steps were taken to remove the Prince Regent, the royal family, and the small Portuguese navy from his power. The whole Braganza court was embarked aboard the flagship, the *Príncipe Real*, and sailed for Portugal's mighty South American colony, Brazil. The escorting warships consisted of four 74-gun ships, three 64s, frigates and some lesser units, together with 20 merchant ships. Some 18,000 people were evacuated, the flagship herself being crowded with 1054 evacuees. Additional escort was supplied by the Royal Navy, consisting of three battleships commanded by Commodore Graham Moore, flying his flag in the 74-gun *Marlborough*.

I subsequently recorded this little-known episode in a painting. After a lengthy Atlantic crossing, calling in first at Bahia (Salvador), the whole fleet is seen arriving in Rio de Janeiro on 7 March 1808, preparations having been made in advance for a suitable reception for the royal family. To the left, the British flagship fires a salute; the *Príncipe Real* herself occupies the foreground. To the right, the remaining Portuguese ships, together with the British *Bedford*, are making their way into the harbour. The *Príncipe Real* had been built as the *Nossa Senhora da Conceição* in 1771 before being refitted and re-named. With the declaration of Brazilian independence in 1822, the ship became one of the first units of the Brazilian navy at its foundation. *GH*

**Arrival of the Portuguese Royal Family in Brazil** (oil on canvas), Geoff Hunt, 1999

[Typical data for an 80-gun ship]: 181ft x 50ft3in x 23ft (55m x 15.3m x 7m).• 1991 tons [BM] • Hull wood.• Armament 30 x 32pdr, 32 x 24pdr, 18 x 9pdr • Complement approx. 800 • Built Portugal, date unknown

# Cutter  Ship's boat c. 1810

The traditional cutter boat was designed for one thing – speed. This came from sharp, but broad lines and a single-mast rigged fore-and-aft. Propulsion could also come from muscle power, as cutters habitually were also fitted out to carry oars. This made the cutter particularly suited to fulfil a number of roles. Large naval vessels would usually carry a cutter for ferrying passengers to and from harbour, carrying dispatches, transporting light stores and conducting reconnaissance, while customs services often favoured them for their speed, hence they were often to be found patrolling water frequented by smugglers. In harbours and rivers the speed and handling qualities of the cutter made them the natural choice for pilot boats.

Local knowledge and experience counts for much and pilots would be used to guide larger vessels through often congested, sometimes dangerous waterways such as the Bristol Channel or the River Thames.

This might seem all rather mundane when set against the glamorous cruising roles fulfilled by frigates or the sheer majesty of a ship of the line, yet sailing fleets could not have survived without smaller vessels such as cutters. They were an important link in the chain, and not just in physical terms, for small boat work was essential for cadets and junior officers to gain valuable seafaring experience – indeed, for many it would have been their first taste of independent command. *MR*

**A Cutter passing astern of a Frigate** *(oil on canvas), Thomas Luny, early nineteenth century, National Maritime Museum, London (BHC1134)*

No data available

# Minotaur   Third Rate ship of the line 1810

Surviving sketches show that J.M.W. Turner began work on 'The Wreck of the Minotaur' some five years before she was lost; the painting was well advanced before his original intention to depict a transport changed to reflect national interest in the *Minotaur*'s loss.

Turner presents the events in a vortex, one of his favourite techniques, which blurs the distinction between sky, sea and spray and forces the viewer to share the disorientation of the frightened victims. The aft end of the *Minotaur* has heeled over to port, revealing the ragged stumps of her main and mizzen masts. The events of many hours are compressed into a single moment as men, boats and wreckage spin in a maelstrom beneath a turbulent sky, and in that respect the painting is surprisingly accurate.

A veteran of the battles of the Nile, Trafalgar and Copenhagen, the 74-gun Third Rate was returning to England from Gothenberg when through navigational error she ran aground on Haak Sands at the mouth of the River Texel during the night of 22 December 1810. Unable to bring her off, the crew cut away her masts to ease the strain as the wind and surf battered her, but the following morning she cracked amidships. Captain John Barrett reluctantly gave permission for 32 men to try their luck in one of the three surviving ship's boats. When after two hours they somehow reached land, Barrett allowed a second party to try with the launch. They, too, succeeded, but the second yawl, with the captain and a hundred men in it, capsized with the loss of all hands. The wreck turned over in the afternoon, drowning the remaining crew, including Lieutenant Salford who went down with his arms clasped round his pet wolf. Around three-quarters of the crew perished. *JH*

**The Wreck of the** *Minotaur (oil on canvas), Joseph Mallord William Turner, 1810, The Art Archive / Gulbenkian Foundation Lisbon / Alfredo Dagli Orti*

172.3ft x 47.8ft x 20.8ft  (52.5m x 14.6m x 6.3m) • 1273 tons [BM] • Armament 28 x 32 pdr, 28 x 18 pdr, 18 x 9 pdr • Complement approx. 500 • Built Woolwich, England, 1793

# Prison Hulks  Obsolete ships c. 1810

The term 'prison hulks' is inextricably linked to Charles Dickens' 1860 novel *Great Expectations* and David Lean's Oscar-winning film adaptation of the book, conjuring up the desolate marshes over which escaped convicts struggled. From 1776-1857 the hulls of decommissioned warships were used as grim gaols, either for the serving of sentences or for holding those awaiting transportation. In 1896 a former hulk, preserved in every detail and complete with wax figures of former convicts, was moored at Blackwall in London as a tourist attraction.

During the Napoleonic Wars hulks were also used to confine increasing numbers of French prisoners of war, including privateer crews. Among them was the French artist Ambrose-Louis Garneray, captured in 1806 while serving aboard the *Belle Poule*. He spent eight years on the hulks at Portsmouth where he was allowed to paint and sell his work for a pittance. His 'Prison Hulks in Portsmouth Harbour' (1810) shows a dismal line of roughly converted hulls, marooning the prisoners so as to make escape extremely difficult. Conditions were so appalling that disease and illness were endemic and thousands died. 'Imagine a generation of the dead coming forth from their graves,' he wrote, 'their eyes sunken, their faces haggard and wan, their backs bent, their beards wild, their bodies terrifying thin and scarcely covered by yellow rags.' As well as the discipline enforced by their captors, the prisoners had their own hierarchies, and fights and bullying were common. Released in 1814, Garneray returned to France where he became the French navy's first official painter.

The tradition of prison ships persisted for years. In 1969 the British Government used the Second World War submarine depot ship, HMS *Maidstone*, for the internment of suspected Irish terrorists, and from 1997-2005 HMP *Weare* was used to ease overcrowding in traditional prisons. *JH*

**Prison Hulks in Portsmouth Harbour** *(oil on panel), Ambrose-Louis Garneray, c. 1810, National Maritime Museum, London (BHC1923)*

# Ariel Brig 1811

*Ariel* is depicted in three different positions in this painting, a popular convention in maritime art. In the centre the vessel is portrayed in a port-broadside view, to the left in stern view and to the right in bow view. The landscape background is believed to be the Isle of Bute, off the Argyll coast of Scotland.

The painter Robert Salmon (originally spelled Salomon) was baptized in the seaport of Whitehaven, Cumberland. He was the son of a silversmith and was related to master mariners and seafarers. There is no record of his formal artistic training but in the early years of the nineteenth century he exhibited at the Royal Academy of Arts in London. His first exhibit there was 'Whitehaven Harbour' (1802).

Salmon's itinerant lifestyle was tied up with his passion for marine subjects, notably mercantile scenes, and including regattas and yacht races, as well as portraits of naval vessels and sea-battles, plus theatrical and panoramic scenes. In addition to Whitehaven he lived in Greenock, Liverpool and London. He travelled extensively in Britain and in 1828 left for America, sailing from Liverpool for New York. Salmon settled in Boston where he resided in a waterfront studio. In America he produced many intense light-suffused compositions inviting comparison with fellow Boston-based artist Fitz Hugh Lane, a master of a style of painting that has become known as 'Luminism', which emphasizes tranquillity, and usually depicts calm, reflective water and soft hazy skies. Salmon's work though was grounded by firsthand experience of the sea and characterized by technical accuracy and careful delineation. *JT*

**The Brig *Ariel*** *(oil on canvas on board), Robert Salmon, 1811, National Maritime Museum, London (BHC3203)*

Dimensions unknown • 160 tons [B] • Hull wood • Armament 14 guns • Built Bombay, India, 1809

# L'Astrolabe  Exploration ship 1811

The *Astrolabe* began her life as a horse-barge, then was refitted as a French naval corvette and christened the *Coquille* in 1814. She was used in the charting of the Black Sea, before embarking on her first circumnavigation under the command of Louis Duperrey in 1822. Upon returning to France, she was renamed the *Astrolabe* in 1826, in memory of the veteran navigator Jean-Francois La Pérouse, whose ship of the same name had vanished in the Pacific in 1788. Under a new captain Dumont d'Urville, *Astrolabe* undertook two further voyages of discovery. The first, from 1826 to 1829 was directed to Australian and western Pacific waters, with a view to finding further traces of the La Pérouse expedition. In 1836, at the request of Parisian scientific societies, French Emperor Louis-Philippe decided to mount an expedition to locate the South Magnetic Pole, with d'Urville as its leader, again in *Astrolabe*.

Departing Toulon in 1837, with sister ship *La Zélée*, the two ships made for Rio de Janeiro and the Strait of Magellan, before heading south into the pack ice of the Southern Ocean. Making little progress that first season, and then spending considerable time among the Pacific islands, they returned south again in 1840 and on 19 January they saw the coast of Antarctica, which they called Terre Adélie (for d'Urville's wife). When they finally returned to France in November 22 crew had died, and another 20 had deserted or left the expedition because of illness, but it was nonetheless hailed as a huge success. *Astrolabe* had returned brimming with natural history specimens, perhaps the largest quantity ever gathered on a single voyage. Although d'Urville died before its publication, his account of *Astrolabe*'s final voyage ran to a staggering 23 volumes. *HLJ*

L'ASTROLABE ET LA ZÉLÉE.
Arrivée à Noukahiva.

*L'Astrolabe* **and** *Zélée* **visiting Nuku Hiva in the French Marquesas Islands** *(colour lithograph), Louis Le Breton, Bibliotheque des Arts Decoratifs, Paris, France / Archives Charmet / The Bridgeman Art Library*

104ft x 61ft x 14ft (31.6m x 18.5m x 4.3m) • 380 tons [B] • Hull wood • Armament 14 x 6 pdr • Complement 75 • Built Toulon, France, 1811

# Chesapeake Frigate 1812

She was an unlucky ship from first to last. Laid down in 1795 as part of the early American Navy's frigate-building programme, *Chesapeake* was the smallest of her class – especially compared to the famous *Constitution* ('Old Ironsides') – due to disagreements over her size and armament. Even her name was undecided until before her launch in December 1799. During her first tour of service, in the 'Quasi-War' with France, she captured a privateer; but during the First Barbary War she failed to establish a blockade of Tripoli and her squadron commander was censured for 'dilatory conduct'.

In 1807 the *Chesapeake* found herself at the heart of Anglo-American tensions when the British Fourth Rate *Leopard* suddenly opened broadsides on her, killing three and wounding 18. Her commanding officer, James Barron, was court-martialled for failing to muster an effective response in time, while the naval affair became an American rallying cry against British high-handedness at sea (the *Leopard* was looking for Royal Navy deserters known to be serving on board the *Chesapeake*). During the subsequent War of 1812, she engaged HMS *Shannon* but was overwhelmed by superior gunnery, which disabled her steering with the first broadside. Mortally wounded, Captain James Lawrence ordered 'Don't give up the ship!', yet *Chesapeake* was boarded, captured and became a much-needed boost to Great Britain after the sensational victories of the *Constitution* the year before. Timbers from the ill-fated ship were used to build *Chesapeake Mill*, which still stands today in Wickham, Hampshire, England. *HF*

**Action between the *Chesapeake* and the *Shannon*, 1 June 1813** *(coloured lithograph), L. Haghe, 1830, Conway Picture Library*

152.5ft x 40.9ft x 13.8ft (46.5m x 12.5m x 4.2m) • 1244 tons [BM] • Hull wood • Armament 28 x 18 pdr, 20 x 32 pdr • Complement 340 • Built Norfolk, Virginia, North America, 1800

# Bellerophon Third Rate ship of the line 1815

The painting by John James Chalon shows the scene at Plymouth Sound in August 1815. According to the artist, 'the time is six-thirty in the evening, when Napoleon usually made his appearance'. A huge crowd in small boats has gathered around the 74-gun ship HMS *Bellerophon* to catch sight of the defeated French emperor. Napoleon had surrendered to Captain Maitland, the commander of the *Bellerophon*, three weeks earlier at Basque Roads off Rochefort. He had been brought to England where it was decided that he should be exiled to St Helena.

The *Bellerophon* had an extraordinary fighting record. She had been the first ship into action at the Battle of the Glorious First of June (1794). She had taken part in the rearguard action known as Cornwallis's Retreat. She had been dismasted and taken heavy casualties at the Battle of the Nile when she anchored opposite the huge French flagship *L'Orient*. And she had played a heroic role at Trafalgar where her captain was shot dead while his ship was under fire from four French warships. Known throughout the fleet as the 'Billy Ruffian', the *Bellerophon* was built to the designs of Sir Thomas Slade, the greatest warship designer of his age. She ended her days as a convict ship on the River Medway before being moved to Plymouth where she was broken up in 1836. *DC*

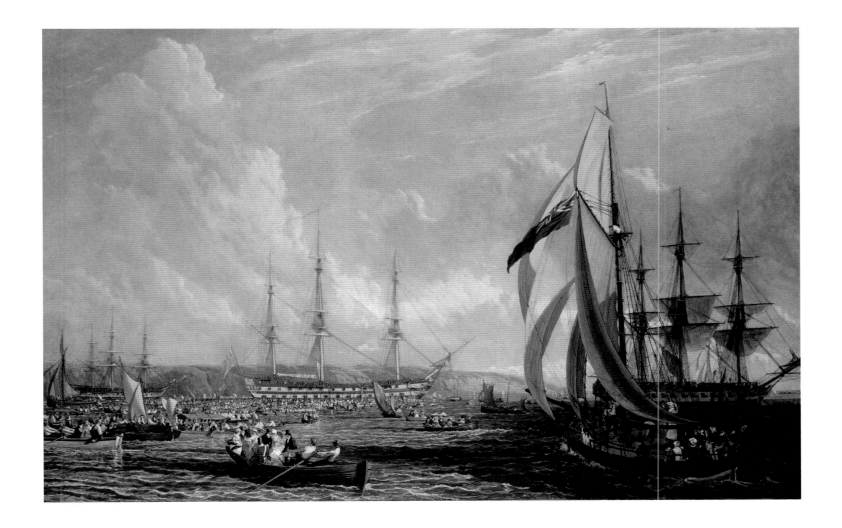

**Scene in Plymouth Sound in August 1815** *(oil on canvas), John James Chalon, 1816, Greenwich Hospital Collection, National Maritime Museum, London (BHC3227)*

168ft x 46.9ft x 19.9ft (51.2m x 14.3m x 6.1m) • 1604 tons • Hull wood • Complement 550 • Armament; gun deck 28 x 32 pdr, upper deck 28 x 18 pdr, quarter-deck 14 x 9 pdr, forecastle 4 x 9 pdr • Built Frindsbury, England, 1786

# Méduse Frigate 1816

Stoked by the shocking revelations of survivors, the story of the loss of the frigate *Méduse* on the treacherous Arguin bank off Mauretania in 1816 en route to Senegal, unleashed a scandal that shook the French Government. Captain de Chaumareys, who despite 25 years ashore had been given command for political reasons, had ignored his officers and handed responsibility for navigation to a passenger. When disaster struck, only the favoured passengers had been put into the boats. The rest, 148 men and one woman, were forced at gunpoint on to an ill-provisioned raft, to be towed by the boats. When towing became difficult, the raft was callously abandoned. Up to their waists in excoriating salt water, without provisions, sails or navigational equipment, those on the raft degenerated from despair into murder, suicide and cannibalism.

After 13 days the 15 remaining survivors sighted a ship and hoisted up a sail, in a vain hope of attracting its attention. The following day, however, the ship – the *Argus* – returned, and this time it found them.

Only two of *Méduse*'s boats reached St Louis in Senegal: those carrying the captain and the governor. The occupants of the others had to land and walk to St Louis under the Saharan sun.

Fascinated by the horrific events, Théodore Géricault began work on his monumental painting now known as 'Le Radeau de La Méduse', taking as his subject the moment when the *Argus* was first sighted. He interviewed some of the survivors, constructed a full-scale model of the raft, and visited hospitals and morgues to see the effects of death and putrefaction on human flesh. Completed in 1819, the painting dismayed the already embarrassed government. Only the King's intervention kept it in France. *JH*

*Le Radeau de la **Méduse** [The Raft of the Medusa] (oil on canvas), Théodore Géricault, 1819, Louvre, Paris/ The Bridgeman Art Library*

154ft x 39.3ft x 16.4ft (47m x 12m x 5m) • 1080 tons [D] • Armament 44 guns • Compement 324 (wartime) • Built Nantes, France, 1810

# Trincomalee Frigate 1817

Built in Bombay of teak by the East India Company in response to timber shortages in the Napoleonic wars, *Trincomalee* spent her first thirty years in reserve at Portsmouth. Cut down into a gun-deck corvette in 1846 *Trincomalee* went to the West Indies from 1847 to 1850 to suppress the slave trade, guard against an American invasion of Cuba, and meet local emergencies. A second commission, from 1852 to 1857 on the Pacific station, took her to war with Russia, although she never fired her guns in anger. Patrols and policing duties on the coast of British Columbia were the main focus before she paid off. For the next forty years *Trincomalee* served as

a harbour drill ship in various locations, including Hartlepool, before being purchased to replace the recently wrecked HMS *Foudroyant*, a name she assumed, and serve as a Boys' Training Ship, latterly at Portsmouth. By the mid-1980s the ship was badly decayed: she was sent to Hartlepool in north-east England in 1987 where HMS *Warrior* had been restored, for a complete rebuild. The restored ship now proudly carries both her original name, and the original Asian figurehead, lying in Jackson Dock, Hartlepool, centrepiece of a dedicated maritime area. *ADL*

*Her Majesty's Ships "Amphitrite" & "Trincomalee" Beating out of San Francisco on Sepr 23d 1854.*

**HM Ships *Amphitrite* and *Trincomalee** (print), National Maritime Museum, London (A1302)

150.1ft x 39.8ft x 13.8ft (45.8m x 12.1m x 4.2m) • 1052 tons [BM] • Hull wood • Complement 284 • Armament 28 x 18 pdr, 8 x 32 pdr, 10 x 9 pdr • Built Wadia, Bombay, India, 1817

# Savannah Hybrid sailing ship/sidewheel paddle steamer 1818

Within a decade of Robert Fulton's first commercially successful steam river boat, the *North River Steamboat*, the same spirit of innovation and enterprise saw the first steam ship cross the Atlantic. The 320-ton ship rigged *Savannah* was launched in August 1818. Initially intended to connect the city for which she had been named with New York, where she was built, an economic downturn and the President's refusal to buy the ship saw the object shifted to a pioneer transatlantic steam service, only for the owners to realise the ship and the technology were unable to deliver, using the ocean passage as a technology demonstration and sales pitch. The target audience was quickly identified as the Russian Czar, Alexander I. She sailed from Savannah on May 24th, and arrived off the coast of Ireland on June 16th, despite being obliged to rely on sail for a large part of the voyage. After causing a sensation in several North European ports the ship reached St. Petersburg, but the Russians were not ready to pay the asking price, and she returned home, to be stripped of her engine and sold off as a sailing coaster. A century later, when the triumph of steam navigation had become a fact, America built a replica to celebrate a pioneering effort, quietly forgetting the commercial failure of the project. *ADL*

*SS Savannah (oil on canvas), Franz Hanfstaengl, 1909, The Art Archive / Eileen Tweedy*

109ft x 25.8ft x 12ft (33.2m x 7.9m x 3.7m) • 320 tons [B] • Hull wood • Complement 20, 22 passengers • Built Fickett & Crockett, New York, USA, 1818

# Hecla  Arctic exploration ship 1819

Launched at the Barkworth & Hawkes yard in Hull on 15 July 1815, just a week after the surrender of Napoleon at the Battle of Waterloo, HMS *Hecla* was denied the fury of war, although she did see active service in an attack on Barbary pirates off Algiers the following year. In peacetime, such a heavily constructed bomb vessel as this (like her sister craft HMS *Erebus* and HMS *Fury*) would find ideal occupation as a polar exploration ship, able to withstand the crushing pressures of sea ice.

She first sailed for the Arctic in 1819, under William Parry, in search of the Northwest Passage and though she was caught in the grip of the ice, she successfully overwintered, the first ship to do so. In 1821, HMS *Hecla* and

HMS *Fury* sailed for Hudson Bay, annually visited by trading ships, but seldom explored. Parry's third expedition in 1824 would return him to Lancaster Sound off the northernmost coast of Canada. Before the stout exploration ship left England on this voyage, she had become so famous that more than 6000 people visited as she lay alongside in the naval dockyard at Deptford. Parry took her north for a fourth time in 1827, in an unsuccessful attempt to reach the North Pole. After this voyage, despite the explorer's protests, the veteran ship was withdrawn from Arctic service. She was dispatched as a survey vessel to the coast of West Africa, where she remained in service until 1831. *HLJ*

**Das Eismeer [The Polar Sea]. This startling painting was inspired by Parry's voyages in the *Hecla*** (oil on canvas), *Caspar David Friedrich, 1824, Hamburger Kunsthalle, Hamburg, Germany / The Bridgeman Art Library*

105ft x 29ft x 14ft (32m x 8.7m x 4.2m) • 372 tons [BM] • Hull wood • Armament 1 x 13in mortar, 1 x 10in mortar, 8 x 24 pdr, 2 x 6 pdr • Complement 67 • Built Barkworth and Hawkes, North Barton, Hull, England, 1815

115

# Vostok Exploration sloop 1820

In 1819 the Tsar of Russia decided to send two scientific expeditions, one to the North and one to the South Pole, to complement and surpass the explorations of the greatest of navigators, Captain James Cook. Although neither expedition reached its goal, it is now accepted by geographers that the first men to sight the icy cliffs of the Antarctic continent were aboard the exploration ships *Vostok* (meaning East) and *Mirnyi* (Peaceful) of Captain Bellingshausen and Lieutenant Lazarev in January 1820.

Although classified as a sloop, the *Vostok* was really a small frigate of about 930 tons displacement, designed as a fast cruiser able to operate in shoal waters. As such, she was not suitable for work in the difficult far southern waters and Bellingshausen spent much time reducing her rig. Her light pine construction without extra strengthening for the ice meant she was very

leaky. She was even so, much faster than her companion, so in this picture, typical of modern Russian representations of the ships near the ice, the *Vostok* would more likely have been found under shorted sail so that both vessels could stay together.

The ships spent two summer seasons probing southwards in the Antarctic, consistently further south than Cook, but constantly bedevilled by adverse weather conditions. Their discovery of Peter I Island was the first actual land ever seen inside the Antarctic Circle. In the intervening winter season they carefully charted many islands in the Tuamotus and visited Tahiti, refitting meanwhile at Sydney in Australia. Although disregarded in its own day, the expedition has been commemorated: Vostok base in the Antarctic is now named for the ship. *CJ*

The Russian corvette **Vostok** and the support vessel **Mirnyi** off the coast of Alaska *(oil on canvas), Mikhail Mikhailovich Semyonov, 1949, State Central Navy Museum, St . Petersburg / Lebrecht Music & Arts Pictures*

129.8ft x 32.7ft x 14.8ft (39.6m x 10m x 4.5m) • 630 tons [D] • Hull wood • Armament 14 x 6 pdr, 6 x 12 pdr carronades • Complement 117 • Built Stoke, Okhta, St Petersburg, Russia, 1818

# Dutton   East Indiaman 1821

Captain Edward Pellew, later Admiral Lord Exmouth, 1757–1833, was a much respected and well-liked commander during the Napoleonic Wars – and he later acquired fictional fame in C.S. Forester's Hornblower novels. On 26 January 1796, while on his way to dine with a friend, he stopped to assist at a major shipwreck in Plymouth Sound.

Chartered as a troopship, the East Indiaman *Dutton* had almost reached Plymouth with some 500 soldiers, passengers and crew when she lost her rudder on Cobbler's Reef and was driven on to the rocks by gale-force winds. Her masts were cut away, and a lifeline with a travelling jib was established to bring people to land. Pellew used the line to go out to the helpless wreck and co-ordinate the rescue, encouraging boats to come in close to take off the women, children and injured, and personally rescuing a baby.

Some accounts suggest he quelled the panic that had broken out because the officers deserted the ship, a charge later vehemently refuted by Captain Charles Grant who had been the *Dutton*'s second mate at the time.

The painting was one of a series commemorating events in his career, commissioned by Pellew from the marine artist Thomas Luny, who had settled in Teignmouth. Luny had previously executed a number of ship portraits of East Indiamen as well as more dramatic paintings of naval battles. 'The Wreck of the East Indiaman Dutton', completed for Pellew in 1821, shows the hulk at the foot of the Citadel, pounded by waves, a line of men hauling on the lifeline run out from the aft end of the ship, and an unconscious woman in the arms of rescuers. Light strikes the figurehead, and people struggle in the angry water. There is nothing to suggest Pellew's presence or his heroism; the painting simply records the event. *JH*

**The Wreck of the East Indiaman Dutton at Plymouth Sound, 26 January 1796** *(oil on canvas), Thomas Luny, 1821, National Maritime Museum, London (BHC3298)*

143ft x 35.1ft x 14.8ft (43.6m x 10.7m x 4.5m) • 761 tons [BM] • Hull wood • Complement approx. 500 • Built Deptford, London, England, 1781

# Boladora Slaver 1829

After the British Parliament passed the Act for the Abolition of the Slave Trade in 1807, the Royal Navy was tasked with suppressing or at least seriously disrupting slave traders of all nationalities, through a combination of treaties with African leaders, attacks on or blockades of slaving ports and the interception and seizure of slave ships. At the same time the government negotiated Right of Search agreements with other nations who opposed the trade, though until 1862 the USA refused to allow the Royal Navy to board its ships.

After 1819 most of the work fell to the newly created West Africa station, an unhealthy posting where, in 1829, the mortality rate among crews was 25 per cent. Officers and men were entitled to 'head money', paid for each freed slave, but courts did not always uphold the actions of the Navy. Nevertheless,

by 1866 more than 500 ships had been captured and the Royal Navy had prevented many others from embarking slaves. The slave traders, particularly those from Spain, used fast and heavily armed vessels, but if brought to battle the standard of gunnery and organization was generally inferior to that of the naval ships.

One notable action was fought on 5 June 1829 by HMS *Pickle*, a five-gun schooner launched in 1827 and commanded by John McHardy. She had spent the day watching a suspicious ship flying US colours and she insinuated herself between it and the Cuban coast. Despite having only half the complement of her opponent – 30 men and six boys – and losing several of them in an hour-long night battle, she managed to capture what proved to be the Spanish slaver *Boladora* vividly depicted in John Moore's painting. *JH*

**The Capture of the Slaver *Boladora*, 6 June 1829** *(oil on panel), John Moore, nineteenth century, National Maritime Museum, London (BHC0624)*

# Beagle Survey barque 1831

HMS *Beagle* is a ship that has shaped all of our lives. The young naturalist Charles Darwin was selected by the ship's captain Robert FitzRoy for her second scientific survey voyage spanning the years 1831 to 1836. During this circumnavigation Darwin acquired many specimens that led to his ground-breaking publication *On the Origin of Species* (1859).

Launched at the Royal Dockyard of Woolwich initially as a 10-gun brig, *Beagle* cost £7803 and was one of a series of vessels known as the Cherokee, Cadmus and Rolla class designed by Sir Henry Peake, the surveyor of the Navy. *Beagle* and some of her sister-ships were not originally intended for survey work – mapping coastlines and seas to create Admiralty Charts. Instead she was originally designed to carry carronades, a type of gun nicknamed the 'smasher' which caused extensive damage at short range, although when Darwin was aboard she carried only one 6lb boat-carronade. Before her first survey voyage to Tierra del Fuego, 1828–1830, under the command of Pringle Stokes, her rig was changed to that of a barque.

To continue the scientific and survey work on the 1831–1836 voyage FitzRoy insisted on further alterations to make her more comfortable and seaworthy. She would, largely thanks to FitzRoy, be one of the finest kitted out ships for survey work and carried a staggering 22 chronometers and a specialist to look after them. He also wanted to create images of the people and places he encountered and to this end personally paid for two artists to accompany him – Augustus Earle and Conrad Martens. Among the supernumeraries onboard was a missionary to accompany three surviving Fuegians FitzRoy had taken on board the *Beagle* during her first survey voyage and whom he now intended to return to their homeland to establish a Christian Missionary settlement.

The painter Owen Stanley was a naval officer who spent four years on the coast of South America, and in 1830 was employed under Captain Phillip Parker King in the *Adventure*, on a survey of the Strait of Magellan. While serving on another ship he came into contact with the *Beagle* again in Australia during her third and last surveying voyage of 1837–1843, under the commands of John Clements Wickham and John Lort Stokes, both of whom served under FitzRoy during *Beagle*'s second celebrated voyage. *JT*

HMS *Beagle* off Fort Macquarie, Sydney Harbour *(watercolour), Captain Owen Stanley, 1841, National Maritime Museum, London (PU8969)*

90ft x 24.6ft x 11ft (21.6m x 5.1m x 1.6m) • 235 tons [BM] • Hull wood • Complement 75 • Armament 5 x 6 pdr, 2 x 9 pdr • Built Woolwich, London, England, 1820

# Amphitrite Convict ship 1833

Between 1787 and 1868, 158,702 male and female convicts were transported from Britain and Ireland to Australia for terms of 7 years, 14 years or life. The ships that took them were ordinary merchant vessels, chartered for the purpose, and they varied in size, from the 842-ton ex-Indiaman *Lady Castlereagh* in 1818 and the last convict transport, the 962-ton *Hougomont*, both owned by major shipowners, to John Hunter's 209-ton *Amphitrite* in 1833. Average voyage lengths depended on the destination: 176 days to Sydney between 1808 and 1809; 127 days between 1839 and 1840.

Conditions on early transports were grim; and only moderately improved in 1817. The *Amphitrite*'s female convicts, some with children, were accommodated three to a bed in bunks down the ship's side and before the ship sailed they spent the daytime on the deck reading and sewing. They had no guards: a naval surgeon had charge of them, and unless they caused trouble he took no interest in them.

*Amphitrite* sailed on 25 August and quickly ran into one of the worst storms of the century. Despite the best efforts of a kind-hearted crew to calm them, the women were terrified. As his ship was pushed dangerously close to the French coast, Captain John Hunter decided to run her on to the sands at Boulogne, not appreciating a worse danger from the wild incoming tide. The Boulogne lifeboat crew braved death to reach the ship; their aid was refused, as was that of local fisherman, Pierre Hénin who swam three quarters of a mile (1200m) with a line. The surgeon refused to launch the ship's boat, and, shortly after the distraught women broke on to the deck, the *Amphitrite* went to pieces in the surf. 133 men women and children died; only three men from the crew of 16 survived. *JH*

**Distraught convicts on the deck of** *Amphitrite* (engraving), Alf Pearse, 1895

93ft x 23 ft (28.3m x 7m) • 209 tons [B] • Hull wood • Complement 16 • Built Appledore, Devon, England, 1801; lengthened 1824

# Thetis   Fifth Rate frigate 1833

This is one of two views of Thetis Cove on the island of Cabo Frio, north of Rio de Janeiro, painted in 1833 by John Christian Schetky. At first sight it seems a romantic interpretation of an exotic landscape in savage weather. Look closely and there is evidence of human activity: figures on the headland and ropes slung across the cove. The title of the painting 'Salvage of Stores and Treasure from HMS *Thetis* at Cape Frio' reveals its inspiration.

The frigate HMS *Thetis* had been wrecked on 30 December 1830 with the loss of 28 lives and a fortune in gold and silver. Captain Thomas Dickinson, in command of HMS *Lightning*, was given the task of mounting what turned out to be one of the most remarkable salvage operations ever undertaken. The treasure lay in 6.5 fathoms in front of cliffs up to 190ft (57m) high; the depth of the seabed fluctuated between 3.5 and 24 fathoms. With no proper equipment available, Dickinson made a diving bell by cannibalizing water tanks from HMS *Warspite*, which can be seen hanging centre-right in the painting. His team built steps and ladders down the cliff, set up a net to stop the treasure being washed away, and adapted air hoses and pumping equipment from *Lightning* and *Warspite* in order to supply the divers. For a year of often dreadful weather the team camped on the exposed headland, fighting illness, and learning by experience. When the expedition finished its work on 9 March 1832 it had recovered almost 300,000 dollars, 138lb of gold and 9106lb of silver bars.

Schetky's concentration on the awe-inspiring grandeur of the location and the elements, rather than the operation, emphasizes both the physical fragility of man and the awesome power of human ingenuity. *JH*

**Salvage of Stores and Treasure from HMS *Thetis* at Cape Frio, Brasil** *(oil on canvas), John Christian Schetky, 1833, Royal United Service Institution Collection, National Maritime Museum, London (BHC3660)*

150.2ft x 125.3ft x 39.9ft (45.8m x 38.2m x 12.2m) • 1052 tons [BM] • Hull wood • Armament 28 x 18 pdr, 8 x 9 pdr, 8 x 32 pdr, 2 x 9 pdr • Complement 284 •
Built Pembroke, Wales, 1817

# Temeraire  Second Rate ship of the line 1838

The Fighting Temeraire was Turner's nickname for the 98-gun HMS *Temeraire,* the British naval ship under the command of Captain Eliab Harvey that became famous for rescuing Vice-Admiral Horatio Nelson's HMS *Victory* at the Battle of Trafalgar, 21 October 1805. Launched on 11 September 1798 at the Royal Dockyard of Chatham, the *Temeraire* was British built, although derived from a French ship name. She was one of the Dreadnought class of Second Rates designed by Sir John Henslow in 1788. She was heavily armed and cost a total of £74,241 to build and fit out. Constructed largely of oak and copper-bottomed, she was part of the 'Wooden Walls' of England and she was the largest of her class.

*Temeraire* remained in service until 1838 when she was decommissioned and towed from Sheerness to the Beatson yard at Rotherhithe to be broken up. Turner almost certainly never witnessed the event himself and traditionally it is thought that the painting represents the decline of Britain's naval power. However, he would have read news reports and, as a patriot, the event appealed as a subject to a painter who had already created images of Nelson's three major sea-battles: Nile (1798), Copenhagen (1801) and Trafalgar (1805). Passionate about Britain's past, Turner was also fascinated by new technology and was a shareholder of Brunel's Great Western Railway Company, and this painting highlights the power and significance of steam propulsion.

Turner was the son of a barber and wig-maker from Covent Garden who had a precocious talent. He exhibited his earliest works in his father's shop window, and later at the Royal Academy of Arts, where he had a long, intimate and rewarding relationship, becoming professor of perspective and temporarily the organization's president. Turner is arguably Britain's greatest painter: that said, his work was criticized by the nautical fraternity, and others, who disliked the extensive technical and artistic liberties taken by him. There was no rigging on *Temeraire* during her final tow; she was tugged by two rather than one tug; the position of the funnel and mast have been swapped on the undersized workhorse, and if the ship is being towed westwards, the brilliant sunset is in  the wrong place. However, in August 2005, BBC Radio 4 ran a poll to find Britain's favourite painting and Turner's 'Temeraire' won. *JT*

**The 'Fighting Temeraire' Tugged to her Last Berth to be Broken up** (oil on canvas), Joseph Mallord William Turner, before 1839, National Gallery, London / The Bridgeman Art Library

185ft x 51ft x 21.6ft (56.4m x 15.5m x 6.6m) • 2121 tons [BM] • Hull wood • Complement 750 • Armament; gun deck 28 x 32 pdr, main deck 28/30 x 18 pdr, upper deck 30 x 18 pdr, quarterdeck 8 x 12 pdr, forecastle 2 x 12 pdr • Built Chatham, Kent, England, 1798

# Charles W. Morgan Whale ship 1841

Preserved at Mystic Seaport Museum, the *Charles W. Morgan* is the USA's last wooden whaling ship, a link to a time before petroleum products were dominant, when whale oil was a vital fuel. Between 1841 and 1921 the *Morgan* sailed on voyages lasting anything from eight-and-a half months, when based on the West Coast, to over four years when she sailed out of New Bedford, Massachusetts. She called at destinations in Chile, Russia and the South Pacific, and on one occasion her captain was accompanied not only by his wife but by their three-week-old baby.

Bowhead, sperm and right whales were caught. The actual hunting was carried out using one or more of the five whaleboats carried by the ship. Each boat was crewed by six men who had to harpoon the whale. The harpoon was attached to a line and the whale would often tow the boat until exhausted, when the crew would kill it and drag it back to the waiting *Morgan* where the blubber was removed and rendered into oil. The *Morgan* could bring home 90,000 gallons, stored in 3000 barrels. The head was also cut off to extract the baleen, spermaceti and ambergris, which were in high demand for corset bones, pharmaceuticals and perfumes respectively.

Even before she had retired from commercial service, the *Morgan* had featured on film: in 1923 she had a major, if implausible, role as an East Indiaman in the silent movie *Java Head*; more recently, she appeared in *Gangs of New York*, and scenes from Steven Spielberg's *Amistad* were shot in her blubber room. In 2008 she was taken out of the water for a major three-year restoration programme. *JH*

The *Charles W. Morgan* at Mystic Seaport *(photograph), John Lee, 2008*

111ft x 27.7ft x 13.7ft (33.8m x 8.4m x 4.2m) • 298 tons [B] • Hull wood • Complement approx. 26 • Built New Bedford, Massachusetts, USA, 1841

# Nemesis East India Company iron paddle frigate 1841

The world's first steam-powered, iron-hulled warship, *Nemesis* was built to a revolutionary design for Britain's Honourable East India Company which maintained its own navy. Her hull was divided into seven watertight compartments – an innovation that saved her when she grounded off St Ives – and, with a keel plate rather than a keel, she was almost flat-bottomed, drawing around 5ft (1.5m). This enabled her to navigate rivers but adversely affected steering; to compensate, a rudder extension and external centreboards could be lowered by winch. Her ratio of length to beam was unusually high, and a 'corrector' was installed to counteract the magnetic influence of the hull on the compass. She was built in just three months and sailed on a secret mission.

The commander of *Nemesis*, William Hutcheon, a Royal Navy midshipman seconded to the HEIC, was given orders to proceed to Ceylon (Sri Lanka);

on arrival in late 1840 he was ordered to join a combined fleet of Company and Royal Navy warships off Macau at the mouth of the Pearl River, to take part in the First Anglo-Chinese War. The conflict had broken out over trade, territorial concessions and particularly over the supply of opium into China where its recreational use was forbidden. The advantage of his ship's radical design and his own brilliance soon became clear. On 7 January 1841 *Nemesis* landed troops, shelled the Chuenpi fort at close range and destroyed 11 junks in nearby Anson Bay. Edward Duncan's 1843 acquatint shows *Nemesis*, background right, firing her first rocket into the largest junk – which immediately exploded. Later she was able to navigate the Pearl River and help capture Canton. Nicknamed Nevermiss, *Nemesis* played a pivotal role in the British victory throughout the controversial war that concluded with major Chinese concessions. *JH*

*Nemesis* **destroying Chinese junks in Anson's Bay, 1841** *(aquatint and etching), Edward Duncan, 1843, National Maritime Museum, London (0792)*

184ft x 29ft x 11ft (56.1m x 8.8m x 3.4m) • 660 tons [D] • Hull iron • Complement 60-90 • Armament 2 x 32 pdr, 10 x swivels, 1 x rocket launcher • Built Cammell Laird, Birkenhead, England, 1839

# Alarm Cutter-rigged yacht c.1842

The sport of yachting which had begun in the Netherlands in the seventeenth century enjoyed a golden age after the Napoleonic Wars, and the wealthy Joseph Weld (1777–1863) was one of its greatest enthusiasts. He helped to build his own yachts, most famously the cutter *Alarm*, the largest of her type. She cost £20,000, equivalent to some £1.5 million in 2010, based on the retail price index, or £16 million in terms of average wages. A founder of the Royal Yacht Squadron, Weld engaged in fierce racing rivalry with other members. *Alarm* won the King's Cup in 1831, 1832 and 1833 but was disqualified after crossing the line half an hour ahead of her nearest challenger in 1834 because Weld had crossed an opponent on the larboard tack in contravention of the rules. The cutter-yacht came to perfection in *Alarm*: she was all but unbeatable in the Solent, but a new type was on the way.

In 1851 the schooner-rigged *America* arrived at Cowes, throwing down the gauntlet to the Royal Yacht Squadron. Six schooners and nine cutters, including *Alarm*, took part in a race around the Isle of Wight. When *Arrow* grounded, *Alarm* went to her aid, probably gifting the race to *America*. Thus began the challenge known as the America's Cup. Weld had *Alarm* lengthened and rigged as a schooner, and she continued to race with great success until her owner's death.

In the painting executed between 1842 and 1851 by Nicolas Matthew Condy the Younger, Joseph Weld is probably the central figure, seated, with the top hat; to his left, hat in hand, could be *Alarm*'s long-serving skipper Edward Cooke. The identity of the others on board this unusual painting are unsubstantiated. *JH*

On board the yacht *Alarm* (oil on mahogany panel), Nicolas Matthew Condy the Younger, c. 1842-1851, National Maritime Museum, London (BHC4178)

82ft [WL] x 24ft (25m x 7.3m) • 193 tons; 218 when rebuilt [BM] • Hull wood • Built Inman, Lymington, England, 1830

# Great Britain Iron screw steamship 1843

The visionary engineer Isambard Kingdom Brunel conceived the *Great Britain* as the first propeller driven transatlantic liner, to provide a fast service from England to New York. Her steam engine was assisted by sails and she was the largest ship in the world. *Great Britain*'s early transatlantic passages were beset with teething problems and bad weather. On the latter part of the ship's second eastward crossing she had to rely on sails alone because her propeller was damaged. The wind freshened to a westerly gale with a high sea, and under reduced sail the ship showed her paces; the log reported, 'Ship scudding and steering beautifully taking spray on the larboard quarter and beam occasionally, but is easier than any ship I ever knew'. After a passage of 20 days her passengers presented a surprisingly forgiving address to the captain, expressing 'the superiority of the *Great Britain* in a heavy gale... For safety, speed and comfort she is unsurpassed, and during this passage of unexpected length we have not suffered the slightest diminution of comfort...'

The lithograph illustration, after an 1845 painting by Joseph Walter, shows the ship in heavy seas off Lundy Island. Unfortunately the fifth outward voyage ended in disaster, with the ship running ashore on the Irish coast. This ended her transatlantic career and she became an emigrant ship, carrying passengers to Australia. *Great Britain* is now on display in Bristol, England. *PB*

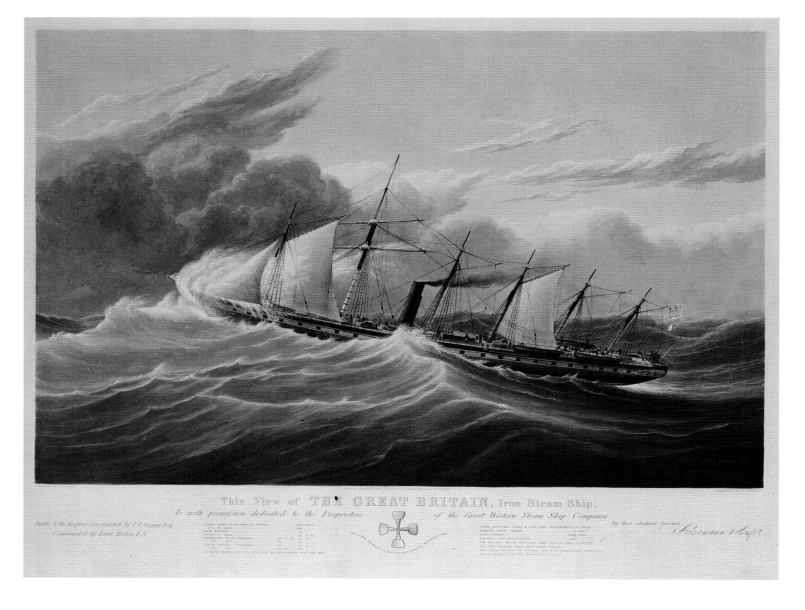

**SS** *Great Britain* (lithograph), Conway Picture Library

322ft x 50.5ft x 16ft (98.1m x 15.4m x 4.9m) • 3443 tons [GRT] • Hull iron • Complement 130, passengers 252 • Built Great Western Steamship Co., Bristol, England, 1843

# Princeton Screw steam warship 1843

At the time of her launch in 1843, the corvette *Princeton* was the most advanced warship in the world. Not only was she the first steam-powered, screw-propelled navy vessel, she boasted an experimental armament of 12in smoothbores firing 225lb shot – far in excess of contemporary naval ordnance. This reflected a strategy of fast, light vessels which could deliver singular knock-out blows against anything they could not outrun. She was one of the US Navy's most controversial men-of-war.

Designed by the brilliant Swedish engineer John Ericsson, *Princeton* was sponsored by Captain Robert F. Stockton, an opportunistic American naval officer who had met Ericsson in England when the eccentric inventor's ideas failed to impress the British Admiralty. While Ericsson closely supervised the construction of his 'Oregon' gun, reinforced by wrought-iron bands around the breech to withstand enormous charges, Stockton attempted to copy the design in his 'Peacemaker', which lacked the same supporting strength. On 28 February 1844, the 'Peacemaker' exploded on board the *Princeton* during a demonstration which nearly succeeded in killing President John Tyler and his entire cabinet (both the Secretaries of State and the Navy were killed in the blast, along with five others, leaving a further 20 wounded). Stockton managed to shift the blame for the catastrophe on Ericsson, whose full claims for payment in building the *Princeton* and her innovations were subsequently ignored by the navy. *HF*

AWFUL EXPLOSION OF THE "PEACE-MAKER" ON BOARD THE U.S. STEAM FRIGATE, *PRINCETON,* ON WEDNESDAY, 28TH FEBY. 1844.

Awful explosion of the Peace-Maker on board the US Steam Frigate *Princeton* on Wednesday, 28th Feb 1844 *(lithograph)*, *1844, Getty Images*

164ft x 31.5ft x 17ft (50m x 9.3m x 5.2m) • 954 tons [D] • Hull iron • Armament 2 x 12in, 12 x 42 pdr • Complement 166 • Built John Lenthall, Philadelphia Navy Yard, USA, 1843

# Rattler Screw steam sloop 1845

Launched in 1843, the 880-ton sloop *Rattler* was the world's first purpose-built screw propeller warship. To test the screw against paddle-wheel propulsion the design of the hull repeated existing paddle sloops. Admiralty technical consultant and engineer Isambard Kingdom Brunel ordered an integrated machinery plant, engines, boilers and shafts from Maudslay Son & Field. Brunel used *Rattler*'s trials to secure critical design data for his gigantic iron screw liner *Great Britain*. Although Brunel's trials validated the screw system, the Admiralty wanted a more public 'demonstration', setting up the famous tug of war between *Rattler* and her paddle-wheel half-sister HMS *Alecto*. Speed tests with and without sail, and tests of comparative towing power were conducted before the famous back-to-back pulling competition of 3 April 1845. The whole process was flawed: the Admiralty knew *Rattler*'s engines were significantly more powerful than *Alecto*'s, but having committed the nation to an expensive screw steamship programme it used a publicity stunt to convince the doubters. Rather than being more 'powerful', screw propulsion was more economical, and easier to combine with sail. Thereafter *Rattler* cruised against slave ships off West Africa, took part in the Burma War of 1852 and fought Chinese pirates before being broken up in 1856. *ADL*

**HM steam sloops *Rattler* and *Alecto* towing stern to stern** *(coloured lithograph), 1845, National Maritime Museum, London (PY0923)*

176.5ft x 32.7ft x 11.8ft (53.8m x 10m x 3.6m) • 1112 tons [D] • Hull wood • Armament 1 x 68 pdr, 4 x 32 pdr carronades • Complement 180 • Built Sheerness, Kent, England, 1843

# Erebus  Expedition ship 1846

Named for the entrance to the underworld in Greek mythology, *Erebus* was a barque-rigged bomb vessel with two huge mortars weighing 3 tons each, designed by Sir Henry Peake as a 'beast of war'. After two years in the Mediterranean , she was adapted for service in polar waters, her toughness making her ideally suited for the rigours of the ice.

In 1839 she came under command of the veteran Arctic explorer James Clark Ross for his scientific voyage to the Southern Ocean. On New Year's Day 1841, *Erebus* and her sister-ship, the bomb vessel HMS *Terror*, crossed the Antarctic Circle and forced their way southward through the pack ice. On 9 January they reached open water, now known as the Ross Sea, and a few days later claimed Victoria Land for Britain. Roald Amundsen, conqueror of the South Pole in 1911, later hailed the voyage of *Erebus*, as a 'brilliant proof of human courage and energy. With two ponderous craft, regular tubs according

to our ideas, these men sailed right into the heart of the pack, which all previous explorers had regarded as certain death'.

Despite much peril and adventure, *Erebus* arrived back in England in September 1843, after a voyage of more than four years. In no time at all she was fitted out for a new voyage in search of the Northwest Passage, under the doughty Sir John Franklin. She was last seen late in the summer of 1845, moored to an iceberg high in Lancaster Bay. She was never seen again. Her fate was partially revealed with the discovery of human remains, relics and one written note, which described the survivors of this fateful expedition abandoning ship on 22 April 1848, in a futile bid to march overland to safety. Where *Erebus* may be remains the subject of fascination and conjecture, inspiring search missions right up to the present day. *HLJ*

**HMS *Erebus* in the Ice, 1846** *(oil on canvas), Francois Etienne Musin, nineteenth century, Caird Collection, National Maritime Museum, London (BHC3325)*

105ft x 29ft x 14ft (32m x 8.7m x 4.2m) • 372 tons [BM] • Hull wood • Armament 1 x 13in mortar, 1 x 10in mortar, 8 x 24 pdr, 2 x 6 pdr • Complement 67 • Built Pembroke, Wales, 1826

# Junk Chinese warship 1850

For 900 years the Chinese naval junk was a formidable vessel, reaching its apogee during the Ming Dynasty. In 1521 and 1522 the Chinese defeated Portuguese fleets at the two battles of Tamao, and in 1661 they overcame the well-armed fleet of the Dutch East India Company which had arrived to support the besieged Fort Zeelandia on present-day Taiwan. With their watertight compartments, well-trained troops, easy handling and often huge size they were at least the equals of their European contemporaries.

However, by the time that this painting was executed by an unknown artist around 1850, the war junk was no match for the European men-of-war, and they were largely at the mercy of heavy, land-based artillery, as was demonstrated during the naval engagements of the First and Second Opium Wars (1838-1842 and 1856-60). The Chinese Imperial Navy would henceforth invest in western-style warships, but junks such as this two-masted craft remained useful as privateers. Despite its size it is heavily manned, and a cannon can be seen on the starboard side of the stern just forward of one of the lamps. Five warriors' shields are hung on the side, and the ship is underway, passing local craft with no need to use the oars, also kown as sweeps, which are raised out of the water. The painting gives excellent detail of the raked bamboo masts and the construction and rigging of the bamboo-stiffened sails. *JH*

**A war junk** *(oil on canvas), artist unknown, 1850, National Maritime Museum, London (BHC1183)*

# America   Racing yacht c.1851

The schooner *America* appears under full sail in this port-broadside view by the artist John Fraser. Perhaps considered the most famous of all racing yachts, she has inspired generations of writers, artists and sportsmen all over the globe. She was designed by George Steers for John C. Stevens, the Commodore of the New York Yacht Club, and built in 1851 in New York with the express purpose of taking on Britain's formidable Royal Yacht Squadron. Nicknamed the 'low, black schooner', she was blessed with exceptional windward abilities and the result was a shock to the nation that had thought of itself as sovereign of the seas.

*America* made her first transatlantic voyage in the summer of 1851 and Stevens duly entered her in the 53-mile race around the Isle of Wight on 22 August, a memorable event attended that year by Queen Victoria. *America* was captained by Richard Brown, a skilled pilot from Sandy Hook, renowned for his expertize in navigating the shoals around New York Harbour. When

*America* crossed the finishing line, her lead was so great that the Queen asked for the name of the vessel in second place. She received the now legendary reply, 'Your Majesty, there is no second'. From then on, the trophy that Stevens won has been known as The America's Cup, which continues to be the most prestigious yachting prize in the world.

*America* was sold to John de Blaguiere in 1851, and in 1856 he passed her to Lord Templeton. In 1857 she was in the Royal Yacht Squadron under the name of *Camilla* and soon changed owners again, sailing to the Mediterranean and Australia. She was for some time used as a blockade-runner during the American Civil War. After many years of racing, cruising and intermittent neglect, she was finally donated to the United States Naval Academy in Annapolis. By 1940 she had become seriously decayed and during a heavy snowstorm, the shed where she was being stored collapsed. In 1945 the piled remains were finally scrapped and burned, a sad end for so famous a ship. *HLJ*

**The Yacht *America*** *(oil on board), John Fraser, c. 1890-1920, National Maritime Museum, London (BHC3192)*

101ft x 23ft x 11ft (30.9m x 7m x 3.3m) • 180 tons [D] • Hull wood • Complement 25 (9 when racing in 1851) • Built William H Brown, New York, USA, 1851

# Assistance  Arctic discovery barque c.1851

In 1845 Sir John Franklin and his two ships, *Erebus* and *Terror*, disappeared in the Canadian Arctic during their search for a Northwest Passage. During more than a decade of anguish, some 30 expeditions were sent out into the labyrinthine waterways of the Canadian Arctic in search of the party. Though traces of the missing expedition's first winter camp on Beechey Island were found in 1850, its route in the years following remained unclear.

HMS *Assistance* was one of these ships sent to search for Franklin. She had begun her career at sea as the *Baboo*, an Indian-built merchant vessel. She was sold to the Royal Navy in 1850 and commissioned as *Assistance*, the sixth vessel to carry the name, from 50-gun warships, naval transports, to a prison ship. Wigrams of Blackwall fitted her for Arctic service at a cost of £8,250. Her first foray north was with Horatio Austin's expedition in 1850 and she over-wintered held fast in the ice; an experience that inspired the artist Thomas Sewell Robins, on reading an account of the voyage, to create this dramatic oil painting. In 1852 she sailed with Edward Belcher's search squadron. Locked in the icy wilderness off Bathurst Island, with her crews unable to extricate her, *Assistance* was abandoned on 25 August 1854.

That same year, the overland traveller Dr John Rae brought back clues to the demise of Franklin's men, with relics and Inuit stories that the expedition had perished somewhere to the west of the Back River. In 1859, the Irish explorer Leopold McClintock returned to London bearing terrible news. With recovered artefacts, he finally confirmed that the whole party had perished. The nation mourned their loss – it was one of the greatest tragedies in the history of naval exploration. *HLJ*

HMS *Assistance* in the Ice *(oil on canvas), Thomas Sewell Robins, 1853, National Maritime Museum, London (BHC4239)*

117ft x 29ft x 14ft (35.8m x 8.8m x 4.2m) • 423 tons [BM] • Hull wood (teak) • Armament 2 x guns • Complement 58 • Built Howrah, Calcutta, India, 1835

# Pequod  Whale ship from *Moby Dick* 1851

'She was a ship of the old school, rather small if anything; with an old-fashioned claw-footed look about her. Long seasoned and weather-stained in the typhoons and calms of all four oceans, her old hull's complexion was darkened like a French grenadier's… Her ancient decks were worn and wrinkled, like the pilgrim-worshipped flag-stone in Canterbury Cathedral where Becket bled. But to all these her old antiquities, were added new and marvellous features…, She was a thing of trophies. A cannibal of a craft, tricking herself forth in the chased bones of her enemies. All round, her unpanelled, open bulwarks were garnished like one continuous jaw, with the long sharp teeth of the sperm whale, inserted there for pins, to fasten her old hempen thews and tendons to. Those thews ran not through base blocks of land wood, but deftly travelled over sheaves of sea-ivory. Scorning a turnstile wheel at her reverend helm, she sported there a tiller; and that tiller was in one mass, curiously carved from the long narrow lower jaw of her hereditary foe.'

This is Herman Melville's description of the fictional Pequod in *Moby Dick*, the story of Captain Ahab's obsessive and fatal pursuit of a malevolent white whale. Fascinated by the story of the whaler *Essex* in 1820 and the killing of a large white whale known as 'Mocha Dick' around 1838, as well as drawing on his personal experience of whaling, the American author published *Moby Dick* in 1851. The novel enjoyed limited success until the 1930 edition with the stark black-and-white illustrations by Rockwell Kent gave an enduring boost to its popularity. In this image, Rockwell captures the helplessness of the boat's crew faced with the vast power of the whale, power that will also take the mother-ship *Pequod* to the bottom. *JH*

**Whalers being tossed from their boat by the tail of Moby Dick** *(illustration for 1937 edition of Melville's* Moby Dick*) Rockwell Kent, 1937, The Art Archive*

No data available

# Red Jacket  Clipper 1853

The *Red Jacket* was built in America in 1853 to the finest standards of her type and in 1854 she was chartered by the White Star Line and put on the run from Liverpool to Melbourne, where many men were hoping for the heady riches of the Australian goldfields. In fact this first voyage was going to be a race around the world against the clipper *Lightning*, commanded by the noted 'Bully' Forbes. Very large wagers were laid. At 2,460 tons register and with strong masting, the *Red Jacket* had already recorded a 24-hour average speed of more than 17 knots. There were 278 passengers for Melbourne, and a double crew for smartness. The clippers would sail down the Atlantic, careful to cross the doldrums on the best heading, to meet the Roaring Forties and then run a great circle, booming up from the Southern Ocean with strong winds to their destination.

On this first voyage the *Red Jacket* had a time of 69 days 11 hours 13 minutes, Rock Light to Port Phillip Heads – against the *Lightning*'s 77 days. She had recorded as much as 18 knots by the patent log. But that was not the end of it. The *Red Jacket* was out of trim for the homeward voyage and the *Lightning*, pushed to her limit, bettered her by a whole 10 days. Money changed hands. The White Star Line was well satisfied, however, and terminated the charter to purchase the *Red Jacket* outright, as she is seen here in a romanticized but typical image. She remained in the Australian service through the 1850s though she never made quite such a fast passage again. After seeing service on the Quebec timber trade in the 1870s, she finished as a coal hulk. *CJ*

CLIPPER SHIP "RED JACKET"
IN THE ICE OFF CAPE HORN ON HER PASSAGE FROM AUSTRALIA TO LIVERPOOL AUGUST 1854.

*Red Jacket* on the ice off Cape Horn during its passage from Australia to Liverpool *(print), 1854, Getty Images*

251.2ft x 44ft x 31ft (76.6m x 13.4 x 9.4m) • 2460 tons [R] • Hull wood • Complement 98, passengers 650 • Built George Thomas, Rockland, USA, 1853

# Arctic  Sidewheel paddle steamer 1854

In February 1852 the American paddle steamer *Arctic* made the fastest eastbound crossing of the North Atlantic, averaging 13.6 knots and just beating the previous record set by her stablemate *Pacific*. For Edward Collins, founder of the New York & Liverpool United States Mail Steamship Company, an aggressive recent entrant into the transatlantic passenger trade, it was further confirmation that his quartet of steamships were not just much larger and more comfortable than the Cunarders, they were faster.

Success came at the cost of taking risks. Outward bound on 27 September 1854 *Arctic* collided in thick fog with the 250-ton French steamer, *Vesta*, 60 miles off Cape Race. Although badly damaged, the *Vesta* was brought safely home through excellent seamanship, but her iron hull had shattered *Arctic*'s timbers. Captain Luce's attempt to steam *Arctic* to Cape Race only forced more water into the hull, and the order to abandon ship was given.

Panic ensued. Boats were lost when being hoisted out; the crew left passengers to fend for themselves. Some boats which did leave the ship foundered without trace, and many people clung to rafts made of wreckage. When the *Arctic* went down and broke up, pieces of timber rushed to the surface, one of which killed the son of Captain Luce as he lay in his father's arms on a raft. Among the 300 or so dead were Collin's wife, daughter and youngest son. No women or children survived.

This 1854 lithograph by Charles Parson based on various sources, shows *Arctic* in the moments before her sinking, accurately depicting her unusual straight stem and reflecting the removal of her mizzen-mast the previous year. In 1856, *Pacific* foundered with all hands. The already faltering passenger confidence in Collins Line collapsed, and in 1858 after the US Government withdrew the mail contract, the company was wound up. *JH*

Wreck of the U.S.M. steam ship *Arctic*: off Cape Race Wednesday 27th September 1854 *(lithograph), Charles Parson, 1854, Library of Congress*

285.5ft x 45.9ft (87.1m x 14m) • 2856 tons [GRT] • Hull wood • Complement 135, passengers: first class 200, second class 80 • Built William H Brown, New York, USA, 1850

# Great Eastern Iron paddle and screw steamship 1854

Originally to be called *Leviathan* and given the nickname 'Great Babe' by her designer Isambard Kingdom Brunel, the ship was officially named *Great Eastern*. She was the largest ship in the world and would remain so for more than 40 years. She was conceived to carry sufficient fuel – 12,000 tons – to sail non-stop as a passenger mail service to the east to India and Australia. Her draught was designed to navigate the Hooghly River. She could accommodate 4500 passengers and 6000 tons of cargo, or convey up to 10,000 troops.

First envisaged by Brunel on paper in the early months of 1852 she was laid down on 1 May 1854 and took several years to build at a site adjacent to John Scott Russell's Millwall shipyard on the north bank of the Thames. After a protracted launching procedure that lasted around three months, involving many mechanical aids, she was eventually pushed – quite literally – into the River Thames on 31 January 1858.

For strength and safety Brunel insisted she had a double bottom with a watertight middle deck and 15 transverse bulkheads for safety. She was built in sections, and encased in metal plates 1in (2.5cm) thick. This revolutionary five-funnelled iron-hulled ship was the first to be powered by both paddle-wheels and screw propulsion, as well as masts to carry sail. She was capable of steaming at around 14 knots but was soon recognized to be underpowered.

Parrott was an accomplished topographical artist who exhibited at the British Institution and Royal Academy of Arts. In the distance of his painting the domes and facades of Greenwich Hospital are visible.

*Great Eastern* was a technological marvel but a financial failure – costing too much money and therefore bankrupting various companies – including the Eastern Steam Navigation Company, and therefore she never went on the eastern run, Instead she was destined in her early years afloat to compete unsuccessfully with the smaller and financially fitter transatlantic liners. Sadly Brunel's death coincided with the completion of the ship. *JT*

**Building the Great Leviathan** *(oil on canvas), William Parrott, 1854, National Maritime Museum, London (BHC3384)*

692ft x 82.7ft x 30ft (210.9m x 25.2m x 9.1m) • 18.915 tons [GRT] • Hull iron • Complement; first class 200, second class 400, steerage 2400 • Built Scott, Russell & Co., Millwall, London, England, 1858

# Edinburgh   Third Rate steam-assisted ship of the line 1855

In the mid 1840s the Royal Navy fitted Napoleonic era 74-gun wooden ships of the line with screw propellers and steam power, creating a powerful, mobile coast defence 'Blockship', initially to repel a French invasion. So successful were the *Edinburgh* and her three sisters that they were reconfigured for coastal assault, as the core element in ambitious plans to destroy the French naval base at Cherbourg by a combination of long range bombardment and close range heavy artillery attack. From 1848 to 1854 *Edinburgh* served as the seagoing gunnery trial ship at Portsmouth, helping to perfect the weapons and tactics of coastal assault. Although the Crimean War (1854–1856) found Britain and France allied, the strategy of coastal assault was equally applicable to other foes. In 1854 the four Blockships were sent to the Baltic, where they took a leading role in the capture and destruction of the Bomarsund fortress on the Åland Islands: in August 1855, *Edinburgh*, left centre, served as flagship at the bombardment of Sveaborg (Suomenlinna), the fortress arsenal complex outside Helsingfors (Helsinki). The old ships were used for coastal operations because they were expendable, unlike the new steam battleships of the Agamemnon type, produced for fleet warfare. By 1860 they were all obsolete. *ADL*

**The Bombardment of Sveaborg, 9 August 1855** *(oil on canvas), John Wilson Carmichael, 1855, Caird Collection, National Maritime Museum, London (BHC0636)*

176ft x 47.6ft x 21ft (53.6m x 14.5m x 6.4m) • 1741 tons [BM] • Hull wood • Armament (1830 onwards): upper deck 6 x 18in + 22 x 32 pdr, quarterdeck 4 x 8in + 18 x 32 pdr • Complement 500 • Built Rotherhithe, London, England, 1811

# Scheveling pink Fishing boat 1855

Seventeenth-century Dutch marine painting has been a constant source of inspiration to later artists both within and beyond the Netherlands. 'Scheveling [Sheveningen] fishermen hauling the pinck out of the surf' by the English artist Edward William Cooke was the result not just of studying paintings by old masters such as the van de Veldes but of periods spent observing the Dutch coast in its different moods. Although Cook executed the painting in his studio, his preliminary drawings were taken 'en plein air'; as a diary entry for October 1855 reveals: 'pottered about the strand, [and] got some sketches'.

Part of The Hague, Scheveningen has been a fishing port since the fourteenth century. Until the heavy storm of 1894 finally led to the building of the harbour, the herring fleet of some 150 flat-bottomed *bomschuiten* and pinks would be drawn up onto the wide beach. In Cook's carefully observed painting, one of the nine-strong crew is carrying the anchor up the beach while another plays out the rope. Inside the boat, four of their colleagues are lowering the sails in the strong wind, a further four heave on the capstan to drag in the net, and a fifth, his back to the viewer, holds the tiller.

The sunlight that breaks through a gap in the angry sky picks out the details of the boat and gives movement and drama to the swirling surf. *JH*

**A North Sea Breeze on the Dutch Coast** (*oil on canvas*), *Edward William Cooke, 1855, National Maritime Museum, London (BHC1246)*

# Bretagne   First Rate ship of the line 1858

The French First Rate steam battleship *Bretagne*, built at Brest between 1853 and 1856, was the flagship of Louis Napoleon III's attempt to challenge British naval mastery. The 6000-ton three decker symbolized the profoundly schizophrenic international policy of the Second Empire, at once seeking to work with Britain, while undermining her global power to secure a dominant role in the partnership. *Bretagne*'s one moment in the spotlight came on 5 August 1858, as the flagship of an ill-advised attempt to improve Anglo-French relations. Louis Napoleon invited Queen Victoria to visit Cherbourg, ostensibly to celebrate the opening of the new railway line linking the port

with Paris. The new railway meant French troops could be sent from Paris to Cherbourg in a matter of hours. For all the pomp and circumstance of her visit to the French ship, Victoria returned home deeply alarmed by the French base, the fleet it contained and the danger of invasion. She demanded that her Ministers do more to maintain naval dominance, and within a few months they had given the order for the construction of HMS *Warrior*, bringing both the French naval challenge and the age of ships like the *Bretagne* to a speedy conclusion. *ADL*

**Napoleon III Receiving Queen Victoria at Cherbourg, 5 August 1858** *(oil on canvas), Jules Achille Noël, 1859, National Maritime Museum, London* (BHC0637)

265.7ft x 59.4ft x 28.2ft (81m x 18.1m x 8.6m) • 5289 tons [D] • Hull wood • Armament; gun deck 18 x 'canon de 36' (43lb shot), 18 x 80 pdr shell gun, main deck 18 x 30 pdr, 18 x 80 pdr shell gun, upper deck 38 x 30 pdr, forecastle 2 x 'canon de 50' (56lb shot), 18 x 30 pdr carronades • Complement 1170 • Built Brest, France, 1855

# Gloire   Ironclad battleship 1859

*Gloire* was the world's first seagoing ironclad battleship, laid down in April 1858 and launched a year before Great Britain responded with HMS *Warrior*. As with the French iron-armoured steam-batteries used during the Crimean War, this revolutionary warship was directly supported by French Emperor Napoleon III.  Designed by the talented naval architect Dupuy de Lôme, the newly appointed Directeur du Matériel, *Gloire* was designed as an armoured version of his previous success, the first steam-powered ship of the line, *Napoleon*.  Given the destructive power of explosive shellfire (as exemplified by the Russian fleet against the Ottomans at Sinope, in 1853), iron shielding was considered crucial for any future naval combat. *Gloire* was therefore protected with iron plates 4.7in (11.8cm) thick around her entire broadside, fore and stern, with slightly thicker armour extending well below the waterline.  At the time this was tested as impervious to any gun afloat.  Her broadside armament was much more traditional; 36 x 6.4in (16cm) rifled muzzle-loaders, with two pivot guns topside.  She was barque-rigged only, comfortable at 11 knots, and intended for limited operations in European waters where French interests were centred (though her sister-ship *Normandie* carried the distinction of being the first ironclad to cross the Atlantic to Mexico, in 1862). The ultimate significance of *Gloire* is that she inaugurated a complete shutdown of France's wooden ship of the line building programme – at the time on a par with Britain's. Though the fourth of her class, the *Couronne*, was iron-hulled, the *Gloire* was acknowledged as a short-term naval equalizer at best, limited by iron construction costs and infrastructure. *HF*

**The French Battleship,** *La Gloire* *(lithograph), Louis Lebreton, nineteenth century, The Art Archive / Eileen Tweedy*

255.6ft x 55.9ft x 27.10ft (77.9m x 17m x 8.5m) • 5630 tons [D] • Hull wood, iron plated • Armament 36 x 6.4in • Complement 550 • Built Toulon, France, 1859

# Warrior Iron-hulled armoured warship 1860

The world's first ocean-going iron-hulled armoured warship was conceived as a frigate, not a battleship. To build a long, fast 9000-ton ship and carry armour required an iron hull, even if the 4½in (12cm) thick wrought iron armour was restricted to a central box battery. Unlike the French *la Gloire*, a seagoing harbour assault ship, *Warrior* was scaled up from the wooden steam frigate *Mersey*, a fact reflected in trial speeds of 14.5 knots under steam, over 17 under steam and sail. 48in smooth bore and 7in rifled guns combined long-range accuracy with armour piercing. Entering service in 1861, *Warrior*

made every other warship afloat obsolete with her combination of speed and firepower, and helped to defeat Imperial France in a major naval arms race. After a decade as the icon of Victorian power *Warrior*, herself rendered obsolete by battleships with thicker armour and heavier guns, joined the reserve. In 1902 she became an engineering workshop at Portsmouth, in 1923 a jetty at Milford Haven. Having been restored to her former glory at Hartlepool *Warrior* returned to Portsmouth in 1986, to take her place at the historic dockyard. *ADL*

HMS *Warrior* (photograph), John Lee, 2009, Conway Picture Library

418ft x 58.4ft x 26ft (128m x 17.8m x 7.9m) • 9137 tons [D] • Hull iron • Armament 26 x 68 pdr, 4 x 40 pdr, 10 x 110 pdr, 2 x 20 pdr, 1 x 12 pdr, 1 x 6 pdr • Complement 700-709 • Built Thames Iron Works, Blackwall, London, England, 1861

# Emigrant Ship Transatlantic passage 1861

During the nineteenth and well into the twentieth centuries, emigration gave a massive boost to shipping. Driven out by poverty or lured by the hope of wealth in the gold fields of Australia and California, millions of Europeans took ships to North and South America, Australia and New Zealand; some as families, some as individuals. Almost all left someone behind.

It is the pain of those on the quayside that Henry Nelson O'Neil captures in his 1861 canvas 'The Parting Cheer'. They are painted with great precision, unlike those on the ship that the tug is pulling out into the river. O'Neil assembles all ages, all emotions and almost all classes – and he includes a black man to demonstrate the shared humanity of the races. The Victorian audience who saw this picture would recognize the clues and stock figures: the man with the rolled-up sleeves indicating he was a member of the honest labouring class; the red-cheeked healthy baby from the countryside; the poor little Irish girl selling fruit; the pale, town-bred man holding his distraught sister – in the orange shawl – whose lover is leaving England; the middle-class woman and her well-dressed son comforting the widow whose faithful dog gazes lovingly at her.

There is no attempt to ground the painting in a particular location, let alone a named ship. This scene is universal. It has taken place many hundreds of times. *JH*

The Parting Cheer (oil on canvas), Henry Nelson O'Neill, 1861, National Maritime Museum, London (F3201)

No data available

# Miami  Sidewheel steam gunboat 1861

The Union Navy during the American Civil War required a wide range of unique warships, expressly built for naval operations in shallow waters and capable of fulfilling a variety of roles. *Miami* was of a very successful class of sidewheel paddle steamers which could reverse direction quickly and easily, without having to turn the entire vessel about in tight situations such as narrow rivers. This 'double-ender' drew less than 9ft (2.7m) of water, could reach up to 8 knots and was fairly heavily-armed with one 80 pdr Parrot rifle, one 9in Dahlgren smoothbore and four 24pdr.

Launched at the Philadelphia Navy Yard in November 1861, *Miami* saw extensive service; from bombardment roles against New Orleans and Vicksburg, deep up the Mississippi River, to blockade duties on the James River approaching the Confederate capital of Richmond, Virginia. On 19 April 1864, *Miami*, accompanied by the paddle-steamer USS *Southfield*, attempted to engage the ram CSS *Albemarle* on the approaches to Plymouth, North Carolina. During the battle, *Southfield* was rammed by the Confederate ironclad which then proceeded to drive off the *Miami*. Personally directing fire against the *Albemarle*, *Miami*'s commanding officer, Charles W. Flusser, was killed when a short-fused shell bounced off the *Albermarle*'s sloping iron armour and exploded on the *Miami*'s gundeck. The battle-scarred Union warship was decommissioned in May 1865, having served virtually the entire war, and was in the American merchant marine until 1869. *HF*

**USS *Miami*'s 9in Dahlgren gun in operation during the American Civil War** *(photograph), photographer and date unknown. Conway Picture Library*

208.2ft x 33.2ft x 8.6ft (63.5m x 10.1m x 2.6m) • 742 tons [D] • Hull wood • Armament 1 x 80 pdr Parrott rifle, 1 x 9in Dahlgren gun, 4 x 24 pdr • Complement 134 • Built Philadelphia Navy Yard, USA, 1861

# Cairo City class ironclad gunboat 1862

The American Civil War was very much a brown-water affair, and the Union's most important victories in the first few years of the conflict were won in the southwest, for control of vital strategic rivers (including the Mississippi) which divided the Confederacy. To this end, the US military initiated an armoured gunboat programme which capitalized on the North's superiority in shipbuilding, marine engine and iron-plate production.

The first of the seven 'City' class of ironclads, the *Cairo* was designed by civilian engineer James B. Eads and naval architect Samuel M. Pook to meet the unique demands of mid-nineteenth century littoral warfare. Flat-bottomed, broad-beamed and drawing only 6ft (1.8m) of water, *Cairo* bristled with 13 guns of medium calibre; three of which were mounted abreast on the forward end of the slanting casemate. Iron shielding was limited to 2.5in (6cm) thick plating on the front and sides only. The necessary compromises in design meant that in combat the unprotected decks were vulnerable to plunging fire. Nevertheless, 'Pook's Turtles' spearheaded the combined attacks against Forts Henry and Donelson, Island No. 10, and destroyed the Confederate gunboat flotilla at Memphis, in 1862. They were also crucial in securing the fall of Vicksburg, Mississippi in July 1863. *Cairo* herself was also the first ironclad sunk by a naval mine, on 12 December 1862; having a wooden hull with no internal compartmentalization proved fatal, though all of her crew were evacuated in time. The remains of this iconic Civil War ironclad are preserved in the Vicksburg National Military Park. *HF*

**USS *Cairo* at the Vicksburg National Military Park** *(photograph), 2009, Ken Lund, Las Vegas, Nevada, USA*

175ft x 51.2ft x 6ft (53.3m x 15.6m x 1.8m) • 512 tons [D] • Hull wood, iron plated • Armament 3 x 8in, 6 x 42 pdr, 6 x 32 pdr, 1 x 12 pdr • Complement 251 • Built James Eads & Co., Mound City, Illinois, USA, 1862

# Monitor Ironclad turret ship 1862

The brainchild of civilian engineer-inventor John Ericsson, the *Monitor* was the first operational turret-ironclad in history, and the early progenitor of the modern warship. She was technically only an armoured gunboat, but the concepts of a limited main armament of the heaviest possible ordnance, and propulsion by steam power alone were revolutionary. Ericsson also devised his vessel as a comprehensive 'machine', reducing sailors to operators of automated life-support, fire-control and propulsion systems.

It took the hasty, crisis environment of the American Civil War for these radical innovations to be even considered by the Union Navy in 1861. The South was known to be constructing its own ironclad from the wreck of the steam-frigate USS *Merrimack*, and European powers were poised to intervene in the conflict. Yet Ericsson's 'battery' had the advantage of making the most

of limited resources; especially money and time. The bizarre 'raft' design with only 12in (30cm) of freeboard and a single steam-rotated turret carrying two 11in Dahlgren smoothbores was launched within a hundred days of the government contract and immediately sent to confront the Confederate *Virginia* at Hampton Roads, Virginia – which she fought to a draw on 9 March 1862.

Life aboard the instantly famous man-of-war was hellish all the same. Ventilation was poor and her complicated engines were prone to breakdown. On the night of 31 December 1862 she foundered in a gale off Cape Hatteras when improper caulking around the turret base overwhelmed the steam pumps. Her wreck was discovered in 1973 and her symbolic turret successfully raised in 2002. *HF*

**Officers beside the turret of USS *Monitor*** *(photograph), photographer unknown, 1862, Conway Picture Library*

179ft x 41.5ft x 10.5ft (54.6m x 12.6m x 3.2m) • 987 tons [D] • Hull iron • Armament 2 x 11in Dahlgren guns • Complement 48 • Built Continental Iron Works, Green Point, New York (hull), Novelty Iron Works, New York (turret), Delamater & Co., New York (engine), USA, 1862

# Numancia  Ironclad frigate 1862

Launched in 1862 and commissioned in 1864, the frigate *Numancia* soon became an icon of the ironclad age, participating in all main Spanish naval actions of the second half of the nineteenth century. A particularly expensive asset for the national economy, the construction of this unit marked Spain's willingness to modernize its fleet in the attempt to re-join the exclusive club of the world's top naval powers and to reaffirm its control over the remote corners of the colonial empire.

To that end, the *Numancia* was assigned to the Spanish Pacific Squadron and left the port of Cádiz on 4 February 1865. This date marked the beginning of an adventurous journey lasting two years, seven months and six days. Returning to Cádiz as the battle-hardened jewel of the Spanish fleet, she became the first ironclad to circumnavigate the globe, earning the motto 'Enloricata navis que primo terra circuivit' (the armoured ship that first circumnavigated the globe).

The *Numancia* entered the world of popular culture as the ship that summarized all the core traits of life at sea: she engaged Spain's enemies in waters far from national shores, travelled the world, met the challenges of nature and returned home. Beyond this glamorous image, *Numancia* was first and foremost one of the cornerstones of Spanish naval expeditions in South America. Joining the fleet under the command of Admiral Casto Méndez Núñez, on 31 March 1866 the *Numancia* fired the first shots against the Chilean port of Valparaíso and again, in the following April, against the fortifications of Callao. In the latter action, the ironclad sustained heavy damage, receiving 52 hits from the coastal defences. Once she returned to Spain, the ironclad continued in her distinguished service, spending her last years in service as a training unit for the next generation of naval leaders, taking her rightful place in Spanish naval history. *AP*

**The frigate *Numancia*, from *Modern Military Vessels*** *(print), Rafael Monleón y Torres, The Art Archive / Museo Naval de Madrid*

315.2ft x 56.9ft x 25.9ft (96.1m x 17.3m x 7.9m) • 7500 tons [D] • Armament 6 x 7.8in, 6 x 10in, 3 x 8in • Complement 590 • Built Forges et Chantiers de la Mediterranée, La Seyne, France, 1863

# Alabama Commerce raider 1864

One of the most controversial warships in history, the Confederate commerce raider *Alabama* began her life as 'No. 290' in the yard of John Laird Sons and Company at Birkenhead, Merseyside. She had been contracted by Southern agents in 1862, who exploited a loophole in Britain's Foreign Enlistment Act. The hull and steam-engines were built by Lairds and she was quietly launched, without any armament fitted, under false identity papers (US Federal agents were unable to convince British authorities of the ship's true nature until it was too late).

Once in international waters the '290' was armed as a sloop-of-war and commanded by Captain Raphael Semmes CSN. The *Alabama* then proceeded on a series of cruises which not only claimed 65 prizes from the US merchant marine worldwide but succeeded in driving many more to switch their

registry to the protection of the Union Jack – somewhat ironic, as most of the *Alabama*'s crew were British.

After two years at sea the *Alabama* put into Cherbourg for much-needed repairs. Within days the sloop USS *Kearsage* arrived, waiting outside the harbour. Rather than risk eventual internment by neutral French authorities, Semmes issued a formal challenge to the *Kearsage*'s Captain John Winslow. The classic ship duel commenced on 19 June 1864. Here *Alabama* proved woefully mismatched against the two 11in Dahlgren guns and cool resolve of the well-prepared Union crew, going down within an hour. After the American Civil War, the US Government successfully sued Great Britain for over $15 million damages in the 'Alabama Claims', for violations of neutrality; the first international arbitration of its kind in modern history. *HF*

USS *Kearsage* Sinking the *Alabama*, 19th June 1864 *(oil on canvas), Xanthus Russell Smith, Private Collection / Christie's Images / The Bridgeman Art Library*

220ft x 31.9ft x 14ft (67.1m x 9.7m x 4.3m) • 1050 tons [D] • Hull wood • Armament 6 x 32 pdr, 1 x 110 pdr, 1 x 68 pdr • Complement 148 • Built Birkenhead, England, 1862

147

# H.L. Hunley   Submarine 1864

The *Hunley* carried two separate test crews with her to the bottom, as well as her final crew on 17 February 1864. But on that date, the hand-powered Confederate submarine did manage to sink the Union steam-sloop *Housatonic* – the first successful kill by a submersible warship in history.

Throughout the American Civil War, the Confederacy was hopelessly mismatched against the maritime, financial and industrial resources of the Northern States. Tennessee-born Horace Lawson Hunley, with two associates, sought a technological equalizer. Their third design was built in Mobile, Alabama and after an initial trial success was shipped by rail to Charleston, South Carolina (the scene of the longest combined arms siege of the entire conflict). *Hunley* was placed under Confederate Army command

but the target was clear: the Union blockading fleet. In addition to the pilot, she was powered by seven men, cranking the propeller and ballast tanks by hand. Somehow the Confederate submarine proved both manageable and undetectable, though her armament consisted of a spar torpedo extended from the bow and she was surfaced when she finally touched the *Housatonic*. The ensuing blast sank both ships; ironically, more men perished on the brave attacker than the unsuspecting victim. As the *Hunley* never returned from her mission, faith in the new 'wonder weapon' collapsed and Charleston remained a doomed symbol of Southern defiance. On 8 August 2000, her wreck was salvaged and the remains of the crew were subjected to forensic analysis before burial with full military honours. *HF*

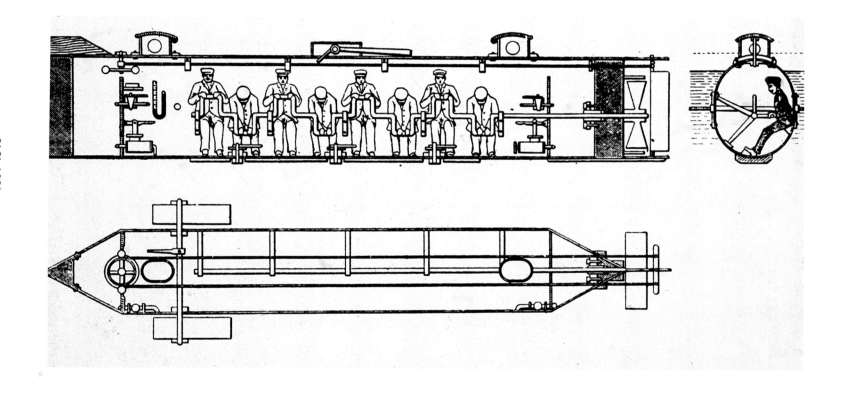

**Diagram Of The *H. L. Hunley*, based on sketches by William A. Alexander** *(pen and ink drawing), 1863, Getty Images*

39.5ft x 3.8ft (12m x 1.2m) • 6.8 tons [D] • Hull iron • Armament 1 x spar torpedo • Complement 8 • Built Horace L. Hunley, Mobile, Alabama, USA, 1863

# Magenta Ironclad battleship 1865

In 1865 the Royal Navy and the Marine Nationale marked the end of a decade of heightened Anglo-French tension by exchanging courtesy visits at Cherbourg, Brest and Portsmouth. On 14 August, Admiral Sir Sidney Dacres led a British squadron into Cherbourg, consisting of the ironclads *Achilles*, *Black Prince* (sister-ship of *Warrior*), *Hector*, *Royal Sovereign* and *Defence*, and the wooden screw ships *Edgar*, *Liverpool*, *Octavia* and *Constance*.

They were met by the French flagship *Magenta*, seen here firing a salute as the British ships enter the harbour. Launched at Brest in 1862, *Magenta* was a two-decker broadside ironclad. Designed by the French naval architect Henri Dupuy de Lôme, she was an imposing ship, carrying 50 rifled 30 pdr guns on two gun-decks. She was also equipped with a large bow ram, a weapon recently reintroduced into naval armament as a stopgap solution to the apparent invulnerability of ironclads to ship-borne artillery.

In reality, however, *Magenta*'s construction reflected the limited capacity of the French iron industry, which dictated armour-on-wood construction, as in the *Gloire* of 1858, as opposed to all-iron hulls like the British *Warrior*. Weight and stability issues also necessitated a limited central armour belt. Arguably then, *Magenta* and her sister-ship *Solférino* compared poorly with the contemporary British ironclads, although they had solved the difficult problem of ironclad ventilation. Nevertheless Geoffrey Hornby, Admiral Dacres' flag-captain, noted that the French were 'active, intelligent men', with a clean, well-organised fleet of generally sound design.

Little more than an opportunity to showcase ships and drill, the courtesy visits did not entail any combined exercises. Instead fetes, banquets and an official ball were held. The British squadron subsequently moved on to Brest, where the French ships were nowhere near as well-ordered as those at Cherbourg. It became apparent that the Cherbourg fleet had hardly been at sea, hence their pristine appearance!

From Brest the two fleets crossed the Channel under easy steam to Portsmouth, where they arrived at the end of the month. *MJ*

**The courtesy visit by Admiral Dacres' squadron to the French fleet at Cherbourg, 1865** *(oil on canvas), Mark Myers, 1991, Conway Picture Library*

282.2ft x 56.8ft x 27.6ft (86m x 17.3m x 8.4m) • 7129 tons [D] • Hull wood, iron plated • Armament 16 x 55 pdr, 34 x 6.4in BLM 1860 guns, 2 x 8.8in RML howitzers • Complement 681 • Built L'Orient, France, 1861

# Ariel  Tea clipper 1866

In the nineteenth century the value of the tea trade from China was so great, and the first tea harvest of the year so highly prized, that ships were built specifically not just to carry tea but to be first home with the cargo. A special premium was paid for the first arrival. So was born the tea clipper, the finest flowering of the sailing ship, a merchant ship built to win races.

The Great Tea Race of 1866 was closely contested, not least by the fastest five ships, which were the first to leave the port of Foochow in China. The first three ships home, *Ariel*, *Taeping* and *Serica*, had left Foochow's Min River on the same tide on 30 May and docked in London on the same tide 99 days later. *Ariel* and *Taeping* had raced together up the English Channel to Dungeness where they took on pilots. When they were telegraphed through the Downs their respective owners agreed to split equally the premium paid by the tea merchants for the first of the new season's tea. One ship's claim would not be disputed by the other, thus avoiding the possibility that the merchants might declare the race a draw, and pay no premium. The illustration, by Thomas Dutton, shows the two clippers passing the Lizard on 5 September: on the next day *Taeping* berthed in the London Docks at 9.45 p.m. while *Ariel* berthed in the East India Dock at 10.15 p.m. The clippers, with their large spread of sail and sleek, almost yacht-like lines were built for speed. *Ariel*'s captain wrote that his ship 'was the most perfect beauty to every nautical man who saw her; in symmetrical grace and proportion of hull, spars, sails, rigging and finish she satisfied the eye and put all in love with her without exception'. *PB*

**The Great China Race** *(coloured lithograph), Thomas Goldsworth Dutton, 1866, National Maritime Museum, London (A7187)*

197ft x 33.9ft x 21ft (60.2m x 10.3m x 6.4m) • 853 tons [D] • Hull wood, iron framed • Built Robert Steele & Co., Greenock, Scotland, 1865

# Cutty Sark Tea clipper 1869

By 1869 advances in technology and metallurgy meant that fast merchant ships like the tea clippers could be very strongly built, with hulls and masts and standing rigging all made of iron, so that they could be driven in all weathers to unprecedented speeds – the American clipper *Sovereign of the Seas* once logged 22 knots, and the *Cutty Sark* once memorably overtook the *Britannia*, a crack steamship. There was a high excitement in all this; the captains drove their ships ever faster, the newspapers reported the progress of the races, and the owners lavished fine workmanship and materials on the clippers as if they were yachts. But the same technological mastery rapidly doomed the tea clipper when steamships, using the newly completed Suez Canal, were able to do the China trip faster and more reliably. *Cutty Sark* was reckoned to be the finest tea clipper ever built – she was designed to beat a rival clipper, the *Thermopylae*, and did so – but she came just too late for the tea trade.

However, for many years steamships remained uneconomical to use on the Australia run, and so the clippers switched to the wool trade, where their captains continued their racing and ship-driving until the end. Hulked, wrecked or broken up, the clippers were all gone by the early twentieth century – except for one glorious survivor, the *Cutty Sark* herself. *GH*

**The *Cutty Sark* being towed into East India Dock on the Thames, London** *(photograph), photographer unknown, 1954, Conway Picture Library*

212.5ft x 36ft x 21ft (64.6m x 11m x 6.4m ) • 975 tons [GRT] • Hull wood, iron framed • Complement 19-28 • Built Scott, Linton & Co., Dumbarton, Scotland, 1869

# Captain Turret ship 1870

Designed by strident turret-ship advocate Captain Cowper Phipps Coles, RN, *Captain* was intended to serve as a bridge between the roving strategic range offered by fast broadside ironclads of the *Warrior* and her sisters, and the tactical perfection in armament and protection represented by the famed American Monitors. Coles, however, was not a trained naval architect or maritime engineer and by 1866 his ideas had been increasingly overshadowed by those of the Chief Constructor, Edward Reed. A bitter 'turret versus broadside' debate ensued in official correspondence, public meetings, the press and finally Parliament (whom Coles was able to convince that 'sea-going' turret ships were not only possible but more economical). Under public pressure the Admiralty finally allowed Coles to contract through Lairds for the construction of his own low-freeboard turret ship, which nevertheless carried the largest masts available.

Upon her launch in 1869 she was considered the 'ship of the future' and a mainstay of British naval supremacy. But she was also much lower in the water than originally intended and inherently unstable (as Reed had feared). On the night of 6 September 1870, HMS *Captain* capsized during a gale off Cape Finisterre, Spain – taking Coles and 472 of her crew down with her; a loss of British lives greater than the Battle of Trafalgar. A highly publicized inquiry followed, which ultimately blamed the pernicious influence of civilians upon modern warship designs, whose technical science was now best left to naval professionals. *HF*

**HMS *Captain*, berthed** *(photograph), date and photographer unknown, Conway Picture Library*

334ft x 53.3ft x 25.5ft (101.8m x 16.2m x 7.8m) • 7767 tons [D] • Hull iron • Armament 4 x 12in, 2 x 7in • Complement 500 • Built Laird Bros, Birkenhead, England, 1870

1861-1918

# Nautilus   Submarine from *20,000 Leagues Under the Sea* 1870

Although many of the celebrated French author's novels took on exploratory themes, Jules Verne had naval technology and power gone mad in mind when he wrote *20,000 Leagues Under the Sea* in 1870. Upon its release it was an instant classic – and an early pioneer of the science-fiction genre. The story revolves around the submarine *Nautilus* – the brilliant invention of the mysterious Captain Nemo. *Nautilus* is advanced far beyond contemporary military science; powered by an endless energy source (foretelling nuclear power), and large enough to cruise at high speeds, deep underwater, for days on end.

Prisoners-turned-guests aboard the vessel are astounded by Nemo's discoveries, impressed by his endless fascination with marine life, and intrigued by his revolutionary ideals against global 'oppression'. But Verne was more concerned with the dangers of rogue inventors, accountable to no one and commanding private, high-tech arsenals. Soon the *Nautilus* is hunted by the navies of the world, and it is revealed that Nemo harbours a smouldering personal desire for revenge against such powers. (In Verne's 1874 sequel, *The Mysterious Island*, Nemo is revealed to be Indian, and his family the victims of the British following the Mutiny of 1857.) Nemo's rage eventually explodes against the fictional steam-frigate USS *Abraham Lincoln* – sunk with all hands. The narrator of *20,000 Leagues* finally comes to describe Captain Nemo as a 'man of the waters, the genie of the sea'; a god. Yet Nemo is also deeply conflicted and finally drives himself, and his machine, into a 'maelstrom'. *HF*

**James Mason as Captain Nemo in the *Nautilus*, from the film *Twenty Thousand Leagues Under The Sea* (1954) *Walt Disney / The Kobal Collection***

No data available

# Challenger Pearl class corvette, steam-assisted expedition ship 1872

During the 1870s the Royal Society began pushing for a huge expedition to probe the mysteries of all three of the world's major oceans, the Atlantic, the Indian and the Pacific. The Royal Navy supplied the screw corvette *Challenger* – easily the largest oceanographic research vessel to date – and a crew under the command of George Strong Nares. Naturalist Charles Thomson led a team of six civilian scientists.

Fitted with a wide array of innovative equipment for gauging water temperature, measuring currents, and taking bottom samples and depth soundings up to 6000 fathoms (36,000ft/10,973m), *Challenger* was in every sense a floating laboratory. She sailed from England on 7 December 1872 and spent the first 10 months of her voyage criss-crossing the Atlantic, recording a mass of data. She pushed on into the Southern Ocean, threading her way through the ice fields. She spent a month in waters off Australia, crossed the Tasman Sea for New Zealand, and traced her way through the maze of archipelagos of the East Indies, the Philippines and the South Pacific.

Two months were spent in Japan, a time of well-needed rest for the crew, and for the ship too. *Challenger* spent a week in dry dock in the government arsenal at Yokosuka, while her rudder was repaired and a general overhaul carried out. After crossing the Pacific, making passage through the Strait of Magellan, she turned north again into the Atlantic. She dropped anchor off England on 24 May 1876, after a voyage of three and a half years and some 68,890 miles (110,868km). *Challenger*'s oceanographic haul really can't be underestimated – in discovering more than 4000 unknown specimens of marine life and in the first comprehensive survey of ocean currents, ocean depths and the composition of the seabed – it may fairly be said that her pioneering voyage laid the foundations of modern oceanography. *HLJ*

**First page from the journal of HMS *Challenger*, a personal diary by Pelham Aldrich** *Royal Geographical Society*

200ft x 41ft x 15ft (61m x 12.3m x 4.6m) • 2306 tons [D] • Hull wood • Armament 20 x 8in, 2 x 68 pdr • Complement 243 • Built Woolwich, London , England,1858

# Mary Celeste Brigantine 1872

The *Mary Celeste* captured public attention when she was found abandoned in December 1872. The strange circumstances surrounding the ship were also popularized in fiction, notably in Arthur Conan Doyle's short story 'J. Habakuk Jephson's Statement', published in 1884. He called his ship the *Marie Céleste*, embellishing certain facts and inventing more dramatic elements. Some sources, however, took the story to be a true account, and the boundaries between fact and fiction have been blurred ever since.

*Mary Celeste* was found by the ship *Dei Gratia* in the Atlantic Ocean, unmanned but under sail. Her cargo of commercial alcohol was intact, save for nine barrels, which it was later discovered were empty. Personal belongings of passengers and crew were still on board. Oliver Deveau, chief mate of the *Dei Gratia*, boarded *Mary Celeste* and found that the ship's papers were missing, except the captain's logbook. Secondary hatches were open,

the compass was destroyed, and the sextant and marine chronometer were missing along with ship's lifeboat, a yawl. A frayed rope was found trailing in the water from the stern.

Many theories were advanced to explain the mystery, from freak weather conditions, to piracy, mutiny and insurance fraud. In his work *Mary Celeste: Odyssey of an Abandoned Ship*, Charles Edey Fay proposed that a minor explosion caused by the alcohol on board persuaded the crew and passengers to think that the ship was going to sink and take to the lifeboat with a tow line fixed, which would allow them to return to the ship if the danger passed. But the rope parted, casting the lifeboat adrift. Published in 1942, Fay's book included this haunting wood engraving of the ship by the prominent artist Rudolph Ruzicka. Fay's theory is both intriguing and plausible, but what really happened to the ship has never been conclusively explained. *MJ*

The brigantine *Mary Celeste*  (wood engraving), Rudolph Ruzicka, 1942, Getty Images

99.3ft x 25.3ft x 11.7ft (30.3m x 7.7m x 3.6m) • 198 tons [GRT] • Hull wood • Complement 10 • Built Joshua Dewis, Spencer's Island, Nova Scotia, Canada, 1861

# Devastation  Turret ship 1873

At the time of her launch, on 12 July 1871, *Devastation* was the most powerful ironclad warship in the world and a forerunner of the modern battleship. Originally conceived as a large 'breastwork Monitor', her designer, Royal Navy constructor Edward Reed, was influenced by the double-turreted USS *Miantonomoh*, which he toured when the American Monitor visited Britain in 1866. Though impressed by the emphasis on twin-screws, super heavy-guns and a concentrated armour scheme along the waterline – and the use of steam-power alone (thus removing all masts, rigging and the need for a large sailing crew) – Reed saw that improvements would be required to make such a vessel suitable for a world-ranging navy.

Accordingly, in Reed's design *Miantonomoh*'s low freeboard, which offered remarkable stability as a gun-platform and a minimal target profile, was increased to 4ft (1.2m) and the turrets, bridge, funnel and 'superstructure' for the crew were mounted upon an armoured citadel. The result was the coastal defence 'turret ship' HMVS *Cerberus*, laid down in September 1867 for the colony of Victoria, Australia.

Reed's concept was further refined in the construction of *Devastation* and her sister-ship *Thunderer*. These ships boasted four 12in, 600pdr rifled guns of 35 tons, with clear fields of fire forward and aft, and protected by 14in (35cm) of iron armour plates on the turret faces. Because the vessel was so unlike anything else in the Royal Navy at the time she was subject to severe criticism. Yet *Devastation* proved stable enough at sea, could manage a respectable 13.8 knots with her Penn trunk engines, and could be docked for coal and repairs virtually anywhere in the British Empire. *HF*

**HM Turret Ship *Devastation* at Spithead on the occasion of the naval review in honour of the Shah of Persia, 23 June 1873** *(oil on canvas), Edward William Cooke, 1875, Greenwich Hospital Collection, National Maritime Museum, London (BHC3287)*

285ft x 62.3ft x 26.5ft (86.9m x 19m x 8.1m) • 9188 tons [D] • Hull steel • Armament 4 x 12in • Complement 400 • Built Portsmouth, England, 1871

# Novgorod  'Popovka' ironclad warship 1873

In an age of extraordinary naval designs and technological innovations, this Russian circular ironclad warship ranks as among the most bizarre. The brainchild of Admiral Andrey Alexandrovich Popov, a veteran of the Crimean War who was well versed in the latest naval developments in America, France and Great Britain, the *Novgorod* and her near-sister *Vitse-Admiral Popov* featured concentrated armour along the waterline and two 26-ton guns. The ship was driven by six engines each driving its own propeller shaft. Launched in 1873, the vessels could operate in less than 15ft (4.5m) of water and were to command the Dnieper River, the Black Sea and Sea of Azov. Popov's vision emphasized 'tactical perfection' to the point where the ship was no longer a ship but strictly a floating weapons-platform; range – even mobility – were largely sacrificed in this pursuit of the maximum weight displacement to killing power ratio. A critical flaw lay in the training of the (exposed) guns themselves; the round hull itself acted as revolving turntable and the sheer concussion of the guns firing sent the ship practically spinning out of control. The design was never repeated.

Both ships served in the Danube Flotilla during the Russo-Turkish War of 1877–8. They were redesignated Coastal Defence Armour-Clad Ships in 1892, and became store ships in 1903. They were not scrapped until 1912. Oddly enough, Admiral Popov succeeded in gaining the enthusiastic approval of the former chief constructor of the British Royal Navy, Sir Edward Reed, who cruised on the vessel while touring Russia and wrote that the concept of a circular ironclad should be 'carefully considered'. *HF*

*Novgorod* on the stocks *(photograph), c. 1873, Conway Picture Library*

101ft x 101ft x 12.6ft (30.8m x 30.8m x 3.8m) • 2490 tons [D] • Hull wood, iron plated • Armament: 2 x 11in, 2 x 4 pdr, 2 x 2.5 pdr • Complement 128 • Built Galerniy Shipyard, St. Petersburg, Russia, 1873

# Trouville boats Fishing vessels 1874

Much of the best-known marine art is concerned with accuracy of detail, capturing significant events, battles or shipwrecks, and, in many instances, promoting a nation's or a company's naval or mercantile power. Such paintings were carefully crafted in the studio using resources that might include a ship's plans. In the nineteenth century the more informal seascape became a popular genre, particularly among artists working in France, perhaps coinciding with the rise of the seaside holiday.

One of the first French landscape artists to work outdoors – 'en plein air' – the Honfleur-born Eugène Boudin, concentrated on the Normandy coastline he knew so well, particularly the beaches of Trouville and Deauville. Boudin was the son of a seafarer. He trained in Paris and recorded what he saw around him, capturing the instant in swift, impressionistic brushstrokes and recording just a few seconds of the constantly changing effect of light on a seascape. 'Trouville, Awaiting the Tide' was painted in 1874, the year of the first Impressionist exhibition in Paris, and it focuses on a simple group of fishing vessels on the beach at low tide. A crisp wind flutters the bright tricolore flags hoisted to celebrate Bastille Day (14 July), and the evocative scene is a reminder that what was in 1874 a fashionable holiday resort used to be a small fishing village.

Boudin was a major influence on Claude Monet, and, through Monet, on other Impressionists. Monet's own paintings of Normandy's coastal resorts reveal a debt to Boudin, as do Sisley's of the English coast. *JH*

**Trouville, Awaiting the Tide** (oil on canvas), Eugene Louis Boudin, 1874, National Maritime Museum, London (BHC2378)

# Benmore  Paddle steamer 1876

A busy scene at the Broomielaw pier in Glasgow shows the paddle steamer *Benmore* departing heavily loaded with passengers who are to sail 'doon the watter' (in the local argot) for a day trip or seaside holiday in the Firth of Clyde. The pier was near Glasgow Central Station and thousands of Glaswegians boarded steamers there every year, not least during the holidays of the Glasgow Fair Week. After sailing past the heavily industrialized banks of the Clyde they would sample the fresh air and scenery of the Clyde estuary. *Benmore* was built for Robert Campbell, who employed her on the Glasgow to Kilmun service. She was sold to Captain Buchanan who maintained her on her original route before switching Benmore to the Glasgow to Rothesay route. She also undertook excursions from Ayr. She was re-boilered in 1887 and acquired a second funnel but this was unsuccessful and short-lived, and she had to be re-boilered again the following year. In 1892 her ownership passed to John Williamson and she was mainly used as a cargo steamer. In 1915 she was chartered by the Caledonian Steam Packet Co., for whom she sailed for a further five years. In 1920 she returned to William Buchanan but was badly damaged by fire in the West Harbour, Greenock, and was laid up before being scrapped three years later. *PB*

1861-1918

*Benmore* **leaving the Broomielaw, Glasgow** (photograph), George Washington Wilson, c. 1890, Conway Picture Library

201.2ft x 19.1ft (61.3m x 5.8m) • 235 tons [GRT] • Hull wood • Complement 16, 934 passengers • Built TB Seath & Co., Rutherglen, Scotland, 1876      **159**

# Pinafore   Setting of Gilbert & Sullivan's comic opera 1878

Almost immediately after the successful launch of 'The Sorcerer', W. S. Gilbert wrote to Arthur Sullivan with his plot for their next collaboration, an 'Entirely Original Nautical Opera'. 'H.M.S. Pinafore; or The Lass that Loved a Sailor', opened in London on 25 May 1878 to great acclaim with the production running for 571 consecutive performances in London, and over 150 unauthorized American productions in the next year alone.

The opera centres around the love story between Josephine, the captain's daughter, and her swain Ralph Rackstraw, a common sailor on her father's ship, HMS *Pinafore*. The most memorable songs are satirical observations on the British class system, patriotism and, most famously, political appointments as embodied in The Rt Hon. Sir Joseph Porter, KCB, First Lord of the

Admiralty's 'When I was a lad'. In 1877 Benjamin Disraeli had appointed the MP for Westminster, W.H. Smith, to First Lord of the Admiralty. Quickly nicknamed 'Pinafore Smith' he was later described by W. S. Gilbert as 'the only man in England who knew nothing whatever about ships'. Gibert on the other hand, took great pains with the accuracy of the first production of 'HMS Pinafore', travelling with Sullivan to Portsmouth to visit HMS *Victory* and commissioning the uniforms for the play from a naval supplier.

The opera's fondly satirical attitude towards British society, and the inspired grounding of the plot in the firmly workaday world of the British navy, has ensured the long-standing appeal of the most famous stage ship, HMS *Pinafore*. KE

**HMS *Pinafore*, theatrical poster** *(coloured woodblock print poster), A.S. Seer, 1879, Library of Congress*

# Vega  Barque 1878

After a number of Arctic voyages, the veteran polar explorer Adolf Nordenskiöld determined to be the first to complete a navigation of a Northeast Passage from European waters across the top of Russia into the Bering Sea. Having finally received the royal support of Oscar II of Norway and Sweden, he was able to convert the German whaler *Vega* for this unique voyage of endeavour.

Accompanied by three support ships, *Vega* departed from Tromsø, Norway in July 1878 and by August had managed to navigate Cape Chelyuskin, the northernmost point of continental Eurasia. Nine days later *Vega* was off the mouth of the Lena River, where Nordenskiöld tried to explore the New Siberian Islands to the north, before being forced back by impassable pack

ice. They continued to the east but became icebound, just 120 miles from the Bering Strait, spending the next ten months locked fast in the ice.

*Vega* was released on 18 July 1879 and within two days was able to make her way into the Bering Strait. Nordenskiöld's team continued conducting scientific observations for many weeks before heading for Japan, where they arrived in September. *Vega* returned to Europe via the Suez Canal, Naples and London and was greeted with huge fanfare when she returned in triumph to Stockholm the following year. After the voyage, *Vega* was sold to pay off many of the expedition's debts and returned to work in the northern fisheries, under the Swedish flag. She sank in 1903, having been caught in the ice off the west coast of Greenland. *HLJ*

The Explorer A. E. Nordenskiöld *(oil on canvas), Count Georg von Rosen, 1886, © Nationalmuseum, Stockholm, Sweden / The Bridgeman Art Library*

142ft x 26ft (43.3m x 7.9m) • 357 tons [GRT] • Hull wood • Complement 35 • Built Bremerhaven, Germany, 1873

# Gannet Doterel class screw sloop 1878

Restored to her original appearance at Chatham Historic Dockyard, HMS *Gannet* is now displayed afloat there in No. 4 Dock. She is a product of the transitional period from sail to steam, having been built with both forms of propulsion. Completed in 1879, she was classified by the Royal Navy as a sloop, and was designed to police the trade routes and colonies of the rapidly expanding British Empire. Retaining sails meant that she could cruise independently in remote parts of the Pacific, Indian and South Atlantic Oceans, where coaling stations were few and far between. When under sail her telescopic funnel could be collapsed and the propeller could be retracted into the stern to reduce drag.

The Victorian exhortation 'Send a Gunboat' led to *Gannet* seeing action at the Red Sea port of Suakin in 1888. She was sent in support of British and Egyptian troops, and local friendly tribes, who were trying to regain control of the Sudan and were under siege from rebel Mahdist forces. *Gannet* shelled the enemy lines and helped prevent the port falling into rebel hands. Her service in the Red Sea also included frequent anti-slavery patrols, stopping and searching suspicious vessels and rescuing any slaves on board. Her operational life ended in 1895 but she survived as a static training ship, at first for reservists on the Thames and, later, for boys on the River Hamble in Hampshire, until 1968. *PB*

1861–1918

*HMS **Gannet** at Chatham (photograph), Paul Brown, 2008*

190ft x 36ft x 15.8ft (57.9m x 11m x 4.8 m) • 1130 tons [D] • Hull wood (teak), iron framed • Armament 2 x 7in muzzle loading guns, 4 x 64 pdr • Complement 139 • Built Sheerness, Kent, England, 1878

# Huáscar  Armoured turret ship 1879

When one thinks of iconic vessels the *Huáscar* will not be on most people's list, yet this turret armed ironclad, built and then launched by Laird Brothers at Birkenhead in 1865, has a remarkable history. *Huáscar* was built for export to the Peruvian navy where she saw action in the Peruvian Civil War (1877) and then the war between Peru and Chile, 1879-84. In this latter conflict *Huáscar* conducted a six-month long raid during which she attacked Chilean ports, destroyed or damaged a number of Chilean naval vessels and liberated two capture Peruvian naval ships. Finally her luck ran out and the *Huáscar* was first captured by and then taken into service with the Chilean navy and participated in the Chilean Civil War of 1891 on the side of the rebels who eventually forced the surrender of the Chilean government.

In one respect the *Huáscar* was an unlucky ship – three senior naval officers were killed while on her deck. First, at the Battle of Iquique on 21 May 1879 while *Huáscar* was still in Peruvian service under the command of Captain Miguel Grau, she was boarded by the crew of the Chilean *Esmeralda*. *Esmeralda*'s Captain, Arturo Prat, was slain on the *Huáscar*. Later that year, at the Battle of Angamos, 8 October 1879, Miguel Grau, now a Peruvian naval hero and raised to the rank of Rear-Admiral was blown to bits by a Chilean shell. After being taken into Chilean service Commander Manuel Thomson was killed while in command of *Huáscar*.

*Huáscar* is one of a handful of surviving nineteenth-century ironclads and, up until the Chilean earthquake of 2010 (though the ship herself was undamaged), could be seen at Talcahuano, Chile. *MR*

**Naval Combat beween the Peruvian Ship** *Huáscar* **and the Chilean** *Blanco Encalada* **and the** *Cochrane* **in 1879,** *Rafael Monleon y Torres,*
*Private Collection / Index / The Bridgeman Art Library*

200ft x 35.5ft x 16ft (37.8m x 10.2m x 3.4m) • 1870 tons [D] • Hull iron • Armament 2 x 10in Armstrong guns, 2 x 4.75in Armstrong guns, 1 x 12lb cannon, 1 x .44 cal Gatling gun, armoured ram bow • Complement 170 • Built Laird, Birkenhead, England, 1865

# Rotomahana  Packet steamer 1879

When the *Rotomahana* was launched in June 1879 by William Denny & Bros of Dumbarton, Scotland for the Union Steamship Company of New Zealand, she was notable as the first ship in the world to be built of mild steel and to have bilge keels. On trials she was described as 'the finest specimen of the shipbuilders' and engineers' skill ever turned out' by the company. She was much admired for her graceful yacht-like lines and for her speed, which set something of a standard on the trans-Tasman trade between New Zealand and Australia.

Far surpassing her colonial contemporaries, she was called the 'Greyhound of the Pacific' and sported a greyhound at the masthead. Her massive compound engine gave her a speed of 15 knots, but like all fast steamers of the

day, coal consumption was high. Named for a New Zealand lake, her figurehead was of a Maori princess. She accommodated 140 first-class, 80 second and 80 third-class passengers. The picture shows her leaving Sydney for Wellington, a passage of less than four days. Propriety demanded that 'Steerage passengers are requested to remove their boots before retiring to bed.'

Following a period during 1891–92 on the express Bass Strait run from Melbourne to Launceston (14 hours), in 1897 she was placed on the overnight ferry service between Wellington and Lyttleton, and with new boilers, she could average 16 knots. Her record between the two cities was 10 hours 35 minutes. In 1908 she was moved again to Bass Strait, where she remained until 1920, when she finally passed from service. *CJ*

Sheep on Nelson wharf, alongside the ship *Rotomohana* (glass negative), Frederick Nelson Jones, c. 1910, Alexander Turnbull Collection, National Library of New Zealand

298.2ft x 35.2ft (90.9m x 10.7m) • 1727 tons [GRT] • Hull mild steel • Complement first class 140, second class 80, third class 80 • Built William Denny & Bros, Dumbarton, Scotland, 1879

# Italia  Battleship 1880

No warship reflected the political, social and economic difficulties affecting the first decades of life of the unified Italian state better than the battleship *Italia*. In the aftermath of the debacle at the Battle of Lissa (20 July 1866), the already precarious political support for a wider contribution from the Royal Italian Navy to national security witnessed a mortal blow – the service experiencing severe reductions to its budget and procurement policies. In a country with a still-fragile economy that shared land borders with powerful states, the construction of particularly expensive naval assets was regarded as low priority. In 1871, the new and charismatic Minister of the Navy, Admiral Augusto Riboty provided the Parliament with a 'vision' for the navy: a service where administrative, educational and procurement reforms were to reflect the nation's ascendency to the world stage. Riboty's ideas found their ideal executor in the thought-provoking naval architect Benedetto Brin.

In 1875, the ironclad *Italia* was the end result of this first revolutionary wave in Italian naval constructions. Her unusual lines reflected her distinctive and highly innovative character. The ship featured powerful guns, it was relatively light and very fast, though fatally unbalanced as a design since these solutions came at the expense of armour protection. The *Italia* joined the fleet in only 1885 and by that time, the rapid pace of technological development in the second half of the nineteenth century had fully exposed the weaknesses in protection intrinsic to her design.

The *Italia* saw no major operational activity throughout her career; instead the construction qualities of her hull and engines enabled her to be transformed in 1919 into a transport ship, remaining in service until 1921. Like the country she served, the *Italia* had been the embodiment of the contradictions in a transition from an age of infancy to one of maturity. *AP*

**The battleship *Italia* early in her career** *(photograph), date and photographer unknown, Conway Picture Library*

409.1ft x 73.8ft x 30.5ft (124.7m x 22.5m x 9.3m) • 13,898 tons [D] • Armament: 4 x 17in, 8 x 6in, 4 x 4.7in, 2 x 3in, 12 x 2.2in, 12 x 1.4in • Complement 756 •
Built Castellamare di Stabia Shipyards, Italy, 1880

# Pall Mall  Thames sailing barge c.1880

The prolific Scottish photographer George Washington Wilton recorded this view of St Paul's Cathedral from the opposite bank of the River Thames between 1880 and 1893, capturing a time when the river was still at the heart of commerce and wharves and warehouses lined its banks. Iron, coal, tea, bricks, cement, plate glass, timber, fish, wine and whisky were among the commodities that came into the metropolis by water – on the far right of the picture can be seen the premises of The London and Lisbon Cork Wood Company at 28 Upper Thames Street, and Paul's Wharf, where stone was offloaded for rebuilding the cathedral after the Great Fire of London. Large ships could not proceed further up the Thames than the Pool of London below London Bridge, so goods arrived by barges and lighters.

A pair of typical spritsail Thames sailing barges are moored in the foreground, just two of thousands that plied the Thames and the shallow waters around the east coast. *Pall Mall* lies closest to the viewer, with *Our Boys* behind her. These flat-bottomed vessels were traditionally crewed by 'a man, a boy and a dog' – the latter performing guard duty. To protect their sails, owners dressed the canvas with a mixture of ingredients as varied as fish oils and horse urine, with red ochre to give the traditional red colour.

Across the river, in front of the elegant warehouse of ironwork manufacturer Carron Company,  a paddle steamer with a white funnel has just passed St Paul's Pier. During the Victorian period and into the twentieth century these small vessels provided a service between strategic landing stages; others offered pleasure trips to the resorts of the Thames estuary, such as Southend-on-Sea. *JH*

**1861-1918**

**View of St Paul's Cathedral, from Bankside** (*photograph*), *George Washington Wilson, late nineteenth century, Conway Picture Library*

*Pall Mall*: 45 tons • Hull wood • Complement 2 • Built Milton, Kent, England, 1875
*Our Boys*: 43 tons • Hull wood • Complement 2 • Built Rochester, Kent, England, 1880

# Polyphemus Torpedo ram 1882

Among the most astonishing nineteenth-century warships, and by far the most misunderstood, the British ship *Polyphemus* was a high speed fleet torpedo vessel, protected against gunfire by a 3in (8cm) steel armoured deck. Concerned that the experimental broadside torpedo tubes might not work *Polyphemus* was completed in 1882 with a ram, carrying the popular sobriquet 'ram' throughout her career. However, her main armament remained the five 14in (35cm) torpedo tubes, and 18 torpedoes.

Displacing 2600 tons, and capable of 18 knots (3 or 4 knots faster than contemporary battleships), *Polyphemus* would have been a very dangerous opponent for any armoured vessel before medium-calibre quick-firing guns were introduced. For all her fighting power she lacked the amenities and 'presence' required for peacetime service, and was only tested at anything like her full potential on one occasion. During the 1885 Fleet exercises at Berehaven, Ireland, she rammed and destroyed a heavy boom defending the 'enemy' fleet anchorage, proving that contemporary harbour defence systems were quite useless. Although a technological dead end, *Polyphemus* demonstrated that contemporary British warship design was anything but conservative. *ADL*

Contemporary artist's impression of HMS *Polyphemus* (line drawing), c. 1882, Conway Picture Library

240ft x 37ft x 20.5ft (73m x 11m x 6.3m) • 2640 tons [D] • Hull steel • Armament 5 x 14in torpedo tubes, 18 torpedoes, 6 x 1in Nordenfelt guns, bow ram • Complement 80 • Built Chatham, Kent, England, 1880

# Leonidas Powder hulk 1885

A sudden squall blows up on the River Medway, while highly explosive gun cotton is being unloaded from the powder hulk *Leonidas*. A shaft of sunlight breaks through the clouds, to set upon the old ship's hull, lashed by the wind and rain. So far now from the storm of war, in her former life *Leonidas* was a 36-gun frigate, launched in 1807 to see service on various stations across the globe throughout the century. By 1872 she had ceased active service to become a powder hulk, anchored on the river, slowly deteriorating. This was the fate of many of the old wooden sailing warships, no longer of fighting use, to wallow sadly in rivers and estuaries close to the naval dockyards. After some years of neglect, *Leonidas* was broken up in 1894.

William Lionel Wyllie's oil on canvas, 'Storm and sunshine: A battle with the elements', was completed in 1885. On his death in 1931, Wyllie was England's most famous marine painter, renowned for his grand seascapes and his late panoramic work of the Battle of Trafalgar. Yet, nearly 50 years before, he had made his name with his unconventional images of the working lives of people on the rivers. He sailed the Thames from London right down to the sea, documenting its industry and landscapes. Borrowing much from Turner's 'Fighting Temeraire', a painting Wyllie frequently praised, this is a vision of the passing of the great days of naval sailing ships, a golden age retiring in the twilight. *HLJ*

**Storm and sunshine: A battle with the elements** *(oil on canvas), William Lionel Wyllie, 1885, National Maritime Museum, London (BHC1348)*

150.1ft x 39.9ft x 13.9ft (45.8m x 12.2m x 4.2m) • 1052 tons [BM] • Armament (as built); upper deck 28 x 18 pdr, quarterdeck 8 x 9 pdr + 6 x 32 pdr carronades, forecastle 2 x 9 pdr + 2 x 32 pdr carronades • Complement 284 • Built John Pelham, Frindsbury, Kent, England, 1807

# Edinburgh Colossus class battleship c.1887

In 1885 Queen Victoria celebrated her golden jubilee with a suitably impressive Naval Review at Spithead, and amidst a fleet of sample vessels that contained examples of every type of warship since *Warrior,* the brand new battleship *Edinburgh* offered both a glimpse of the future, and the last hurrah for a lost age. She combined three major firsts for a British battleship; the first to use steel for the hull, the first with heavy breech loaders, in this case 12in rifled guns, and the first use of compound, rather than simple wrought iron armour.

However her low freeboard and *en echelon* arrangement of her two heavy gun turrets was utterly useless for naval combat. Her true function was coastal bombardment. This was hardly surprising in an age when the Royal Navy possessed more first class warships than the rest of the world combined. The main threat to the Victorian battle ship of 1885 came from small torpedo craft: here *Edinburgh* displays new anti-torpedo nets and small calibre guns for a royal and popular audience. While the new technologies seen in the *Edinburgh* would revolutionise warships, her design was a dead end. *ADL*

**HMS *Edinburgh* on anti-torpedo exercise** *(oil on canvas), Eduardo de Martino, c. 1887, National Maritime Museum, London (BHC1674)*

325ft x 68ft x 25.9ft (99m x 21m x 7.8m) • 9420 tons [D] • Hull steel • Armament 4 x BL 12in Mk IV, 5 x BL 6in, 20 smaller calibre guns.
2 x 14in torpedo tubes • Complement 396 • Built Pembroke, Wales, 1882

# Dupuy de Lôme Armoured cruiser 1890

Named after a renowned French naval architect, the cruiser *Dupuy de Lôme* was the first of a series of fast, heavily-armed cruisers intended to prey on commerce on the high seas. These cruisers were an essential element in the maritime strategy favoured by the Jeune Ecole, which envisaged using massed small craft armed with torpedoes to counter an anticipated British blockade of French ports, while fast cruisers broke out for independent operations against the shipping lanes essential to Britain's economy. The *Dupuy de Lôme* was of revolutionary design, with an armoured belt of steel that extended from 4.5ft (1.4m) below the waterline to the upper deck. A 0.8in (2cm)

protective deck extended from the lower edge of the belt to the waterline amidships, and a cellulose-filled cofferdam ran along the ship's sides above the protective deck. Coal bunkers located between the protective deck and a splinter deck over the engines completed this advanced protection system. The two 7.6in guns were in beam turrets amidships, with the 6.4in mountings grouped fore and aft. In 1905 *Dupuy de Lôme* was reconstructed with new boilers. She subsequently had three funnels, and the original military masts were removed. She was a second-line ship by the First World War, and was sold to Belgium in 1920. *JJ*

**The French armoured cruiser *Dupuy de Lôme*** *(photograph), Conway Picture Library*

364ft x 51.5ft x 24.5ft (111m x 15.7m x 7.5m) • 6700 tons [D] • Hull steel • Armament 2 x 7.6in, 6 x 6.4in Modèle 1893, 4 x 9 pdr, 2 x 18in torpedo tubes • Complement 525 • Built Brest, France, 1890

# Infanta Maria Teresa Armoured cruiser 1890

The *Infanta Maria Teresa* was the lead ship of a class of three cruisers that joined the Spanish Navy between 1889 and 1893. Built in the naval shipyard located along the River Nervión in Bilbao, all three met a tragic end in the 1898 Battle of Santiago de Cuba at the hands of the US Navy.

At the turn of the twentieth century, foreign possessions were one of the defining parameters of a major international player and navies were the prime tool that enabled governments to maintain and safeguard vast colonial empires scattered throughout the globe. The *Maria Teresa* was the result of Spain's need to maintain the degree of naval power necessary to protect her widely dispersed colonial interests in an increasingly volatile and competitive international arena. Following the 1890 crisis with the German Empire in the Caroline Islands, the Spanish Government was forced to renounce its desire to build more battleships of the class of the *Pelayo* and decided to procure the *Maria Teresa* instead.

Fast and well-armoured with two powerful 11in guns and ten 5.5in guns, the *Maria Teresa* nicely met the necessities of colonial service thanks to her longer endurance and speed. Her valuable cruising qualities were, however, off-set by the limits of her armour protection. The armour belt was narrow and limited only to two-thirds of her hull, while her naval guns were only lightly protected. The *Maria Teresa* was beautifully decorated and furnished with wood, an element that did not contribute to her safety. The *Maria Teresa* was the best compromise to meet the security requirements of Spain's increasingly strained imperial resources. She was the jewel of a fading empire soon to be seized by the United States. *AP*

**Launch of the Spanish warship** *Infanta Maria Teresa in the Nervión shipyard* (print), Juan Comba y Garcia, nineteenth century, The Art Archive / Private Collection

366.8ft x 65ft x 21.6ft (111.8m x 19.8m x 6.6m) • 6890 tons [D] • Armament 2 x 11in, 10 x 5.5in, 8 x 12 pdr QF, 10 x 3 pdr Hotchkiss revolvers, 8 x Nordenfeld machine guns, 2 x Maxim machine guns, 8 x torpedo tubes (2 submerged) • Complement 484 • Built Nervión, Bilbao, Spain, 1890

# Mayer de Rothschild  Sandgate lifeboat 1891

The hurricane-force winds that sprang up across England shortly before dawn on 11 November 1891 caused havoc at sea. The Sydney-bound sailing ship *Benvenue* was being towed down the English Channel by tug when at 5.30 a.m. off Folkestone the tow parted and Captain James Moddrel dropped anchor to stop his ship being thrown ashore. It was a fatal error. The square-rigger struck and settled a hundred yards from land, her decks underwater, forcing her crew to scramble up the masts and tie themselves to the yards

The self-righting Sandgate lifeboat, named *Mayer de Rothschild* in honour of her donor's father, put to sea but capsized in the maelstrom, drowning one man. Throughout the day the coastguard and a field artillery unit tried in vain to fire a line across, injuring some of the crew in the process, and the lifeboat made a second, unsuccessful attempt to reach the ship – all watched by thousands of spectators. Wet and frozen, 27 crewmen of the *Benvenue* clung

on, trusting that their ship's iron hull would support the masts. Four men had gone into the water and drowned; the captain was also dead, trapped below after going back for his pipe.

In the evening the *Mayer de Rothschild* tried again, manned by two of her original crew – Coxwain Hennessy and Second Coxwain Sadler – and some volunteer local fishermen. Helped by the tug and the soldiers and civilians on the beach she managed to get out to sea and reach the *Benvenue* at 9.30 p.m. The 27 survivors were successfully taken off to great cheers from the beach.

Honours were showered on the lifeboat crew, including a silver medal bearing Queen Victoria's image. Sadler and Hennessy were awarded the Royal National Lifeboat Association's silver medal, and Hennessy also received the Albert Medal. *JH*

**Crew of the *Mayer de Rothschild* after service to *Benvenue*, Sandgate, near Hythe, 1891** *(photograph). photographer unknown, Conway Picture Library*

Dimensions unknown • Hull wood • Complement 18 • Built Hythe, England, c. 1890

# Fram   Polar expedition ship 1892

When the Norwegian zoologist Fridtjof Nansen hit upon the novel idea that a 'current passes across or very near the Pole into the sea between Greenland and Spitzbergen', he determined to use that current to make a pioneering drift across the Arctic Ocean. For this bold attempt he would need a new kind of exploration ship, and Nansen turned to the naval architect Colin Archer to design a craft that differed 'essentially from any other previously known vessel'. *Fram* was stoutly built, smooth-sided and double-ended, without a keel or sharp strakes and thus able 'to slip like an eel out of the embraces of the ice'. Withstanding the pressure of the pack, *Fram* would be raised up out of the water undamaged.

She sailed from northern Norway in July 1893, heading east across the Barents Sea, hugging the Russian coast until turning north into the Arctic Ocean. On 22 September *Fram* lodged into the ice and, as predicted, she was carried to the northwest. All the while her crew took extensive magnetic, astronomical and hydrographic measurements, but their minds were fixed firmly to the North. *Fram* finally emerged from the ice in August 1896, floating freely into open water off the northwest coast of Spitzbergen. In the meantime, Nansen and a companion had left the ship, in an effort to reach the North Pole on ski and by kayak. They were lucky to return alive. Finding their way blocked by impenetrable ice they turned south to Franz Josef Land, where they were rescued by the English explorer Frederick Jackson.

In 1898, Otto Sverdrup, who commanded the ship after Nansen left for the Pole, took *Fram* on a three-year expedition to Greenland. In 1910, she was brought out of retirement by fellow Norwegian Roald Amundsen in his successful bid for the South Pole, a plan he revealed to his crew only when the ship was heading toward Antarctica. Surprisingly, the intrepid craft spent much of the next 20 years decaying in storage, before she was installed in a new museum in Oslo built in her honour in 1936. *HLJ*

*Fram* **in winter** *(watercolour), Wally Herbert, Polarworld*

128ft x 34ft x 15ft (39m x 11m x 4.8m) • 402 tons [GRT] • Hull wood • Complement 16 • Built Colin Archer, Larvik, Norway, 1892

# Olympia Protected cruiser 1892

This famous armoured cruiser of the Spanish-American War of 1898 remains as a museum ship in Philadelphia, Pennsylvania; a unique specimen of her era. Built in 1891–2, she epitomized America's decision to become a leading naval power by the twentieth century and featured the latest improvements in naval design (including electricity).

*Olympia* became flagship of the US Asiatic Squadron in 1898 under the command of Commodore George Dewey. A Spanish fleet was known to be based at Manila Bay in the Philippines and Dewey set sail from China to attack at the first opportunity. When he arrived in the vicinity on 30 April, Dewey discovered the enemy fleet was anchored beyond the effective firing range of the surrounding fortifications. He steered *Olympia* and three other cruisers through outer harbour mines, which failed to inflict damage, so that by the early morning of 1 May, Dewey informed the captain of the *Olympia*: 'You may fire when ready, Gridley.'

The ensuing battle was a lopsided affair. The Spanish cruisers were obsolete and largely immobile – and their gunnery was worse. *Olympia* led the American battleline up and down the enemy position until Admiral Patricio Montojo Passaron attempted a futile charge which American guns left in flames. The Battle of Manila Bay saw one American dead and nine wounded, and Spanish power in the Philippines – a legacy of the sixteenth century – was broken. A brief attempt by an Imperial German squadron at the scene to muscle the Americans out of the region was then quietly rebuffed. *HF*

**Museum ships moored at the river; the cruiser *Olympia* and submarine *Becuna*, Independence Seaport Museum, Delaware River, Penn's Landing, Waterfront District, Philadelphia, Pennsylvania, USA** *(photograph), Richard Cummins / SuperStock*

344.1ft x 53ft x 21.5ft (104.9m x 16.2m x 6.6m) • 5586 tons [D] • Hull steel • Armament 4 x 8in, 10 x 5in, 4 x 6 pdr, 6 x 1 pdr, 6 x 18in torpedo tubes • Complement 411 • Built Union Iron Works, San Francisco, USA, 1895

# Rome   Iron screw steamer 1892

P&O built the four-masted single-screw iron steamer *Rome* for the Australian trade, in which she enjoyed an uneventful career. She was re-engined and lengthened in 1892, her new bow section adding 19ft (5.8m) to her length but before she could re-enter service, fire ripped through her accommodation. Her most famous passenger would prove to be the young Winston Churchill who in 1897 travelled to Brindisi to board her for his return to India after three months' leave in England. Two years earlier Churchill had written: 'I do not contemplate ever taking a sea voyage for pleasure and I shall always look upon journeys by sea as necessary evils…', but there were others who took a different view.

In 1900, the German line HAPAG launched the first purpose-built cruise ship, the *Prinzessin Victoria Luise*, aimed at wealthy clients with leisure to spare. Four years later, P&O replied not with a new ship but the conversion of *Rome*

into what they termed a 'cruising yacht' under the new name *Vectis* (the Roman name for the Isle of Wight). Beginning with a voyage to Norway and the North in July 1904, cruises ran for ten months of the year and lasted between two weeks and one month, with shore excursions organized by Thomas Cook. In August 1907 *The Bystander* magazine advertised two forthcoming itineraries: a September cruise from London to Spain and the Balearics, and one in October starting at Marseilles and taking in Greece, the Holy Land, Syria and Naples – with reductions for clients taking both.

The French Government bought *Vectis* in 1912, ostensibly for conversion into a hospital ship. Those plans came to nothing and she was broken up in Italy in 1913. *JH*

SS *Rome*, **port side view looking aft** *(photograph), date and photographer unknown, Conway Picture Library*

430.1ft x 44.4ft x 33.5ft   (131.1m x 13.5m x 10.2m) • 5013 tons [GRT] • Hull iron • Complement: first class 150 • Built Caird and Co., Greenock, Scotland, 1881

# Britannia  Racing cutter 1893

The racing cutter *Britannia* is seen here locked in a close contest with the schooner *Westward* in the Solent during Cowes Week, 1935. This was to be her last season, for in the following year, after the death of King George V, she was towed out to St. Catherine's Deep, south of the Isle of Wight, and sunk by HMS *Winchester*, thus fulfilling the King's dying wish.

Her sinking symbolized the end of an era. For more than 40 years *Britannia* had been at the centre of 'Big Class' yacht racing, lending social status and royal prestige to a sport that could only be indulged in by the super-rich. Their yachts needed costly maintenance, constant updating to remain competitive, and large professional crews. *Britannia* had been ordered by the Prince of Wales, later King Edward VII, in 1892 and in her first season (1893) she won 24 of the 43 races she entered. Indeed, she became one of the most successful racing yachts ever, winning a total of 231 out of her 635 races.

In 1910 when Edward VII died, her ownership passed to George V, who also took a keen interest in yacht racing and had often sailed in *Britannia* with his father. Originally a gaff cutter, she was converted to a Bermuda rig in 1931 to meet the rules of the J-class, the leading (and biggest) class of yachts of the 1930s. *PB*

**HMY *Britannia* racing the yacht *Westward* in the Solent, 1935** *(oil on canvas), Norman Wilkinson, mid-twentieth century, National Maritime Museum, London (BHC3750)*

121.5ft x 23.7ft x 15ft (37m x 7.22m x 4.6m) • 221 tons [D] • Hull composite • Complement 28 plus owner's party • Built D. & W. Henderson, Partick, Glasgow, Scotland, 1893

# Campania  Cunard ocean liner 1893

When completed the Cunard liner *Campania*'s two triple expansion steam engines were the largest in the world. They were fed by 12 boilers (with 102 furnaces) and had five cylinders each: the illustration shows an engine seen from the stern. Each engine had its own watertight compartment and drove one propeller. The twin propellers could produce a speed of up to 23.5 knots, enough for *Campania* to win the Blue Riband for the fastest transatlantic crossings each way in 1893. In the following year her record westbound crossing of August 1894 logged 2776 nautical miles at an average speed of 21.44 knots. The engines of *Campania* and her sister-ship *Lucania* were near to the limits of steam-reciprocating engine technology and the next generation of transatlantic liners was to have turbine propulsion.

*Campania* remained in service between Liverpool and New York until 1914 when she was purchased by the Admiralty from ship breakers for conversion to an aircraft carrier. And it was a success: in August 1915, the first aircraft to successfully take off from a ship that was underway did so from the *Campania*. Her planes were intended to scout ahead of the Grand Fleet looking for the German High Seas Fleet. By a curious accident with signals she missed the Battle of Jutland, and only six days before the end of the First World War, on 5 November 1918, *Campania* dragged her anchors during strong winds in the Firth of Forth, was holed in collision with nearby battleships, and sank. *PB*

Cutaway drawing of one of *Campania*'s two reciprocating five-cylinder triple expansion steam engines, seen from stern, *The Art Archive / John Meek*

622ft x 65.3ft x 29.9ft (189.6m x 19.9m x 9.1m) • 12,950 tons [D] • Hull steel • Complement 424, passengers first class 600, second class 400, third class 1000 • Built Fairfield Shipbuilding & Engineering Co., Govan, Scotland, 1892

# Spray  Oyster sloop 1895

Joshua Slocum was a Nova Scotian who, while still a boy, was drawn to the sea and took the post of cook on a fishing schooner. He later became an American citizen and commanded deep-sea sailing ships until about 1890. In 1892 he was given a derelict sloop named *Spray* which he rebuilt himself; effectively she was a new boat.

On 24 April 1895, aged 51, Captain Slocum left Boston in her to sail single-handed around the world. This first ever solo circumnavigation was completed when he sailed into Newport, Rhode Island, on 27 June 1898, after a voyage of 46,000 miles (74,030km). Slocum altered *Spray*'s sloop rig

to yawl rig partway through his voyage, which improved her sailing qualities on the wind. His many adventures included being chased by Moorish pirates off Morocco, being boarded by thieves and chased by natives in canoes in the Strait of Magellan, being 'visited' by the ghost of one of Columbus's crew, and battling through gales and snowstorms. His book, *Sailing Alone Around the World* became an instant bestseller. The photograph shows Slocum aboard *Spray* and was taken in 1895 by his son: it has appeared in some editions of the book. Tragically the *Spray* was lost with Slocum aboard in 1909 when sailing from Martha's Vineyard, Massachusetts, to South America. *PB*

**Joshua Slocum, the first person to sail alone around the world** (*photograph*), *Benjamin Aymar Slocum, 1895, Bibliotheque Nationale, Paris, France / Archives Charmet / The Bridgeman Art Library*

36.8ft x 14.2ft x 4.2ft (11.2m x 4.3m x 1.3m) • 13 tons [GRT] • Hull wood • Complement 1 • Built c. 1800, rebuilt Fairhaven, Massachusetts, USA, 1894

# Standart Imperial Russian yacht 1896

Laid down in 1893 by Tsar Alexander III, the Russian Imperial yacht *Standart* was launched two years later, serving as a handsome ship of state and a floating palace for the family of the new Tsar, Nicholas II. Rigged as a three-masted fore-and-aft schooner, with three decks, two funnels and a clipper stem, *Standart*'s elegant lines, opulent fittings and advanced technical features marked her out as a truly grand vessel and an emblem of Romanov Imperial majesty. She was the largest Royal yacht afloat throughout the late nineteenth and early twentieth centuries; the envy of the crowned heads of Europe, notably Kaiser Wilhelm II and Edward VII.

Tsar Nicholas and his family were holidaying on *Standart* in the Finnish fjords when Archduke Franz Ferdinand was assassinated in June 1914; the catalyst for the First World War. By order of the Tsar, she was placed in dry dock. This proved to be the end of her glory days; after the 1917 Revolution the yacht was renamed *Vosemnadtsate Martza* and stripped of her luxurious fittings. In 1932 she was renamed *Marti* and fitted as a minelayer in the Soviet navy. During the Second World War she laid some 3159 mines and bombarded shore positions near Leningrad. After hostilities ended, *Marti* was refitted and converted to a training ship, renamed *Oka*. During the refit her steam engines were replaced by diesels. She was scrapped at Tallinn, Estonia in 1963. *MJ*

**The Russian Imperial yacht Standart** (photograph). Conway Picture Library

370.1ft x 51.8ft x 19.7ft (112.8m x 15.8m x 6m) • 5557 tons [D] • Hull steel • Armament 8 x 47mm Hotchkiss • Complement 355 • Built Burmeister & Wain, Copenhagen, Denmark, 1895

# Holland  Submarine 1897

The first official submarine of the US Navy was launched in May 1897, and named after her designer, Irish-American John Philip Holland – who also built the first submarine for Great Britain's Royal Navy three years later. (Ironically enough, Holland had constructed a prototype submarine 'ram' in 1881 for US-based Fenians against the British.) He had been developing his ideas for more than 20 years; ballast tanks for controlling depth and attitude, an electric engine, which could operate fully underwater for extended periods; an internal combustion petrol engine when surfaced: and an armament that included Whitehead torpedoes launched from an internal tube when the vessel was submerged. The *Holland* also featured a conning tower, characteristic of modern submarines ever since.

Considered a practical success, the US Navy purchased several more units which developed into the Plunger 'A-Class' submarines. There is some suggestion that construction of these novel warships directly led to the establishment of the General Dynamics Corporation. But the chief importance of the vessel was its reliability as a working prototype for the improved submarine classes that followed. By 1914, such 'underwater boats' were ready to challenge the traditional definition of naval power. *Holland* was only 53ft (16.2m) long with a beam just over 10ft (3m) but housed a crew of six. She was decommissioned in 1910. *HF*

**John P. Holland in the conning tower of USS *Holland* (SS–1)** *(photograph), date and photographer unknown, Conway Picture Library*

53.3ft x 10.3ft x 8.5ft (16.2m x 3.1m x 2.6m) • 65 tons [D] • Hull steel • Armament 1 x 18in torpedo tube, 1 x 8.4in pneumatic gun • Complement 6 • Built Crescent Shipyard, Elizabeth, New Jersey, USA, 1897

# Majestic  Majestic class battleship 1898

Few ships have so fully taken on the character of their age as HMS *Majestic*. The very embodiment of late Victorian power, the flagship of the old Queen's navy, and guardian of her empire, *Majestic* was the first of nine, the largest class of steel battleships ever built, and progenitor of a decade of capital ships armed with four 12in guns, and 12–16 secondary 6in guns. The buff, white and black livery, inherited from mid-Victorian ironclads such as *Warrior*, reflected anticipated battle ranges of under 2 miles, and the overriding importance of deterrence in contemporary British policy. By building nine of these ships and parading them, Britain warned off potential rivals. Conspicuous displays of power maintained peace, and supported the expanding wealth of Empire based on trade, capital and investment.

The decision to build these ships, and a full range of contemporary cruisers and torpedo boats, ended the political career of Prime Minister William Gladstone, and ushered in an era of naval arms races. With her stern walk and luxuriously fitted admiral's quarters *Majestic* carried the flags of many senior officers as she steamed up and down the English Channel, reminding the French who ruled the oceans.

Few ships suffered so much when naval paint schemes shifted to battleship grey; there could be little majesty in a dull monotone, leaving her profile cluttered and imprecise. *Majestic* met her doom off the Gallipoli beachhead, still flying an Admiral's flag, sunk by a threat unimagined when she was built 20 years before – a U-boat torpedo. The pomp and circumstance of Victorian empire gave way to the new brutality of mechanized total war. *ADL*

**The Channel Squadron** *(oil on canvas), Eduardo de Martino, 1898, National Maritime Museum, London (BHC0646)*

413ft x 75ft x 27.5ft (126m x 23m x 8.4m) • 14,900 tons [D] • Hull steel • Armament 4 x BL 12in Mk VIII, 12 x 6in QF, 16 x 12 pdr, 12 x 3 pdr QF, 5 x 18in torpedo tubes (four submerged, one above waterline) • Complement 757 • Built Portsmouth, England, 1895

# Thunder Child H.G. Wells' torpedo ram 1898

Though a fictional torpedo ram, HMS *Thunder Child* of H. G. Wells's *War of the Worlds* (1898) stands as an important symbol of mankind's last, best hope – in the form of high-tech naval power. To the late-Victorian readership it made sense for the Royal Navy to stand up to the previously unstoppable Martian Tripod-machines, and indeed Wells sets this up as the climax of his novel: London has been overrun; the Martians employ a heat-ray that vaporizes steel as well as people; and evacuees crowd in boats off the coast of Essex, when Tripods appear. Burning, but still under steam, a lone ironclad manages to ram one Martian machine, toppling it over, so that it crashes into a second one. For a brief moment, humanity has hope. 'Everyone was shouting. The whole steamer from end to end rang with frantic cheering that was taken up by all in the crowding multitude of ships and boats that was driving out to sea.' Still, the navy is unable to stem the tide of humanity's collapse.

*Thunder Child* is typically shown as a pre-dreadnought battleship; notably on the sleeve of the popular musical adaptation of 'War of the Worlds' and in the sketch below by Brazilian illustrator Henrique Alvim Corrêa, produced for a Belgian edition of Wells' novel, published in 1906. The 1954 movie version replaced the ship with the A-Bomb – which failed to inflict any damage upon the Martians; a thermonuclear strike in the 1996 film, *Independence Day*, also proves useless. As with *Thunder Child*, technology is pointless without people, whose civilization is breaking down. *HF*

**'The torpedo-boat's brave attack on the Martians'** *(pen and ink drawing), Henrique Alvim Corrêa, 1906, Mary Evans Picture Library*

# Wittelsbach   Wittelsbach class battleship 1899

An emblem of doomed ambition, *Wittelsbach*, named for the Bavarian royal family, was the first of five battleships built to the same design. Ordered shortly after the passage of the 1897 German Navy Law to fulfil the dreams of Kaiser Wilhelm II and Admiral Alfred Tirpitz, they helped start a naval arms race. Although noticeably smaller than their British contemporaries, the Wittelsbach class ships were the first German 'pre-dreadnoughts' to mount 11in heavy guns. Designed to fight somewhere between Heligoland and the Thames Estuary they were, albeit briefly, the acme of German world power politics, and a fitting subject for Carl Salzman's carefully constructed composition. Placing the Imperial German Naval ensign and the Emperor's monogram at the centre Salzman highlighted his ability to combine the fluid qualities of sea and smoke with the hard edged, potent masculinity of 11in guns and battleship grey. By 1914 these ships were perfectly obsolete; they saw no combat, and ended the war in subsidiary harbour service roles. Converted into a depot ship for motor minesweepers, *Wittelsbach* survived to serve the new Republic until 1921, outlasting the Imperial regime, the men responsible for her construction, and the dynasty she celebrated. *ADL*

German Fleet Manoeuvres on the High Seas *(oil on canvas), Carl Saltzmann, c. 1900, National Maritime Museum, London (BHC0648)*

416ft x 74ft x 26ft (127m x 23m x 7.9m) • 12,798 tons [D] • Hull steel • Armament 4 x 9.2in, 18 x 5.9in, 12 x 3.4in, 5 x 17.7in torpedo tubes • Complement 683 • **183**
Built Kaiserliche Werft, Wilhelmshaven, Germany, 1900

# Mikasa  Battleship 1900

The pre-dreadnought battleship *Mikasa* holds a special place in Japanese history and social memory. Paraphrasing a historian of modern Japan, this ship and her successes on the high seas symbolized the ascendancy of Japan as a modern state in the international arena and justified to the eyes of the nation the heavy price paid to build up a fleet of state-of-the-art naval platforms.

Adapted from the design of the Royal Navy's Majestic class, by the time she was completed the *Mikasa* was arguably the most powerful ship in the world. She had a larger displacement, stronger Krupp armour and greater firepower than her British counterpart; with a maximum speed of a little more than 18 knots she was also faster.

Acting as Admiral Heihachirō Tōgō's flagship in the Russo-Japanese War (1904–05), the battleship *Mikasa* met her destiny at the Battle of Tsushima (27 May 1905), where the Japanese fleet annihilated the Russian Baltic Fleet, leaving Japan with the command of waters of the Western Pacific while shattering Russian hopes of victory.

The quality of her design enabled her to sustain considerable damage both at Tsushima and in the other major naval encounter of the war, the Battle of the Yellow Sea (10 August 1904). Her speed was a key asset at Admiral Tōgō's disposal and was combined with her crew's professional expertise; the line of battle headed by the *Mikasa* outpaced the slower, less trained Russian units, crossing their 'T' and giving superior Japanese gunnery the opportunity to fire full broadsides. In engaging the enemy, a 'Z' flag flew from the *Mikasa*'s main mast carrying the following message: 'the fate of the Empire rests upon this very battle. Let every man do his utmost.' By the end of the battle, the *Mikasa* had been the centrepiece of the greatest naval success since Trafalgar. She had saved the fate of the emerging Japanese empire. In doing so, she secured an everlasting place in the Olympus of Japanese national history. *AP*

**Admiral Togo on the deck of *Mikasa*** *(photograph), Keystone / Getty Images*

432ft x 76.2ft x 27.2ft (131.7m x 23.2m x 8.3m) • 15,140 tons [D] • Hull steel • Armament 2 x 12in, 14 x 6in, 20 x 3.4in, 4 x 1.8in, 5 x 17.7in torpedo tubes • Complement 904 • Built Vickers Naval Yard, Barrow-in-Furness, England, 1900

# Discovery Antarctic survey ship 1901

The first polar command of explorer Robert Falcon Scott, *Discovery* was a purpose-built research vessel. The ship's name had a proud heritage: the collier *Discovery* had distinguished itself in the Pacific during James Cook's last voyage; the 10-gun sloop *Discovery* was the lead ship in George Vancouver's explorations of the North American west coast; and the screw-propelled *Discovery* had engaged the floes during George Nares' polar expedition in 1875.

Much was expected therefore of this Dundee-built vessel as she departed Cowes amid fanfare in the summer of 1901. After stops at the Cape of Good Hope and New Zealand, she entered the Ross Sea, where Scott established his winter quarters near the volcano Mt Erebus on Ross Island in McMurdo Sound. Among a number of firsts from the ship were a tethered balloon flight and electricity generation with the help of a windmill. An extensive scientific programme was also undertaken. Later that Antarctic summer, Scott, Ernest Shackleton and Edward Wilson reached 82°16'S, about 500 miles (800km) from the Pole and set a new record for farthest south.

*Discovery* remained locked in the ice through 1902–03, but with the help of supply ships *Terra Nova* and *Morning* (which sailed to her rescue), she finally broke free in February 1904. On returning to England, she was purchased by the Hudson's Bay Company and converted for use as a merchant ship. In the 1920s *Discovery* made a series of scientific cruises in the Southern Ocean and a second Antarctic expedition, this time under explorer Douglas Mawson. She was laid up until 1936 when she was bought by the Boy Scouts Association as a training ship, and later used jointly by the Sea Scouts and the Royal Naval Reserve. Restored to her former glory, in 1986 *Discovery* was opened to the public as a museum ship in Dundee. *HLJ*

Commander Scott and his officers on the bridge of the *Discovery* (photograph), Conway Picture Library

171ft x 33.8ft x 15.8ft (52.1m x 10.3m x 4.8m) • 1570 tons [D] • Hull wood • Complement 39-43 • Built Stevens Yard, Dundee, Scotland, 1901

# Gjøa  Expedition sloop 1901

Under the command of the pioneering Norwegian explorer Roald Amundsen, *Gjøa* was the first ship to complete a transit of the Northwest Passage. Named for the fighting Valkyrie of the Vikings, the shallow-draught sloop was originally built for the herring fishery. Amundsen bought her in 1900 and spent a year testing her between Norway and Greenland. After these trials he gave her 3in (8cm) oak sheathing, iron strapping on the bow, and a paraffin-fuelled internal combustion engine.

*Gjøa* sailed from Norway on 16 June 1903 with Amundsen and a crew of six. They made quick progress to the west coast of Greenland, where they embarked sleds, dogs and kayaks, and then continued westwards through Lancaster Sound to King William Island, where they spent two years taking magnetic observations. By August 1905 they were free of the ice and continued west along continental Canada and wintered again off King Point, Alaska. From here, Amundsen set out up the Porcupine and Yukon Rivers, skiing some 500 miles to reach the settlement of Eagle, where he telegraphed the news of his success to the world. By October 1906, *Gjøa* had reached San Francisco where the crew were given a heroes' welcome.

Despite an invitation to be the first ship to pass through the Panama Canal, then under construction, at the instigation of the Norwegian community in San Francisco, *Gjøa* remained in the city as an exhibit in Golden Gate Park. She drew large crowds there for many years, admired but slowly rotting. She remained in the city until 1974, when she was finally restored and returned to Oslo to be housed in the Norwegian Maritime Museum. *HLJ*

*Gjøa (oil on canvas), Lauritz Haaland, Norsk Sjöfartsmuseum, Oslo*

70ft x 20.6ft x 7.7ft (21.3m x 6.3m x 2.3m) • 67 tons [GRT] • Hull wood, with ice-sheathing • Built Kurt Johannesson Skaale, Hardanger, Norway, 1872

# Shamrock II J class racing yacht 1901

*Shamrock II* was launched at William Denny & Brothers at Dumbarton in Scotland on 30 April 1901. She was designed by the brilliant Glasgow-born naval architect George Lennox Watson (1851–1904). Perhaps his best-known yacht was the *Britannia* built for the Prince of Wales, who later became Edward VII. But *Shamrock II* was a pioneering vessel: the first to be built after extensive testing of models in a tank. Watson compared 12 wax models in the William Denny test tank and made 60 modifications before adopting the final hull form. Of metal construction her frames were steel, hull of plated immadium bronze, boom of steel, bowsprit of wood, ballast of lead and deck of pine wood. She was built for retail magnate Sir Thomas Lipton

Unfortunately *Shamrock II* was an accident-prone and unlucky yacht for both designer and owner. A few days after she was launched, on 4 May 1901, she snapped her gaff on the first day of her trials. She proved to be slower in sea trials than her predecessor *Shamrock I* and on 22 May her mast collapsed, injuring King Edward VII who was onboard at the time. During the America's Cup races against *Columbia* from 28 September to 4 October 1901, off New York, she was beaten three wins to nil.

Sir Thomas Lipton was born in a Gorbals tenement, near Glasgow. He left school at 10 and as a teenager temporarily settled in America after stowing away on ship, and it was there he developed his business acumen and flair. He later returned to Glasgow where he established his first shop in what would become a hugely successful multi-million pound retail empire best known for Lipton's tea. He attempted to win the America's Cup with five yachts; all were named *Shamrock*, and all failed to win the coveted trophy. In super-market-speak they were all 'loss-leaders' which made sure many more people were drinking his tea on the east coast of America and elsewhere. *JT*

Accident to *Shamrock II*, 22 May 1901 (photograph), Conway Picture Library

# Herzogin Cecilie Barque 1902

Named after Duchess Cecilie of Mecklenburg and built to train the future officers of Germany's famous Norddeutscher Lloyd line of transatlantic steamships, the *Herzogin Cecilie* was indisputably one of the world's finest sailing ships. The huge four-masted barque carried 31 sails, spreading some 40,000ft² (4180m²) of canvas; her mainmast soared 200ft (70m) from the deck, and the fine lines of her steel hull made her swift as well as elegant. Little wonder she was the de facto flagship of the German mercantile fleet, but having been interned in Chile during the First World War, she was afterwards allotted to the French Government as part of war reparations.

Rebuffing German offers to buy her back, the French sold her to Gustaf Erikson of Mariehamn for £4000, less than a tenth of her original cost, and she began a second brilliant career under the Finnish flag carrying grain from Australia. During the previous century, clippers had raced home from China with the tea cargo; the 1920s and 30s saw the Grain Races, and *Herzogin Cecilie* had her share of victories. In 1927 she came home a month ahead of her rivals, having run from Port Lincoln to Queenstown, Ireland, in just 88 days. Instead of her training crew of 88, she was now handled by 20 men.

On 25 May 1936, after another excellent passage and with 4000 tons of grain on board, she was sailing up the English Channel in poor visibility when she struck the Ham Stone, near Salcombe. Following a botched salvage operation, the wreck of the majestic ship, affectionately nicknamed 'the Duchess', now lies in 25ft of water in Starehole Bay. Her figurehead and panelling are on display at the Mariehamn Maritime Museum in Finland. *JH*

*Herzogin Cecilie (oil on canvas), Geoff Hunt, Conway Picture Library*

336.9ft x 46.3ft x 24.2ft (102.6m x 14.1m x 7.3m) • 3111 tons [D] • Complement: 88 as a training ship/approx. 20 post-1920 • Built Rickmers A.G., Bremerhaven, Germany, 1902

# Renown Centurion class battleship 1903

Obsolete before the First World War, the last Second Rate battleship built for the Royal Navy, HMS *Renown*, enjoyed a high-profile early career as a flagship and occasional royal yacht. Fast and beautiful, she was the favourite ship of Vice Admiral 'Jackie' Fisher who helped design her. He chose his new creation for his flagship at the 1897 Review marking Queen Victoria's Diamond Jubilee, and subsequently on the North American, West Indian and Mediterranean Stations where she hosted lavish entertainments. The flash plates beneath her main guns were removed to make her deck more suitable for dancing.

In 1902 she was refitted to take the Duke of Connaught to India where he represented his brother, the newly crowned King Edward VII at the Delhi Durbar on 1 January 1903. She returned from this spectacular ceremony in March, carrying an unusual additional passenger: a baby elephant which had been presented to the Duke and which had to be hoisted onboard and ashore in a sling. Further royal duty followed in 1905; she lost her secondary 6in guns during refit before taking the future King George V and Queen Mary on their state visit to India. Her last royal engagement came at the end of that year when she provided transport for a visit by the Spanish royal family, but thereafter, displaced by the new dreadnoughts, she dwindled into a training ship for stokers before being scrapped in 1913.

Her social life overshadows her technical features. She may have been the last to load her main guns manually, but with her speed, her heavy secondary armament and the use of the Harvey process to create a thinner but stronger armour belt, this unique ship, built to create work at Pembroke Dockyard, showed how Fisher wished to take the Navy forward. *JH*

**Loading a baby elephant onboard HMS *Renown*, a gift from an Indian Rajah to the Duke of Connaught, 1903** *(photograph), Conway Picture Library*

402ft x 72ft x 26.8ft (123m x 22m x 8.2m) • 12,590 tons [D] • Hull Harvey steel • Armament 4 x BL 10in, 10 x QF 6in, 12 x QF 12 pdr, 12 x 3 pdr, 2 x machine guns, 5 x 18in torpedo tubes • Complement 674 • Built Pembroke, Wales, 1895

# Duke of Wellington  First Rate ship of the line c.1904

For most ships, great or small, famous or workaday, the end is sad. For the British 131-gun wooden screw steam battleship HMS *Duke of Wellington*, once the mightiest ship afloat, that end was long delayed. Began as the 120-gun sailing ship *Windsor Castle* in 1849, the ship was cut in half and lengthened for a second-hand steam plant, and launched on the day the hero of Waterloo died. Quickly renamed, and fitted with a mighty figurehead of the Iron Duke, she took part in the Crimean War as flagship of the British Baltic Fleet in 1854 and 1855, and served out her days in Portsmouth harbour. In 1904

Admiral Sir John 'Jacky' Fisher swept away all the old wooden hulks, and the Duke went to Castle's Ship-breaking Yard at Charlton on the River Thames. Some timbers from the old warrior remain on the foreshore at Charlton, an archaeological testament to the glories of a mighty past age, when as John Ruskin observed, 'a Ship of the Line is the most honourable thing that man, as a gregarious animal, has ever produced'. The figurehead, with many more, was destroyed during a Luftwaffe bombing raid. *ADL*

**Figurehead of HMS *Duke of Wellington* on the wharf at Charlton** (photograph), 1904, Conway Picture Library

(as sailing ship) 210ft x 60ft x 24.8ft (64m x 18.3m x 7.6m); (as screw ship) 240.6ft x 60ft x 24.8ft (73.3m x 18.3m x 7.6m) • 3759 tons [BM] • Hull wood • Armament; gun deck 30 x 8in, main deck 30 x 32 pdr, upper deck 32 x 32 pdr, spar deck 8 x 32 pdr + 14 x 32 pdr (short) • Complement 970 • Built Pembroke, Wales, 1852

# Potemkin  Battleship 1905

The infamous *Potemkin*, a pre-dreadnought battleship of the Imperial Russian Fleet, is notable neither for battle honours nor distinctive design but is chiefly remembered for the rebellion of her crew, rising up against their oppressive officers in June 1905. It was one of a chain of events that led towards the Russian Revolution of 1917. The ship remained in the hands of the mutineers, despite being faced by two squadrons of the Black Sea Fleet, but was shortly afterward handed over to Romanian authorities.

Returning to the Russian Navy, and in an effort to dismiss the humiliation of the event, the ship's name was changed to *Panteleimon* (after Saint Pantaleon, the 'all-compassionate'). However, after the revolution, she would be proudly renamed, *Boretz za Svobodu*, the Freedom Fighter. She was destroyed at Sevastopol in 1919 and later scrapped.

The battleship's ongoing notoriety is owed chiefly to Sergei Eisenstein's 1925 silent film, imagining the uprising; a masterpiece of propaganda, frequently hailed as one of the 'influential films of all time'. In celebrating the mutiny, and demonizing the Tsarist regime, the ship became a stage for the reworking of history; a potent symbol of cultural mythmaking to serve the Bolshevik cause. The film was for many years banned in Britain and France for its violence and revolutionary zeal. *HLJ*

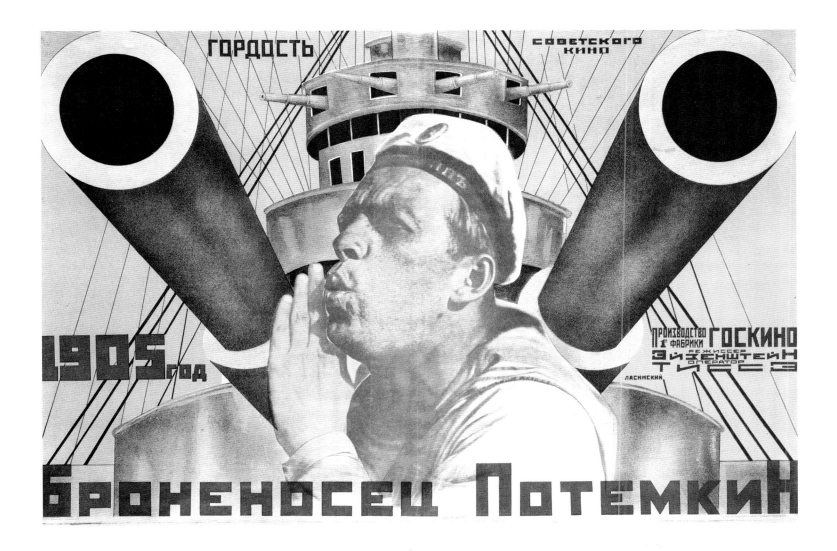

Poster for Sergei Eisenstein's film, 'Battleship Potemkin' *(colour lithograph), Anton Lavinsky, 1926, Russian State Library / The Bridgeman Art Library*

377ft x 73ft x 27ft (115m x 22.3m x 8.2m) • 12,500 tons [D] • Hull steel • Armament 4 x 12in guns in two turrets, 16 x 6in, 14 x 3in, 5 x 15in torpedo tubes • Complement 730 • Built Nikolayev Shipyard, Mykolaiv, USSR (now Ukraine), 1900

# Dreadnought All-big-gun battleship 1906

The brainchild of British Admiral John Fisher, *Dreadnought* introduced a revolution in battleship design so profound that all subsequent ships of the type were known as 'dreadnoughts' and earlier battleships as 'pre-dreadnoughts'. *Dreadnought* introduced the all-big-gun battery to battleships (and subsequently to cruisers), a development made possible by higher rates of fire for the latest 12in guns. The fire control problem was simplified by having uniform main guns firing shells with the same trajectories, and the all-big-gun battery would eventually make it possible to engage at distances where guns of medium calibre would be effectively outranged.

The decision to build *Dreadnought* involved considerable political and technological risks. The adoption of an all-big-gun armament did not initially meet with universal acceptance, with many commentators championing the quicker-firing medium-calibre gun. The adoption of turbine propulsion for such a major vessel was a considerable gamble, given that Royal Navy destroyers with turbines had entered service only four years previously. Arguably the greatest risk lay in building a vessel which at a stroke made all previous battleship construction obsolete, thereby undermining the substantial superiority that the Royal Navy had built up over the years. Fisher himself was well aware of this, and *Dreadnought* was built in great secrecy in little over 12 months, with follow-on battleships and 'battle cruisers' laid down while she was completing. *JJ*

1861-1918

England. Linienschiff „Dreadnought." 1906.

*Dreadnought*, from a German postcard. The construction of an all-big-gun, turbine-powered battleship created huge interest in all the navies of the world *(photograph), Conway Picture Library*

526ft x 82ft x 29ft (160.3m x 25m x 8.8m) • 21,845 tons [D] • Hull steel • Armament 10 x 12in, 24 x 12pdr, 5 x 18in torpedo tubes • Complement 695 • Built Portsmouth, England, 1906

# Mauretania  Cunard ocean Liner 1907

Seen here under her own steam, with her hull still in its grey rustproofing undercoat paint prior to completion, Cunard Line's *Mauretania* along with her sister-ship *Lusitania* were the first express transatlantic liners to be propelled by modern turbine machinery. Audaciously demonstrated at the 1897 Spithead Naval Review by its inventor, Charles Algernon Parsons (1854–1931), who skilfully zigzagged his private yacht *Turbinia* in and out among the assembled battle tonnage of the world navies assembled for the event, and even outran the fast Royal Navy patrol boat dispatched to chase him off, the marine turbine revolutionized marine propulsion for naval and merchant shipping until well into the late twentieth century. The turbine's higher performance greater compactness over earlier reciprocating compound piston marine engines allowed for the building of much larger and faster ships with a greater amount of space available for passenger accommodations and facilities.

Perhaps most significantly for Cunard was the great prestige and trading advantage of regaining the North Atlantic Blue Ribband speed record from Germany, which had wrested the honours from Cunard's *Lucania* in 1898, first with North German Lloyd's *Kaiser Wilhelm der Grosse* and then Hamburg America's *Deutschland*. It was *Lusitania* that first took the Blue Riband in October 1907 and then *Mauretania* from 1909 until conceding to *Bremen* in 1929. *Mauretania* was an immensely popular and reliable ship that served until 1935 with railway-like punctuality throughout her long and happy service career. Nicknamed by her loyal passengers as 'The Rostrun Express' in honour of her long-time captain Arthur Rostrun (1869–1940) who commanded the ship from September 1915 to April 1916 and later from June 1919 until July 1928, when he was given command of Cunard's then flagship *Berengaria* and appointed as the Line's Commodore Captain in 1930. When *Mauretania* was broken up at Rosyth in 1935, the inner workings of her boilers, and condensers were found to still be in remarkably good condition after some 28 years in service. *PD*

*Mauretania* **at Wallsend, Tyne and Wear** (*photograph*), *1907, Conway Picture Library*

790ft x 88ft (240.8m x 26.8 m) • 31,938 tons [GRT] • Hull steel • Complement 802, passengers 2165 • Built Swan, Hunter & Wigham Richardson, Wallsend, Tyne and Wear, England, 1906

# Bertha L. Downs Four-masted schooner 1908

Seen here off Boston in a modern painting by Geoff Hunt, the *Bertha L. Downs* was built in 1908, by which time steam had all but ousted the sailing cargo ship. However, plentiful timber for hulls and masts, wire for the standing rigging and steam-powered donkey engines to carry out labour-intensive tasks such as setting the gaff sails and raising the anchor, made the large wooden schooner a viable proposition in the US coastal trade. Traditionally schooners are small two-masted vessels, their overall size constrained by an upper limit in the size of gaff sail. These late schooners had four, five or six masts, greatly increasing the amount of canvas they could set, and unlike their European cousins with their square topsails, they were rigged entirely fore-and-aft. The optimum was the four-masted vessel.

One of many such schooners built on the Kennebec River in Maine, from a model rather than from plans, *Downs* had the elegance of a yacht. Her construction was of such high quality that she outlasted most of her contemporaries and more than repaid the $55,000 she had cost her first owners, the Benedict-Manson Marine Company of New Haven, Connecticut. With a capacity of 1200 tons of coal or 600,000ft (18,288m) of timber, she served them for eight years, until she was sold – at a profit – to her master. He disposed of her to Danish owners who renamed her *Atlas*. In 1923, under Finnish ownership, she entered the Anglo-Baltic timber trade before being sold to Estonian owners. During the Second World War the Germans found her laid up at Copenhagen, the Baltic being too heavily mined for sailing ship operations, and moved her to Kiel. She was finally broken up on the River Stör in 1950. *JH*

**The schooner *Bertha L. Downs*** (oil on canvas), Geoff Hunt, 1994

1861-1918

**194**  175.4ft x 37.1ft x 14.2ft (53.5m x 11.3m x 4.33m) • 716 tons [GRT] • Hull wood • Complement 8 • Built Edward W. Hyde, Bath, Maine, USA, 1908

# Emden  Light cruiser 1909

The graceful small cruiser *Emden*, built in the Kaiserliche Werft Danzig shipyard and commissioned on 10 July 1909, was one of the most successful commerce raiders of the twentieth century. Its construction marked the end of a technological era, as it was the last German warship to be equipped with reciprocating steam engines. By contrast, her sister *Dresden*, also a successful commerce raider, was given steam turbines.

In 1910 the *Emden* left European waters destined for service with the East Asia Squadron, based at the port of Tsingtao in northern China. Here she operated along Chinese rivers and patrolled Germany's disparate Pacific island possessions. Sensing the imminence of hostilities, Korvettenkapitän Karl von Müller took the *Emden* out of Tsingtao at the end of July 1914 to rendezvous with the rest of the squadron under Vice Admiral Maximilian von Spee in the Marianas. The *Emden* did not join Spee in his Pacific campaign, but was detached to wage commerce warfare in the Indian Ocean to distract Allied attention. She was able to take shipping by surprise and it was not until mid September that the Allies realised a commerce raider was operating in the area. In just under two months the *Emden* captured or destroyed 23 vessels, an old Russian cruiser and a French torpedo boat destroyer.

The strategic and economic disturbance was considerable, with troop convoys from Australia being temporarily suspended and a large number of Allied ships involved in hunting the *Emden*. In an audacious move Müller also bombarded the oil installations at Madras and later attacked the harbour at Penang. The *Emden* was finally brought to battle and sunk by the more powerful HMAS *Sydney* on 9 November in the Cocos Islands, where Müller had attempted to destroy a vital communications link across the Indian Ocean. *MF*

**The cruiser *Emden* off the Cocos Islands** *(photograph), 1914, Conway Picture Library*

388ft x 44.3ft x 18ft (53.5m x 11.3m x 4.33m) • 4268 tons [D] • Hull steel • Armament 10 x 10.5 cm (4.1in) rapid fire guns, two torpedo tubes • Complement 378-394 • Built Kaiserliche Werft, Danzig (now Gdańsk, Poland), 1909

# Neptune  Neptune class battleship 1909

Both in her appearance and in her technical characteristics *Neptune* typified the later 12in-gun dreadnoughts built for the Royal Navy. In a departure from HMS *Dreadnought* and her immediate predecessors, the wing turrets were disposed *en echelon*, which in theory permitted both turrets to fire on either broadside – although in practice this was possible through only very limited arcs. In order to minimize the increase in hull length this implied, 'X' turret was superimposed above 'Y' as in contemporary U.S. Navy battleships; the upper turret was not, however, permitted to fire directly aft as the design of the turret hoods meant that the gunlayers in 'Y' turret would have been concussed.

*Neptune* was the first British dreadnought to have cruise turbines, adopted because the direct-drive turbines of the early dreadnoughts had high coal consumption at lower speeds. When completed in early 1911 *Neptune* was considered the most powerful battleship in the Royal Navy, and in May she became flagship of the Home Fleet under Admiral Sir Francis Bridgeman. She was present at the Coronation Review of June 1911, and in the autumn of that year led the First Battle Squadron out of Portsmouth to give a send-off to the liner *Medina*, in which King George V and Queen Mary embarked for the Delhi Durbar in India. She subsequently joined the First Battle Squadron, being present at the Battle of Jutland in 1916. *JJ*

*HMS **Neptune** (photograph), Library of Congress*

546ft x 85ft x 28ft (166m x 25.9m x 8.7m) • 19,700 tons [D] • Hull steel • Armament 10 x 12in, 16 x 4in, 3 x 18in torpedo tubes • Complement 760 • Built Portsmouth, England, 1909

# Terra Nova   Antarctic expedition barque 1909

Built for the Dundee whaling and sealing fleet, *Terra Nova* was ideally suited for service in the polar regions. She acted as a relief ship for the Jackson-Harmsworth Arctic Expedition from 1894 and later, in company with fellow Dundee whaler *Morning*, she sailed to Antarctica to assist in freeing Robert Falcon Scott's expedition ship *Discovery*, trapped in the ice in McMurdo Sound in 1903.

In 1909 she was purchased for Scott's new British Antarctic Expedition (which would soon be known popularly at the *Terra Nova* Expedition), and was reinforced from bow to stern with oak to help her withstand the crushing grip of the pack ice. Captain Scott described her as 'a wonderfully fine ice ship… as she bumped the floes with mighty shocks, crushing and grinding a way through some, twisting and turning to avoid others, she

seemed like a living thing fighting a great fight'. Iconic photographs of *Terra Nova* and her crew among challenging ice conditions would make the ship world famous.

After the fateful expedition, which saw the death of Scott and his four companions clawing their way back from the South Pole across the Ross Ice Shelf, *Terra Nova* was bought back by her former owners and returned to work in the Newfoundland seal fishery. In 1943 her stern was damaged by sea ice off the coast of Greenland. Though her crew were rescued by a US Coastguard patrol ship, *Terra Nova* eventually burst into flames. So she would not pose a hazard to Atlantic shipping, 22 rounds were fired into the 'burning derelict', and she slowly sank; a devastating end for one of the most famous polar expedition ships. *HLJ*

Geologist T.G. Taylor and meteorologist Charles Wright in the entrance to an ice grotto during Scott's *Terra Nova* Expedition to the Antarctic. The ship is in the background *(photograph)*. *Herbert Ponting, 5 January 1911, Scott Polar Research Institute, University of Cambridge/Getty Images*

187ft x 31.4ft x 19ft (57m x 9.6m x 5.8 m) • 764 tons [GRT] • Hull wood • Complement 65 • Built Alexander Stephen & Sons Ltd., Dundee, Scotland, 1884

# Friedrich der Grosse  Kaiser class battleship 1911

Launched some 16 months before her British counterpart *Iron Duke*, *Friedrich der Grosse* was the flagship of Admiral Reinhard Scheer, Commander in Chief of the German High Seas Fleet. Like most of her German contemporaries she was broader in the beam and more heavily armoured than the British dreadnoughts of the period, and retained the standard 12in gun in the face of an increase in gun calibre in the British super-dreadnoughts to 13.5in. German dreadnought battleships were generally ordered in classes of four and operated as a homogeneous division, but the five-ship Kaiser class was intended to provide a fleet flagship as well as a four-ship division. The design

of this class marked a break with the two previous classes, which had four of their six turrets on the beam amidships and particularly compact machinery spaces amidships. In contrast the Kaisers had superimposed turrets aft, and the midships pair of mountings were *en echelon*, the fore and after machinery spaces being widely separated to enable these mountings to fire across the beam. *Friedrich der Grosse* was the German flagship at Jutland, and led the fleet into internment at Scapa Flow in November 1918. She was scuttled, together with the remainder of the German ships at Scapa, in June 1919. *JJ*

*Friedrich der Grosse* at Scapa Flow during the German Fleet surrender to Admiral Beatty *(photograph), 21 November 1918, Getty Images*

565ft x 95ft x 30ft (172m x 29m x 9m) • 24,350 tons [D] • Armament 10 x 12in, 14 x 5.9in, 12 x 88mm (3.4in), 5 x 19.7in torpedo tubes • Complement 1250 •
Built A.G. Vulcan, Hamburg, Germany, 1911

# Iron Duke  Iron Duke class battleship 1912

The four 'super-dreadnoughts' of the Iron Duke class were the last British battleships to be armed with the 13.5in gun and the first to carry a heavy secondary battery of 6in guns for use against enemy torpedo-boats and light cruisers. The increase in calibre of the secondary guns was considered necessary to counter the improvement in range of the latest torpedoes. The 6in battery was in armoured casemates and required a 25ft increase in length compared to the previous class, but the aftermost guns were mounted so low that the ports were washed out in anything short of flat calm and the guns were subsequently removed. *Iron Duke* entered service in March 1914, and in August became the flagship of Admiral John Jellicoe, C-in-C Grand Fleet. She served in that capacity until 1917, taking part in the only major fleet action of the war, the Battle of Jutland, in May 1916. Together with her three sisters, *Iron Duke* continued in active service after the Washington Treaty of 1922, serving in the Mediterranean and the Atlantic. She was then disarmed, serving as a gunnery training ship throughout the 1930s and as a depot ship during the Second World War. Damaged by a German bombing raid in October 1939, she was beached and broken up in 1946. *JJ*

**HMS** *Iron Duke* (photograph), c. 1914, Conway Picture Library

# Lion   Lion class battlecruiser 1912

The first of four 'Splendid Cats', *Lion* epitomized the British battlecruiser of the First World War. Due to the limitations of the steam technology of the day she was huge – and hugely expensive. In comparison with her battleship contemporaries she had 2 per cent greater length and displacement, and 150 per cent greater power. The steam for her 27 knots had to be provided by no fewer than 42 Yarrow coal-burning boilers, and at speed she created such huge volumes of black smoke that care had to be taken with her heading in order not to hinder fire control. Her great size meant that only moderate protection could be provided, and much of her armour could be penetrated by German 11in shells. Following completion, *Lion* became the flagship of

the First Battlecruiser Squadron (under Rear-Admiral David Beatty), and subsequently became flagship of the newly created Battle Cruiser Force (BCF). *Lion* took part in most of the significant naval actions of the war, including Heligoland Bight in 1914 and Dogger Bank in 1915 (in which she was seriously damaged and had to be towed home). At Jutland she sustained 13 major shell hits from the German battlecruiser *Lützow*, and almost suffered the catastrophic fate of her half-sister *Queen Mary* when a hit on 'Q' turret resulted in a fire which all but ignited the central magazine. *Lion* was finally paid off under the Washington Treaty of 1922. *JJ*

**HMS *Lion*** *(photograph), Conway Picture Library*

700ft x 89ft x 28ft (213.5m x 27m x 8.5m) • 26,250 tons [D] • Hull steel • Armament 8 x 13.5in, 16 x 4in, 2 x 21in torpedo tubes • Complement 995 • Built Devonport, Plymouth, England, 1910

# Texas   New York class battleship 1912

*Texas* and her sister *New York* were were the first US Navy battleships to be armed with 14in guns. Like other American battleships of the period, they were slow, broad-beamed, heavily armoured ships and were fitted with distinctive cage masts fore and aft of two close-spaced funnels. Despite the adoption of steam turbines for the previous two classes, this class reverted to reciprocating turbines to give them sufficient endurance to make the transit from the West Coast to the Philippines. Both ships served with the American 6th Battle Squadron of the Grand Fleet 1917–18.

*New York* underwent a major modernization in 1925 during which she was converted to oil-burning, the cage masts were replaced by a heavy tripod,

and her fire control systems were upgraded. In 1939 she became flagship of the Atlantic Squadron. Following the neutrality patrols of 1939–41, she was assigned to Operation Torch in November 1942 in the fire support role. She was subsequently the Bombardment Force Flagship for Omaha Beach during Operation Overlord, the Allied landings in France, and also took on the German shore batteries at Cherbourg. In early 1945 she was transferred to the Pacific, where she provided fire support at Iwo Jima and Okinawa. She became a museum ship postwar, and is now housed in a purpose-built dry dock at San Jacinto, California. *JJ*

**USS *Texas* in New York Harbour** *(photograph), c. 1918, Schenectady Museum; Hall of Electrical History Foundation/Corbis*

573ft x 95.5ft x 28.5ft (175m x 29m x 8.5m) • 27,000 tons [D] • Hull steel • Armament 10 x 14in, 21 x 5in, 4 x 21in torpedo tubes • Complement 1040 • Built Newport News, Virginia, USA, 1912

# Titanic  White Star ocean liner 1912

Famous for all the wrong reasons, the maiden voyage of White Star liner RMS *Titanic* and the artefacts associated with the ship have continued to fascinate the public more than any other maritime disaster. In her dying hours on the night of 14–15 April 1912, the stricken liner sent many distress messages using her Marconi wireless apparatus, the recently developed equipment that had first been fitted to the liner *Kaiser Wilhelm der Grosse* in 1900. The illustration shows a message received by the White Star Line's *Baltic*, giving *Titanic*'s final position as 41°46'N, 50°14'W, when she hit the iceberg off Nova Scotia, and saying simply 'Sinking wants immediate assistance'. Ironically about ten hours earlier the *Baltic* had sent *Titanic* a message warning of icebergs in that vicinity. *Titanic* sank at about 2.20 a.m. with the loss of 1503 lives. A wireless message received by the Cunard liner *Carpathia*, 'Come at once we have struck an iceberg', led to that ship being first on the scene, about 3 hours later, when she rescued 705 survivors who were in *Titanic*'s boats. Both of the wireless operators aboard *Titanic* made it into a collapsible boat but one died of exposure before being rescued. In 1985 the wreck of the *Titanic* was found on the seabed, some 13.5 miles (21.7km) east-south-east of the last position reported by the ship. *PB*

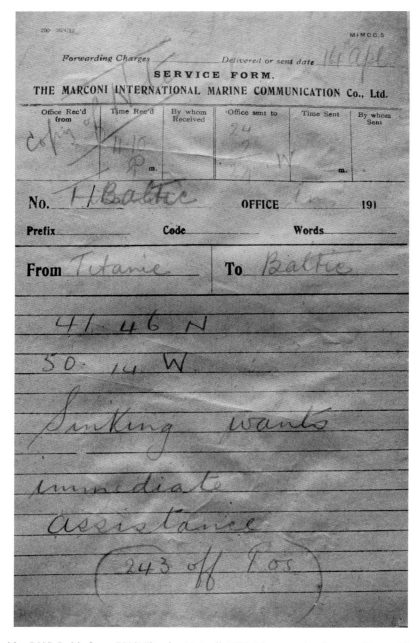

**Marconi wireless message received by RMS *Baltic* from RMS *Titanic*, 14 April 1912** *(photograph), Conway Picture Library*

883ft x 92.5ft x 34.6ft (26.91m x 28m x 10.5m) • 46,329 tons [GRT] • Hull steel • Complement 860, passengers 905 first class, 564 second class, 1134 third class • Built Harland & Wolff, Belfast, Northern Ireland, 1911

# Aquitania  Cunard ocean liner 1913

The bow of *Aquitania* towers above a quartet of bowler-hatted gentlemen at the John Brown Clydebank shipyard shortly before her launch in April 1913. With its dimensions expanded, cranes and other equipment modernised and surrounding buildings reconfigured through the years, this building berth and inclined slipway hosted virtually all of the largest and most famous Clyde-built ships. Seven years earlier *Lusitania* had been launched there. After Canadian Pacific's *Empress of Britain* was launched there in June 1930, hull no. 534 was laid down there in December that year. 534 languished silent and empty in this same berth, with her destiny in jeopardy from December the following year until April 1934 when Government loan guarantees could be secured and work finally resumed. No. 534 was launched as *Queen Mary* in September that year. *Queen Elizabeth* was launched from this same dock four years later, before her outfitting was completed and she made her secret maiden Atlantic crossing to New York in March 1949, where she was made ready for her six years of Wartime service as a troopship, before finally making her commercial maiden voyage in 1946.

The last great hull to occupy that famous building berth was no. 736, launched in September 1967 as Cunard's *Queen Elizabeth 2*. Her bows too were frequently photographed high above many of the same buildings, workshops and other structures that surrounded that birthplace of so many famous Clyde-built ships, both merchant and naval. The yard has since been closed and the properties it once occupied redeveloped for other purposes. Shipbuilding too has changed, with today's supertankers, bulk carriers, container vessels and cruise ships now being block-built in drydocks. Gone too is the heart-stopping thrill of the traditional launch, when, upon the shattering of a magnum of Champagne against the bows, upwards of 16,000 tons of steel would be sent thundering down the greased launching ways into the Clyde, to tumultuous cheers from the yard's amassed workforce. Such spectacles have generally replaced by naming ceremonies for cruise ships upon delivery to their home ports. *PD*

*Aquitania* **under construction by John Brown & Co. Ltd at Clydebank** *(photograph), Bedford Lemere & Co., 1913, National Maritime Museum, London (G10689)*

901ft x 97ft x 36ft (275.2m x 29.6m x 11m) • 45,647 tons [GRT] • Hull steel • Complement 972, passengers (as built) first class 618, second class 614, third class 1998 • Built John Brown & Co., Clydebank, Scotland, 1913

# Fuso  Fuso class battleship 1914

Even at a first glance, the battleship *Fuso* provides a statement of power and status of uniquely Japanese flavour. Laid down in 1912 in the navy's Kure shipyard, she represented Japan's response to the international naval race, a concentration of firepower of unmatched level. Intended to rival the American battleships *Texas* and *New York*, she mounted twelve 14in guns as opposed to the *Texas*'s ten; in terms of propulsion, her engines produced approximately 40 per cent more horsepower than her American counterparts, giving her a considerable advantage in speed.

Regardless of the unorthodox placement of six in-line turrets (two forward, two alternating with the funnels, and two aft), this ship of the line had the world's most powerful broadside until the Nagato class of battleships joined the fleet. As Japan played only a secondary role in the naval operations of the First World War, powerful battleships such *Fuso* had no opportunity to prove their destructive power, seeing no direct action. This picture captures the battleship after she underwent a major reconstruction in the early 1930s, together with her sister-ship, *Yamashiro*, and all other Japanese capital ships. Reflecting the Imperial Navy's obsessive quest for maintaining superiority in firepower and the ability to outrange its opponents, the *Fuso* was equipped with a complex 'director system' of fire control, eventually adopted by the Japanese navy for all its warships. The result was a very tall and top-heavy bridge superstructure that lent a distinctive 'pagoda' style to the ship's foremast.

The *Fuso* took part in some of the engagements of the Second World War, most notably as part of Admiral Shoji Nishimura's southern force in the Battle of the Leyte Gulf (23–26 October 1944). She sunk in a dramatic explosion that broke her in two during the action at Surigao Strait (25 October 1944), after the main magazines caught fire following torpedo hits. *AP*

**The Japanese battleship *Fuso*, post-1933 refit** *(photograph), Conway Picture Library*

672.5ft x 94.2ft x 28.5ft (205m x 28.7m x 8.7m) • 30,600 tons [D] • Hull steel • Armament (c. 1939) 12 x 14in, 16 x 6in, 8 x 5in DP, up to 95 x 1in AA guns, up to 10 x 0.52in AA machine guns • Complement 1272 • Built Kure Naval Shipyard, Hiroshima, Japan, 1914

# U-9 U-boat 1914

A heroes' welcome from the German Fleet greets *U-9* and her crew as they return to Wilhelmshaven on 24 September 1914. Kapitänleutnant Otto Weddigen salutes from the conning tower and crew members stand to attention on the deck in this drawing by *Titanic* survivor Professor Willy Stöwer which captures the euphoria of their arrival two days after sinking three 12,000-ton British cruisers with the loss of more than 1400 lives. They had proved just what this newest naval weapon could accomplish.

Nicknamed 'the live bait squadron', the old cruisers were vulnerable and unescorted, but *U-9* was also outdated: her paraffin engines emitted smoke and a tell-tale oily slick, and the pressure hull was so cramped that reloading the bow tubes meant stripping out two compartments. The crew cooked meals on deck using a paraffin stove because the galley oven always shorted out.

Kapitänleutnant Otto Weddigen had spotted his targets when he surfaced in the morning of 22 September: they were in slow procession and not even zigzagging. At 7.20 a.m. he lined up the middle ship and fired a single torpedo at HMS *Aboukir*. It exploded below the magazine and the cruiser sank rapidly, some 50 miles (80.5km) off Hoek van Holland. Before 8.00 a.m., the empty bow tube was reloaded and both tubes were fired at HMS *Hogue* which had come to rescue the survivors. After *Hogue* sank, Weddigen turned *U-9* and put two torpedoes into *Cressy*. By now his last torpedo had been loaded, and he used it to finish off *Cressy*.

Oberleutnant zur See Johannes Spieß had watched the sinkings through the periscope and later wrote: 'a horrifying scene unfolded. We ... tried to suppress the terrible impression of drowning men, fighting for their lives in the wreckage, clinging on to capsized lifeboats'. *JH*

**Postcard of sailors welcoming the U-boat *U-9* on its return to Wilhelmshaven, 23rd September 1914** *(lithograph), Willy Stöwer, Private Collection / The Bridgeman Art Library*

196.8ft x 19.6ft (57.4m x 6m) • 493 tons [D] • Hull steel • Armament 6 torpedoes (2 bow tubes; 2 stern tubes), 1 x 105mm deck gun • Complement 35 • Built Kaiserliche Werft, Danzig (Gdańsk, now Poland), 1908-1910

# Ajax  King George V class battleship 1915

By early 1914 the British had won the naval arms race with Germany. William Lionel Wyllie captured the mood and majesty of the occasion in 'Masters of the Sea', reflecting the urgent, potent identity of a nation obsessed with its navy and on the brink of war. Few artists ever captured the size, speed and power of a super-dreadnought with such skill, with just a hint of humanity to ensure that while the 13.5in guns of HMS *Ajax* and the size of her hull dominate the image, they remain under human direction.

Like the classical hero whose name she bore, *Ajax* emphasized size and strength over sophistication; her vestigial bridge hinted that something was missing at the top, but her flaws lay deeper, a veritable Achilles heel. Her sister-ship the *Audacious* would be sunk by a single mine in 1914, in full sight of a liner loaded with American tourists. Wyllie's carefully crafted image hid a flaw that left Admiral Sir John Jellicoe more concerned to save his fleet than to sink the enemy. At Jutland on 31 May 1916 he feared that torpedoes and mines, or rash subordinates, might lose the battle, the fleet and the Empire. If the reality of British power never quite matched up to the image, it was still enough to win the war at sea: by 1918 *Ajax* and her type were once again 'Masters of the Sea'. *ADL*

**Masters of the Seas** *(oil on canvas), William Lionel Wyllie, 1915, National Maritime Museum, London (BHC1467)*

598ft x 89ft x 27.5ft (182m x 27m x 8.4m) • 23,400 tons [D] • Hull steel • Armament 10 x 13.5in Mk V, 16 x BL 4in Mk VII, 4 x 3 pdr, 3 x 21in torpedo tubes • Complement 900 • Built Scotts, Greenock, Scotland, 1912

# Endurance Barquentine 1915

Arguably the most famous polar expedition ship, *Endurance* began her life as a Norwegian-built tourist vessel destined for Arctic cruises and hunting trips. One of her first owners was Adrien de Gerlache, captain of *Belgica*, the first ship to winter in Antarctica. Shortly after hearing news that the South Pole had been claimed for Norway by Roald Amundsen, Ernest Shackleton began planning the Imperial Trans-Antarctic Expedition, in his words, 'the last great Antarctic adventure'. He chose *Endurance* as his ship. Queen Alexandra visited her as she lay alongside in London, shortly before leaving London just as war broke. Shackleton offered to turn *Endurance* over to the navy, to assist with the war effort, but he was given the all clear to proceed.

*Endurance* entered the pack ice in December 1914, and navigated a maze of constantly shifting leads for some 1000 miles (1609.3km) until 19 January 1915, when she stuck fast, just 85 miles (136.8km) short of her intended landing site at Vahsel Bay on the Weddell Sea. The ship drifted at the mercy of the ice for nine months, but was so battered by it that Shackleton would write in October that 'she was doomed: no ship built by human hands could have withstood the strain'. All hands were ordered out on to the floe, taking off stores and supplies, adrift some 350 miles (563.3km) from land. On 21 November, as the ice began to thaw, *Endurance* eventually sank.

The crews made slow progress across the ice and, having taken to the ship's boats, finally staggered ashore on Elephant Island in April the following year. With five companions, Shackleton completed an epic navigation in the small whaleboat *James Caird* across 800 miles (1287.5km) of treacherous ocean, to reach the island of South Georgia and raise a rescue. *HLJ*

*Endurance* **frozen into the ice floe, Weddell Sea, Antarctica** (photograph), August 1915, National Maritime Museum, London (P00016)

144ft x 25ft x 16ft (43.9m x 7.5m x 4.7m) • 300 tons [GRT] • Hull reinforced wood • Complement 28 • Built Framnaes Mek Verstad, Sandefjord, Norway, 1912

# Blücher   Blücher class armoured cruiser 1915

The *Blücher* was laid down on 15 February 1907 at the Kaiserliche Werft Kiel shipyard in response to reports that the British were constructing a new, larger class of armoured cruiser. In common with all German warships of the era, the emphasis was placed on the vessel's defensive characteristics at the price of its speed and armament. Owing to a lack of intelligence on the British Invincible class that did not anticipate the revolutionary nature of the design and its 12in guns, the *Blücher* was equipped with a primary armament of 8.3in guns. This made the design obsolete before work even commenced. Within two years of being commissioned in October 1909 she was employed as a training vessel.

After the outbreak of the First World War the *Blücher* served briefly in the Baltic before being attached to Admiral Franz von Hipper's I Scouting Group in the North Sea with which she took part in the bombardment of English east coast towns in the autumn. On 24 January 1915 a British trap foiled a German attempt to ambush British light forces off the Dogger Bank. Slower than Hipper's battlecruisers the *Blücher*, at the rear of the German line, quickly came into range of superior British battlecruisers. As a running battle developed throughout the morning, to save his force Hipper was forced to abandon the *Blücher* as she increasingly sustained damage and lost speed. This allowed the British to concentrate the fire of four battlecruisers, as well as cruiser and destroyer attacks, on to the *Blücher*. Although her tough construction took considerable punishment, shortly after 1 p.m. she rolled over, remained briefly afloat, when this photograph was captured, before sinking. Of the crew, 792 died and 260, including the captain, Fregattenkapitän Alexander Erdman, were taken prisoner. *MF*

**SMS *Blücher*** sinks after receiving multiple hits from British warships at Dogger Bank on 25 January 1915 *(photograph), Conway Picture Library*

525.9ft x 79.6ft x 28.6ft (161.8m x 24.5m x 8.8m) • 17,500 tons [D] • Hull steel • Armament 12 x 8.2in, 8 x 6in, 16 x 8.8cm, 4 x 18in torpedo tubes • Complement 929 • Built Kaiserlicher Werft, Kiel, Germany, 1909

# Warspite Queen Elizabeth class battleship 1915

The battleship *Warspite* served with distinction in both World Wars. Completed in March 1915 as one of a revolutionary class of fast battleships armed with 15in guns and burning oil rather than coal, she and three of her sisters were with the 5th Battle Squadron at Jutland, where they provided invaluable support to the battlecruisers, particularly during the 'Run to the North' when they held off the powerful vanguard of the German High Seas Fleet. *Warspite* had a lucky escape when her steering gear jammed and she turned two full circles, but she survived the action and was subsequently repaired. She was completely rebuilt during 1934–7, when new machinery was fitted and she received a modern bridge structure and new AA guns with the latest fire control systems. During the Norwegian Campaign of April 1940 she played a major part in the Second Battle of Narvik, when in company with nine destroyers she entered the Narvik Fjord to finish off eight German destroyers that had survived the first battle. After three years as flagship of the Mediterranean fleet, she was hit by a German radio-controlled glide bomb and near-missed by a second in September 1943, while off Salerno. These caused extensive damage, but the ship was repaired in time to provide fire support during the Normandy landings and at Walcheren, after which she was retired. *JJ*

**HMS *Warspite* in the Mediterranean,** *(photograph), 10 June 1940, Alexandria, Egypt, Bettmann / Corbis*

646ft x 90.5ft x 29ft (197m x 27.5m x 8.5m) • 27,500 tons [D] • Hull steel • Armament 8 x 15in Mk I, 14 x 6in Mk XII, 2 x 3in AA, 4 x 3 pdr, 4 x 21in torpedo tubes • Complement 925 • Built Devonport, Plymouth, England, 1913

# Lusitania  Cunard ocean liner 1915

The chilling reality behind this seemingly benign photograph is that it is reputed to be the last picture ever taken of Cunard Line's *Lusitania* before she was torpedoed and sunk by a German U-boat at 2.10 p.m. on 8 May 1915. *Lusitania*, approaching Queenstown for a scheduled stop on her way home to Liverpool, was expected to arrive on that evening's tide. She had continued to run a monthly round trip to New York at reduced speed while many other liners were withdrawn from service during the War. As a precaution against attack, *Lusitania*'s name and port of registry were painted over and she flew no company or national flags. All watertight doors throughout the ship's lower decks were kept closed throughout the voyage, and as she approached the British Isles her lifeboats were swung out ready for immediate lowering if need be as an added safety precaution.

The single torpedo fired by German U-boat *U-20*, the last one aboard, struck a deadly blow to *Lusitania*, hitting the ship just below the waterline on her starboard side slightly aft of the bridge, causing an immense explosion in the vicinity of her boiler rooms. Still making headway, with her propellers turning, though out of control, the stricken ship immediately began to list, sinking in only 20 minutes with the loss of 1198 innocent lives, including 124 Americans. *Titanic* had foundered only three years earlier after grazing an iceberg off Cape Race during her maiden voyage in April 1912, taking the lives of some 1500 passengers and crew. Once again people on both sides of the Atlantic were caught up in shock, dismay and grief at the loss of loved ones on the high seas.

America's decision to enter the First World War against Germany and its allies in April 1917 was motivated largely by the belligerent sinkings by German U-boats of American merchant vessels and other ships carrying American citizens, particularly *Lusitania. PD*

**Probably the last picture ever taken of RMS *Lusitania*, 1915** *(photograph), Conway Picture Library*

787ft x 87ft x 33.6ft (26.5m x 10.2m x 239.9m) • 31,550 tons [GRT] • Hull steel • Complement 850, passengers 552 first class, 460 second class, 1186 third class • Built John Brown & Co., Clydebank, Scotland, 1906

# Arizona   Pennsylvania class battleship c. 1916

In many respects the most famous American warship of the Second World War, the spectacular loss of the battleship *Arizona* became a rallying cry for revenge against Imperial Japan for her surprise attack at Pearl Harbor, Hawaii. Launched in June 1915, this Pennsylvania class battlewagon was powerfully armed with twelve 14in guns, boasted improved underwater protection against contemporary torpedoes and could squeeze through the Panama Canal for operations in any 'Two-Ocean War'. On the morning of 7 December 1941, the *Arizona* was specially targeted by 'Kate' bombers from the Japanese aircraft-carrier *Hiryu*. Within minutes a 16in, 1763.7lb (800kg) armour-piercing shell modified as a bomb struck between the two forward gun turrets, penetrated the comparatively thinly armoured topdeck and

triggered an explosion in a gunpowder compartment used for her catapult planes – which instantly spread to the forward ammunition magazine. The results were catastrophic. Witnesses reported the sight of the *Arizona* lifting out of the water with the force of the blast, as she split in two and quickly sank. More than 1100 of the crew of 1400 perished; the lion's share of casualties suffered by the US Navy that day. In 1962 the remains of the battleship were designated a national memorial. What is left of *Arizona* contrasts sharply with the USS *Missouri* now permanently moored nearby: the former battleship initiated America's entry into the greatest war in history; the ending of which was signed on the deck of the latter. *HF*

USS *Arizona* passing out to sea under the Brooklyn Bridge on her first voyage since being put in commission *(photograph), 10 November 1916. Bettmann / Corbis*

608ft x 97.1ft x 28.10ft (185.4m x 29.6m x 8.8m) • 31,400 tons [D] • Hull steel • Armament 12 x 14in, 22 x 5in, 4 x 3in, 2 x 21in torpedo tubes • Complement 915 • Built New York Navy Yard, 1915

# Invincible Invincible class battlecruiser 1916

For a decade *Invincible*, the first battle cruiser was the poster-child of the Fisher revolution: she introduced the key components of the modern capital ship, all big gun armament, turbine propulsion and high speed. Like so much of Admiral John Fisher's best work, her true function was to deter war, not to fight: it was never intended that the proud boast of her name should be tested. Designed to secure British global communications against Russian and French cruisers, she proved the concept in spectacular style off the Falkland Islands on 8 December 1914, annihilating Admiral von Spee's German armoured cruisers in a one-sided battle.

Having secured the world ocean, *Invincible* came home to face the High Seas Fleet in the North Sea. In her next battle she would face altogether more formidable opponents, bigger and more heavily armoured German battlecruisers. At Jutland in 1916 Vice Admiral Sir Horace Hood's aggressive handling of *Invincible* and her two sisters shattered the German light cruiser screen, and inflicted mortal damage on leading German battlecruisers before a salvo of 12in shells hit amidships, exposing her thin armour and haphazard magazine procedures. The resulting explosion turned the ship into a pair of colossal steel memorials for the thousand men who had perished in an instant. In that moment it seemed that the legacy of the Fisher era and the reputation of the battlecruiser had been fatally damaged. In retrospect it was tragic but glorious. The next *Invincible* won another battle off the Falklands Islands in 1982. Hopefully Jacky Fisher would have approved. *ADL*

**The wreck of *Invincible*, approximately half an hour after the explosion that ripped her apart. The destroyer *Badger* approaches to pick up the few survivors** *(photograph), 31 May 1916, Conway Picture Library*

567ft x 78.5ft x 30ft (173m x 23.9m x 9.1m) • 17,530 tons [D] • Hull steel • Armament 4 x 2 BL 12in Mk X, 16 x 4in QF Mk III, 7 x Maxim guns, 5 x submerged 18in torpedo tubes • Complement 784 (up to 1000 in wartime) • Built Armstrong, Whitworth & Co., Newcastle-on-Tyne, 1908

# Paris French ocean liner 1916

*Paris* was a luxurious French ocean liner built in Saint-Nazaire for the Compagnie Générale Transatlantique (CGT), known as the French Line. Laid down in 1913 her launch was delayed until 1916, and because of the First World War she was not finally completed until 1921. *Paris* was the largest liner flying the French flag. Powered by oil-fired turbines (in place of the pre-war coal system) she was capable of 21 knots.

The vessel's interiors spurned earlier heavier Tudor, Jacobean and Baroque styles in favour of greater refinement and simplicity and she is especially remembered for her Art Nouveau and Art Deco features. The ship possessed some novel elements. In most of the first-class staterooms you would find square windows rather than the usual round portholes, and in a first-class cabin it was possible to use a private telephone. Service and accommodation were notable but all passengers who travelled on the French Line ships were hooked on the haute cuisine.

She sailed between France and the United States and during the Great Depression was also operated for cruising. On 18 April 1939 *Paris* caught fire while docked at Le Havre, where she capsized and sank. The French Line also owned the celebrated Art Deco masterpiece *Normandie* and for a while the capsized *Paris* prevented this super-liner from leaving dock. *Paris* was scrapped in 1947. *JT*

*Paris* **lying on her side at Le Havre after she caught fire and capsized on 19 April 1939** (*photograph*), *Central Press/Getty Images*

764ft x 85ft (233m x 26m) • 34,569 tons [GRT] • Hull steel • Complement 648, passengers 565 first class, 460 second class, 1100 third class • Built Penhoët, Saint Nazaire, France, 1916

# Aurora  Pallada class protected cruiser 1917

The Russian *Aurora* has the distinction of spearheading one of the most important political and social revolutions in modern world history. Laid down in 1897, this First Rate protected cruiser of the Pallada class managed to escape the annihilation of Imperial Russia's Second Pacific Squadron at the Battle of Tsushima (27–28 May, 1905) and was interned for the remainder of the Russo-Japanese War in Manila by the Americans.

With the outbreak of the First World War, *Aurora* operated in the Baltic and was undergoing repairs in Petrograd (St. Petersburg) at the end of 1916 when the military and political fortunes of Tsar Nicholas II had finally reached the point of no return. Many of *Aurora*'s sailors joined the February Revolution that deposed the Romanov dynasty; the mere presence of the cruiser within sight of the Winter Palace was enough to help convince police forces of the futility of opposing disaffected soldiers who had supported revolutionaries in the streets.

Lenin also recognized the vital strategic importance of *Aurora* as a floating fortress when he staged the October Revolution against the Provisional Government of Alexander Kerensky. On 25 October 1917 the largely Bolshevik crew commandeered the vessel and manoeuvred her to command the Nikolayevsky Bridge on the Neva River while Red forces mounted the final coup. During the Second World War, *Aurora* acted as an anti-aircraft platform during the Siege of Leningrad. She remains today as a museum-ship, permanently moored where she helped steer history. *HF*

**1861-1918**

LE CROISEUR *AURORE* BOMBARDANT LE PALAIS D'HIVER
*Reconstitution de CARREY, d'après des documents authentiques.*

**The cruiser *Aurora* bombarding the Winter Palace** *(colour lithograph), Georges Carrey, Private Collection / Archives Charmet / The Bridgeman Art Library*

416ft x 55ft x 24ft (126.8m x 16.8m x 7.3m) • 6731 tons [D] • Hull steel • Armament 8 x 6in, 24 x 75mm, 8 x 37mm, 3 x torpedo tubes • Complement 590 •
Built Admiralty Shipyard, St Petersburg, Russia, 1900

# Furious Modified Glorious class aircraft carrier 1917

Laid down as one of Admiral John Fisher's 'large light cruisers', *Furious* was to have been armed with single 18in guns fore and aft, but was completed with a short flying-off deck and hangar in place of the forward mounting. The aft 18in turret was then removed and replaced with a flying-on deck with a second hangar beneath. This arrangement proved unsatisfactory, and following the Washington Conference *Furious* was taken in hand for a more radical reconstruction as a fully fledged aircraft carrier. A two-tier hangar was built atop the original hull. The upper hangar exited on to a short flying-off deck over the bow, which was used by fighters. Above it there was a three-quarter length unobstructed flight deck served by two cruciform lifts. The

ship was conned from a streamlined bridge at the forward end of the flight deck, to starboard, with a similar flying control position to port. The exhaust gases from the boilers were led aft in horizontal smoke ducts which vented at the stern. This proved to be a most unsatisfactory arrangement due to the heat generated in the after part of the ship. In 1939 a small island superstructure was provided, and the ship was rearmed with six twin 4in high-angle mountings and three eight-barrelled pompoms. Although obsolescent, *Furious* gave useful service in the Second World War, taking part in Operation Pedestal for the resupply of Malta in 1942 and in attacks on the German battleship *Tirpitz* in 1943. *JJ*

**The First Deck Landing** *(gouache on paper). Wilfred Hardy, twentieth century. Private Collection / Look and Learn / The Bridgeman Art Library*

786ft x 90ft x 28ft (224m x 27.5m x 8.6m) • 22,450 tons [D] • Hull steel • Armament (1925) 36 aircraft; 10 x 5.5in, 2 x 4in, 4 x 2 pdr • Complement 1218 • Built Armstrong, Elswick, England, 1916

# Australia  Indefatigable class battlecruiser 1918

The Indefatigable class battlecruiser HMAS *Australia* was built as the first flagship of the newly formed Royal Australian Navy. After completion she embarked on a tour of Australian ports, but following the outbreak of the First World War she served as a flagship, moving from the North America and West Indies Station to the Pacific, to respond to any threat posed by Vice-Admiral von Spee's squadron. In 1916 she became the flagship of the Second Battlecruiser Squadron, missing the Battle of Jutland through damage sustained in a collision with HMNZS *New Zealand*.

During 1918 Australia became closely involved in the development of naval aviation. Its Royal Navy was experimenting with the launch of single-seater biplanes such as the Sopwith Pup from a platform erected on the gun turrets of capital ships and extending over the barrels. Instead of the ship having to turn into the wind to allow the aircraft to take off, the turret could be turned into the wind. On 7 March 1918 aboard *Australia* the future Air Marshal Sir [David] Grahame Donald became the first to fly a two-seater Sopwith Ship Strutter reconnaissance plane from the ramp on Q turret. The photograph below was taken the following day, showing Flight Sub-Lieutenant Simonson flying off into a stiff wind, with a boat standing by in case the Strutter ditched on take-off. The ship in the background is the third of the Indefatigable class, HMNZS *New Zealand*. On 4 April Flight Commander Cox successfully took off carrying an observer and wireless gear for the first time. With no landing-on facilities, planes could only land ashore or, if fitted with flotation gear, ditch in the sea.

*Australia* returned to Australia in 1919, but was scuttled off Sydney Heads in 1922 as a consequence of the Washington Disarmament Treaty signed earlier that year. *JH*

**A Sopwith 1½ Strutter takes off from a platform fixed to 'Q' turret of HMS *Australia*, 8 March 1918** *(photograph), Conway Picture Library*

590ft x 80ft x 26.6ft  (179.8m x 24.4m x 8.1m) • 18,500 tons [D] Hull steel • Armament: 8 x 12in Mk X, 16 x 4in Mk VII, 4 x 3 pdr, 3 x 18in torpedo tubes • Complement 800 • Built John Brown & Co., Clydebank, Scotland, 1913

# Coastal Motor Boat  Motor torpedo boat c.1918

The British Coastal Motor Boats (C.M.B.s) of the First World War were intended to penetrate German naval bases in the North Sea and torpedo ships at anchor, using their high speed for surprise and their shallow draught to pass over defensive minefields. The hull was a stepped planing type, and the single 18in torpedo, carried not in a tube but in a trough in the stern, was launched tail-first. The only other armament comprised Lewis 0.303in machine guns, although there was provision for carrying mines and depth charges in place of the torpedo. Their powerful, lightweight petrol engines gave them a speed in excess of 30 knots even when fully loaded, and sufficient fuel was carried to give a considerable radius of action.

The C.M.B.s were designed by Thornycroft, who had considerable experience in designing and building small fast boats. In 1917 the early 40ft boats were superseded by an enlarged 55ft (17m) variant that could carry one or two torpedoes. The C.M.B.s were used extensively in the raids on the Belgian coast in 1917; at Zeebrugge a force of C.M.B.s attacked German destroyers, sinking one of their number. In 1919 they were deployed to the Baltic and Caspian Seas against the Bolsheviks. In June of that year two C.M.B.s attacked the Baltic base of Kronstàdt and sank the Soviet cruiser *Oleg*. In August, a larger combined operation with aircraft managed to sink a depot ship and damage two battleships. *JJ*

**55ft Coastal Motor Boat 65A at speed, c. 1918** *(photograph), Conway Picture Library*

60ft x 11ft x 3ft (18.3m x 3.4m x 0.9m) • 11 tons • Hull wood • Armament: 1/2 x 18in (457mm) torpedo tubes or four depth charges, 4 Lewis MG • Complement 3-5 • Built various locations (65A, pictured, built at Thornycroft, Hampton, England, 1918)

# MAS   Motor torpedo boat 1918

At dawn on 10 June 1918 off the Dalmatian island of Premuda, MAS 15 and 21 under the command of a young officer of Sicilian origins, Lieutenant Commander Luigi Rizzo, engaged an Austrian squadron of nine warships led by the dreadnoughts *Szent István* and *Tegetthoff*. In a 'David versus Goliath' action, the small Italian torpedo boats closed in on the enemy, launched their torpedoes and within minutes mortally wounded one of the larger, slower dreadnoughts. By the time Lt. Cdr. Rizzo and his MAS 15 returned to his base in Venice, the centre piece of the Italian 'mosquito fleet' (the nickname of the Regia Marina's fast coastal forces), had entered the Italian Olympus of national heroism.

The MAS (*Motobarca Armata Silurante*) was originally developed from an idea by the navy's Chief of Staff Paolo Thaon di Revel, who drew inspiration from the motor boats produced by the Società Veneziana Automobili Navali (SVAN), operating in the Venetian lagoon. After a series of unsuccessful tests,

in 1915 the first two torpedo boats joined the fleet, to be followed shortly after in 1916 by other enhanced units.

In the First World War, the MAS proved an invaluable asset in the waters of the Adriatic Sea, when handled by crews combining seamanship and initiative. In this respect, these small vessels had a distinctive Italian character, highlighting the traits of the individuals manning them. This painting of Rizzo's action at Premuda captures the nation's pride in one of the most celebrated encounters of the war. Famous Italian poet and novelist Gabriele D'Annunzio crystallized the heroism of the crews of fast coastal forces by using the term MAS as reference for the acronym of the Latin saying 'Memento audere semper' (Remember always to dare). Today, the MAS 15 rests in the inner chapel of the Vittoriano in Rome, while the Italian Navy adopted 10 June as its day of celebration. *AP*

**L'affondamento della corazzata** *Szent Istvan*, **10 Giugno 1918** *(oil on canvas), Rudolf Claudus, c. 1920, courtesy of the Ufficio Storico della Marina Militare, Rome, Italy*

52.5ft x 8.6ft x 3.9ft (16m x 2.6m x 1.2m) • 12.3 tons [D] • Hull wood • Armament 2 x 17.7in torpedo tubes, 2-3 x 6.5mm (0.25in) • Complement 8 • Built SVAN, Venice, Italy, 1916

# Rewa Hospital ship 1918

HMHS (His Majesty's Hospital Ship) *Rewa* was a steamship launched on 14 February 1906 and built by William Denny & Bros for the British India Steam Navigation Company. During the First World War she was requisitioned as a British hospital ship and was torpedoed by a German U-boat (*U-55*) on 4 January 1918 at Hartland Point, off the North Cornish coast. She was returning from Malta with around 550 men (including 279 wounded officers) aboard. Fortunately almost everyone apart from several engine men were rescued. The ship's personnel details indicated in David Wilson's poster (700 men) have been exaggerated for propaganda effect.

Frustrated by the convoy system of Allied navies, German U-boats adopted the strategy of 'total war' in a desperate effort to win the war. Hospital ships were unarmed, painted white with a green band around the hull and large red crosses that were highly visible durng the day and illuminated at night. To avoid conviction the captain of *U-55* wrote in his ship's log that he had sunk a cargo vessel.

David Wilson was remembered by the influential English artist William Roberts who met him in the studio of Sir Joseph Causton's company in 1910, which was 'a firm of law stationers, producers of posters and other kinds of commercial art. Their offices were in Eastcheap, near the Billingsgate fish market.' Roberts described Wilson as 'the star of the studio… a tall middle-aged Scotsman… well-known as a freelance illustrator and cartoonist [who] … seemed much concerned with his family troubles'.

Wilson produced several hard-hitting home-front and service propaganda posters highlighting the atrocities of the Germans during the First World War several involving U-boats and the Red Cross, others featuring the cruelty inflicted upon captured servicemen who were deprived of medical services, food and water. He also produced work for the London Underground in the 1920s. *JT*

**What a red rag is to a bull – The Red Cross is to the Hun** *(colour lithographic poster), Art Archive / Eileen Tweedy*

456ft x 56.2ft x 30ft (139m x 17.1m x 9.1m) • 7308 tons [GRT] • Hull steel • Complement 550 approx. • Built William Denny & Brothers, Dumbarton, Scotland, 1906

# Hermes   Aircraft carrier 1919

In 1917 the Royal Navy, the largest and most successful naval air arm of the age, used the hard won experience of the First World War to design and build the world's first purpose-built aircraft carrier. *Hermes* reflected the uncertain, experimental era in which she was built. Initially designed to carry seaplanes she was modified for wheeled aircraft during construction. Combining the power plant and guns of a contemporary light cruiser with hangar storage and an axial flight deck – cleared for landing by shifting the superstructure and funnel to the starboard side – *Hermes* had everything but size. After 1918 the Royal Navy, with several converted ships in hand, slowed construction, only completing the ship in 1924. In the meantime the Japanese *Hosho* became the first purpose-built carrier to enter service. That said, *Hermes*

proved to be a better ship. She provided the Royal Navy and the Royal Air Force squadrons that operated at sea (before the Fleet Air Arm was revived in 1937) with an excellent training platform. By 1939 *Hermes'* small size and limited aircraft capacity rendered her obsolete. When war broke out she was deployed on the broad oceans to hunt raiders, not with the battle fleet. Ironically she became the first carrier to be sunk by other carriers. Caught at sea off Sri Lanka she was shattered by 40 hits scored by dive bombers from the *Kido Butai*, the pioneering Japanese carrier task force that had already savaged Pearl Harbor. The Japanese *Akagi* alone was four times bigger, and carried eight times as many planes. *ADL*

**HMS *Hermes* in 1938** *(photograph), Conway Picture Library*

598ft x 70ft x 19ft (182.3m x 21.4m x 5.7m) • 10,850 tons [D] • Hull steel • Armament up to 20 aircraft, 6 x 5.5in, 3 x 4in AA • Complement 664 (excluding aircrew) • Built W. G. Armstrong-Whitworth and Company, High Walker, Tyne, England, 1919

# Hood   Admiral class battlecruiser 1919

When completed in 1920 *Hood* was by some way the largest and fastest capital ship in the world, and would remain so during the interwar period due to Washington Treaty restrictions on displacement. Three sister-ships were cancelled. Initially designed as a comparatively lightly armoured battlecruiser, *Hood* was redesigned in the aftermath of the Battle of Jutland with protection comparable to that of the Queen Elizabeth class battleships. She was given a raked bow and a hull with pronounced flare and sheer, a deep anti-torpedo bulge, and had the secondary battery at forecastle deck level, where it could be worked even in heavy seas. However, the ship had 'pre-Jutland' horizontal protection, with multiple thin decks intended to resist shell splinters rather than plunging heavy shell.

Although *Hood* remained the most prestigious unit of the Royal Navy throughout the interwar period, it was recognised by the late 1930s that she was overweight and in desperate need of modernization. A refit similar to that of the battlecruiser *Renown* was envisaged but was preempted by the outbreak of war. *Hood* served with distinction with the Home Fleet and Force H during 1939–41, and was Admiral Somerville's flagship at Mers el-Kebir, but when despatched with the new battleship *Prince of Wales* to intercept the German *Bismarck* in May 1941 she was lost to a catastrophic magazine explosion; only three members of her crew survived. *JJ*

HMS *Hood* seen from between two of HMS *Rodney*'s 16in guns as she returned from the Mediterranean *(photograph), Lt. R.G.G. Coote, 1940, Imperial War Museum (A 111)*

860ft x 104ft x 28.5ft (262m x 31.5m x 8.5m) • 42,500 tons [D] • Hull steel • Armament 8 x 15in Mk I, 12 x 5.5in BL Mk I, 4 x 4in QF Mk V AA, 4 x 3 pdr, 6 x 21in torpedo tubes • Complement 1477 • Built John Brown & Co., Clydebank, Scotland, 1918

# Nagato   Nagato class battleship 1919

In the first three decades of the twentieth century, Japanese warships featured designs with technological solutions of great sophistication, which combined the need to meet specific operational requirements with a unique look. The imposing 'pagoda' masts of Japanese capital ships were their most distinct feature. Some of these warships came to reflect the ascendancy of the Japanese nation to the world stage and its dramatic downfall at the end of the Second World War more than others.

The battleship *Nagato* was such a case. Designed in 1917 by one of Japan's most famous and controversial naval architects, Yuzuru Hiraga, she was the first warship to include the lessons learned from the Battle of Jutland in terms of main armament, displacement, speed and distribution of weight. She was modern and powerful, mounting only eight of the heavier and more powerful 16in guns, with the armour concentrated around the ship's more vital parts, below the waterline. Equipped with 15 oil-fired and 6 mixed-fired boilers, she reflected the Japanese Navy's progressive conversion to oil and constant efforts to keep abreast of innovations. The *Nagato* served as the flagship of the Combined Fleet until the gargantuan *Yamato* was commissioned and for years she was an iconic symbol of the might of Japan's naval power. As one of the centrepieces of the country's first line of defence, she took part in all main naval actions of the Second World War until in November 1944 she returned to Yokosuka for major repairs. Lack of fuel and materials prevented her from resuming active service.

At the end of the war, the *Nagato* was Japan's last surviving battleship and in July 1946 she was included among the ships to be used in the atomic bomb tests in Bikini Atoll. In the post-war era, her story was popularized in a multi-volume series by famous novelist Hiroyuki Agawa. Through his narrative, the *Nagato* ceased to be just a warship; she became a metaphor of Japan's experience in peace and war. *AP*

**Nagato** *(glass negative), date and photographer unknown, Library of Congress*

705.3ft x 95ft x 32.3ft (215.8m x 29m x 9.8m) • 32,720 tons [D] • Hull steel • Armament 8 x 16.1in, 20 x 5.5in, 8 x 3.14in, 8 x 21in torpedo tubes • Complement 1333 • Built Kure Naval Shipyards, Hiroshima, Japan, 1919

1919-1946

# Felucca   Nile trader c.1920

In many minds, the wooden felucca with its Nubian captain in his long white jellaba is inseparable from the River Nile, a link between the present and the Egypt of Tutankhamun, or a way for tourists to relax and view the temples and pyramids as they pass slowly by. In fact, the felucca is nothing like the boats that plied the Nile in ancient times. It was introduced by the Arabs much later, and it also existed for centuries in many parts of the Mediterranean – the word itself is Italian, derived from the Arabic.

With their shallow draught and broad beam, feluccas are still used to transport cargoes up and down the Nile, and the vessel shown is a traditional commercial boat. It can journey up-river relying on the prevailing wind, travelling downriver with the current. The huge lateen sail, made from panels of locally woven cotton is tied along its hypotenuse to two poles that have been lashed together to form a single yard, longer than the boat itself and carried obliquely. A second, much smaller sail, set on a shorter mast, is also common, and the boat is steered by a tiller. It can be handled by a single person or by a crew of two or three. *JH*

**Gaiassa on the River Nile, Egypt** *(photograph), c. 1925, Waterline Collection, National Maritime Museum, London (P93837)*

No data available

# Dhow Arabian vessel c.1920

The dhow is a term that westerners have given to traditional Arab sailing vessels. These ships have been in use since the Greeks, and their design has changed little over the centuries. Dhows have several distinguishing characteristics. One of these is a lateen sail arrangement. Another is that, traditionally, the hull is stitched together. Classic dhows were pointed at both ends, although many modern dhows have square-shaped sterns, larger stems and ornately carved transoms – from the deep-sea baghlah, to the shallow-draught badan, the large sambuq, and the common, medium-sized shu'ai.

The modern dhow has several different uses. Originally, they were used for simple tasks such as offshore fishing. As the Arabian and Islamic population grew and expanded, with an energetic mercantile system connecting with the rest of the known world, dhows were adapted for voyaging and trade – laden with oils, dates, perhaps even mangrove timbers or slaves. Even to the present day, dhows make long journeys between the Persian Gulf and the East African coast, often using sails as their only means of propulsion. *HLJ*

1919-1946

**An Arabic boum off the coast of Kuwait,** *(photograph), Alan Villiers, 1938-1939, National Maritime Museum, London (PM5019)*

# Garthsnaid Three-masted barque 1920

Even in peacetime the sea has always been a hazardous workplace and never more so than in the days of sail, whether merchant or naval ship. The four crewmen furling sail in heavy weather on the *Garthsnaid* (ex-*Inversnaid*) off Chile in 1920, have a footrope to assist them, attached at intervals along the yard by short lengths of rope known as stirrups. Before the middle of the seventeenth century, at the earliest, they would have had to run along the yard with nothing to save them in the event of a slip. As it was, men working aloft had to contend with the pitching and rolling of the ship, as described by the narrator of Jack London's 1904 novel *The Sea Wolf*. 'Sometimes she would lift and send across some great wave, burying her starboard rail from view,

and covering her deck to the hatches with the boiling ocean. At such moments, starting from a windward roll, I would go flying through the air with dizzying swiftness, as though I clung to the end of a huge, inverted pendulum, the arc of which, between the greater rolls, must have been 70 feet or more. Once, the terror of this giddy sweep overpowered me, and for a while I clung on, hand and foot, weak and trembling…'.

Bad weather was to end the career of Montreal-registered *Garthsnaid* in 1922. Dismasted in bad weather on a voyage from Iquique to Melbourne, she was fortunately found by the Shaw Savill liner *Zealandic* which managed to take her in tow. On arrival at Melbourne she was condemned. *JH*

*Garthsnaid* in a heavy sea, hands securing foresail, during a passage from Iquique to Delagoa Bay in 1920 *(photograph), Conway Picture Library*

238ft x 36.2ft x 21.7ft (72.5m x 11m x 6.6m) • 1319 tons [GRT] • Hull steel • Complement 23 • Built A. McMillan and Son, Dumbarton, Scotland, 1892

# Birkdale  Barque 1922

On 22 April 1920, the marine artist John Everett sailed from Bristol for Texas as third mate on the barque *Birkdale*. The voyage resulted in many innovative paintings, unusual at the time for their challenging sense of composition, inspired by his adventurous photographs. Everett had a modest independent income, and neither sought nor achieved fame or recognition during his lifetime. He sold very few of his remarkable seascapes and dynamic ship portraits and at his death, in London in 1949, he bequeathed the majority of his work (including some 1000 oil paintings and more than 2000 prints and drawings) to the National Maritime Museum in Greenwich, London.

The *Birkdale*, built in 1892, spent nearly all her working life in the Chilean nitrate trade. For a short while after the First World War she switched to other cargoes. During the voyage in 1920 she was due to take sulphur from Sabine Pass, Texas, to Cape Horn, but on arrival was re-chartered to Australia. Everett left her reluctantly and came home by steamer. *Birkdale* returned to the nitrate trade but was wrecked on the Chilean coast after catching fire in 1927. *HLJ*

The barque *Birkdale*, **view aft from the bowsprit** *(oil on canvas)*, Herbert Barnard John Everett, 1922, National Maritime Museum, London *(BHC4126)*

# Gamble   Wickes class flush deck destroyer 1922

Between 1917 and 1922, 273 four-funnelled destroyers popularly known as 'flush-deckers' were built for the US Navy in three classes: 11 shipyards participated in the programme. Built for the First World War, there was little immediate need for these ships after 1918 and many of them were laid up after only brief service. Fourteen ships were converted as fast minelayers in July 1920, with their torpedo tubes removed. These were later scrapped and replaced by eight further converted 'flush-deckers', of which *Gamble* was one (reclassified DM-15 after conversion in 1930). All eight of these active destroyer-minelayers were present at Pearl Harbor when the Japanese attacked on 7 December 1941.

Their ensuing careers in the Pacific War were eventful, with mining operations commencing in 1942 in the Solomon and Aleutian Islands. On 29 August 1942 *Gamble* became the first US destroyer to sink a Japanese fleet submarine, the *I-123*, using depth charges. She subsequently took part in minelaying operations off Kolombangara which resulted in the sinking of three Japanese destroyers belonging to the island resupply force – known as the 'Tokyo Express'.

*Gamble*'s luck finally ran out when she was seriously damaged in an air attack off Iwo Jima on 18 February 1945 while screening the battleship *Nevada*. Towed to the Marianas, she was scuttled off Guam. *JJ*

Wickes class destroyers laid up in San Diego harbour, California. USS *Gamble* is DD-123, front row, third from right *(photograph), late 1922, Conway Picture Library*

314ft x 31ft x 9ft (96m x 9.4m x 2.8m) • 11,090 tons • Hull steel • Armament (as minelayer) 4 x 4in, 1 x 3in, 80 mines • Complement 114 • Built Newport News, Virginia, USA, 1918

# Albert Ballin  Hamburg America ocean liner c.1923

The Hamburg Amerikanische Packetfahrt Actien Gesellschaft, or HAPAG for short, is usually referred to in English as the Hamburg America Line and was a transatlantic shipping enterprise established in Hamburg, Germany in 1847. It developed into the largest German, and for a time one of the world's largest, shipping companies, cashing in on the huge demand for the movement of German immigrants to the United States. On 1 September 1970 HAPAG ceased to be an independent company when it merged with the Bremen-based North German Lloyd to form Hapag-Lloyd AG.

Koeke's poster personifies the Art Deco style of the 1920s and 1930s. The two-funnelled ships pictured here are a group of four all built at the Blohm & Voss yard in Hamburg: *Albert Ballin* (1923), *Deutschland* (1923), *Hamburg* (1926) and the *New York* (1926). The *Albert Ballin* was originally built as a 16 knot ship – named after the visionary founder of the company, who enjoyed the support of Kaiser Wilhelm I. The Kaiser was the first to hire celebrated interior designers and chefs de cuisine for his vessels.

Little biographical information is known about Koeke but he was a follower of Adolphe Mouron Cassandra, the influential Ukrainian-French painter, commercial poster artist and typeface designer. *JT*

Hamburg-Amerika Linie to New York *(colour lithographic poster), Henning Koeke, 1930, Swim ink / Corbis*

602.4ft x 78.7ft (183.6m x 23.9m) • 20,815 tons [GRT] • Hull steel • Complement 1650 • Built Blohm & Voss, Hamburg, Germany, 1922

**1919-1946**

# Jääkarhu  Icebreaker 1926

The *Jääkarhu* (Polar Bear), built in Rotterdam in 1926, was the last Finnish steam icebreaker. Unusually the ship was fitted with three propellers, two in the stern and one in the bow, providing an aggregate power output of 9200hp. Her eight steam boilers were oil fired, considerably enlarging her effective radius of operation compared to conventional coal-fuelled ships.

In severe winters ice covers the whole of the Gulf of Finland. Historically, the freezing of the Baltic waters from November or December each year paralyzed shipping, and the closure of the sea routes was a major disadvantage to the trade of Finland. The commission of *Jääkarhu* meant that the sailing period for fishermen from several Finnish harbours could be extended until January. The task of rescuing fishermen from floating ice was an interruption to the daily winter chores of the Finnish icebreakers. Indeed, the most extensive rescue operation ever recorded was undertaken by *Jääkarhu* in March 1932. In just one trip she collected 550 men and 40 horses from ice floes drifting in the eastern part of the Gulf of Finland.

During the Second World War *Jääkarhu* was often the target of enemy bombing expeditions as she assisted ships loaded with provisions and military material into Finnish harbours. She came through the war without major damage, only a few bullet holes in funnels and superstructure. After the end of hostilities in 1945 she had to be surrendered to the Soviet Union by way of compensation. She was renamed the *Sibirjakov* on entering Russian service. Her familiar shape often appeared in the southern parts of the Gulf of Finland, as she assisted ships heading to or from Leningrad. She was still sailing in early 1972, but later in the year she was taken to Italy and scrapped in La Spezia. *SL*

*Jääkarhu, Hjelmaren, Gertrud* and *Huxter* ner Utö (*gouache on canvas*), Adolf Bock, 1926, John Nurminen Foundation, Helsinki

257.5ft x 63ft x 21ft (78.5m x 19.3m x 6.4m) • 4825 tons [D] • Hull steel • Armament (wartime) 4 x 102mm Obuhov, 2 x 40mm Vickers MG • Built Machinefabriek en Sheepswerf van P. Smit, Jr., Rotterdam, Netherlands, 1926

# Delta Queen  Stern-wheel paddle steamer 1926

Perhaps the most famous of all American steamboats, *Delta Queen* was in fact built by William Denny & Sons, the famous Clyde shipbuilders. Ordered by the California Transportation Co. in 1924, her hull, lower decks and some of her machinery were constructed at Dennys yard in Dumbarton, using removable bolts rather than rivets, before being shipped across the Atlantic in pieces to be reassembled by the CN&L shipyard in Stockton, California. *Delta Queen* and her sister-ship *Delta King* were completed in 1927 and began overnight passenger service between San Francisco and Sacramento.

In 1946, having seen wartime service as a troop carrier in San Francisco Bay, she was bought by Greene Lines and towed to Mississippi for service on the Western Rivers. Plying the cargo and passenger trade throughout the region, she regularly steamed west to Omaha, Nebraska, south to New Orleans, north to Stillwater, Minnesota, and east to Charleston, West Virginia, and Knoxville, Tennessee. Luxuriously appointed and exuding a unique glamour, she was a much-loved sight on the Mississippi and its tributaries and became an important part of the cultural and historical heritage of these regions.

Despite changing ownership numerous times, *Delta Queen* continued working throughout the 1960s and 70s. Her significance was acknowledged when she was awarded a presidential exemption from the 1971 maritime safety law that prohibited the operation of overnight passenger vessels with wooden superstructures. Indeed, President Jimmy Carter cruised on board in 1979, as did a Royal party that included Princess Margaret in 1986. In 1989 she was designated a National Historic Landmark, testament to the enduring appeal of this long-serving Southern belle. She was finally withdrawn from service in 2008 and is now a floating hotel, permanently moored at Chattanooga, Tennessee. *MJ*

The *Delta Queen* Steam Boat *(oil on canvas), Paul Anthony John Wright, twentieth century, Private Collection / Gavin Graham Gallery, London, UK / The Bridgeman Art Library*

285ft x 58ft x 11.5ft (86.9m x 17.7m x 3.5m) • 1650 tons [GRT] • Hull steel • Complement 200 • Built Stockton, California, USA, 1926

# Yankee J class yacht 1930

The iconic J-class of the 1930s were large, extravagant and wildly expensive racing yachts built to compete for the prestigious America's Cup. The class developed from Nathanael Herreshoff's Universal Rule, which used a yacht's dimensions to calculate an equivalent rating in feet. The rule enabled boats of equal rating to race against each other directly in head-to-head contests. J-Class yachts were the largest boats constructed under the Universal Rule, and the first America's Cup yachts to be governed by such regulations.

The new criteria meant that considerable sums of money were spent on purpose-built J-class yachts in preparation for the 1930 America's Cup match. *Yankee* was designed by Frank Paine and built by the Boston shipbuilder George Lawly and Son, just one of four American yachts constructed that year to defend the cup from British tea magnate Sir Thomas Lipton's challenger, *Shamrock V*. *Yankee* proved to be an excellent all-rounder. Solid, well-balanced and very distinctive, she was an elegant and powerful contender. However, she was not as finely tuned as some of her US rivals, and thus was not selected to compete against *Shamrock V*. That honour went instead to the *Enterprise* – which proved to be an inspired choice, as she beat *Shamrock V* in the 1930 series 4-0.

*Yankee* never did represent USA in the America's Cup, despite being a strong contender once again in 1934 and 1937, after her rig was altered to carry more sail, and her bow had been lengthened and reshaped. She was a frequent participant in other races on both sides of the Atlantic, however, and was regularly seen at Falmouth and Cowes.

In 1941, as Europe was engulfed in war, *Yankee* was sold. The May 1941 edition of *Yachting Monthly* applauded owner Mr Gerard Lambert 'for his thoughtful act in selling his J-Class *Yankee* and giving the proceeds of about £2,500 to Lord Queensborough, Commodore of the Royal Thames Y.C., towards buying a Spitfire fighter plane.' *MJ*

Crew members on the deck of the *Yankee* as she leans to port during the New York Yacht Club cruise *(photograph), Edwin Levick, August 1936.* © *The Mariners' Museum/Corbis*

125ft x 22.6ft x 14.6ft (38.1m x 6.9m x 4.4m) • 148 tons [D] • Hull composite • Complement 16-30 • Built Lawly of Boston, Massachusetts, USA, 1930

# Amerigo Vespucci Sailing ship 1931

Laid down in Castellammare di Stabia in 1930 and commissioned on 15 October 1931, the *Amerigo Vespucci* is the oldest ship in the pennant list of the Italian navy and one of the oldest sailing ships to be in service in any navy worldwide. Together with her sister-ship, *Cristoforo Colombo*, she constituted, until the end of the Second World War, the Regia Marina's 'Divisione Navale d'Istruzione' (Naval Training Squadron), and was one of Italy's most valued international cultural and goodwill ambassadors.

Named after the famous Italian explorer and cartographer of the second half of the fifteenth century, the ship is a graceful reminder of the allure of the sea. As the ship's motto has it, 'Not those who begin, but those who persevere' can achieve the high level of seamanship and experience required by a professional naval organization. The *Amerigo Vespucci* is designed to accustom young midshipmen to the harsh conditions and the insecurity of life at sea. Every detail and practice on the ship serve this purpose; sails and ropes are still made of natural fibres; orders are given by the captain through the sailing master with a whistle and executed manually as was standard practice in the age of sail.

In 2006, after 75 years of service, and 71 training cruises stretching from the Mediterranean Sea to the waters of South America, the *Vespucci* underwent a major refit that sought to preserve her unique features. Today her double mission as training laboratory for future naval officers and iconic testimony of national culture remain at the heart of her operational activity. In recent years the ship has taken part in major events such as the America's Cup in New Zealand (2002), the Olympic Games in Athens (2004) and the Trafalgar 200 celebrations (2005). *AP*

**1919-1946**

*Amerigo Vespucci* **drying her sails at Dartmouth, Devon** *(photograph), August 1962, Conway Picture Library*

270.3ft x 51.2ft x 22.3ft (82.4m x 15.6m x 6.8m) • 4083 tons [D] • Hull steel • Armament: 2 x 6 pdr • Complement 24 + 421 • Built Castellammare di Stabia Shipyards, Naples, Italy, 1930

# Royal Oak  Revenge class battleship 1931

The Grand Harbour, Malta, was home to the Royal Navy's powerful Mediterranean Fleet and this 1931 photograph shows a typical scene in the inter-war years. Following the opening of the Suez Canal in 1869 Malta's importance increased greatly due to its strategic position on British trade routes to the Middle and Far East, and the Royal Navy built its largest overseas dockyard there. The harbour had been heavily fortified by the Knights of St John in the sixteenth century and British control dated from 1800. The illustration shows the battleships *Queen Elizabeth* (nearest) and *Royal Oak*, to the right of which are two County class heavy cruisers. In the foreground is a group of dghajsa (pronounced 'dicer'), traditional Maltese

craft which ferried sailors between their ship and the shore, and had their origins in Phoenician times. *Royal Oak* was part of the Grand Fleet at Jutland in 1916 but was to be an early casualty of the Second World War, after being struck by torpedoes from the German submarine *U-47* at Scapa Flow on 14 October 1939. She rolled over and sank about 30 minutes after the first torpedo hit and 786 of the ship's company lost their lives. *Queen Elizabeth* was at the Dardanelles in 1915 but missed Jutland because she was in refit. She served in the Mediterranean and Eastern fleets during the Second World War and was scrapped in 1948. *PB*

Dghajsas in Grand Harbour, Valetta, Malta, with the battleships *Queen Elizabeth* and *Royal Oak*, and two London class cruisers of the 1st Cruiser Squadron *(photograph), unknown photographer, 1931, Waterline Collection, National Maritime Museum, London (P92968)*

624.3ft x 88.6ft x 28.6ft (190.3m x 27m x 8.7m) • 28,000 tons [D] • Hull steel • Armament 8 x 15in Mk I, 14 x 6in BL Mk XII, 2 x 3in AA, 4 x 3 pdr, 4 x 21in torpedo tubes • Complement 908-997 • Built Devonport, Plymouth, England, 1914

# Strathnaver   P&O ocean liner 1931

In 1931 the P&O Line introduced the first of a group of liners that were to define its service for the future. The *Strathnaver* was the first of five vessels built by Vickers Armstrong at Barrow-in-Furness that were to become known and loved as 'the Straths'. She had turbo-electric drive for a service speed of 21 knots. At 22,547 tons gross, she was larger than previous ships, as well as being comfortably faster and with a larger passenger capacity. Her 498 first-class and 668 tourist-class passengers all enjoyed a much higher standard than on rival liners on the route from London to Sydney, via exotic ports including Bombay and Colombo. The name came from the company's chairman, the Earl of Inchcape, Viscount Strathnaver. Her overall white paint scheme and three yellow funnels were an innovation that gave her a new and stylish appearance that was to become the badge of the P&O subsequently, so unlike their previous drab livery. As well as the liner service to Australia, she and her sister *Strathaird* ran cruises to Norway or the Mediterranean in the northern summer.

In 1939 she was requisitioned as a troop transport and managed to survive bombing by the Luftwaffe in Algeria in 1942, where other ships around her were sunk. She returned to the company in 1948. Following an extensive refit at Belfast which resulted in the removal of her two dummy funnels, she returned to service from 1950 to 1961. In 1954 she was converted to all-tourist class for 1252 berths. Overtaken finally by larger and more modern ships such as the *Canberra*, she was scrapped in Hong Kong during 1962. *CJ*

*The White Sisters*, **P&O Archives** *(book cover), The Art Archive / P&O Archives / Eileen Tweedy*

664ft x 80ft x 29ft (202.4m x 24.4m x 8.8m) • 22,547 tons [GRT] • Hull Steel • Complement 480, passengers first class 498, tourist 668 • Built Vickers Armstrong, Barrow-in-Furness, England, 1931

# Parma  Four-masted barque c.1932

In this photograph we look down from aloft, through the sails towards the shifting deck, as the four-masted barque *Parma* races up the Atlantic in 1932. She was launched in 1902 as the *Arrow*. Originally owned by the Anglo-American Oil Company, she was used for carrying paraffin in small cases, one of a fleet of 10 trading between New York, Philadelphia, Australia and Japan. In 1911 the *Arrow* was sold to F. Laeisz, Hamburg, there renamed *Parma* and used to carry nitrates from Chile. At the outbreak of the First World War she was interned there at Iquique, and later, in 1920, was assigned as war damage reparations to Britain. For the next 10 years, she traded between Europe and Talcahuano, Chile, continuing to carry nitrates, with an average eastbound passage of 96 days.

In 1931 she was sold to Ruben De Cloux and the well-known mariner and author Alan Villiers, sailing under the Finnish flag. She was used to transport grain from Australia; carrying up to 62,000 bags of wheat, *Parma* was the largest and most successful of the large sailing ships, making a record passage of 83 days from Port Victoria, South Australia to Falmouth, England in 1933. It was aboard this ship and a number of other square-riggers that Villiers created film documentaries and majestic photographs to record the last sailing ships operating commercially. Villiers later sold his shares in the *Parma* and after a minor collision at Princes Dock in Glasgow, she was used as a storage hulk at Haifa, Israel. She was eventually scrapped in 1938. *HLJ*

**Looking down through the sails of the barque 'Parma' towards the deck, with the sea below. Full sail** *(photograph), Alan Villiers, 1932-1933, National Maritime Museum, London (N61487)*

327ft x 47ft x 28ft (99.9m x 14.2m x 8.5m) • 3090 tons [GRT] • Hull steel • Built A. Rodger, Port Glasgow, Scotland, 1902

# Normandie  French ocean liner 1932

One of greatest ever so-called 'ships of state', French Line's magnificent 1930s flagship *Normandie* was created as the ultimate ocean-going expression of contemporary France. At the time of her 1935 debut she was the largest and fastest liner ever built. Her sleek hull minimized bow wave, flank turbulence and wake at high speed; a design that was the brainchild of the French-domiciled naval architect Vladimir Yurkevich, who had grown up in Russia and trained at the St Petersburg Polytechnic Institute. *Normandie* was propelled by 20,000kW turbo-electric machinery, with enough generating power to run the entire central Paris Métro system's 150km of track. She was also a ship of remarkable structural daring, boasting a three-deck-high first-class dining salon that extended nearly a third of the ship's whole length. The ship was also equipped with a magnificent suite of large public rooms, arranged along a central processional route with broad open vistas through much of its length.

Yet she was more than simply an array of superlatives of size, power and speed. *Normandie* was the consummate expression of the Gallic grand gesture; exhibiting flair, style and panache. Without being overpowering or overwhelming, *Normandie*'s public spaces, as well as her private accommodations, from the largest suites to the smaller standard-grade cabins, were remarkably contemporary in the 1930s sense of style and décor, and promoted an altogether more informal onboard lifestyle than had hitherto been seen on the North Atlantic. *Normandie*, with her axial layout, open plan and extensive use of glass was a veritable ship of light that created an altogether different passenger experience.

Sadly this great ship was only in service for five years before the outbreak of the Second World War. She was destroyed in a disastrous fire while undergoing conversion as a troopship in early 1942. A planned sister ship was, alas, never realized. *PD*

*Le Normandie (poster), 1935, The Art Archive / Musée de la Poste Amboise / Gianni Dagli Orti*

1029.4ft x 118.1ft (313.8m x 36m) • 79,280 tons [GRT] • Hull steel • Complement 1345, passengers; first class 828, second ('tourist') class 670, third class 454 • Built Penhoët, St Nazaire, France, 1935

# Penang    Three-masted barque 1932

The Finnish barque *Penang* undergoing repairs in the Britannia Dry Dock during July 1932; she had just arrived in London from Adelaide, laden with a cargo of grain. Tucked in from the Thames, her bowsprit looms over the backyards of Millwall's West Ferry Road – a vivid illustration, perhaps, of the pervasive influence of the sea in everyday life during that period. The dock itself has long since been filled in and today expensive apartments crowd the riverside.

Launched in 1905, under the name of *Albert Rickmers*, she was soon acquired by the Laeisz transport company and put on the South American nitrate trade. In 1923 she was passed to the famous Finnish ship owner Gustaf Erikson and excelled in the Australian wheat trade. She operated across the oceans until 1940, when she disappeared without trace. It was not until some 30 years later that the truth was uncovered – she was torpedoed in the North Atlantic by a German submarine and lost with all hands. *HLJ*

*Penang* **3 masted barque, in dry dock at Millwall 1932** *(photograph), unknown photographer, 1932, National Maritime Museum (P39610), London*

265.7ft x 40.2ft x 24.3ft (81m x 12.3m x 7.4m) • 2019 tons [GRT] • Hull steel • Complement 18 • Built Rickmers Reismühlen Rhederi & Schiffsbau AG, Bremerhaven, Germany, 1905

# Le Terrible   Fantasque class fast destroyer 1933

The six ships of the Fantasque class marked the high point in the construction of 32 'super-destroyers', designated *contre-torpilleurs* (counter-torpedo), for France's Marine Nationale. They were intended to operate in divisions of three with a primary mission of screening and scouting for the heavy ships. Each ship in the division fired shells with a different splash colorant to enable it to identify its fall of shot. They were heavily armed for flotilla craft, with five quick-firing 5.4in guns in single mountings complemented by three triple banks of 21.7in torpedo tubes. They were also exceptionally fast, being designed to sustain a speed of 37 knots even when fully loaded. *Le Terrible* attained just over 45 knots for a short period on trials – a world record which

has never been surpassed by a displacement ship. However, their machinery was fragile and subject to regular breakdown, and generator capacity was inadequate for their elaborate electrical systems. *Le Terrible* served with Force Y at Dakar 1940-3, being engaged by the British cruisers during General De Gaulle's failed attempt to bring the Vichy colony into the Allied camp. She was subsequently refitted in the United States, receiving eight 40mm AA guns in one quad and two twin mountings, reclassified as a 'light cruiser' and served in the postwar Marine Nationale until the late 1950s. *JJ*

*Le Terrible* (photograph), Wright & Logan collection, Royal Naval Museum, Portsmouth

435ft x 39ft x 16ft (132m x 12m x 5m) • 2600 tons [D] • Hull steel • Armament: 5 x 5.4in, 4 x 37mm, 9 x 550mm (21.7in) torpedo tubes • Complement 220 • Built A. C. Loire, France, 1933

# Queen Mary  Cunard White Star liner 1934

From 1938 until 1952 the *Queen Mary* was the fastest transatlantic liner, having gained the Blue Riband in August 1938 with average speeds of 30.99 knots westbound and 31.69 knots eastbound. Her construction for Cunard Line began in 1930 but was halted for three years because the company had financial problems. The illustration shows the ship lit by dockside floodlights and her own lights, in the final stages of fitting out at Clydebank in March 1936 – two months before her maiden voyage. She was the first of two great new liners designed to provide an express service from Southampton to New York, with a call at Cherbourg in each direction. Her half-sister *Queen Elizabeth* was completed four years later, and was slightly larger.

Stripped of many of her luxurious fixtures and fittings, *Queen Mary* served as a troopship from 1940 to 1946, carrying up to 15,000 troops on each voyage. She twice took Winston Churchill across the Atlantic, to New York and Canada, for conferences with President Roosevelt and for these voyages many luxury fittings were reinstated.

*Queen Mary*'s post-war service continued until 1967, with some interludes in the 1960s for cruising. However, the size of the Queens made them unsuitable for cruising at that time because there were many ports that they could not enter. After her sale by Cunard, *Queen Mary* steamed to Long Beach, California, where she became a static floating hotel, museum and tourist attraction. *PB*

1919-1946

*Queen Mary* **fitting out at John Brown's yard, Clydebank** *(photograph), 5 March 1936, Conway Picture Library*

1019.4ft x 118.6ft x 39ft (310.7m x 36.1m x 11.9m) • 80,774 tons [GRT] • Hull steel • Complement 1101, passengers; cabin 776, tourist 784, third class 579 • Built John Brown & Co., Clydebank, Scotland, 1934

# De Ruyter   Light cruiser 1935

Authorized in 1930 as the third cruiser for the Dutch East Indies station, *De Ruyter* was originally to have been restricted to 5250 tons and a main armament of six 6in guns in twin turrets for budgetary reasons, but the design was subsequently enlarged and a single semi-enclosed mounting was added in 'B' position. The ship had a powerful, modern anti-aircraft armament comprising five twin 1.6in Hazemeyer mountings, which were grouped together on the low after superstructure, and fire control systems were also particularly advanced, featuring remote power control (RPC), stabilization and a high level of automation. Soon after her arrival in the Far East *De Ruyter* became flagship of the Netherlands East Indies Squadron. In January 1942, when the unified ABDA command was formed to coordinate resistance to the Japanese in the Far East, the Combined Striking Force, comprising American, British, Dutch and Australian (ABDA) cruisers and destroyers, was placed under the command of Rear-Admiral Karel Doorman in the *De Ruyter*. The force at first held its own against the Japanese heavy cruisers *Haguro* and *Nachi* during the Battle of the Java Sea (26 February 1942), but just after 11.32 p.m. *De Ruyter* was hit by a 'long lance' torpedo, and sank two hours later with heavy loss of life. *JJ*

**HNLMS *De Ruyter* in 1936** *(photograph), Conway Picture Library*

560ft x 51.5ft x 17ft (171m x 15.7m x 5.1m) • 6000 tons [D] • Armament 7 x 5.9in, 10 x 40mm, 2 aircraft • Complement 435 • Built Wilton-Fijenoord, 1935

# Junk Fishing vessel 1935

A Chinese fishing junk sails across Hong Kong harbour. This 1935 image is almost timeless. For more than 1500 years the Chinese junk has been used for war, commerce, fishing, exploration and transport. Junks ranged massively in size and the number of masts they carried; they varied according to their specific purposes, but all shared unmistakable features that made them one of the most efficient ships afloat.

Constructed without a keel, the flat-bottomed hull could work in shallow coastal and estuary waters. A heavy stern-mounted rudder, hung beneath the high, projecting stern, was developed for deepwater voyages far earlier than in similar vessels in the west. Bulkheads that divided the hull into watertight compartments were introduced into western ships at the turn of the nineteenth and twentieth century; junks had them by the twelfth century.

The lug sails were easy to handle and could be turned until they were almost parallel to the sides, allowing a junk to sail into the wind, while bamboo battens stiffened the sails and made them easy to roll up. In the foreground of the image, a group of typical flat-botomed sampans, possibly used to store fish, lie at anchor.

In 1405 Admiral Zhung He led the first of seven treasure expeditions that saw huge fleets of up to 63 ships and 30,000 men reach far beyond India to Hormoz, Jeddah and East African ports as far south as Mozambique. Historians debate whether his huge nine-masted junks were as large (400ft, 122m) as has been claimed, but Ibn Battuta, a visitor to Calcutta during the previous century, certainly encountered 12-masted Chinese junks.

Junks are still built today and are popular with tourists. *JH*

**Sampans and a fishing junk, Hong Kong** *(photograph), 1935, Waterline Collection, National Maritime Museum, London (P92302)*

No data available

# Schlesien  Deutschland class battleship 1936

By the time *Schlesien* entered service in 1908 she was already obsolete, a victim of the dreadnought revolution. Yet that very obsolescence saved her from an early demise after 1918 when Germany was restricted to a fleet of obsolete warships, dating back to the pre-dreadnought era. Modernised and maintained, *Schlesien* spent the inter-war years as a sea-going training ship, preparing officers and men for the revived fleet.  Seen here at Curaçao in the Netherlands Antilles in 1936, the modernised ship, her fore-funnel neatly trunked back to join the second, and very well painted, wears a Nazi naval ensign and a prominent Nazi eagle on her aging flanks. However, a destination better known for cruise liners, the obvious holiday mood, Hollywood posters and pristine white uniforms subvert the numerous guns of a ship that had fought at Jutland, and would go to war again in 1939. Along with her sister ship the *Schleswig-Holstein* this small battleship was still in service in 1939, taking an active role in Baltic operations against Poland and the Soviet Union, surviving to the last days of the Nazi regime. In May 1945 the old warrior was mined, bombed and then scuttled off Swinemünde. *ADL*

**German battleship *Schlesien* at Curaçao, Lesser Antilles** *(photograph), unknown photographer, 1936, National Maritime Museum, London (P84925)*

419ft x 73ft x 25ft (127.6m x 22.2m x 7.7m) • 13,200 tons [D] • Hull steel • Armament 4 × 11in SK L/40, 14 × 6.7in, 22 × 3.5in, 6 × 18in torpedo tubes • Complement 743 • Built Schichau, Danzig (Gdańsk, now Poland), 1906

# Admiral Graf Spee 'Pocket battleship' 1936

The Treaty of Versailles restricted the new German Republic to ships of 10,000 tons with a maximum gun calibre of 11in. However, rather than building the expected slow coast defence vessels, the German navy opted for a radical new design which combined the protection and speed of a cruiser with the armament of a capital ship. The Panzerschiffe were powered by two-stroke diesel engines which gave them a maximum speed of 27–28 knots and an endurance of some 33,357.3km. Their 11in guns, which could range to 36,000m, gave them a considerable advantage over any foreign cruiser, while the later addition of torpedo tubes and a catapult for reconnaissance aircraft made them ideal commerce raiders.

Shortly before the outbreak of the Second World War two of the three Panzerschiffe, *Deutschland* and *Admiral Graf Spee*, were slipped into the North Atlantic, and *Graf Spee* then proceeded to the South Atlantic and the Indian Ocean, sinking nine merchant ships. She was finally cornered off South America by the British cruisers *Exeter*, *Ajax* and *Achilles* on 13 December 1939, and received moderate damage in the Battle of the River Plate. She docked for repairs in the neutral port of Montevideo, but was forced by international law to leave within 72 hours. Faced with what he believed to be overwhelming odds, Captain Langsdorff scuttled his ship. *JJ*

The *Admiral Graf Spee* scuttled and in flames off Montevideo, Uruguay, 17 December 1939 *(photograph), Conway Picture Library*

610ft x 70ft x 19ft (186m x 21.7m x 5.8m) • 12,100 tons [D] • Hull steel • Armament 6 x 11in, 8 x 5.9in, 6 x 4.1in, 8 x 37mm, 8 x 21in torpedo tubes, 2 aircraft • Complement 1150 • Built Wilhelmshaven, Germany, 1936

# Littorio   Littorio class battleship 1937

Laid down on 28 October 1934 together with her sister-ship, *Vittorio Veneto*, this warship represented the embodiment of Italy's quest for the status as one of the world's top superpowers. Though its nominal displacement was given as 35,000 tons, *Littorio* was a much larger and imposing battleship, reaching almost 46,000 tons full load. Designed by the successful naval architect Umberto Pugliese, the four units of this class were to become the defining icons on the high seas of Italian taste for balanced and graceful naval designs. The Littorio class featured excellent vertical armour as well as the revolutionary Pugliese system for underwater protection from torpedoes; *Littorio* mounted reliable and effective 15.2in long-barrelled naval guns on triple turrets, and was very fast. As an Italian national newspaper remarked reporting on *Littorio*'s launching ceremony on 22 August 1937, the battleship was a majestic and terrifying celebration of the achievements of the Italian nation as a whole in the fields of advanced technology, engineering and international affairs. In fact, originally conceived to engage the French battlefleet in the relatively confined spaces of the Mediterranean Sea, *Littorio* encapsulated the virtues and limitations of Italian industrial might. At the test of fire, the Pugliese system proved less effective than conventional multiple torpedo bulkhead systems, whilst the ship's powerful main guns suffered from barrel lives more rapidly than equivalent systems adopted by other navies and was affected by inconsistent shell patterning. *Littorio* took part in 46 war missions, including some of the main naval actions of the Second World War; notably at the Second Battle of Sirte, where with her main guns she hit the destroyer HMS *Havock* and severely damaged HMS *Kingston*. *AP*

*Littorio, Vittorio Veneto* (foreground and far left) and the destroyer *Grecale* (background) make for Alexandria following the Italian surrender (photograph), Lt. R.G.G. Coote, 14 September 1943, Imperial War Museum (A 19481)

780.2ft x 107.9ft x 34.4ft (237.8m x 32.9m x 10.5m) • 43,835 tons [D] • Hull steel • Armament: 9 x 15in, 12 x 6in, 12 x 3.5in, 20 x 1.4in, 24-30 x 20/65mm (0.7in), 4 x 4.7in • Complement 1920 • Built Ansaldo Shipyards, Genoa, Italy, 1937

# Lince   Spica class torpedo boat 1938

With her awnings rigged against the sun, the *Lince* proceeds in state past the great Venetian basilica of Santa Maria della Salute that rises between the Bacino di San Marco and the Grand Canal, probably on a goodwill visit to the city after crossing the Adriatic at Fiume, in 1938. Although she has the air of a handsome pleasure steamer, she was one of 32 Spica class torpedo boats built by the Italian navy between 1934 and 1937, all named after stars and constellations; *Lince* translates as Lynx.

The inter-war Washington Naval Treaty that capped the tonnage and so restricted the number of warships of the main navies passed no restrictions on vessels of 600 tons or less, making the Spica class attractive. In reality,

however, it was rendered obsolete by the destroyer classes, and though the boats had some capability in anti-submarine work, they proved extremely vulnerable during the war, *Lince* being among the casualties.

Her fate was in complete contrast to the image of tranquillity she presented at Venice. On 4 August 1943, she grounded at Punta Alice in the Bay of Taranto, Italy (39°24'N, 17°09'E), and on the 28th she was spotted by the submarine HMS *Ultor*, commanded by Lieutenant George Hunt DSO, DSC. Two torpedoes hit the aft end, killing 12 of the crew, injuring local fishermen and killing a child on the beach. *JH*

**The Italian fleet torpedo boat *Lince* at Venice, Italy** *(photograph), 1938 or 1939, Waterline Collection, National Maritime Museum, London (P83949)*

263.4ft x 26ft x 10.2ft (81.4m x 8.2m x 3.1m) • 995 tons [D] • Hull steel • Armament (from 1941) 3 x 100/47 mm, 6-10 machine guns, 4 x 450 mm torpedo tubes, 2-4 depth charge throwers • Complement 116 • Built Cantieri del Quarnaro, Fiume, Italy, 1938

# Gneisenau   Scharnhorst class battlecruiser 1939

Although launched later than her sister-ship *Scharnhorst*, *Gneisenau* was commissioned some months earlier, in May 1938. Their protracted construction meant that both ships were a compromise of German technical limitations and political necessity. Nevertheless their design proved to be essentially sound, and the ships were adequate for their primary role as commerce raiders. As such they were equipped with 11.1in (283mm) guns. The long range, high muzzle velocity and good rate of fire of the 11in meant the ships were perfectly capable of destroying merchant vessels and convoy escorts, but were vastly inferior to the 15in (380mm) guns of first-class battleships. Instead, superior speed was prioritized to avoid such encounters.

Both *Scharnhorst* and *Gneisenau* operated together throughout the early part of the war, and merchant navy sailors dubbed the pair the 'ugly sisters'. They scored some notable successes, sinking the British aircraft carrier *Glorious* and her two escorts, the destroyers HMS *Acasta* and *Ardent* during the British withdrawal from Norway. This was followed in January 1941 with a sustained anti-shipping operation in the Atlantic in which *Gneisenau* accounted for 14 ships and *Scharnhorst* 8 ships. After returning to the German-occupied port of Brest, they successfully completed Operation Cerberus, the audacious 'Channel Dash', in 1942. Unfortunately, the damage *Gneisenau* suffered meant that she would not see action again – an impact with a mine off Terschelling meant that she was forced to put in at Kiel, where RAF attacks destroyed her entire bow section. After emergency repairs, she steamed to Gotenhafen, where she was decommissioned in order to carry out reconstruction work. This was to allow for the replacement of her 11.1in battery with twin 15in turrets, which would have made her a formidable opponent. However, the work was abandoned after *Scharnhorst* was sunk by British cruisers in December 1943, and *Gneisenau* was scuttled in Gotenhafen harbour as a blockship in March 1945. She was subsequently raised by the Poles, broken up, and scrapped after the war. *MJ*

**A Kriegsmarine sailor signals to the German battlecruiser** *Gneisenau* *(photograph), August 1939, Scherl/SZ Photo/Mary Evans*

772ft x 98.4ft x 31.9ft (235m x 30m x 9.7m) • 31,500 tons [D] • Hull steel • Armament 9 x 11in, 12 x 5.9in, 14 x 4.1in, 16 x 37mm, 10 (later 16) x 2cm, 6 x 533 mm torpedo tubes, 3 Arado Ar 196 A-3 aircraft • Complement 1669 • Built Deutsche Werke, Kiel, Germany, 1936

1919-1946

# Richelieu   Richelieu class battleship 1939

*Richelieu* was laid down in late 1935 in response to the Italian Littorio class. Like her immediate predecessors, *Dunkerque* and *Strasbourg*, she was heavily influenced by British design practices of the 1920s; she had the same all-forward main armament, a shortened armoured citadel, and a high tower topped by the directors for the main and secondary guns. The planned secondary armament of five triple 6in dual-purpose mountings was modified during construction, and she received six twin 4in high-angle guns in lieu of the two midships turrets. *Richelieu* had exceptionally heavy horizontal protection, the main armoured deck being backed by a 1.5in (40mm) 'splinter deck' above the machinery and magazines. She was also exceptionally fast, easily attaining her designed speed of 32 knots on trials. When the Germans invaded northern France in June 1940 *Richelieu* escaped to Dakar, Senegal, where she became the focus of repeated British attempts to disable her. She was patched up following an aerial torpedo hit, and when West Africa was liberated she was sent to the United States for a major refit, during which her aviation facilities were stripped away and she was given a powerful battery of quadruple AA guns. *Richelieu* subsequently served with distinction in the British Eastern and East Indies Fleets. In 1952 she became a gunnery ship, paying off in 1956. *JJ*

*Richelieu* en route to the Pacific, 24 March 1944. View looking aft from the bow *(photograph), US Naval Historical Center*

813ft x 108ft x 31ft (248m x 33m x 9.2m) • 37,250 tons [D] • Hull steel • Armament 8 x 15in, 9 x 6in, 12 x 3.9in, 12 x 37mm, 3-4 aircraft • Complement 1570 •
Built Brest, France, 1939

# Robert Ley  KdF cruise ship 1939

One of the first purpose-built cruise ships, *Robert Ley* was ordered by the Nazi party for members of the Deutsche Arbeitsfront (DAF); the German Labour Front. She became a visible symbol of economic success and a potent propaganda tool as the Nazis projected a vision of a unified and happy German *Volk* across Europe through the 'Kraft durch Freude' programme. Initiated in 1934, this scheme was introduced to give German workers the opportunity to take subsidized cruises to various destinations. Several vessels were initially requisitioned from Germany's largest shipping companies for this purpose, but when the success of the programme became apparent, two new ships were ordered. The first of the two vessels was the *Wilhelm Gustloff*, while the second was the *Robert Ley* (named after the leader of the DAF). She was launched on 29 March 1938 in a ceremony personally attended by Adolf

Hitler. Yet other, more sinister Nazi designs meant that she would serve for only two months as a KdF cruise ship.

In late May 1939 she was sent to Spain to bring back the Condor Legion, who had assisted Franco's nationalists in seizing power. *Robert Ley* was subsequently commissioned as a hospital ship for the German navy following the invasion of Poland. Later, she became an accommodation and garrison ship, serving in this capacity until the early weeks of 1945, when she was again pressed into service to evacuate soldiers and Germans from the Eastern territories of the Reich back to the Fatherland.

By March 1945, the *Robert Ley* was at Hamburg, awaiting further transport duties. She was targeted in a RAF bombing raid, leaving little more than a fire-ravaged hulk. In 1947 she was towed to Britain and scrapped. *MJ*

Passengers crowd the deck of the German cruise ship *Robert Ley* during a voyage to Norway *(photograph), Hugo Jaeger, May 1939, Timepix / Time Life Pictures / Getty Images*

667.2ft x 78.6ft (203.8m x 24m) • 27,288 tons [GRT] • Hull steel • Complement 1470 • Built Blohm & Voss, Hamburg, Germany, 1938

# U-47 Type VIIB U-boat 1939

'But as we approached and the band raised their gleaming instruments to their lips, and the national anthem blazed across the water to us, as the people in their hundreds cheered and waved, and our submarine glided through the lock and made fast, as I gazed from the conning tower across the crowd on the mole to the man in the blue coat, then I felt the glory of the hour crash over me in a great wave.'

So wrote Korvettenkapitän Gunther Prien as he and *U-47* had returned to a hero's welcome after sinking the battleship HMS *Royal Oak* at her anchorage in Scapa Flow in the Orkney Islands off Scotland, just after 1a.m. on 14 October 1939. The penetration of the well-defended British base was one of the most audacious raids of the Second World War.

Prien's *U-47* was a Type VIIB, of which 24 were built between 1936 and 1940. They carried more fuel than the Type VIIA, were slightly faster than the far more numerous Type VIIC that followed, and in the hands of commanders such as Prien, Kretschmer, Endrass, Schultze and Schepke caused heavy losses among Allied convoys in the Atlantic. Like all the U-boats of the time they were essentially motor torpedo boats with diving capability, rather than true submarines, and operating in 'wolfpacks' they would locate a convoy, shadow it by day and then attack by night on the surface.

As a class, they sank 252 ships, representing more than 1,300,000 gross register tonnage, and seriously damaged others. Four Type VIIBs survived hostilities to be scuttled; the rest were sunk, mostly with all hands. Prien and *U-47* were last heard of on 7 March 1941 near Rockall Banks. *JH*

**U-47 returns from Scapa Flow, October 1939** *(photograph), Conway Picture Library*

238.6ft x 22.8ft x 15.6ft (66.5m x 6.2m x 4.74m) • 753 tons [D] • Hull steel • Armament 5 x 53.3 cm torpedo tubes, 14 torpedoes; 1 x 88mm/45 C35, 1 x 20mm C30 deck gun • Complement 44 • Built F Krupp Germaniaweft AG, Kiel, Germany, 1938

# Comandante Cappellini Marcello class submarine 1939

Commanded by C.C. Salvatore Todaro, the Italian Marcello class submarine *Comandante Cappellini* sailed from La Spezia on 29 September 1940, negotiated the Straits of Gibraltar and began a patrol in the Atlantic. On 15 October she was attacked by the *Kabalo*, an armed Belgian merchantman. Todaro returned fire and, after giving the crew time to abandon ship, sank it. One lifeboat was found by a neutral ship, but Todaro, already with five survivors on board, took the other in tow, anxious about its survival in the heavy seas. Three times the tow broke, and on the 17th Todaro brought everyone into the *Cappellini*, stowing them in the sail. Proceeding of necessity on the surface, *Cappellini* made for the Azores, where she landed her passengers by rubber dinghy.

On 5 January 1941, *Cappellini* sank the British freighter, *Shakespeare*, and once again Todaro, bottom left, first towed the survivors' lifeboat, then took the men on board, putting them safely ashore in the Cape Verde Islands.

Todaro's chivalry in breaking off patrol to assist survivors found little favour with his superiors. He was killed in 1942, but in 1943, under T.V. Marco Revedin, the *Cappellini* famously became one of four Axis submarines involved in the rescue of survivors from the *Laconia*.

At the Italian Armistice in September 1943 the *Cappellini* was at Singapore loading vital supplies of raw materials including rubber for Italy and Germany. Against the wishes of the officers, most of the crew opted to continue the fight on the Axis side, and, now renamed *UIT-24*, *Cappellini* became part of the German Navy until Germany's surrender. She then joined the Japanese Navy as *I-504*, and after capture by the US Navy was scuttled off Kobe in April 1946, one of two submarines to serve in three Axis navies. *JH*

**Survivors of the torpedoed British freighter *Shakespeare* climb aboard the fore deck of the Italian submarine *Comandante Cappellini* (photograph), *January 1941, Conway Picture Library***

238.6ft x 22.8ft x 15.6ft (73m x 7.2m x 5.1m) • 1060 tons [D] • Hull steel • Armament 8 x 21in torpedo tubes (16 torpedoes; 2 x 3.9in, 4 x .52in) • Complement 58 • Built O.T.O, La Spezia, Italy, 1939

# Schnellboot Motor torpedo boat 1939

Schnellboote, referred to as E or Enemy-Boats by the British, were small, fast torpedo boats used by the Kriegsmarine throughout the Second World War. During the First World War the German navy fitted airship engines to small vessels to create an improvised force of high-performance craft for operations in littoral waters. The Lürssen Werft shipyard in Bremen continued the development after the war and in 1928 produced the plans for the S-1 based on an enlarged motor yacht. From 1929 onwards the production for naval use was undertaken. The basic design had doubled in size by 1939 and wartime boats displaced around 100 tons, had a wooden hull, were 111.5ft (35m) long and carried two torpedo tubes in the bow. They were also equipped with light calibre weapons and could carry about 6 mines. Initially petrol engines were fitted but, as these were prone to catch fire, from 1933 newly developed high-performance diesel engines were used. With these the boats could develop speeds of up to 42 knots and had a combat radius of between 300 and 350 nautical miles (345–403 miles, 556–648.6 km). The key characteristic of the Schnellboote was their round-bottomed hull that enabled them to operate in rough open waters and at high speed without leaving a detectable wake.

Originally the boats were designed for operations against the Soviets in the Baltic Sea, but during the war they were used in all coastal regions and were particularly effective at attacking Allied coastal shipping in the English Channel. In total around 200 boats were built and together they accounted for more than 350,000 tonnes of shipping sunk by torpedoes or mines. On 28 April 1944 Cherbourg-based Schnellboote were able to inflict heavy damage on an American LST flotilla during a training exercise for Operation Overlord, killing more than 600 servicemen. *MF*

'**Schnellbooten on the march against England**' *(photograph). July 1940. Conway Picture Library*

111.5ft x 16.7ft x 5.9ft (35m x 5.1m x 1.8m) • 78.9-100 tons [D] • Hull composite (wood over alloy frames) • Armament 2 x 533mm torpedo tubes (4 torpedoes), 1 x twin 20mm, 1 x single 20mm, 1 x 37mm Flak 42 • Complement 24-30 • Built various yards, Germany, 1939-45

# Glengyle  Cargo liner 1939

The *Glengyle* was a real merchant ship although the rescue incident depicted here derives from the artist's imagination. She was a cargo liner built for the Glen Line in 1939. Constructed by the Caledon Shipbuilding & Dry-Dock company at Dundee, she was the fifth vessel to bear that name.

On the outbreak of the Second World War she was requisitioned by the Admiralty and converted into a fast supply ship, and as such she flew the white ensign and was given the prefix HMS.

In April 1940 HMS *Glengyle* was converted into a Landing Ship, Infantry (Large) capable of carrying 700 troops and commissioned on 10 September of that year. She was fitted with a naval bridge, carried six 4in guns in twin mountings and 22 landing craft. She had a distinguished and lengthy service history in the Mediterranean and Far East (notably in Bombay and Hong Kong), playing a part in the raid on Bardia, North Africa on 19–20 April 1941, and later that month was involved in the evacuation of Greece and later the evacuation of Crete. By January 1942 she was part of the Malta Convoys carrying supplies from Alexandria before returning to Britain for preparations for the Dieppe Raid. She transported US troops for the Operation Torch landings of November 1942, the Allied Invasion of French North Africa, and was present during Operation Husky – the Allied invasion of Sicily in July 1943. She was also used as General Montgomery's headquarters.

The artist Arthur Burgess was born in Bombala, Australia and studied art in Sydney. In 1901 he settled in England where he continued his studies in St Ives, Cornwall, finally settling in London. He exhibited regularly at the Royal Academy of Arts, London, and worked as an illustrator for *The Graphic* and the *Illustrated London News*. Burgess was appointed the official naval artist for the Commonwealth of Australia in 1918, and was art editor of *Brassey's Naval and Shipping Annual* from 1922 to 1930. He painted a wide range of maritime subjects and was a founder member of the Society of Marine Artists and a member of the Wapping Group. Formally founded in 1946 this group initially met to record the busy life of London's dockland. *JT*

**The Brotherhood of Seamen: rescue of a fishing vessel by the steamship** *Glengyle* (oil on canvas), *Arthur James Wetherall Burgess*, c. 1945, National Maritime Museum, London (BHC1536)

507.6ft x 66.4ft x 30.6ft (154.7m x 20.2m x 9.3m) • 9919 tons [D] • Hull steel • Armament 3 x QF 4in Mk XVI, 2 x 2 pdr Mark VII, 12 x 20mm Oerlikon • Complement 523 • Caledon Shipbuilding & Engineering Company, Dundee, Scotland, 1939

# Queen Elizabeth Cunard White Star liner 1940

Although completed in 1940 for Cunard Line, the passenger liner *Queen Elizabeth* had to wait six years before her maiden transatlantic voyage, which started at Southampton on 16 October 1946. During the Second World War she served as a troopship, at first in the Pacific and later on the North Atlantic run, transporting a total of 811,000 troops. She did not travel in convoy, making use of her speed to elude the preying U-boats.

The elegant profiles *Queen Elizabeth* and her sister ship *Queen Mary* complemented their elaborately decorated and luxurious public rooms and epitomized the golden age of the liner. This, together with their impressive speed, quickly made them favourites amongst regular liner passengers. *Queen Elizabeth* remained the world's largest liner (by tonnage) for all her working life. The illustration shows workmen dismantling scaffolding at the bows of the ship during her annual overhaul at Southampton in 1961. In the foreground are her three anchors, each weighing 17 tons.

By the early 1960s jet aircraft were wresting the transatlantic traffic from ships and the *Queen Elizabeth* turned, unprofitably, to cruising to supplement her regular work. Her final, 907th, Atlantic crossing was made in 1968: in total she had carried 2.3 million passengers and covered 3.4 million miles (5.5 million km). She was sold to become a floating university at Hong Kong but just before her conversion was complete she caught fire there in January 1972, capsizing to become a total loss. *PB*

Workmen dismantle scaffolding at the bows of *Queen Elizabeth* after carrying out overhaul work at Southampton docks *(photograph), 28 February 1961, Conway Picture Library*

1029ft x 118ft x 39 ft (314.2m x 36.1m x 11.9m) • 83.673 tons [GRT] • Hull steel • Complement , passengers; first class 823, cabin class 662, tourist class 798 • Built John Brown & Co., Clydebank, Scotland, 1938

# Cossack  Tribal class destroyer 1940

*Cossack* was the most famous of a class of 16 large destroyers built for the Royal Navy during the late 1930s. Using the maximum 1850-ton displacement figure permitted by treaty for flotilla leaders, the destroyers of the Tribal class were built to match the large Imperial Japanese Navy destroyers of the Special Type and those serving with the Italian and French navies in the Mediterranean.

In contrast to earlier British fleet destroyers the primary emphasis in the design was on guns rather than on torpedoes. The four twin CP Mk XIX mountings for the 4.7in guns were hydraulically powered, and had a maximum angle of elevation of 40°. They were complemented by a quadruple 2pdr pompom and two quadruple 0.5in MG mountings for close-range AA fire. There was only a single bank of torpedo tubes.

In February 1940, while on patrol off the Norwegian coast, *Cossack* received a report that the German naval tanker *Altmark*, with British prisoners of war on board, was attempting to shelter in Norwegian waters. Under the direct orders of First Lord of the Admiralty Winston Churchill's orders, she boarded the *Altmark* and rescued 299 merchant seamen and officers. *Cossack* subsequently took part in the Norwegian Campaign and the *Bismarck* chase, before succumbing to a U-boat torpedo while escorting a convoy in the Mediterranean in October 1941. *JJ*

**HMS *Cossack* and the store ship *Altmark*, 16 February 1940** *(oil on paper), Herbert Barnard John Everett, early to mid twentieth century, National Maritime Museum, London (BHC1628)*

377ft x 36.5ft x 13 ft (114.9m x 11m x 4m) • 1850 tons [D] • Hull steel • Armament 8 x 4.7in, 4 x 2 pdr pompom, 4 x 21in torpedo tubes • Complement 190 • Built Vickers Armstrong, High Walker, Tyne, England, 1937

# Eskimo Tribal class destroyer 1940

The Tribal class destroyer HMS *Eskimo* sits forlornly in the Norwegian port of Skelfjord after being torpedoed during the Second Battle of Narvik in April 1940. Hastily patched up, she limped home, was completely repaired and promptly embarked on a second, eventful wartime career. Following operations with the Home Fleet she took part in further actions around the Lofoten Islands and recovered a set of Enigma machine rotors from a German trawler. In 1942 she escorted Russian convoys, screened the carrier, HMS *Victorious* during attacks on the *Tirpitz*, participated in the epic Operation Pedestal convoy that saved Malta from capitulation and provided cover during Operation Torch in North Africa.

Bombed during the Sicily landings in 1943 she suffered major damage and casualties but returned to service in time to form part of the defensive screen for the D-Day landings, torpedoing the German destroyer *ZH1* and subsequently helping to sink *U-971*. She spent the last year of the war in the Indian Ocean operating against the Japanese, and, shortly after her return, she was converted to an accommodation ship and later used for target practice before being broken up in 1949.

*Eskimo*'s career was typical of her famous class of 27 large, fast destroyers that were armed with large guns as well as with torpedoes and which came into service between 1938 and 1944. They were frequently found in the thick of the action, and only four of the Royal Navy's allocation of 16 survived the war. Eleven served with the Royal Australian and Royal Canadian Navies, and a solitary survivor of the class, RCN *Haida*, which shared with *Eskimo* and an aircraft the sinking of *U-971*, is preserved at Hamilton, Ontario. *JH*

Damage to HMS *Eskimo* after she was torpedoed at Narvik, Norway *(photograph), April 1940, Imperial War Museum (N 233)*

377ft x 36.6ft x 13ft draught (114.9m x 11.1m x 4m) • 2519 tons [D] • Hull steel • Armament 8 x 4.7in QF Mk XII, 4 x 2 pdr pompom, 4 x 21in torpedo tubes • Complement approx. 190 • Built Vickers Armstrong, High Walker, Tyne, England, 1938

# Illustrious  Illustrious class aircraft carrier 1940

*Illustrious* was the first of six armoured carriers laid down for the Royal Navy during the late 1930s. Although she bore a superficial resemblance to *Ark Royal* she was designed with only a single hangar which, for the first time, was fully protected against 6in cruiser fire and 500lb (227kg) bombs. In contrast to American aircraft carriers of the period, *Illustrious* was to use her embarked fighter aircraft not for self-defence but to accompany her torpedo attack planes on long-range strikes. When attacked by hostile enemy bombers, it was envisaged that the ship would strike down her aircraft in her armoured hangar and use her powerful anti-aircraft battery for self-defence. Unfortunately AA guns alone proved insufficient, and on 10 January 1941

*Illustrious* was seriously damaged by six 500kg bombs delivered by German Ju87 dive-bombers, necessitating lengthy repairs in the USA.

*Illustrious*'s most famous exploit was the night attack on Taranto, Italy in November 1940, which resulted in the crippling of three Italian battleships and at a stroke changed the balance of naval power in the Mediterreanean. *Illustrious* went on to serve with the British Eastern and Pacific Fleets, by which time she was able to embark more than 50 aircraft by operating with a permanent deck park. The armoured hangar made post-war modernization difficult and costly, and *Illustrious* was sold for scrap in 1956. *JJ*

**Deck Landing Officer on HMS *Illustrious* guides in the pilot of a landing aircraft** *(photograph), c. 1942, Hulton Archive / Getty Images*

753ft x 96ft x 28.5ft (229.5m x 29m x 8.5m) • 23,000 tons [D] • Hull steel • Armament 33 aircraft, 16 x 4.5in, 48 x 2 pdr pompom • Complement 1230 • Built Vickers Armstrong, Barrow-in-Furness, England, 1939

# Dunkirk ships  'Little ships' 1940

'…we shall fight on the beaches, we shall fight on the landing grounds, we shall fight in the fields and in the streets, we shall fight in the hills; we shall never surrender…'

Winston Churchill's famous speech of 4 June 1940 encapsulates one of the most enduring of British qualities: to be able to turn a defeat into a glorious tale of heroism and self sacrifice, to find victory of some kind in adversity, whether a moral, emotional or humanist victory. In the pantheon of glorious retreats perhaps nothing ranks higher than Operation 'Dynamo', the evacuation of over 300,000 men of the British Expeditionary Force and their French allies from Dunkirk between 27 May and 4 June 1940. The evacuation was planned by Vice-Admiral Sir Bertram Home Ramsay, an expert in littoral warfare. Moreover, learning from defeat is an important part of war and

Dunkirk was the first of several hard learning experiences which would eventually culminate in the success of Operation 'Overlord', the invasion of Europe via the Normandy beaches, in 1944 and for which Ramsay was the senior naval commander.

Dunkirk cannot be mentioned without the 700-odd flotilla of 'Little Ships' which evacuated troops as and where they could or acted as ferries between the shore and larger vessels. Despite being highly organized and mainly manned by naval personnel, the 'Little Ships' story was cast as something more organic, a spontaneous, important and highly visible example of the qualities Churchill was referring to in his speech and which he thought would see Britain through the war. *MR*

**Withdrawal from Dunkirk, June 1940** *(oil on canvas), Richard Ernst Eurich, 1940, National Maritime Museum, London (BHC0672)*

# Sydney Leander class light cruiser 1940

HMAS *Sydney* was completed in 1935, a light cruiser of 9000 tons full load, armed with 8 x 6in and 4 x 4in guns, as well as eight torpedo tubes. During the Second World War following the entry of Italy into the conflict, she distinguished herself as part of the Royal Navy's Mediterranean Fleet in action with Italian forces in 1940. She saw action on 27–28 June when she sank the destroyer *Espero*, and at the Battle of Calabria on 9 July. On 19 July in company with five British destroyers she encountered two fast Italian light cruisers off Cape Spada, Crete. Her long range gunfire slowed then stopped the second cruiser, *Bartolomeo Colleoni*, which was subsequently sunk, while the *Bande Nere* managed to outpace the pursuit and escape. The *Sydney* had just one shell hit in the action, right through one of the funnels, but she had

shot off almost all her main ammunition. In six weeks, 2200 rounds had been fired, including 956 in this action. The painting by Frank Norton illustrates the drama of this celebrated battle. A busy schedule continued, with contested convoy escort work and operations in support of forces in Greece. Then in February 1941 she made a triumphant return to Australia.

On 19 November 1941 she encountered the German auxiliary cruiser *Kormoran* off the Western Australian coast and, in a short fierce fight at close range, both ships were sunk. All 645 of the *Sydney*'s crew tragically perished. The mystery of her fate was fuelled over the years by several theories that were not laid to rest until the final discovery of her wreck in 2008. *CJ*

**HMAS *Sydney* and *Bartolomeo* in action off Crete** *(oil on canvas), Frank Norton, 1942, The Art Archive / Australian War Memorial*

555ft x 56.8ft x 19.5ft (169.2m x 17.3m x 5.9m) • 9000 tons [D] • Hull steel • Armament 8 x 6in, 4 x 4in, 12 x 0.5in Vickers Mk III MG, 9 x 0.303in Lewis MG, 8 x 21in torpedo tubes, 1 aircraft • Complement 645 • Built Swan Hunter & Wigham Richardson, Wallsend-on-Tyne, England, 1934

# King George V King George V class battleship 1940

Laid down with her sister *Prince of Wales* on 1 January 1937, *King George V* was the first of a new generation of British battleships, which followed the expiry of the 'battleship holiday' agreed at the Washington Naval Conference of 1922. For the final treaty in the series, the London Treaty of 1936, the British had proposed and secured a reduction in the maximum gun calibre to 14in. As the Italians, followed by the French, had already laid down battleships with 15in guns and the USA would take advantage of an 'escalator clause' in the treaty to revert to the original 16in limitation, the British ships would be outgunned by all their foreign contemporaries. Nevertheless, the adoption of a ten-gun main battery was some compensation, and these were otherwise well-balanced and well-protected ships, with a powerful dual-purpose secondary armament of 5.25in guns able to provide a barrage against level bombers and torpedo planes or to stop a destroyer. For close-range air defence there were four 8-barrelled pompoms, later increased to eight and supplemented by 40mm Bofors and 20mm Oerlikons.

As the flagship of Admiral Sir John Tovey, *King George V* had the distinction of leading the pursuit and sinking of the German battleship *Bismarck* in May 1941. She later served with the British Pacific Fleet. *JJ*

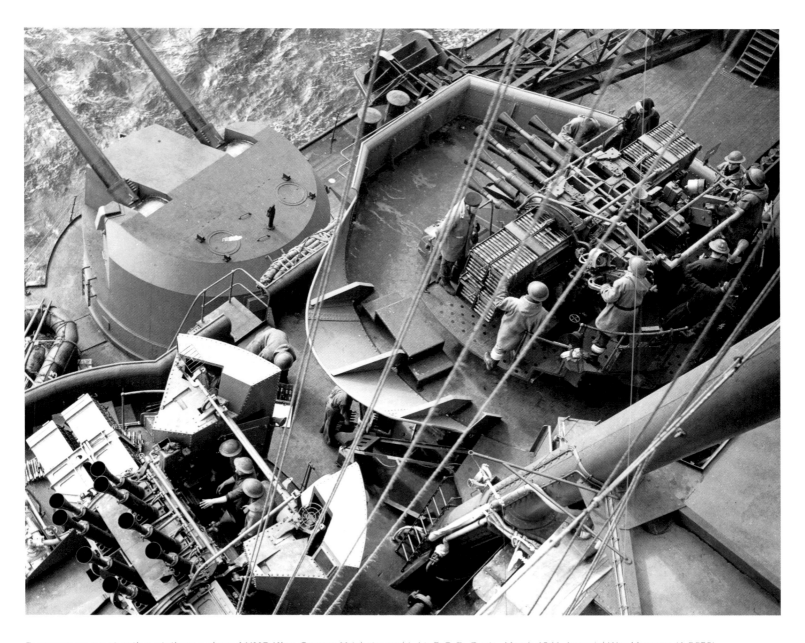

1919-1946

Pompom crews at action stations onboard HMS *King George V* (photograph), Lt. R.G.G. Coote, March 1941, Imperial War Museum (A 3650)

745ft x 104ft x 30ft (239m x 31.7m x 9.1m) • 36,700 tons [D] • Hull steel • Armament 10 x 14in, 16 x 5.25in, 32 x 2 pdr pompom, 2 aircraft • Complement 1420
• Built Vickers-Armstrong, High Walker, Tyne, England, 1939

# MTB   Motor torpedo boat c.1940

While many famous vessels are big capital ships, battleships, aircraft carriers and so on, the real white-knuckle excitement was to be found in the small boats built for speed and manoeuvrability – and none were more glamorous than the Second World War's Motor Torpedo Boats. Their role was simple, to hit the enemy hard and fast with their torpedoes before making a swift escape. Royal Navy MTBs came under the jurisdiction of Coastal Forces and saw much action in the English Channel, North Sea and Mediterranean Sea. In particular they made for excellent raiding craft and played an integral role in the famous attack on St Nazaire to blow up the lock gates using the destroyer HMS *Campbeltown* on 28 March 1942.

One of the few surviving examples is *MTB 102*, now owned and operated by the *MTB 102* Trust. Built by Vospers and launched in 1937 she was,

perhaps, the fastest ship in service with the Royal Navy during the war, reaching the phenomenal speed of 43 knots while loaded. Her service record is similarly remarkable. In assisting with the evacuation of Dunkirk in the summer of 1940, for two nights she became the flagship of Rear Admiral Wake-Walker. Four years later her distinguished guests for a review of the D-Day preparations were Winston Churchill and General Dwight 'Ike' Eisenhower, Supreme Allied Commander in Europe. Despite her unique history, by the 1970s *MTB 102* was in a sorry state and was effectively saved by Kelso Films who refurbished her as an operational seagoing vessel for a role in the 1976 film 'The Eagle has Landed'. *MTB 102* still regularly takes to sea and can be seen at numerous events around the coastline of South and South East England. *MR*

**Motor torpedo boats** *(oil on canvas), Norman Wilkinson, twentieth century, Norman Wilkinson Estate from collection at National Maritime Museum, London (BHC1602)*

**260**   [Data for *MTB 102*] 68ft x 14.9ft x 3.3ft (20.4m x 4.3m x 1.1m) • 32 tons [D] • Hull wood • Armament 1 x 20mm, 2 x 21in torpedo tubes • Complement 10 (2 officers and 8 ratings) • Built Vosper Thornycroft, Portsmouth, England, 1937

# Rodney Nelson class battleship 1940

On 31 July 1970 the last tot of rum was issued to the men of the British Royal Navy, ending a tradition dating back to 1655. The official report stated: 'The Admiralty Board concludes that the rum issue is no longer compatible with the high standards of efficiency required now that the individual's tasks in ships are concerned with complex, and often delicate, machinery and systems on the correct functioning of which people's lives may depend.' A bottle of beer was substituted for the rum, and the right of officers to buy spirits on board ship was extended to chiefs and petty officers.

Originally, the rum allowance was half a pint (284ml), issued twice-daily and drunk without water. In 1740 Admiral Vernon ordered that the rum be mixed 2:1 with water before being issued. Because the water tasted foul, sugar and lime were added. Angry sailors soon turned the admiral's nickname 'Old Grog' against him, referring to the new ration as 'grog'. Unexpectedly, the incidence of scurvy among his crew diminished thanks to the previously unknown vitamin C content of citrus fruit. Over the decades the quantity of rum and the level of dilution changed; prior to abolition, the measure was 2.5fl oz (71ml).

Whether in the days of the sailing navy, the Second World War convoys or the Cold War, the piping of 'Up Spirits' heralded the beginning of ritual for those who were not teetotal or under-age. In this 1940 photograph the crew of the battleship HMS *Rodney* are queuing up for their ration during the Second World War. The keg of rum bears the words of the toast: The King – God bless him. *JH*

The noon rum issue on board HMS *Rodney* (photograph). Lt. R.G.G. Coote, 1940, Imperial War Museum (A 103)

710ft x 106ft x 28.1ft (216.4m x 32.3m x 8.6m) • 33,730 tons [D] • Hull steel • Armament 9 x 16in, 12 x 6in, 6 x 4.7in, 8 x 2 pdr, 2 x 20mm, 8 x 0.5in, 2 x 24.5in torpedo tubes • Complement 1361 • Built Cammell Laird & Co., Birkenhead, England, 1927

# Scharnhorst Scharnhorst class battlecruiser 1940

Designed as an enlarged Deutschland class *Panzerschiff*, the *Scharnhorst* was first laid down in February 1934, but within months was broken up to be redesigned, taking into account the larger French battlecruisers then under construction. Laid down again in June 1935 the construction was plagued by delays and she was not commissioned until January 1939. Although very elegant, the ship was under-gunned for a vessel of its size owing to initial political considerations against adopting larger calibre guns and an emphasis on defensive characteristics. Plans were drawn up to replace the triple 11in gun turrets with twin 15in ones, but the outbreak of the Second World War prevented this. The high-pressure steam propulsion gave her a high speed of 31 knots, but was susceptible to defects requiring lengthy maintenance periods. Despite the retrofitting of an 'Atlantic' bow, the *Scharnhorst* was a notoriously 'wet' ship.

During the first years of the war the *Scharnhorst* operated alongside her sister, the *Gneisenau* and together they sank the AMC *Rawalpindi*, the carrier *Glorious* and her attendant destroyers. The zenith of the partnership's success was a two-month raid into the Atlantic between January and March 1941 in which they sank 22 vessels totalling more than 115,000 tonnes. Withdrawn to Germany in February 1942 owing to British air raids on Brest, the *Scharnhorst* underwent lengthy repairs and in March 1943 was sent to Norway to help disrupt Allied convoys to the Soviet Union. On 26 December while attempting to intercept two Allied convoys in heavy seas off the North Cape the *Scharnhorst* was engaged and sunk by a powerful British force, led by HMS *King George V*, which used radar to direct its gunnery to great effect in the winter darkness. Only 36 of the crew of 1968 men survived. *MF*

*Scharnhorst*, c. 1940 *(photograph),Hulton-Deutsch Collection/Corbis*

770.5ft x 98.4ft x 32.5ft (234.8m x 30m x 9.9m) • 38,100 tons [D] • Hull steel • Armament 9 x 11.2in, 12 x 6in, 14 x 10.5cm, 16 x 3.7cm, 34 x 2cm, 6 x 21in torpedo tubes • Complement 1800 • Built Kriegsmarinewerft, Wilhelmshaven, Germany, 1939

# Surcouf Submarine 1940

Authorized under the 1926 Estimates, *Surcouf* was designed for long-range commerce warfare. She would take more than five years to build and on completion was the world's largest submarine – a position she would hold until 1942. Two large Sulzer diesels, each rated at 3800bhp, provided a maximum speed of 18.5 knots on the surface, and she carried sufficient stores for a 90-day patrol. A floatplane intended to locate potential targets was stowed in a watertight hangar abaft the conning tower. Other novel features included a boarding launch and, to conform with Prize Laws, accommodation for 40 prisoners. The 8in guns, which were in a watertight trainable twin turret, could open fire just over two minutes after surfacing. There were four 21.6in bow torpedo tubes, and two triple trainable mountings each comprising one tube flanked by two 15.7in tubes, all of which were reloadable; the smaller torpedoes were for use against small surface warships and merchantmen. When completed *Surcouf* was plagued with technical problems, some of which were never completely resolved. After the fall of France in 1940, she served with the Free French, largely as a transatlantic convoy escort. She was lost in a collision with a US freighter off Jamaica in February 1942. *JJ*

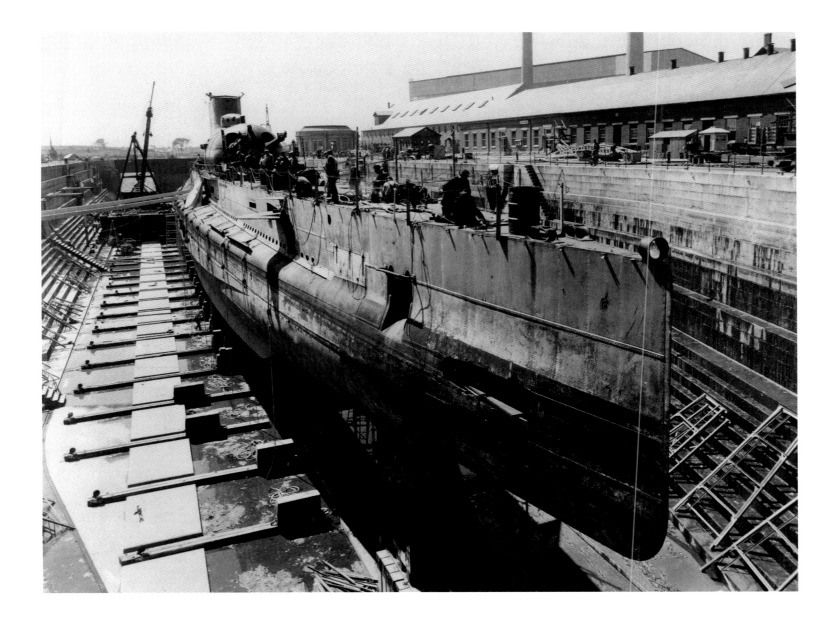

*Surcouf* in Dry Dock No. 2 at Portsmouth, 1 September 1941 *(photograph), Royal Navy Submarine Museum*

361ft x 30ft x 23ft (110m x 9m x 7m) • 3250 tons [D] • Hull steel • Armament 2 x 8in, 6 x 21.7in + 4 x 15.7in torpedo tubes, 2 x 37mm cannon, floatplane • Complement 118 • Built Cherbourg, France, 1931

# U-99 Type VIIB U-boat 1940

*U-99* was one of the most successful U-boats of the Second World War. She was laid down as one of the 24 boats of the Type VIIB group, which, with their successors of the Type VIIC group, became the workhorses of the U-boat flotillas. She was commissioned in 1940 under the command of Otto Kretschmer, who would become one of Germany's greatest U-boat aces. Assigned to the 7th Flotilla, based first at Kiel and then at Lorient, *U-99* began her patrols in the North Atlantic in July 1940, and during her relatively short career sank no fewer than 38 merchant ships for a total of 244,658 gross register tonnage, damaged five more ships and captured one ship as a

prize. For this Kretschmer received the Knights Cross with Oak Leaves and Swords. During the first four patrols of *U-99* Kretschmer attacked convoys at night on the surface, sinking merchant ships with a single torpedo in order to save ammunition. He earned a reputation for chivalry towards the crews of the merchantmen he sank. *U-99* was finally hunted down and attacked south of Iceland by HMS *Walker* and *Vanoc*. With his boat severely damaged and forced to the surface, Kretschmer ordered her to be scuttled. Forty crew, including Kretschmer were rescued and became prisoners of war, while three crewmen lost their lives. *JJ*

**Oberfähnrich zur See Volkmar König leans out of the starboard side of U-99's conning tower** *(photograph). Völkmar Konig*

218ft x 20ft x 15ft (66.5m x 6.2m x 4.7m) • 740 tons [D] • Hull steel • Armament 5 x 53cm (21in) torpedo tubes, 1 x 8.8cm (3.4in) • Complement 44 • Built Germaniawerft, Kiel, Germany, 1939

# Washington North Carolina class battleship 1940

USS *Washington* and her sister North *Carolina* were the first US battleships laid down after the 'battleship holiday' agreed at the Washington Conference. The calibre of the main guns was increased at a late stage in the design process when, faced with the reported construction of new Japanese battleships armed with 16in guns, the USA invoked the escalation clause in the London Treaty of 1936. This meant that while the ships were armed with 16in guns, they were protected only against 14in shells, a deficiency corrected in the following South Dakota class. Unlike contemporary European and Imperial Japanese navy battleships, *Washington* had a lightweight secondary armament of dual-purpose 5in guns in lightly-protected enclosed mountings. Although the 5in shell was arguably incapable

of stopping an enemy destroyer, it proved to be an excellent anti-aircraft weapon. The initial close-range battery of four quadruple 1.1in guns was soon supplemented by multiple 0.8in Oerlikon guns, and from 1943 was replaced by the formidable new 1.6in Bofors quad. The impressive AA capabilities of these ships, together with their relatively high speed of 28 knots, led to their incorporation into the carrier task groups from which they could be extracted, if required, to form a conventional battle line. Following an initial deployment in support of the British Home Fleet in the North Atlantic, *Washington* took part in the Solomons Campaign of mid-1942, sinking the Japanese battleship *Kirishima*, and then served primarily as a carrier escort for the remainder of the war. *JJ*

USS *Washington* and USS *Lexington* (background) as part of Task Force No. 50, en route to the Gilbert Islands, November 1943. An SBD Dauntless dive bomber is on escort patrol top right *(photograph)*. *Conway Picture Library*

729ft x 108ft x 33ft (222m x 33m x 10m) • 37,500 tons [D] • Hull steel • Armament (as built) 9 x 16in, 20 x 5in, 16 x 1.1in • Complement 1880 • Built Philadelphia Navy Yard, USA. 1941

# Trento  Trento class cruiser 1940

The Italian cruisers *Trento* and *Trieste* were among the first of the so-called 'treaty cruisers', and made a huge impact when they were first commissioned. Powerfully armed and moderately protected, *Trento* attained 35.6 knots on her eight-hour power trials, making her by a comfortable margin the fastest cruiser of her time. This led to export orders for similar cruisers, notably from Argentina.

Unusually, the Italians used longitudinal construction for the midships (protected) section, and transverse construction for the ends of the ship. Other noteworthy features included: a unit machinery layout – advantageous for damage control purposes; fixed athwartships torpedo tubes; and a fixed catapult and hangar for three reconnaissance aircraft set into the forecastle. However, *Trento* was a flawed design: the turrets were cramped and the closeness of the gun axes resulted in dispersion problems; the legs of the tripod mast were not firmly seated on transverse bulkheads, leading to severe vibration which affected fire control; and she emerged from the shipyard several hundred tons overweight. *Trento* served with her sister and the modified *Bolzano* in the 3rd Division, and took part in virtually all the major actions of the early war period. She was finally torpedoed and sunk by the British submarine *Umbra* during the Malta convoy operations of 1942. *JJ*

**The inner harbour at Taranto showing two damaged Trento class cruisers, an RAF reconnaissance photograph taken after a raid by Fleet Air Arm Fairey Swordfish aircraft** *(aerial photograph), 12 November 1940, Conway Picture Library*

646ft x 68ft x 22ft (197m x 20.6m x 6.8m) • 13,110 tons [D] • Hull steel • Armament 8 x 8in, 16 x 3.9in, 4 x 40mm, 8 x 21in torpedo tubes, 3 aircraft •
Complement 730 • Built OTO, Leghorn, Italy, 1927

# Bismarck    Bismarck class battleship 1941

One of the most well-known ships of the Second World War, *Bismarck* was to have been the first of a series of battleships designed to operate in a conventional battle fleet. In the event only her sister-ship *Tirpitz* was completed; construction of their successors was abandoned, and it was decided that *Bismarck* should be used instead as a commerce raider, a role for which her characteristics made her poorly suited. She was a powerful ship, with excellent guns and fire control systems and a good turn of speed, but her protection system was dated: she carried her horizontal armour one deck lower than her foreign contemporaries, which exposed significantly more of her internal volume to plunging shell fire.

Following work-up *Bismarck* was earmarked for Operation Rheinübung, in which she would break out into the North Atlantic in company with the cruiser *Prinz Eugen* and attack Allied shipping. The German ships were intercepted in the Denmark Strait by the British battlecruiser *Hood*, a powerful unit desperately in need of modernization, and the new battleship *Prince of Wales*. She sank the *Hood*, but damage sustained in the action led to a decision to head for the French port of Brest. After a prolonged chase, her rudder crippled by an aerial torpedo, she was finally caught and sunk by the battleships *King George V* and *Rodney*. JJ

'The sinking of the *Bismarck*', 27 May 1941 *(oil on canvas)*, *Charles E. Turner, c. 1941, National Maritime Museum, London (BHC0679)*

814ft x 118ft x 29ft (248m x 36m x 8.7m) • 41,700 tons [D] • Hull steel • Armament 8 x 15in, 12 x 5.9in, 16 x 4.1in, 16 x 37mm, 4 aircraft • Complement 2090 •
Built Blohm & Voss, Hamburg, Germany, 1940

# Ark Royal  Aircraft carrier 1941

One of the most famous ships of the Second World War, *Ark Royal* was the British Royal Navy's first purpose-built fleet carrier. In common with her immediate predecessors, the converted battlecruisers *Courageous* and *Glorious*, she had a two-tier hangar and a short island structure dominated by a tall, broad funnel to starboard. However, unlike the latter ships she had a full-length flight deck with considerable overhang aft. Her lower hull, housing the propulsion machinery, the aviation fuel tanks and the ordnance magazines, had cruiser-scale protection, and her anti-aircraft armament, comprising a mix of medium-calibre 4.5in high angle guns and multiple 2pdr pompoms for self-defence, was impressive for the period. As first designed

she was intended to operate 72 aircraft, but this figure was subsequently reduced to 60; in wartime she generally carried 30 Swordfish torpedo biplanes and 21 Sea Skua fighter/dive-bombers.

*Ark Royal* was very active in the first two years of the war, operating with the Gibraltar-based Force H and taking part in the pursuit of the *Bismarck*. It was a torpedo from one of her Swordfish which secured the crippling hit that delivered the German battleship to her executioners. *Ark Royal*'s career was prematurely ended by a single torpedo from a German U-boat. A heavy list resulted in extensive flooding of the machinery spaces via the low funnel uptakes, and the ship lost power and was subsequently abandoned. *JJ*

**HMS *Ark Royal* lists heavily to starboard after being torpedoed by U-81 off Gibraltar** (photograph), Lt. S.J. Beadell, 13 November 1941, Imperial War Museum (A 6334)

800ft x 95ft x 28ft (244m x 29m x 8.5m) • 22,000 tons [D] • Hull steel • Armament 60 aircraft; 16 x 4.5in, 48 x 2 pdr pompom • Complement 1580 • Built Cammell Laird & Co., Birkenhead, England, 1937

# Prince of Wales King George V class battleship 1941

The loss of HMS *Prince of Wales* along with the battlecruiser HMS *Repulse* on 10 December 1941 was a shock to Churchill, the Admiralty and the wider British public. It marked a turning point in the Pacific theatre, hastening the fall of Singapore to the Japanese and severely weakening the Eastern Fleet, which withdrew to Ceylon and the Dutch East Indies. Most significantly, the sinkings illustrated the effectiveness of aerial attacks against naval forces that were not protected by air cover, sounding the death knell for the battleship and emphasizing the importance of the aircraft carrier in major fleet actions.

A modern battleship launched in 1939, *Prince of Wales* had already seen considerable action when she was deployed to Singapore, in an effort to curb Japanese aggression and deter any invasion attempt on the British colony. There she became part of Force Z, along with the ageing HMS *Repulse* and four destroyers; HMS *Electra*, HMS *Express*, HMS *Encounter*, and HMS *Jupiter*. The intended air component of this force, HMS *Indomitable*, had run aground while working up in the Caribbean and had thus returned to dry dock in Virginia, USA for repair.

On 8 December the Japanese landed in Malaya and began to push towards the Johor–Singapore Causeway that connected Singapore to Malaya. Force Z sailed to intercept a Malaya convoy, but was unsuccessful, instead identifying targets of opportunity on the east coast of Malaya. On the morning of the 10th, the ships were attacked by waves of Japanese bombers and torpedo-bombers. *Prince of Wales* was hit by 4 torpedoes, taking a catastrophic hit to her outer port propeller shaft. Listing to port and severely damaged, she rolled over and sank at 1.18 pm. 327 sailors were lost. *MJ*

1919-1946

The crew of HMS *Prince of Wales* abandoning ship, after torpedo attacks by Japanese aircraft in the South China Sea. Alongside, the destroyer HMS *Express* takes on survivors *(photograph), Lt. Cmdr Cartwright, 10 December 1941, Imperial War Museum (HU 2675)*

745ft x 103ft x 29ft (227.1m x 31.4m x 8.8m) • 43,786 tons [D] • Hull steel • Armament 10 x 14in, 16 x 5.2in, 32 x 2 pdr, 3 rocket projectors, 2 aircraft • Complement 1560 • Built Cammell Laird & Co., Birkenhead, England, 1941

# West Virginia Colorado class battleship 1941

This American super-dreadnought battleship, laid down in April 1920, represented the durability and flexibility of these types of weapons-platforms even up to the end of the Second World War. During the Japanese attack on the US Pacific Fleet at Pearl Harbor (7 December 1941), *West Virginia* (*BB-48*) was a frequent target of enemy torpedo and dive-bomber aircraft, positioned at the centre of 'Battleship Row' off Ford Island and sheltering the battleship *Tennessee*, moored inboard. In this she suffered at least seven hits, as well as two direct armour-piercing bombs – which penetrated but failed to explode. Her captain was killed in the morning's action; a cook, Doris Miller, earned the distinction of being the first African-American to receive the Navy Cross for gallantly manning an anti-aircraft gun while the ship burned around him and eventually settled to the bottom. In a grisly reminder of the perils of naval service, the remains of three sailors were found months later when the *West Virginia* was finally salvaged. They had been trapped in an airtight compartment and had survived on rations for 16 days following 7 December.

After an extensive refitting which emphasized improved anti-aircraft defences, the 'Wee Vee' helped sink the Japanese battleship *Yamashiro* with radar-controlled gunnery at the Battle of Leyte Gulf (Surigao Strait, 25 October 1944). She went on to pound enemy coastal positions in the Philippines, Iwo Jima and Okinawa, where she was struck by a kamikaze, suffered light damage yet resumed her fire-support to US Marines later that evening. *HF*

**The USS *West Virginia* and USS *Tennessee* after the Japanese attack on Pearl Harbour, 7 December 1941** *(photograph), Conway Picture Library*

624ft x 97.3ft x 30.5ft (190m x 29.7m x 9.3 m) • 33,590 tons [D] • Hull steel • Armament 8 x 16in, 12 x 5in, 4 x 3in, 2 x 21in torpedo tubes. After reconstruction; 8 x 16in, 16 x 5in, 40 x Bofors 40mm, 50 x Oerlikon 20mm • Complement 1407 • Built Newport News Shipbuilding, Virginia, USA, 1921

# Siluro a Lenta Corsa Manned torpedo 1941

The boom guarding the British base at Alexandria opened at 1 a.m. on 19 December 1941 to admit the 15th Cruiser Squadron and, unbeknown to the sentries on high alert, three pairs of Italian frogmen riding 'Siluri a Lenta Corsa' (slow speed torpedoes). Led by Luigi Durand de la Penne, they belonged to the Decima Flottiglia MAS, the Italian navy's elite special force, and had been transported to Alexandria by the specially adapted submarine *Scirè* commanded by Lieutenant Commander Borghese.

Five hours later three massive explosions ripped though HMS *Queen Elizabeth*, HMS *Valiant* and the Norwegian oiler, *Sagona*, putting the battleships *hors-de-combat* for many months.

Developed by two naval engineers, Sub-Lieutenants Tesei and Toschi, the 'human torpedo' was, in fact, a torpedo-shaped, battery-powered, mini-submarine on which a two-man crew rode at 2 knots, their feet in stirrups. Its fore-end was a detachable, time-fused warhead filled with some 66lb

(300kg) of explosive. Behind the clutch, a windscreen protected the officer-pilot who steered the machine and controlled the trim-tank, resting his back against the externally mounted crash-submersion tank that separated him from his petty-officer diver. The latter braced himself against a tool box, the contents of which included cutters to break though defensive torpedo-nets and clamps and wires to attach the warhead to the keel of the target. Using breathing apparatus the frogmen could ride partially or totally submerged, and go down under their targets to a maximum 98.4ft (30m).

The job done, the operators had to set the self-destruct on their machines, hide their frogmen suits and endeavour to escape.

The Alexandria attack was the unit's most spectacular success. All six men were captured, but after the Armistice, Italian expertise in this area assisted the British with the 'chariot' programme that had been set up to emulate and refine the Italian model. *JH*

*Siluro a lenta corsa; Italian slow-running torpedo (drawing). Erminio Bagnasco*

24ft/21ft without warhead x 1.9ft x 3.3ft* at shield (7.3m/6.7m x 0.5m x 1m) • 3500lb (1588kg) • Hull steel • Armament 300kg explosive warhead • Complement 2 • Built various yards, Italy, 1942

# Prinz Eugen   Admiral Hipper class heavy cruiser 1942

*Prinz Eugen* was the third of a class of heavy cruisers laid down for the Kriegsmarine shortly before the Second World War. The ships were designed as fleet units, but with the abandonment of the 'Z Plan' it was envisaged that they would be employed as commerce raiders, for which purpose they were given an exceptionally heavy armament of torpedoes. They were to prove poorly suited to this role, as their high-pressure steam turbine machinery proved unreliable, and their endurance was inferior to that of the Panzerschiffe. *Prinz Eugen* sortied into the North Atlantic in company with the *Bismarck* in May 1941, and when the latter was compelled to abandon her mission conducted her own short campaign against merchant shipping before proceeding to Brest, where she joined the battleships *Scharnhorst* and *Gneisenau*. In early 1942 it was decided to bring these three heavy units back to Germany. In a well-planned operation christened 'Cerberus', and heavily escorted by torpedo-boats and the Luftwaffe, *Prinz Eugen* and the two battleships made their way up the Channel under the noses of the British (see photo). *Prinz Eugen* entered German waters unscathed, but shortly afterwards was torpedoed while attempting to transfer to Norway. She was subsequently employed as a training ship, and was finally sunk while under the US flag following the atomic weapons tests off Bikini Atoll in 1946. *JJ*

View from *Prinz Eugen*, looking aft, with the German *panzerschiffs Scharnhorst* and *Gneisenau* steaming behind through a grey and misty English Channel, 13 February 1942 *(photograph), Conway Picture Library*

697 ft x 72 ft x 24ft (212.5 m x 21.8m x 7.2m) • 15,240 tons [D] • Hull steel • Armament 8 x 20.3cm, 12 x 10.5cm, 17 x 4cm Flak, 8 × 37mm, 28 x 2cm MG, 12 x 53.3cm torpedoes, 3 x Arado Ar 196 floatplanes • Complement approx. 1600 • Built Germania shipyards, Kiel, Germany, 1938

# Campbeltown ex-US Wickes class destroyer 1942

HMS *Campbeltown* was one of fifty destroyers transferred to the Royal Navy as part of the 1940 Anglo-US 'Destroyers for Bases' agreement. Formerly the USS *Buchanan*, she was an obsolescent ship dating from 1919, a Wickes class flush-decker, a type nicknamed 'four-pipers' or 'four-stackers' due to their four prominent funnels. After being refitted and modernised she worked on Atlantic convoy escort. In January 1942 however, she was taken out of service and specially modified to play her part in one of the most daring operations of the Second World War.

At this time the German battleship *Tirpitz* was anchored in Norway, a potential threat to the Atlantic convoys that supplied the Allied war effort and the beleaguered British nation. Were she to start commerce-raiding operations she could wreak havoc on the merchant ships. To do so, however, *Tirpitz* needed a base, and the only suitable dry-dock on the Atlantic seaboard was at St Nazaire, in German-occupied France.

The Allies determined that the dock had to be put out of commission to eliminate the *Tirpitz* threat. Accordingly, Operation Chariot was devised – a raid in which *Campbeltown*, her appearance altered to resemble a German Möwe class destroyer, would ram the St Nazaire lock gates and blow up the dock with a delayed-action explosive charge. She would be accompanied by 18 shallow draught boats including MTB74, MGB314 and Fairmile B motor launches, which would land commandos to destroy other key dockyard structures before fighting their way out.

The operation, which was carried out on the night of 28 March 1942, was a success, despite incurring heavy losses. Out of 611 Commandos engaged in the operation, all but 27 were either killed or captured; 22 escaped back to Britain and 5 escaped to the Spanish border. Five Victoria Crosses were awarded to men involved in the raid, including Lieutenant-Commander Stephen Halden Beattie RN, who commanded *Campbeltown. MJ*

**HMS *Campbeltown* at St Nazaire, 27 March 1942** *(oil on canvas), Norman Wilkinson, twentieth century, National Maritime Museum, London (BHC1597)*

314.4ft x 31.8ft x 9ft (95.8m x 9.7m x 2.7m) • 1090 tons [D] • Hull steel • Armament 4 x 4in, 1 x 1 pdr, 2 x 3 pdr, 2 x .30 cal, 12 x 21in torpedo tubes • Complement 113 • Built Bath Iron Works, Bath, Maine, USA, 1919

# Takao  Takao class heavy cruiser 1942

*Takao* was the lead ship of a class of four heavy cruisers built by the Imperial Japanese Navy at the end of the 1920s in response to the limit of 10,000 tons displacement imposed by the Washington Treaty on warships of this category. Designed as an improvement of the Myókó class, Japan's first 'treaty cruisers', the *Takao* had several substantial differences, the most visually notable being her ten-level massive bridge structure. The complex installations in her superstructure, including communications, command, navigation and fire-control stations, reflected the cruiser's function as fleet flagship and command centre in day and night engagements involving gunnery and torpedoes. The result was a ship that proved to be top-heavy, highly resistant to the wind and that, in principle, presented a larger target for enemy fire. These considerations notwithstanding, the *Takao* was a very successful design, reflecting the navy's constant demand for offensive power

on its warships. This cruiser had a stunning top speed of more than 33 knots, 10 x 8in guns with a maximum elevation of 70° (enabling them – in principle – to double as AA guns) and eight torpedo tubes. This combination of firepower and speed made the *Takao* a particularly effective combat platform.

In the battles that took place in the first year of the war in the Pacific, the *Takao* and her sister-ships performed with remarkable results, especially in night combats. In the Battle of the Savo Island (8–9 August 1942), the third cruiser of the class, *Chókai*, acting as flagship of the 8th Fleet under the command of Vice-Admiral Gunichi Mikawa, was at the centre of a most devastating defeat inflicted on the Allied forces, sinking four cruisers. In the darkness of the summer night over southeast Asia, the distinctive battleship-like features of the cruiser *Takao* came to be associated with a formidable adversary. *AP*

**Japanese Heavy Cruiser *Takao*** *(oil on canvas), Ross Watton, 1993*

669ft x 68ft x 21ft (204m x 20.7m x 6.4m) • 9850 tons [D] • Hull steel • Armament 10 x 8in, 8 x 4.7in, 66 x 0.9in, 16 x 24in torpedo tubes • Complement 773 • Built Yokosuka Naval Shipyard, Japan, 1930

# Enterprise Yorktown class aircraft carrier 1942

The 'Big E' was part of the U.S. Navy's pre-war carrier programme and went on to become the most decorated warship in American naval history. She was the second of the Yorktown class of fast aircraft carriers, and pushed the limits of the 1922 Washington Naval Treaty at 19,800 tons. Laid down in 1934, *Enterprise* joined the fleet in 1938 as tensions mounted with Imperial Japan. On 7 December 1941 she arrived in Hawaiian waters to find Pearl Harbor under attack. She avoided detection by Japanese attack planes but was unable to discover enemy carriers before they retired. *Enterprise* joined the task force which launched the famous 'Doolittle Raid' against Tokyo in April 1942 and missed participating in the Battle of the Coral Sea the following month. Her role in the subsequent Battle of Midway (4-7 June 1942), however, was

crucial. In conjunction with *Yorktown*, it was her Dauntless dive-bombers which sank three Japanese carriers, followed by the fourth after *Yorktown* herself was stricken. This was the turning of the tide in the Pacific War, and one of the most decisive naval battles in history. *Enterprise* went on to serve in nearly every major campaign that followed, as Japanese naval power waned in the face of American mobilization.

Several other ships have taken the name; one served successfully in the War of 1812; another entered service as the world's first nuclear-powered aircraft carrier (1961). The tradition continues into space with Gene Roddenberry's 'Star Trek' franchise, and the naming of the first space shuttle 'Enterprise' in 1974. *HF*

Douglas Dauntless dive-bombers and Grumman Wildcat fighters on the forward deck of USS *Enterprise* (photograph), c. early 1942, Conway Picture Library

[As built] 809.5ft x 83ft x 21.5ft (246.7m x 25.3m x 6.6m) • 19,800 tons [D] • Hull steel • Armament 8 × 5in, 4 × quad 1.1in, 24 × .50 calibre MG, 90 aircraft • Complement 2217 • Built Newport News, Virginia, USA, 1936

# Lexington Lexington class aircraft carrier 1942

*Lexington* and her sister-ship *Saratoga* were the first fleet carriers built for the US Navy, and were used extensively during the interwar period to develop carrier tactics and air operations. They were built using battlecruiser hulls which would otherwise have had to be scrapped following the Washington Treaty of 1922. The treaty restricted carriers to 27,000 tons displacement, but an exception was made to enable the conversion of these two ships. They were completed with twin 8in gun mountings fore and aft of the prominent island superstructure and funnel for self-defence against similarly-armed 'treaty cruisers', but these were removed from *Lexington* shortly before her

loss. The exceptionally large flight deck was complemented by a relatively small hangar which was used only for maintenance. This prompted the development of a large deck park allied to a crash barrier, aircraft being moved forward on landing and then re-spotted aft for take-off; as a result, US Navy carrier air strikes were typically much larger than those of other navies.

Struck by two torpedoes and three bombs at the Battle of Coral Sea on the morning of 8 May 1942, *Lexington* was later shaken by a massive explosion caused by a build-up of petrol vapour and had to be scuttled. This disastrous loss prompted a revision of damage control arrangements in US carriers. *JJ*

**Survivors from the USS *Lexington* are pulled aboard a cruiser after the Battle of the Coral Sea** *(photograph), 8 May 1942, Conway Picture Library*

888ft x 105.5ft x 33ft (259m x 32m x 10m) • 36,000 tons [D] • Hull steel • Armament 90 aircraft, 8 x 8in, 12 x 5in • Complement 2300 • Built Bethlehem, Quincy, Massachusetts, USA, 1925

1919-1946

# Akagi Aircraft carrier 1942

Originally laid down as a battlecruiser, *Akagi* was named after a mountain – standard practice in the Japanese navy for warships of this type. Converted to an aircraft carrier following the disposition of the 1922 Washington Treaty, the *Akagi* became the jewel in the crown of Japan's carrier striking force, flying the colours of Vice-Admiral Chúichi Nagumo in the attack on Pearl Harbor and in the Battle of Midway. In the interwar period, the *Akagi* constituted the navy's testing ground for the development of tactical and technological solutions in the emerging field of naval aviation. Her initial design, incorporating three superimposed decks and 8in surface guns, proved the experimental character of these new capabilities.

Maintaining lean lines deriving from her cruiser hull and a rather tall profile due to the number of decks, the *Akagi* underwent major modifications between 1935 and 1938. The transformation reflected the coming of age of naval aviation and the navy's intention to maximize its offensive potential. As the multiple flight decks proved to be ineffective, especially with the constantly growing dimensions and weight of aircraft and ordnance, they were removed together with the naval guns; the lower hangars and the upper flight deck were extended to a capacity of 91 aircraft, and an island superstructure on the port side of the ship. This was an unusual arrangement that coupled with her downturned starboard funnel, gave the *Akagi* a unique design for a specific purpose. The carrier was conceived to operate with starboard-sided carriers as a way to improve the flight pattern of the formation increasing the effectiveness of the long-range punch of the fleet. Though the experiment was not continued beyond the carrier *Hiryú*, the design and technical features of the *Akagi* well summarized the spirit of the force it served: it was a platform designed to strike first and strike hard. *AP*

The Battle of Midway: US SBD-3 Dauntless bombers attacking the Japanese carriers *Akagi* and *Kaga*, 1942 *(oil on canvas), Keith Woodcock*

855ft x 103ft x 28.7ft (260.7m x 31.3m x 8.7m) • 36,500 tons [D] • Hull steel • Armament 10 x 8in, 12 x 4.7in, 28 x 25mm (0.9in) • Complement 1630 • Built Kure Naval Shipyard, Hiroshima, Japan, 1925

# Soryu · Aircraft carrier 1942

The 'Blue Dragon' was the first of a class of two aircraft carriers constructed by the Imperial Japanese Navy in the mid-1930s. The first of Japan's third-generation carriers, the design of *Soryu* incorporated all the basic features that characterized subsequent Japanese carrier designs. These included a high-aspect cruiser-like hull propelled by powerful engines with twin down swept funnels to vent exhaust gases away from the flight decks, dual hangar decks, small island structure, and light construction with little or no armament. The peculiar features of the *Soryu* were largely the result of the desire of her naval architects to circumvent the limitations on carrier tonnage imposed by the naval treaties. Taking advantage of the definition of aircraft carriers as ships designed exclusively for air operations, Japanese designers initially drafted plans for a 'hybrid' warship, one that would include cruiser-class armament and that could remain, as a result, outside the calculations for the total carrier tonnage allocated to Japan. By the time her keel was laid down, the Imperial Japanese Navy had already set its heart on withdrawing from the treaties and the ship was completed maintaining the hybrid configuration but without the 6in gun cruiser armament. The ultimate result was a particularly light platform with an astonishing maximum speed of 35 knots which could accommodate an air wing of 68 aircraft (51 operational and 17 as reserve). Similarly to other classes of warship operated by the Imperial Japanese Navy, the *Soryu* was meant to maximize speed of action and firepower, it represented the tip of the sword of the navy. To obtain these results, the carrier sacrificed defensive protection. In this respect, *Soryu* well summarized Japanese preference for naval assets capable to deliver devastating blows, a choice that contributed to give them their reputation as aggressive and fearless modern samurais. Speed and firepower represented the contributions of the carrier *Soryu* to Japan's undisputed ascendancy in the opening stages of the war in the Pacific. Nonetheless, her lack of defensive protection proved to be a fatal Achilles' heel, one that was fully revealed at the Battle of Midway when she became the first Japanese carrier to be sunk since the outbreak of the hostilities. *AP*

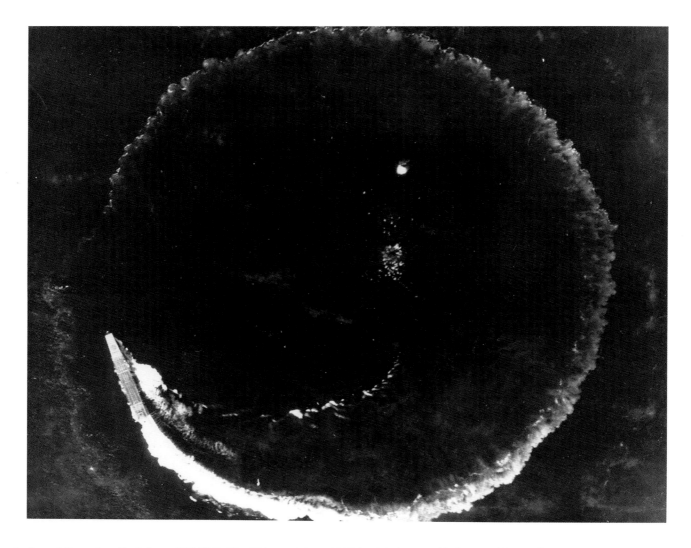

*Soryu* circling while under attack from USAAF B-17s, Midway, 4 June 1942 *(aerial photograph)*, *Conway Picture Library*

728.5ft x 70ft x 24.5ft (222m x 21m x 7.4m) • 18,800 tons [D] • Hull steel • Armament 12 x 5in, 28 x 0.9in • Complement 1100 • Built Kure Naval Dockyard, Hiroshima, Japan,1935

# Victorious   Illustrious class aircraft carrier 1942

The aircraft carrier is the only military asset capable of projecting power at sea and from the sea on a sustainable global scale. Its reach and hitting power are formidable and aircraft carriers are an integral, some might say central, component of modern maritime war. One only has to think of the War in the Pacific during the Second World War or the Royal Navy's ski-jump carriers during the Falklands campaign to appreciate the vital contribution made to winning those wars.

Yet, as so often with the operations of navies, their roles are hidden from the wider public. Such is the case with HMS *Victorious*, a ship with a glittering service record in the Second World War. In 1941 she was involved in the hunt for the *Bismarck* and the *Prinz Eugen*, and later ferried aircraft to the defence of Malta. Among all her triumphs, however, perhaps the most vital was her participation in Operation Tungsten, the attack on the German battleship

*Tirpitz* in April 1944. The *Tirpitz* was the biggest battleship built in Europe and had just undergone repairs from previous action and was ready to take to the sea again – and at a critical time with the Allies planning Operation Overlord, the invasion of Europe. Nothing would be left to chance, and the *Tirpitz* could have caused immense damage upon the invasion flotilla or the vital Atlantic sea lines of communication from Britain to America. Operation Tungsten took place on 3 April and although *Tirpitz* was not sunk, the damage inflicted put her out of action for two months. Further attacks continued during April and into May and, though not a success, the *Tirpitz* did not put to sea until August 1944 – two months after D-Day and the Allied invasion of Europe. So, even though the individual raids did not achieve their aim, the higher strategic aim of negating the *Tirpitz* had been achieved. *MR*

**Aircraft carriers in the Malta convoy** *(oil on canvas), Charles Pears, c. 1942, National Maritime Museum, London (BHC1575)*

673ft x 95ft x 28ft (205m x 29m x 8.5m) • 29,500 tons [D] • Hull steel • Armament 16 × 4.5in, 48 × 2 pdr, 21 × 40 mm AA, 45 × 20 mm AA, 36-54 aircraft •
Complement 730 • Built Vickers Armstrong, High Walker, Tyne, England, 1939

# Iowa  Iowa class battleship 1942

In 1938, following rumours of Japanese battleships displacing 46,000 tons, the USA invoked the Escalator Clause of the 1936 London Treaty: capital ships could now be armed with 16in guns and displace 45,000 tons. Faced with a choice between more guns, heavier armour and higher speed for their next class of battleships, the US Navy opted for the latter. This made the *Iowa* class well-suited to operations with the fast carrier task forces, and the advantages of the long hull adopted to achieve 32.5 knots included the ability to pass through the Panama Canal – the beam was unchanged from the South Dakota class – and to accommodate large numbers of light AA guns without interference from the main battery. Two ships were launched in 1942 and completed in early 1943, two in mid-1944; two further ships were cancelled.

In November 1943 *Iowa* carried President Roosevelt to Casablanca for the Tehran Conference, and subsequently joined her sister *New Jersey* in the fast carrier task forces for the early raids on the Japanese island chains of the central Pacific. *Missouri* and *Wisconsin* took part in the later operations against the Japanese islands, and it was on the quarterdeck of *Missouri* that the Japanese surrender took place. Following a lengthy period in reserve *Iowa* was reactivated in 1984 as part of the 600-Ship Navy Plan, and was fitted with Tomahawk land attack cruise missiles. She was decommissioned in 1990. *JJ*

**1919-1946**

**USS Iowa (BB-61) firing her 16in guns** (*photograph*), *August 1984, Conway Picture Library*

887ft x 108ft x 36ft (270m x 33m x 11m) • 48,000 tons [D] • Hull steel • Armament 9 x 16in, 20 x 5in, 80 x 40mm • Complement 1920 • Built New York Navy Yard, New York, USA, 1942

# Laconia  Cunard ocean liner 1942

Exuding a sense of grandeur and elegance, and much admired for her clean lines, in her 1920s heyday the Cunard liner RMS *Laconia* was a luxurious ship. In 1922 she made the first round-the-world-cruise to be navigated by gyrocompass.

During the Second World War she was requisitioned by the Admiralty as a troop carrier, albeit a slow and smoky one, and Saturday, 12 September 1942 found her sailing unescorted north of Ascension Island with 2700 crew, armed forces personnel, women, children and Italian prisoners. At 8.15 p.m. *U-156* put two torpedoes into her hold, causing carnage among the Italians and fatally damaging the ship. Evacuation was a chaotic affair; the prisoners were held below deck until a few moments before the ship went down.

Discovering he had sunk a ship containing his country's allies, Kapitänleutnant Werner Hartenstein took the extraordinary step of breaking

off hostilities, appealing by radio for help from any nation willing to send ships, and rescuing as many people as he could. Women, children and the injured were brought into the submarine and cared for; supplies were distributed to the lifeboats, which he then took in tow towards a rendezvous with Vichy French warships. He abandoned his mercy mission only after a US B-24 Liberator, with orders to sink him, attempted to bomb the submarine.

Two lifeboats reached the African coast while other survivors were assisted by *U-506*, *U-507* and the Italian submarine *Comandante Cappellini* to reach the Vichy ships. Determined that no other German submarines would ever again be put at such risk, Admiral Dönitz issued the 'Laconia Order', forbidding his commanders to assist survivors. Two days afterwards, Hartenstein assisted the crew of the *Quebec City*.

*U-156* was lost with all hands in 1943. *JH*

**The Sinking of the *Laconia* in 1942** *(gouache on paper), Graham Coton, Private Collection / Look and Learn / The Bridgeman Art Library*

601ft x 73ft (183.2m x 22.4m) • 19,860 tons [GRT] • Hull steel • Complement 463, passengers: 347 first class, 350 second class, 1500 third class • Built Swan Hunter and Wigham Richardson, Wallsend-on-Tyne, England, 1921

# Belfast Town class light cruiser 1942

*Belfast* and her sister *Edinburgh* were the last in a series of large British cruisers armed with 6in guns intended to match the Imperial Japanese navy Mogami and US Brooklyn classes. Initial proposals were for four quadruple turrets of new design, but this was rejected in favour of the triple turrets of their predecessors. The increase in displacement was used instead to provide increased endurance and a more powerful anti-aircraft armament. The funnels and mainmast were widely separated from the bridge, giving these ships their distinctive appearance. However, the magazines for the 4in guns were well forward of the mountings, which slowed the rate of replenishment, and there was a structural weakness where the belt armour

was stepped down between the bridge and the fore funnel. This was largely responsible for *Belfast* breaking her back when mined in November 1939. Repairs took almost three years, the hull being reinforced at this point by a bulge which increased beam by 6ft (1.8m).

*Belfast* then served with distinction in northern waters, providing cover for the Arctic convoys and playing an active part in the sinking of the *Scharnhorst* in December 1943. In June 1944 she took part in the bombardment of enemy positions in support of the D-Day Landings. Modernized during the 1950s, *Belfast* was paid off in 1963 and is preserved as a memorial ship close to Tower Bridge, London. *JJ*

HMS *Belfast*, **exploded view** *(pen and ink drawing), Ross Watton, 1985*

613ft x 63ft x 21ft (187m x 19.3m x 6.5m) • 10,500 tons [D] • Hull steel • Armament 12 x 6in, 12 x 4in, 16 x 2 pdr pompom, 6 x 21in torpedo tubes, 3 aircraft • Complement 850 • Built Harland & Wolff, Belfast, Northern Ireland, 1938

1919-1946

# Intrepid Essex class aircraft carrier 1943

*Intrepid* was the third of the Essex class carriers, which formed the backbone of the carrier task forces that took the war to Japan in 1943–45. Twenty-four ships of the class were completed; two further ships were cancelled. This industrial-scale production could not have been matched by any other nation, and certainly not by Japan. The design was an enlarged *Yorktown*, with a unit machinery layout and a designed aircraft capacity of 90 – initially 36 Hellcat fighters, 36 Dauntless or Helldiver dive-bombers and 18 Avenger torpedo planes. Only the hull was armoured, the hangar and flight deck being totally unprotected. In addition to the two large square aircraft lifts at the ends of the hangar there was a side lift, which folded against the side of the ship when not in use.

Unlike the British armoured carriers, *Intrepid* depended on her aircraft for both attack and defence, a decision which was to be proved correct once air surveillance radar and plotting were sufficiently developed, and combat air patrol techniques perfected. *Intrepid* began operations against the Marshall Islands in late January 1944, and subsequently took part in all the major Pacific operations. During 1945 she was twice seriously damaged by kamikazes. In the mid-1950s *Intrepid* was modernized as an antisubmarine support carrier (CVS). She was finally decommissioned in 1974, becoming a museum ship in New York City. *JJ*

**USS** *Intrepid* *(oil on canvas), John Roberts, 1982*

870ft x 93ft x 28ft (265m x 28.5m x 8.5m) • 27,200 tons [D] • Hull steel • Armament 90 aircraft; 12 x 5in, 40 x 40mm • Complement 2700 • Built Newport News, Virginia, USA, 1943

# Giorgios Averoff  Armoured cruiser 1943

'Lucky Uncle George', as the cruiser was nicknamed by the crews of the Royal Hellenic Navy, served as flagship of the fleet from the Balkan War of 1912–1913 until she was decommissioned in 1952. Ordered in 1909, this armoured cruiser was initially commissioned from the Orlando shipyards in Livorno for the Regia Marina, but the Italian Government cancelled the order for budgetary reasons. Substantial financial assistance from Greek businessman and philanthropist Georgios Averoff enabled the Hellenic government to step in instead and secure the warship.

In a fleet of fast-ageing platforms, the modern solutions of the *Averoff*, featuring Italian engines, French boilers, German generators, and British guns, gave her a good blend of speed and firepower; she was an ideal military asset to operate in the Aegean Sea. More importantly, the choice to name her after her benefactor transformed the warship into an emblem of the Greek identity-building process; the *Averoff* was a statement of national gratitude towards the dedication of a most distinguished patriot.

The *Averoff* did not fail the nation's expectations. Under the command of Rear-Admiral Pavlos Kountouriotis, the outstanding officer of his generation, the warship was instrumental in the successes in the Battles of Elli (3 December 1912) and Lemnos (5 January 1913), giving Hellenic forces the command of the Aegean against Turkish naval power for the reminder of the war. In particular at Elli, Admiral Kountouriotis gave a distinctive naval character to the emerging Greek national martial identity. Following the professional footsteps of Admirals Nelson and Tógó, he hosted the 'Z' flag signalling 'independent action' and sailed 'by the power of God and the wishes of our King and in the name of justice (…) towards the victory against the enemy of the nation'. A little less than a hundred years later, the *Averoff* is today a museum, but she still flies the Greek jack as if she were in active service – testimony to the resolute character of her nation. *AP*

**Morning divisions on board *Giorgios Averoff*, as sailors make preparations for the celebration of Greek Independence Day, 25 March 1943** (*photograph*), *Imperial War Museum (A 15185)*

459.7ft x 68.9ft x 23.6ft (140.1m x 21m x 7.2m) • 10,200 tons [D] • Hull steel • Armament: 4 x 9.2in, 8 x 7.5in, 16 x 3in, 4 x 1.85in, 3 x 17in torpedo tubes • Complement 670 • Built Orlando Shipyards, Livorno, Italy, 1911

# Minesweeper   Defence ship 1943

During the Second World War, minesweeping operations were used by both sides to keep open safe channels for friendly vessels and to clear thousands of mines laid by the enemy. Minesweepers operated in home waters and on convoys and were an integral part of the protection for many amphibious landings. They had to deal with three types of device: the simple tethered contact mine, the acoustic mine that was set off by the sound of a ship's propeller, and the magnetic mine that exploded under the influence of the magnetic field created by a ship.

British war artist Leslie Cole recorded sweeping operations on an unnamed minesweeper off Gibraltar in 1943. The crew are swinging out an Oropesa: a float named after a First World War Admiralty trawler. This was towed astern on a long wire. Two contraptions – a 'kite' and an 'otter' –

were attached to this wire: the first near to the ship to determine the depth; the second towards the float, to hold the wire level and position the Oropesa. The serrated middle section was fitted with cutters, and if the cable of a tethered mine was caught, it would pass down the wire on to the cutter. Magnetic mines were detonated at a safe distance by towing a long and a short wire together and passing an electric current down them. Acoustic mines were set off by creating a sound similar to that of a propeller.

The specification given below is for the Bangor class HMS *Rye*, part of the 17th Minesweeping Flotilla at Gibraltar in 1942–3. She had a dramatic war, participating in the toughest Malta convoys, including Pedestal, and the landings in Sicily and at Salerno. On D-Day *Rye* swept for the Omaha beach landings and was decommissioned in 1946. *JH*

**Minesweeping in the Straits of Gibraltar, swinging out an Oropesa** *(watercolour), Leslie Cole, 1943, National Maritime Museum, London (PZ0548)*

174ft x 28.6ft x 9.8ft • 780 tons [D] • Hull steel • Armament 1 x 3in/20cwt HA, 40DC as escorts • Complement 60-87 • Built Ailsa Shipbuilding Company Ltd, Troon, Ayrshire, Scotland, 1941

# Jeremiah O'Brien  Liberty ship 1943

Allied victory in the Second World War owed much to the *Jeremiah O'Brien* and the other 2769 Liberty ships built in American shipyards between 1941 and 1945. This unique construction effort was organized by Henry J. Kaiser, an industrialist with no experience of shipbuilding. By standardizing and mass producing, Kaiser transformed an industry used to building individual ships into a car plant for the oceans. In essence, these ships replaced every single vessel sunk by U-boats during the war, maintaining the Allies decisive advantage, the ability to move men and material between theatres of war by sea. Although American built, the original design of these strong, simple and capacious ships was British. In the interests of mass production, basic triple-expansion engines and auxiliary machinery replaced diesels or turbines. Sold off in large numbers after 1945 Liberty ships helped revive the shipping industry postwar, and many carried on serving through the 1960s.

Built in Portland, Maine, in only 40 days, *Jeremiah O'Brien* went to sea in June 1943, made 11 supply runs to the D-Day beachhead and served in the Pacific War before being reduced to reserve in San Francisco Bay. In 1963 the mothball fleet was sent for scrap, but *Jeremiah O'Brien*, the best-preserved Liberty was saved as a memorial. From her base in San Francisco she made an emotional return to Europe and the Normandy beachhead in 1994 to mark the 50th anniversary of the invasion, and continues to steam around the Bay. She provided engine room scenes and sounds for James Cameron's blockbuster film *Titanic*. *ADL*

**Jeremiah O'Brien** *(photograph), Paul Holland / Flickr*

441.6ft x 57ft x 27.9ft (135m x 17.4m x 8.5m) • 14,245 tons [D] • Hull steel • Armament 8 x 20mm AA, 1 x 3in, 1 x 5in gun • Complement approx. 80 • Built New England Shipbuilding Corporation, South Portland, Maine, USA, 1943

# Cavalier C class destroyer 1944

A late development of the standard War Emergency Programme destroyers, *Cavalier* had many of the characteristics of her predecessors of the O–W classes, but had the new 4.5in, 45-calibre Mk IV gun in place of the 4.7in of the earlier ships. Although the gun had a lower velocity, the shell was heavier and had less air resistance. To speed the ship's construction the bow and stern sections were welded, the midships section being riveted to ensure strength.

On completion *Cavalier* joined the 6th Destroyer Flotilla Home Fleet, taking part in operations off Norway. In February 1942 she escorted convoy RA-64 from the Kola Inlet in Russia, surviving attacks by aircraft and U-boats

and a force 12 hurricane; this action earned her a battle honour. Following the German surrender she was transferred to the Pacific. She was subjected to various modifications during the post-war era, including the fitting of the Seacat surface-to-air missile system. *Cavalier* maintained her high speed even into old age, and in 1970 was the winner in a race with the frigate HMS *Rapid* to decide which was the fastest ship in the fleet. Following her decommissioning in 1972, by which time she was the last surviving warbuilt destroyer in the Royal Navy, she was preserved as a memorial ship in various locations, finding a final resting place at Chatham dockyard in 1998. *JJ*

1919-1946

**HMS *Cavalier* at Chatham** *(photograph), Paul Brown, 2008, Conway Picture Library*

363ft x 36ft x 14.5ft (111m x 11m x 4.5m) • 1750 tons [D] • Hull steel • Armament 4 x 4.5in QF Mk IV, 2 x 40mm Bofors, 10 x 21in torpedo tubes, 4 throwers and 2 racks for 96 depth charges • Complement 190 • Built White, East Cowes, Isle of Wight, 1944

# Convoy ships  Arctic convoy ships c.1944

Presented by the War Artists' Advisory Committee to the National Maritime Museum in 1946, this painting portrays survivors of a convoy entering the prominent port of Murmansk, Russia. The dramatic display of Northern Lights reveals the location to be within the Arctic Circle. Convoy conditions were harsh and dangerous, and especially this particular route, served by American and British servicemen, not just because of the brutal icy weather but also because of the attacks from German-occupied Norway.

Charles Pears was a painter, printmaker and poster designer. He was educated at the East Hardwick and Pomfret College. During the First World War he held a commission in the Royal Marines and was an official war artist to the Admiralty. Pears was the first President of the Royal Society of Marine Artists, established in 1939. During the Second World War he worked as an official war artist for Sir Kenneth Clark's War Artists' Advisory Committee, which was established to create an historical record of the war in all its aspects. Although Pears did not personally witness this convoy he was able, through his expert knowledge of ships, to create a highly accurate and atmospheric reconstruction.

In addition to working as a professional illustrator for the *Illustrated London News*, *The Graphic* and *Punch* magazine, Pears also illustrated maritime books and novels – many reflecting his passion for yachting. He was also commissioned to produce designs and posters for London Underground. *JT*

**Convoy to Russia** *(oil on canvas), Charles Pears, c. 1944-45, National Maritime Museum, London (BHC1576)*

No data available

# LSI Landing Ship, Infantry 1944

Although some thought had been given to small-scale amphibious raids on an enemy coastline during the interwar period, it was only after the fall of France in June 1940 that Britain gave serious consideration to the need to transport a vast army of men and their equipment across the English Channel. Prototypes of assault landing craft had been developed, but these would need to be carried close to the beachhead by larger ships. The Landing Ships Infantry (LSI) were merchantmen converted to carry Landing Craft, Assault (LCA) under gravity davits. There were three categories: Large (L: 8000–12,000 tons), Medium (M: 4000–7000 tons) and Small (S: 2000–3000 tons). The most uniform group was the 13 Lend/Lease ships of the US Maritime Commission C1-S-AY1 type, which could carry 18 LCAs

and 900–1500 troops. Heavy equipment was delivered to the beaches by Landing Craft, Mechanized (LCM), or Landing Craft, Tank (LCT), for which a purpose-built vessel designated Landing Ship, Dock (LSD) was designed. The LSD was essentially a self-propelled floating dock with a ship-shape bow added, the stern closed by a gate, and the bridge and accommodation arranged across the dock walls at the forward end. Heavy equipment could also be delivered directly to the beach by the Landing Ship, Tank (LST), which had bow doors and an articulated ramp and could transport up to 15–25 tanks. These and other types of amphibious landing ship saw extensive employment in the Mediterranean in 1943–4 and in the Normandy Landings of June 1944. *JJ*

**Troops embarking on a Landing Ship during Exercise Fabius** *(photograph), Sgt. Wooldridge, 6 May 1944, Imperial War Museum (H 38288).*

[Data for LSI(L) of C1-S-AY1 type] • 418ft x 60ft x 26ft (127.4m x 18.3m x 7.9m) • 11,650 tons • Hull steel • Armament 1 x 4in (102mm), 1 x 12 pdr AA, 12 x 20mm AA • Complement 250 • Built Consolidated Steel Corporation, Wilmington, California and Orange, Texas, USA, 1942–45

# LCI Landing Craft, Infantry 1944

D-Day, 9 a.m. on Juno Beach at St Aubin-sur-Mer: under German sniper fire, Marines from the British 48 Royal Marine (48 RM) Commando, some with bicycles, disembark from their transport using bow ramps. Two of the craft carrying their comrades had already sunk; some men were dragged under to their deaths by their heavy equipment; and half of those who reached the beach were killed by small-arms fire from heavily defended German positions. Percentage casualties were equally high among the Canadians who formed the majority of the troops landing on Juno.

More than four thousand assorted landing craft took part in the Normandy Landings on 6 June 1944. Many of 48 RM Commando crossed the Channel in wooden-hulled vessels designated LCI(S) Landing Craft, Infantry (Small). Although a lightweight vessel, the LCI(S) was capable of carrying 102 troops and their equipment below deck. Once empty, the LCI(S)' were directed to the large troop ships to pick up more troops and bring them to the beach.

The LCI(S) had been built to a design by Fairmile Marine, a company founded by car maker Noel Macklin (later Sir Noel), and run from his home at Cobham Fairmile in Surrey. At maximum speed, they had a range of only 330 nautical miles, and their protective armour plating came in the form of steel scales: 40 Small and 10 Large were produced. *JH*

**48 (RM) Commando disembark from LC(I)s at St Aubin-sur-Mer, Normandy** *(photograph), 6 June 1944, Conway Picture Library*

158.6ft x 23.3ft x 5.4ft (48.3m x 7.1m x 1.6m); 5.11ft (1.8m) aft • 238 tons [D] • Hull steel • Armament 2 (or more) x 20mm Oerlikon, 2 x .303 Lewis Guns • Complement 17 crew, 102 soldiers • Built various yards, 1943

# Glasgow  Southampton class light cruiser 1944

Following the London Treaty of 1930 the Royal Navy had hoped that new cruisers laid down by the other major powers would be limited to 8000 tons displacement. However, it quickly became apparent that neither Japan nor the United States was prepared to accept this ceiling, laying down ships of the Mogami and Brooklyn classes armed with 15 x 6in and 15 x 6.1in guns in triple turrets respectively.

Britain was compelled to respond with the cruisers of the 'Town' class, which although less heavily armed, were powerful and well-balanced ships with arguably the most handsome appearance of all the British interwar designs. The eight ships of the class saw extensive use in the Second World War, both in northern waters and in the Mediterranean. *Glasgow* played an active part in the Norwegian campaign of April 1940, and was then transferred to the Mediterranean, suffering extensive damage in late 1940 when she was struck by two torpedoes launched by Italian aircraft. She was patched up sufficiently to continue operating, albeit at a much-reduced speed, and in 1942 underwent permanent repairs in the U.S.A. She returned to the Home Fleet, escorting Arctic convoys in early 1943. In June 1944 she provided gunfire support for the U.S. Army landings on Omaha Beach (see image). Hit and seriously damaged by German coastal batteries during operations against Cherbourg, she was repaired and subsequently served in the East Indies Fleet. *JJ*

**D-Day Ships. The Allied Invasion Fleet, 6 June 1944** *(oil on canvas), Peter Hogan, 1993*

592ft x 62ft x 20ft (180m x 18.8m x 6.2m) • 9100 tons [D] • Hull steel • Armament 12 x 6in, 8 x 4in, 8 x 2 pdr pompom, 6 x 21in torpedo tubes, 3 aircraft • Complement 750 • Built Scotts, Greenock, Scotland, 1936

# Type XXI U-boats Submarine 1944

The Type XXI U-boat marked an important step in the development of the submarine. Prior to this, submarines were little more than submersible torpedo boats, vulnerable to attacks on the surface and limited by slow underwater speeds and battery capacity that required frequent surfacing to recharge. Although development work on the revolutionary Walter propulsion system, using hydrogen peroxide to produce steam for turbines without the need to surface, was underway at the outset of the Second World War, it was not sufficiently developed for operational service.

After the collapse of the U-boat offensive in the Atlantic in May 1943, the Kriegsmarine decided to use the hull of the proposed Walter boat and equip it with a conventional diesel-electric propulsion system as an interim measure. The two key features of the Type XXI were its streamlined hull, optimized for underwater rather than surface sailing, and the size of the boat.

The Type XXI was between two and three times the displacement of existing U-boat types, enabling the fitting of a substantially larger battery capacity, which in turn allowed either an unprecedented high underwater speed of 16 knots to be reached or a lower speed of 8 knots to be maintained for more than a day.

Other innovations included an advanced sonar system, a hydraulic torpedo reloading system allowing three full 6-tube salvoes to be fired in less than 20 minutes, as well as substantially improved crew accommodation. From late 1943 Type XXIs were manufactured in prefabricated sections, often far inland, before final assembly in shipyards. Although 118 were built, by May 1945 they were plagued by technical problems and poor workmanship so that only four entered operational service and only two conducted actual wartime patrols in the last days of the war. *MF*

**Type XXI U-boats after Allied bombing, c. 1944** *(photograph), Conway Picture Library*

251.8ft x 26.3ft x 17.5ft (76.7m x 8m x 5.3m) • 1621 tons • Complement 57 officers and men • Armament 6 x torpedo tubes; 4 x 20mm cannon • Built Blohm & Voss of Hamburg, AG Weser of Bremen, Germany, and F. Schichau of Danzig (Gdańsk, now Poland), 1943–5

# Zuikaku Shokaku class aircraft carrier 1944

'Tennouheika Banzai! Long live the Emperor!' A quarter of an hour after the crew of the *Zuikaku* raised their arms and shouted this traditional salute the Japanese carrier capsized, taking half of her complement to their deaths in the waters off Luzon, in the Philippines. She was the last of Japan's fleet carriers: with her demise, Japan had lost what remained of its decimated naval air power.

Completed in September 1941, *Zuikaku* had been one of the six carriers that attacked Pearl Harbor in 1941. The following April, while operating in the Indian Ocean, her aircraft had sunk HMS *Hermes*. She did not participate in the Battle of Midway but later in 1942 she caused damage to the USS *Enterprise* and fatally crippled USS *Hornet*. However, her luck finally ran out in the Leyte Gulf Campaign of October 1944 when the US sent a powerful force to begin the liberation of the Philippines. Admiral Halsey's Third Fleet, which included the fleet and light fleet carriers, was to take care of the main Japanese navy while the escort carriers supported the opposed landing. The Japanese plan was for Admiral Ozawa's small carrier force – three light carriers with *Zuikaku* as the only remaining fleet carrier – to lure away Halsey's powerful ships. Halsey fell into the trap and went after Ozawa but the US operation was saved by the escort carriers and the 7th Fleet. Halsey caught Ozawa and on 25 October, at the Battle of Engaño, two of the light carriers were sunk by superior US air power and *Zuikaku* was hit 16 times and began to list. Ozawa transferred to the *Oyodo* and at 1.58 p.m. the crew were ordered to abandon ship. They saluted their flag, and at 2.14 p.m. *Zuikaku* went down with her captain and 800 men. *JH*

**Crew members of the sinking Japanese carrier *Zuikaku* salute as the naval ensign is lowered, 25 October 1944** *(photograph). Conway Picture Library*

844ft 10in x 85ft 4in x 29ft 1in (257.50m x 26m x 8.87m) • 32,105 tons • Armament: 16 x 5in/40(DP (8 x 2); 42-25mm AA; 72 operational aircraft • Complement 1660 • Built Kawasaki, Kobe, Japan, 1940

# Tirpitz   Bismarck class battleship 1944

Following the loss of *Bismarck*, Adolf Hitler was determined that her sister *Tirpitz* should not meet the same fate. Rather than being used for commerce raiding, *Tirpitz* was despatched in early 1942 to Norway, where she formed the centrepiece of a 'fleet-in-being', which tied down two or three of the available modern battleships of the Royal Navy for almost three years. She was also available for the defence of Norway, which Hitler considered strategically crucial to the German war effort, and together with *Scharnhorst* and the two remaining *Panzerschiffe*, posed a constant threat to the security of the British Arctic convoys. A brief sortie in July 1942 panicked the British Admiralty into scattering convoy PQ17, with disastrous consequences.

Hidden away under camouflage in the Norwegian fjords, surrounded by torpedo nets and smoke floats, and protected by the fighters of the Luftwaffe, *Tirpitz* was a difficult target, and for a long period of time she frustrated all attempts by the British to cripple or sink her. In September 1943 midget submarines (X-craft) succeeded in placing and detonating charges beneath the hull. *Tirpitz* was repaired, but was then subject to numerous bombing attacks by aircraft of the Fleet Air Arm before an attack by RAF Lancaster bombers armed with 5-ton 'Tallboy' bombs finally caused her to capsize in November 1944. *JJ*

*Tirpitz* **protected by anti-torpedo nets, anchored at Alten Fjord, Norway in 1943** *(aerial reconnaissance photograph), Imperial War Museum (A 19625)*

248m x 36m x 8.7m (814ft x 118ft x 29ft) • 42,900 tons [D] Hull steel • Armament 8 x 15in, 12 x 5.9in, 16 x 4.1in, 16 x 37mm, 4 aircraft • Complement 2600 •
Built Wilhelmshaven, Germany, 1939

# S-class Submarine 1944

'On Board an S Class Submarine: up the conning tower' is one of a series of paintings of submarine life executed by the official war artist, Stephen Bone, towards the end of the Second World War. Stripped to the waist, a tattooed crewman climbs the ladder that leads from the hot and humid control room with its harsh electric lighting, up the conning tower and into the welcome daylight and fresh air. He is being followed by another man while, up on the bridge, one of the look-outs holds the periscope standard and scans the sea for enemy ships and aircraft.

Built between 1930 and 1945, the 63 S-class boats fell into three groups, each larger than its predecessor and incorporating noticeable modifications. But as a class they were of medium size, easy to handle, and adequately fast; they were also the first class to be fitted with radar for surface searches.

Success came in every theatre of the war in which they served. In December 1939, HMS *Salmon* sank *U-36* and badly damaged the two light cruisers *Leipzig* and *Köln* while operating in the North Sea. She was lost with all hands the following year, probably as a result of hitting a mine. In the Mediterranean, HMS *Shakespeare* sank the Italian submarine *Velella* in the hours before the Italian Armistice.

Although built for the North Sea and Mediterranean, a number of them went out to the Far East after changes had been made to increase their fuel load. HMS *Stygian* sank 21 miscellaneous vessels in the Pacific, as well as towing the midget submarine *XE-3* which attacked the Japanese cruiser *Takao* in Singapore Harbour in 1945. Seventeen of the class were lost during the war, six of them in the North Sea in 1940 alone. *JH*

**On Board an S-Class Submarine: Up the Conning Tower** *(oil on canvas), Stephen Bone, c. 1944, National Maritime Museum, London (BHC1555)*

217ft x 23.6ft x 11ft (66.1m 7.2m x 3.4m) • 814-872 tons [D] • Hull steel • Armament 6 x 21in forward torpedo tubes,1 x external stern tube (13 torpedoes). 1x 3in (76mm) gun • Complement 48 • Built Scotts, Greenock, Scotland; Cammell Laird & Co Ltd, Birkenhead, England, also at Chatham, Kent, England and Vickers Armstrong Ltd, Barrow-in-Furness, England, 1940-1945

# Wilhelm Gustloff  KdF cruise ship 1945

The sinking of the liner *Wilhelm Gustloff* in the evening of 30 January 1945 by the Soviet submarine *S-13* ranks as the single greatest loss of life in a maritime disaster. The *Wilhelm Gustloff* was built by Blohm & Voss in Hamburg and launched in May 1937 for the *Kraft durch Freude* (Strength through Joy) organization that arranged leisure activities on behalf of the state-sponsored workers movement. The ship was named after the leader of the Swiss section of the National-Socialist party's overseas wing who was assassinated in February 1936. Designed from the outset as a cruise-liner for the middle classes, the 682ft (208m) long vessel displaced 25,500 tons and offered berths for 1500 passengers in identical cabins. On the outbreak of war she was converted into a hospital ship, before being employed as an accommodation vessel for a U-boat training division based in Gotenhafen (present day Gdynia). On 13 January 1945 the Red Army launched its East

Prussian offensive that cut off German military personnel and civilians in the Courland peninsula and East Prussia. Admiral Karl Dönitz, Commander-in-Chief of the Kriegsmarine, ordered the large-scale seaborne evacuation, Operation Hannibal on the 21st. In the afternoon of the 30th the *Wilhelm Gustloff* left Gotenhafen accompanied by another liner and two torpedo boats. She was carrying approximately 10,500 people – 9000 civilians and 1500 naval personnel. Shortly after 9 p.m. three torpedoes, fired from close range, struck the *Wilhelm Gustloff*, which had its navigation lights on to avoid collision with a minesweeper flotilla suspected to be operating in the area. After an hour the ship sank around 23 nautical miles off the Pomeranian coast and although rescue vessels arrived quickly only 1252 people could be saved from the freezing Baltic Sea. *MF*

**Adolf Hitler and his Nazi party entourage launching the KdF liner *Wilhelm Gustloff* at the Blohm & Voss shipyard in Hamburg** *(photograph), 5 May 1937, Keystone / Getty Images*

684.1ft x 77.4ft x 21ft (208.5m x 23.6m x 6.5m)• 25,484 tons [GRT] • Hull steel • Complement (as cruise ship) 417, passengers 1465; (as naval ship) 173 • Built Blohm & Voss, Hamburg, Germany, 1937

# Yamato   Battleship 1945

The *Yamato* was the ultimate symbol of pre-Second World War Japanese naval power and martial prowess. As her name was meant to suggest, she was the supreme embodiment of the qualitative superiority of the people of the ancient Japanese province of Yamato, a visually majestic and terrifying response to the larger material resources of the American and British navies.

The plans for this battleship went through 23 designs before final approval in 1936, and with them the navy sought no economy of scale. It was to be the finest tool in Japan's naval armoury and the entire industrial and logistical apparatus of the service were mobilized to build her. Naval yards in Kure, Nagasaki, Yokosuka and Sasebo were expanded and improved to accommodate her immense hull and lift her outsized armour plates and main naval guns. Unprecedented security measures were taken to prevent foreign observers getting information on her technical characteristics. No detail in the design process was neglected. As a result, when she was completed, she was not only the most powerful battleship ever to set sail on the high seas,

but she was also one of the most luxurious combat platforms of the first half of the twentieth century, featuring air-conditioning and ice-cream makers. The standard of her living quarters were unmatched within the Japanese navy – a navy with a reputation for very few comforts on its combat units – and earned the ship the nickname 'The Yamato Hotel'. At the heart of this gem of elegance and design were nine powerful guns capable of firing shells of approximately 1½ tons. The ship was designed to resist hits of similar calibre, while reaching a top speed of 27 knots. On 7 April 1945, the *Yamato* fulfilled her destiny by engaging the fast advancing American forces in a suicide mission of unprecedented scale. In one last desperate operation codenamed 'Ten-Go', she was sent to stop the invasion of the sacred islands that her name represented. Almost her entire crew was lost and the ship that had defined the image of Japan's military might at sea became a symbol of the unwavering commitment of its people. *AP*

**The battleship *Yamato* as completed** *(oil on canvas), Ross Watton, 1987*

839.9ft x 121ft x 34.1ft (256m x 36.9m x 10.4m) • 64,000 tons [D] • Hull steel • Armament 9 x 460mm (18.1in), 12 x 155mm (6.1in), 12 x 127mm (5in), 24 x 25mm (0.9in), 4 x 13.2mm (0.5in) • Complement 2300 • Built Kure Naval Shipyard, Hiroshima, Japan, 1940

# Formidable Illustrious class aircraft carrier 1945

*Formidable* was the second of the armoured carriers of the Illustrious class to be completed. She replaced *Illustrious* in the Eastern Mediterranean when the latter was heavily damaged by German dive-bombers, and subsequently played a prominent role in the Battle of Matapan, when her Albacore aircraft succeeded in torpedoing first the Italian battleship *Vittorio Veneto* and then the heavy cruiser *Pola*, which was stopped. The result was a night battle in which *Pola* and her two half-sisters *Zara* and *Fiume* were sunk by British battleships under Vice-Admiral Andrew Cunningham.

In May, while supporting operations off Crete, *Formidable* was heavily damaged by two 2200lb (1000kg) bombs and underwent six months of repairs in the USA. She subsequently served in the Indian Ocean, the Mediterranean and the Home Fleet, taking part in operations against the German battleship *Tirpitz* in the summer of 1944. In April 1945 *Formidable* joined the British Pacific Fleet and took part in air strikes against the Japanese islands. On 4 May and again on 9 May she was struck by kamikaze aircraft. However, the heavy armoured deck provided a level of protection which was not available to her US counterparts, and although the first incident resulted in a fire between decks in which eight personnel were killed and 11 aircraft destroyed, on both occasions flight operations were resumed within hours. The Battle Honours board in the accompanying photograph tells the story of *Formidable*'s eventful wartime career, with no fewer than seven honours awarded between 1941 and 1945. *JJ*

**Shipkeepers on board HMS *Formidable* at Portsmouth, beneath her scroll of battle honours** *(photograph), c. 1954, Conway Picture Library*

753ft x 96ft x 28.5ft (229.5m x 29m x 8.5m) • 23,000 tons [D] • Hull steel • Armament 33 aircraft, 16 x 4.5in, 48 x 2 pdr pompom • Complement 1230 •
Built Harland & Wolff, Belfast, Northern Ireland, 1939

# Glory  Colossus class aircraft carrier 1945

In 1941 the urgent need for more aircraft carriers – which led to temporary expedients such as the small Escort Carriers, capable of carrying only between 6 and 20 aircraft – prompted British design studies for an intermediate type called the Light Fleet Carrier, of which the *Glory* was one. Smaller and slower than the main battle carriers, they could nevertheless carry some 40 aircraft at 25 knots. And since they were designed to be capable of construction to mercantile standards and in merchant shipbuilding yards, they could be completed in two and a half years, whereas the contemporary Implacable class battle carriers were taking four and a half years to build. They proved to be an excellent and useful design, of which 20

were built in three developments. Four of them – *Colossus*, *Glory*, *Venerable* and *Vengeance* – were completed in time to form the 11th Carrier Squadron, which arrived in the Pacific just before the end of the Second World War. *Glory* was then given the task of receiving the surrender of the Japanese forces occupying New Guinea, New Ireland and Bougainville, following which she was used on repatriation duty for thousands of Allied servicemen. The ship's own taste of war came in 1951–53, when she carried out 11 combat patrols off Korea. Post-war the ubiquitous Light Fleets were an economical means of supporting naval aviation and they went on to give good service, some of them for more than 40 years, in eight different navies. *GH*

**HMS Glory** *(oil on canvas), Geoff Hunt*

695ft x 80ft x 23ft 3in (211.3m x 24.4m x 7m) • 18,040 tons [D] • Hull steel • Armament 24 x 2 pdr, 40 aircraft • Complement 1300 • Built Harland & Wolff, Belfast, Northern Ireland, 1945

# Missouri Iowa class battleship 1945

*Missouri*, known to those who served in her as the 'Mighty Mo', was the last battleship ever built by the USA. Ordered in 1940, she was commissioned in June 1944, and subsequently took part in the operations off Iwo Jima, Okinawa and the Japanese home islands, becoming the flagship of Admiral William Halsey, Commander in Chief of the Third Fleet, in May 1945. Following her service in the Korean War 1950–53 she was placed in reserve. Reactivated and modernized in 1984 as part of the Reagan administration's 600-Ship Navy Plan, *Missouri* received Tomahawk land attack cruise missiles and Phalanx anti-missile guns and subsequently fought in the 1991 Gulf War. The ship was finally decommissioned in 1992. In 1998 *Missouri* was donated to the USS *Missouri* Memorial Association and became a museum ship at Pearl Harbor, Hawaii.

The pivotal moment in *Missouri*'s long and distinguished career took place on 2 September 1945, when she hosted the formal surrender of the Empire of Japan while anchored in Tokyo Bay. The ceremony was attended by high-ranking military officers of all the Allied powers, including the British, the Dutch, the French and the Soviets. The USA was represented by Fleet Admiral Chester Nimitz and General of the Army Douglas MacArthur, the Supreme Allied Commander; the Japanese delegation was led by Foreign Minister Mamoru Sigemitsu. *JJ*

**General MacArthur signs the peace treaty with Japan aboard USS *Missouri* during formal surrender ceremonies** *(photograph), 31 August 1945, Conway Picture Library*

887ft x 108ft x 36ft (270m x 33m x 11m) • 48,000 tons [D] • Hull steel • Armament 9 x 16in, 20 x 5in, 80 x 40mm • Complement 1920 • Built New York Navy Yard, New York, USA, 1944

# I-400 Submarine 1945

In the interwar period, Japanese studies analyzing a potential war with the USA were based on an 'interception-attrition' strategy in which long-range submarines were to ambush American units crossing the Pacific or to attack ports on the American West Coast. The gigantic Sen Toku I-400 class of submarines was conceived and built for that purpose. The project for this class, which featured an unprecedented standard displacement of more than 5000 tons surfaced, was developed in 1942 but the lead boat of the class and her sister-ship *I-401* were not completed until the end of 1944 due to the stringencies of the war.

Initial plans were to build a fleet of 18 units, but only these two submarines entered service before the end of the war. The *I-400* remained the largest submarine ever built prior to the appearance of nuclear ballistic missile submarines in the 1960s and possessed some unique characteristics. The pressure hull had a figure-eight shape developed by the Japanese to give the boat strength and stability, a solution later adopted by the Soviet navy in some of her larger nuclear submarines. The boat was outfitted with a German-supplied snorkel system and could conduct operations along the American coast and return to Japanese waters without refuelling.

Yet what made the *I-400* stand out among her peers was an impressive hangar that enabled her to carry three Seiran dive-bomber aircraft (Aichi M6A1s). Her operational history brought only limited results. After the surrender, *I-400* and her sister submarine, *I-401*, were inspected by American technicians before taking their place in history as Japan's extreme attempt to turn the tide of the war. *AP*

**Imperial Japanese Submarines** *I-14*, *I-401* and *I-400* in Tokyo Bay moored to a US submarine tender *(photograph), c. 1945, Ric Hedman*

400ft x 39ft x 23ft (122m x 12m x 7m) • 6,560 tons [D] • Hull steel • Armament 3 Aichi M6A1 Seiran sea-planes, 8 x 21in torpedo tubes, 1 x 5.5in, 3 x 25mm, 1 x 25mm • Complement 157 • Built Kure Naval Shipyard, Hiroshima, Japan, 1944

# Ocean  Colossus class aircraft carrier 1945

On 4 December 1945, Lieutenant Commander Eric Brown MBE DSC AFC RN approached the light fleet carrier HMS *Ocean* in a modified de Havilland Vampire, a prototype jet aircraft capable of 504mph. The weather in the Channel off the Isle of Wight was far from ideal: the carrier was pitching and rolling as Brown came round and began his approach. His anxiety was that, if required to abort the landing on the 690ft (210.3m) flight deck, the Vampire's turbojet Goblin engine would not be able to accelerate rapidly enough to regain the necessary speed. In the event, he made a perfect landing. It was the first time that a true jet had landed on any aircraft carrier. Coincidentally, the last Fairey Swordfish to take off from a British carrier had done so from *Ocean*'s flight deck on 15 October, earlier that same year.

Initially designed for night fighter operations, the Colossus class *Ocean*, remained in service until 1960, serving with distinction in the Korean War for two and a half years. During the conflict one of her Sea Furies became the only piston-engined aircraft to shoot down a jet fighter in air-to-air combat when a flight from 802 Naval Air Squadron, led by Lieutenant Peter Carmichael RN, downed a MiG-15 during 1952. No jet squadrons served on *Ocean*, but in 1956 she embarked the Joint Helicopter Unit and achieved another first when she and HMS *Theseus* landed Royal Marines ashore by helicopter during the Suez Crisis. She was scrapped in 1962. *JH*

**A mooring party takes the strain as HMS *Ocean* is tied up at Faslane prior to being broken up** (*photograph*), *7 May 1962, Conway Picture Library*

693ft x 80ft x 23.3ft (211.2m x 24.4m x 7.1m) • 18,300 tons [D] • Hull steel • Armament 31 x 2 pdr pompom, 37 aircraft • Complement 1300 • Built Alexander Stephen and Sons, Glasgow, Scotland, 1944

# Orcades  Ocean liner 1947

*Orcades* was the first of three replacement liners built for the Orient Line's Australia route after the Second World War, the others being *Orsova* and *Oronsay*. Four of the company's liners had been lost during the war. The illustration shows one of *Orcades*' two propellers being inspected at the works of J Stone & Co. Ltd, in Charlton, London, where it had been cast and finished. This company had first been established at Deptford by Josiah Stone in 1831 and later expanded with new foundries at Charlton. The propeller was delivered to the yard of Vickers-Armstrong at Barrow-in-Furness, where the *Orcades* was launched on 14 October 1947.

The ship left London on 14 December 1948 on her maiden voyage to Melbourne and Sydney, reaching Melbourne in 26 days. She continued in service on this route, with some voyages being extended to San Francisco and Vancouver, and was later based at Southampton. On 15 June 1953 she was at the Coronation Review of the Fleet, at Spithead, and proceeded through the lines carrying government guests. In the latter part of her career she spent time cruising from Britain and Australia.

*Orcades* was withdrawn in October 1972 and was broken up in Taiwan during the following year. *PB*

**Making propellers for the liner *Orcades* at J. Stone & Co. Works, Ltd, Charlton** *(photograph). c. 1947, Conway Picture Library*

709ft x 90.6ft x 30 ft (216.1m x 27.6m x 9.1m) • 28,164 tons. [GRT] • Hull steel • Complement 733 first class, 772 tourist class • Built Vickers-Armstrong Ltd, Barrow-in-Furness, England, 1947

# Bibb Coast Guard cutter 1947

*George M. Bibb*, as she was officially known for the first weeks of her operational life, was completed as a US Coast Guard cutter in 1937. The expansion of commercial aviation had created a need for ships to respond to emergencies, but the *Bibb* spent the Second World War as a convoy escort before resuming her role as a weather ship, operating out of New Bedford, Massachusetts and providing meteorological reports and search-and-rescue services for transatlantic flights.

At 8.16 a.m. on 13 October 1947 the American International Airlines flying boat *Bermuda Sky Queen* which had left the Republic of Ireland for Newfoundland, radioed: 'I have only 2.7 hours fuel left and am returning to weather ship for landing on sea, due to severe head wind.' The four-engined Boeing, with 69 crew and passengers on board, made what was later described as an 'incomparable landing' on the stormy Atlantic. Unable to set up a tow in the conditions, a perilous transfer operation began. *Bibb*

reported: 'Darkness approaching, plane leaking. Passengers mostly prostrated by seasickness. Rough sea. Three persons removed unharmed with small lifeboat. Continuing operations with boat and raft. Second successful boat and raft operation brings total saved thus far to five men, two women, two little boys and one baby...'.

With the wind turning galeforce, Captain Paul Cronk asked for volunteers to continue manning the shuttle. By the time darkness suspended operations, 48 terrified passengers were safe; the remainder survived the night in the aircraft and were transferred the following morning. An enquiry revealed that the aircraft's crew had little experience of flying boats and none of transatlantic flight.

*Bibb*'s later career with the US Coast Guard included successful anti-drug smuggling patrols and interception. Withdrawn from service in 1985 she was sunk off Florida in 1987 as an artificial reef. *JH*

**USCGV *Bibb* (photograph)**, *US Naval Institute*

327ft x 41ft x 12.6ft (99.67m x 12.5m x 12.6m) • 2350 tons [D] • Hull steel • Armament 2 x 5in, 2 x 6 pdrs, 1 x 1 pdr; 1 aircraft • Complement 123 • Built Charleston Navy Yard, South Carolina, USA, 1937

# Kon-tiki Raft 1947

Named after the legendary sun king of the South American Indians, *Kon-Tiki* was the raft made by Thor Heyerdahl for a Pacific expedition in 1947. The Norwegian scientist and adventurer believed that the Polynesian islands were in part settled by the peoples of Peru – the Incas and their predecessors. This ran counter to the general accepted theory at the time that Polynesia must have been populated from Asia. The Pacific migration theory had been dismissed, as it was believed that the indigenous wood, balsa, would not have been seaworthy, making it impossible for the inhabitants of South America to reach Polynesia before the arrival of European ships.

To this end Heyerdahl built a raft based on the type described by the first Europeans to arrive in Peru and Ecuador, which operated along the coast. It was made from the trunks of nine balsa trees, lashed together, with balsa cross beams bound across these for lateral support. The vessel was rigged with a short mast and single square sail. Behind it was a bamboo cabin, and there was a long steering oar fitted at the stern. On 28 April 1947, *Kon-Tiki* was towed out from Callao harbour with Heyerdahl and five other men on board into the Humboldt Current. From there she drifted 4300 miles (8000km), surviving two storms, to beach on the Raroia Reef in the Tuamotos 101 days later, and thus proving the feasibility of this form of migration. *Kon-Tiki* is now on display in the Kon-Tiki Museum, Oslo. *AM*

**Heyerdahl and his crew aboard the raft *Kon-Tiki*** (photograph), 1947, *Keystone / Getty Images*

45ft x 18ft x 2ft (13.7m x 5.5m x 60cm) • tonnage unknown • Hull wood (balsa, pine, bamboo and hemp) • Complement 6 • Built Callao, Peru, 1947

# Herring drifters Steam fishing boats 1947

By 1947 the ports of Lowestoft and Great Yarmouth had long been established as the major centres of the North Sea herring fleets. They were ideally placed to catch the shoals that concentrated off the East Anglian coast over autumn as the herring migrated from summer feeding grounds to their winter spawning grounds further south.

Through October and November Lowestoft thrived as the herring harvest was landed and processed. Thousands of cran of herring were caught each year – a cran being the standard measurement for the sale of fresh herring. One cran was 37.5 gallons, on average 700 to 1,500 fish, or about 392lbs. The fleets were comprised largely of steam drifters, who worked with specially-treated cotton nets that were laid vertically, suspended at a pre-determined depth to drift on the tide. The boats shown here are all from Lowestoft, with the exception of *Boyds*, FR294, a Scottish boat out of Fraserburgh. Scots often came south to help take the annual catch; the men

worked the boats while the women processed the fish in the curing sheds. 1947 was a solid year for herring, if unspectacular; the best single catch was 253 cran. This was lower than the previous year's best catch, which had been 264¾ cran. The all-time record was taken a few years later in 1953, when *Fruitful Bough*, a Peterhead boat, landed 323 cran at Yarmouth. Such figures were carefully recorded because from 1936 to 1966 the boat that caught the biggest single haul was awarded the Prunier Trophy, £25 and an invitation for the crew to dine at the Maison Prunier restaurant in London, with two days sightseeing in the capital at the restaurant owner's expense.

Still, it was scant reward for a difficult and dangerous job. The industry suffered as yields fell; although Lowestoft's drifting fleet struggled on until the late Sixties, the local fishermen, along with their Scottish counterparts and latterly the fishermen from the European Common Market, hunted the herring to virtual extinction in the North Sea. *MJ*

**Herring drifters unloading at Lowestoft** *(photograph), 13 November 1947, Conway Picture library*

[Typical data for type] 92.1ft x 20.1ft x 11.6ft (28m x 6.1m x 3.5m) • 115 tons [GRT] • Hull wood • Complement 10-12 • Built J. Chambers, Oulton Broad, Lowestoft, England, 1930

# Seattle  Cargo liner 1947

Building anew after the Second World War, Sweden's Rederi Ab Nordstjernen, which traded at the Johnson Line, commissioned a series of eight very innovative new refrigerated cargo liners for services from Scandinavia to the Americas. The lead ship of a new class of seven was the 6910 ton *Seattle*, delivered in 1947. Built by Kockums Varv Ab, Malmö, the *Seattle*'s progressive design attracted a great deal of attention. For starters, her superstructure and funnel casing were streamlined, rather than having the flat and vertical look of most cargo vessels of the era. Secondly, where other freight-carrying ships used derricks with cargo booms, which required lengthy preparation by a large crew, the *Seattle* was the first to use instead electric cranes for cargo handling.

A twin-screw vessel, she was powered by Kockums-MAN diesels. (Scandinavian ship owners had long been enthusiastic users of marine diesels, and this method of propulsion became increasingly common elsewhere as the 1950s progressed.) Come the 1960s, further advances were made in cargo-handling techniques – for example, using forklift trucks to load goods on palettes via side hatches and, slightly later, containerisation. In 1962, the *Seattle* was lengthened at the Rheinstahl Nordseewerke, Emden to accommodate containers.

As well as carrying general cargo, the *Seattle* and her sisters also transported up to twelve passengers in considerable comfort (back then, it was typical that cargo liners carried a small number of passengers – twelve being the maximum permitted without a vessel having to meet passenger ship certification standards).

Eventually, time rapidly advancing, technology caught up with the *Seattle*. Johnson Line joined a consortium of operators who introduced fully containerised services to South America in the early 1970s, jointly marketed as ScanStar. The *Seattle* was sold out of the fleet in 1972 and went for scrap the following year in Kaosiung, Taiwan. *BP*

The cargo liner *Seattle* in Johnson Line livery *(advertisement), Bruce Peter Collection*

Dimensions unknown • 6910 tons [GRT] • Hull steel • Complement passengers 12 • Built Kockums Varv Ab, Malmö, Sweden, 1947

# City of New York Cargo liner 1947

By 1945, Vickers-Armstrongs was one of the most important ship manufacturers in the world. Their yard on the Tyne, the Walker Yard, was one of the major sites of British shipbuilding, although it had experienced lean periods and even closure in a long history. Wartime demands had revitalized Walker, however, and the battleship *King George V* and the aircraft carrier *Victorious* were both built there, along with 3 cruisers, 24 destroyers, 16 submarines, a series of Empire ships and numerous landing craft.

In the post-war period Vickers-Armstrongs modernized the Tyne yard to prepare for prospective work on passenger and cargo vessels. These ships were built to new designs for customers all over the world, principally for commercial shipping concerns eager to rebuild their merchant fleets after the Second World War.

One such order came from Ellerman Lines, one of the world's largest operators of cargo ships. Ellerman had lost 60 of their fleet of 105 ships during the war, and planned to replace the losses with new fast steam cargo liners with limited passenger capacity in a bid to re-establish global trade routes. The first of these ships was *City of Bristol*, lead ship of an entire class of City cargo liners, which included the *City of New York*, launched on the Tyne in 1947.

Here a dockyard worker is varnishing the hull of a model of the ship. Such models were a long-established shipbuilding tradition, often made concomitant to the construction of their full-size counterparts. Even by the 1940s a model remained the best way of visualizing the lines and general appearance of the ship, particularly useful when presenting aspects of her construction to those unfamiliar with technical details. Often the models were presented to the new owners, but most yards also kept large collections. Remarkably, the *City of New York* model survives today, outlasting the real ship, which was broken up in 1969. *MJ*

**Mr J.A. Barrie, a dockyard painter at the Walker Naval Yard, works on a model of the cargo liner** *City of New York*, **to be presented to the ship's owners** *(photograph), photographer unknown, 1947, Conway Picture Library*

Dimensions unknown • 8420 tons [GRT] • Hull steel • Complement passengers 12 • Built High Walker, Tyne, England, 1947

# Caronia  Cunard ocean liner 1948

'Sorry chaps, nothing on tap yet' – Clydebank shipyard workers complete the outfitting of a cocktail bar aboard the Cunard Liner *Caronia*, before her January 1949 debut. A little less than half the size of the Cunard *Queens*, this more agile two-class ship was built with the dual purpose of transatlantic service during the 'season' – as the time of year from about mid April to late autumn was known in the North Atlantic trade – and during those months when the Atlantic was less hospitable, cruising out of New York. Apart from the addition of cruising features such as a swimming pool and lido, *Caronia*'s most distinguishing feature was her unique paint scheme in four different shades of pale green rather than the traditional Cunard black hull and white upperworks. This unusual livery earned *Caronia* the popular nickname 'The Green Goddess', and also had a practical advantage in that the colour helped to deflect the heat of the sun away from the ship's decks and superstructure.

Despite her smaller size, this ship nonetheless conveyed virtually the same look and feel on board as the *Queens*. She shared the same standard of accommodation in spacious and comfortable hotel-room style cabins and public rooms of characteristic Cunard style, with their rich and exotic veneers and snugly upholstered furnishings. Moreover, *Caronia*'s more human scale and lower passenger capacity was ideally suited to the longer cruises she provided to her wealthy and mostly elderly clientele, where a Caribbean cruise from New York lasted three or four weeks with extended port stays, and the annual around-the-world cruise each winter was a 3–4 month odyssey. Passengers, many of whom sailed frequently aboard the ship, had time to become acquainted with each other and the crew, creating a friendlier atmosphere than is to be typically found aboard today's larger economy-of-scale cruise ships. *PD*

Workmen fitting out the cabin class cocktail bar on board the liner *Caronia* (photograph), 17 November 1948, Conway Picture Library

714.9ft x 91.2ft x 31.7ft (217.9m x 27.8m x 9.66m) • 34,183 tons [GRT] • Hull steel • Complement 932 passengers (581 first class, 351 tourist class) • Built John Brown and Co., Clydebank, Scotland, 1948

# X-craft Midget submarines 1949

The British X-craft, inspired by the midget submarines built for the Imperial Japanese Navy, were developed in 1942–3 to penetrate the Norwegian fjords, where the major German surface units were now based. The British boats were, however, significantly smaller than their Japanese counterparts, and were quite different in conception. They had conventional dual propulsion, with a diesel engine for surfaced operation; underwater speed using the electric motor was only 5–6 knots, and they were towed to the target area by larger submarines rather than being carried 'piggy-back'. They were not armed with torpedoes, but carried 2-ton side charges with clockwork time fuzes, which were to be laid on the seabed directly beneath the target vessel. Their complement of four included a specialist diver, whose job was to clear net defences and attach other small charges to the hull of the vessel by lines attached to magnetic clamps. The X-craft were operated with conspicuous success against both the German battleship *Tirpitz*, which was effectively crippled, and later against the Imperial Japanese Navy cruiser *Takao* at Singapore. Six boats were lost in the *Tirpitz* operation, one during transit due to problems with the manila ropes used for towing, but the remaining craft had a major impact on the strategic situation in northern waters. X-craft also landed beach reconnaissance parties prior to the Normandy landings in 1944. The boats which operated in the Far East were of the modified XE type, which had air-conditioning. Three of these were retained in service after the war. *JJ*

**Royal Navy midget submarines *XE8* and *XE9* tied up after harbour penetration exercises** (photograph), 13 June 1949, Conway Picture Library

53ft x 5ft 9in x 7ft 2in (16.2m x 1.8m x 2.17m) • 30 tons [D] • Armament two 2-ton detachable explosive charges • Complement 4 • Built XE8: Thomas Broadbent & Sons, Huddersfield; XE9: Markham, England, 1944

# Ark Royal Audacious class aircraft carrier 1950

The largest and most long-lived of Britain's post-war carriers, *Ark Royal* was launched in 1943 as a successor to the armoured fleet carriers of the Illustrious/Implacable classes, but was subject to considerable redesign to enable her to operate jet aircraft and was not completed until 1955. She entered service with a 5.5-degree angled deck, two steam catapults capable of launching aircraft weighing up to 30,000lb (14,000kg), a deck-edge lift on the port side (the first British ship to be fitted with such a device), and the new mirror landing system. She had a complement of up to 50 aircraft comprising Sea Hawks, Sea Venoms, Gannet ASW aircraft and Skyraider AEW aircraft. The side lift, which served only the upper of the two hangars, was found to obstruct flight operations and was removed in 1959. Following the cancellation of the CVA-01 new generation fleet carrier in 1966, *Ark Royal* underwent a major modernization to enable her to operate the US Phantom F-4K fighter and the Buccaneer S-2 strike aircraft. More powerful catapults were fitted and the original armament was removed. She would serve as Britain's only remaining attack carrier until 1978, when she was finally paid off.

*Ark Royal* managed to avoid all the major post-war conflicts in which Britain was involved – she was too late for Suez and paid off four years before the Falklands War. Her main claim to fame was arguably her starring role in the 13-part BBC TV documentary series *Sailor* shortly before she decommissioned. *JJ*

**HMS *Ark Royal*** goes down the slipway at the Cammell Laird shipyard, Birkenhead *(photograph). 3 May 1950. Conway Picture Library*

812ft x 164ft x 36ft (247m x 50m x 11m) • 43,500 tons [D] • Hull steel • Armament 48 aircraft, 8 x 4.5in, 28 x 40mm • Complement 2600 (incl. air group) •
Built Cammell Laird, Birkenhead, England, 1950

# Oronsay Ocean liner 1950

Swift calculations by a senior engineer at Vickers-Armstrong in Barrow-in-Furness saved the brand new Orient Line passenger ship *Oronsay* from worse damage after fire spread through her on the night of 28 October 1950. The huge volume of water pumped into the ship's port holds to extinguish the blaze had given the ship a 20-degree list to port and threatened to capsize her. Len – later Sir Len – Redshaw, a future chairman of the company, had the level in the dock lowered and stabilized the ship by calculating how much water to pump into her starboard side and how much to release from the port side through holes burned into it for the purpose.

Launched on 30 June, *Oronsay* had been fitting out in the Buccleugh Dock. Welders in Number Two hold had ignited cork insulation material which smouldered until bursting into flames at 9 p.m. and spreading to Number

One hold. Fire engines from 23 towns helped to extinguish the blaze and, despite the damage, *Oronsay*'s maiden voyage to Australia was put back only five weeks to 16 May 1951.

Over 24 years *Oronsay* made 64 world voyages and 37 cruises. In November 1951 she assisted in the evacuation of Suez, and the outbreak of the Six Day War in 1967 caused her to be re-routed via the Cape. Her passengers included many emigrants on free or assisted passages, but for those who paid in full, a bed in a first-class cabin cost £110, one way, and a berth in a tourist-class cabin started at £62. In 1972 she became a one-class ship for 1400 passengers, and at the end of her final cruise in 1975 she was taken to Taiwan to be scrapped. *JH*

**The burning liner *Oronsay* heels over at Buccleugh Dock, Barrow-in-Furness** *(photograph), 31 October 1950, Conway Picture Library*

708ft x 93.6ft x 31ft (216m x 28.5m x 9.4m) • 27632 tons [GRT] • Hull steel • Complement 622; passengers 668 first class, 883 tourist class • Built Vickers Armstrong, Barrow-in-Furness, England, 1950

# Arromanches  Light fleet aircraft carrier 1951

Completed for the Royal Navy as HMS *Colossus*, the first of a series of unarmoured light fleet carriers, *Arromanches* was transferred on loan to the Marine Nationale in 1946 and subsequently purchased outright in 1951. By this time she had already made two deployments to Indo-China, flying British Seafires and US Dauntless, Hellcat and Helldiver aircraft, and would make two further deployments before the collapse of the French military position in 1954. She took part in the Suez Operation of 1956, and then underwent a major modernization in which she received a 4-degree angled deck and a mirror landing sight; her original armament was removed. After this modification *Arromanches* became a training carrier, operating the new Alizé

ASW aircraft in addition to Fouga Zéphir trainers. She thus helped to build up a supply of pilots for the jet squadrons which would operate from the new French carriers *Clemenceau* and *Foch*. In 1962 *Arromanches* embarked a squadron of HSS-1 troop-carrying helicopters and took on the assault role in addition to her primary training role. Following a further major refit in 1968 she was redesignated 'helicopter carrier', with multiple missions which included intervention, ASW, troop/aircraft transport and training. She was to have been replaced by a nuclear-powered purpose-built helicopter carrier, PH 75, but the latter was not funded and *Arromanches* was paid off in 1974. *JJ*

The French carrier *Arromanches* (photograph), date unknown, Conway Picture Library

693ft x 80ft x 23ft (211m x 24.5m x 7.2m) • 14,000 tons [D] • Hull steel • Armament (as completed) 24 aircraft, 24 x 2 pdr pompom, 19 x 40mm •
Complement 1400 (incl. air group) • Built Vickers-Armstrong, Tyne, England, 1943

# Lamorna  Schooner 1951

Four days after leaving Gosport, England, to search for the buried wealth of Captain Kidd in the South China Sea, a disconsolate party of treasure hunters retrieved personal effects from the hulk of their schooner, *Lamorna*, beached near Christchurch, Dorset). They had got into difficulties south-south-east of Durlston Head in heavy weather on 4 November 1951 and been taken in tow by HMS *Redpole*. When the tow broke and the yacht lost her masts, the Yarmouth lifeboat went out to her and with difficulty took off the crew. *Lamorna* was damaged beyond repair: a miserable end for a once renowned schooner yacht.

Built for Cecil Quentin in 1902 as a fast cruiser with a clipper bow and setting nearly 1000ft² (93m²) of canvas, the steel-framed wooden-planked *Cecily*, as she was originally named, competed at the most prestigious regattas, and during her first season she was unbeaten in her class, even trouncing the Kaiser's new yacht *Meteor (III)*. A subsequent owner renamed her *Lamorna* in 1913, fitted her with an engine and used her for cruising; in the 1920s she was owned by Captain Wilfred Dowman who rescued the *Cutty Sark*. At the time of her loss she was registered to the Prospero Shipping Company.

The hunt for Kidd's treasure was the result of a strange and elaborate hoax played on Hubert Palmer, a collector of pirate artefacts. During the early 1930s he was offered several items with a link to Kidd. Coincidentally, each one he purchased turned out to contain a secret compartment holding a map indicating the treasure was buried on an island in the South China Sea. Although he made no use of his maps, beyond having one authenticated by the British Museum, he willed them to his nurse who made them available to the *Lamorna* expedition. *JH*

**Treasure seekers salvage belongings, Christchurch, Dorset** *(photograph)*, 1951, Conway Picture Library

113.6ft x 23.4ft x 12.2ft (34.6m x 7.1m x 3.7m) • 120 tons [D] • Hull composite • Complement (at time of loss) 14 • Built G. Fay and Co, Southampton, England, 1902

1947-2010

# Maipu Argentinian liner 1951

A brand new addition to the fleet of Compañía Argentina de Navegacion Dodero, the *Maipu* was on her first voyage from the coast of South America to Hamburg via Spain and Amsterdam carrying 107 passengers, among them the mathematician Dr Julio Rey Pastor, and a cargo that included dried fruit and frozen meat. There was thick fog in the North Sea around the Frisian islands in the early hours of 4 November 1951, and when the officer of the watch informed the master that due to rapidly diminishing visibility he was reliant on radar, Captain Juan Marquez took over control. The radar showed up another vessel, but it was thought to pose no danger. Visibility was down to 200ft (61m).

At around 7.30 a.m., while approaching the Elbe estuary, the US troopship *General M. L. Hersey*, bound for Bremerhaven with some 3000 troops for the NATO commitment to Germany, loomed out of the fog. Despite her captain's attempts to cut inside the *Maipu*'s track and avoid a collision, she struck the liner's port side amidships at an angle of 45 degrees. The troopship's engine went astern, and when her bows pulled out, water rushed into the *Maipu* pulling her into a heavy list to port. Both ships launched their boats and salvage vessels put out from Bremerhaven and Cuxhaven. Captain Marquez ordered passengers and crew to abandon ship, and in an orderly evacuation there were no casualties. Most were taken aboard the American ship; a US corporal recalled that one passenger arrived aboard the *Hersey* wearing little more than a fur coat.

The *Maipu* sank in three hours; the badly damaged *Hersey* underwent repairs at Norddeutscher Lloyd's Bremerhaven yard before returning to the USA with more than 1300 Second World War refugees classed as 'stateless persons'. *JH*

**Lifeboats pull away from the sinking Argentinian liner *Maipu** (photograph). 4 November 1951. Conway Picture Library*

522.9ft x 64.2ft x 35ft (159.36m x 19.6m x 10.7m) • 11,515 tons [D] • Hull steel • Complement 143 approx. when lost; passengers, 13 first class; 740 tourist class • Built Koninklijke Maatschappij de Schelde, Flushing, Netherlands, 1951

# Flying Enterprise Type C1-B cargo freighter 1952

She was originally built as *Cape Kumukaki*, one of hundreds of merchant ships churned out by the USA during the Second World War for the Allied war effort, but as the cargo freighter *Flying Enterprise*, she hit the international headlines in 1952 as no other merchant ship had done since *Titanic*.

En route from Hamburg to New York over Christmas 1951 the New York registered cargo ship ran into appalling weather 350 miles off Land's End, Cornwall. Her deck cracked; she listed as her cargo shifted. Passengers and crew abandoned ship by jumping into mountainous seas to be rescued by nearby ships, but her captain, Henrik Kurt Carlsen, decided to remain on board. A succession of US naval vessels stood by, managing to get food across; the Admiralty tug *Turmoil* came to fix a tow, but, alone, Carlsen could not catch the line and make it fast. On 4 January, when tug and ship suddenly came alongside, the *Turmoil*'s first mate, Ken Dancy, grabbed the stern rail and hauled himself aboard to help Carlsen. The next day they managed to secure a line, and *Turmoil* headed slowly for Falmouth, the *Enterprise* rolling to 80 degrees.

The US Navy set up a London press HQ to satisfy the hunger of the world's media, as the unfolding drama became front-page news. Early on 9 January the towline broke and could not be re-established; *Flying Enterprise*'s dangerous list worsened: by the following day she was on her beam ends. That afternoon, Carlsen and Dancy walked along the now horizontal funnel, jumped into the sea and were picked up by *Turmoil*. Minutes later, with the ships around her setting off flares and sounding their sirens in salute, *Flying Enterprise* foundered – just 39 miles (73km) from Falmouth. *JH*

**Captain Carlsen clings to the stern rails of the listing *Flying Enterprise*** *(photograph), 8 January 1952, Conway Picture Library*

396.5ft x 60.1ft x 25.8ft (120.8m x 18.3m x 7.8m) • 6711 tons [GRT] • Hull steel • Complement 40, passengers 10 approx. • Built Consolidated Steel Corporation, Wilmington, California, USA, 1944

# United States  Ocean liner 1952

*United States* is seen here docked alongside Southampton's then new Ocean Terminal on Tuesday, 8 July 1952 after her illustrious maiden voyage. She had just decisively clinched the Blue Ribband record for a stellar eastbound Atlantic crossing from the Ambrose Channel Light Ship at the entrance to New York harbour to Bishop's Rock at the south-western of the British Isles. The 2942-nautical mile passage between these two reference points was made at an average speed of 35.59 knots, 3.9 knots faster than *Queen Mary*'s 1936 record. Sailing against prevailing winds and currents, the westward passage back home to a tumultuous welcome in New York took only two hours longer, at an average speed of 34.51 knots.

The USA had played a major role in winning the Second World War, and at a time of euphoric pride and patriotism, to have then put to sea the world's fastest ever ocean liner was a crowning glory of the era. The celebrations on board the ship at the end of the voyage were justifiably triumphant.

SS *United States* was built to US Navy specifications for alternative use as a fast troop carrier if needed in times of war. As such, she was propelled by powerful steam turbine machinery similar to that of the USS Midway class aircraft carriers, yielding a maximum speed for commercial service of 38 knots. While much of her technical details were never disclosed to the public, it is generally believed that she was capable of considerably higher speeds — well over 40 knots in calm seas. *PD*

1947-2010

**Streamers hang from the Southampton Ocean Terminal following the arrival of the liner *United States* after her record-breaking maiden voyage** (photograph), 9 July 1952, Conway Picture Library

990ft x 101ft x 31ft (301.8 m x 30.8m x 9.4m) • 53,330 tons [GRT] • Hull steel • Complement 900, passengers 1928 • Built Newport News, Virginia, USA, 1952

# Britannia  Royal yacht 1953

The construction of a new Royal Yacht had first been mooted in the latter 1930s, but the plan was interrupted by the outbreak of the Second World War. In 1951, the requirement for a new yacht came back on the national agenda; King George VI was ill and it was hoped that such a vessel would aid his convalescence. John Brown & Co. of Clydebank was selected as best able to meet the specification and short timeframe. Alas, the King died on 6 February 1952 – the day John Brown received a letter confirming the contract, worth £1,615,000.

Political sensitivities about spending so much on a Royal Yacht while rationing was still in force were assuaged by the argument that the vessel had dual use as a hospital ship in wartime. The yacht's design was carried out in consultation with Queen Elizabeth II, and her consort, HRH Prince Philip. The interiors were designed by J. Patrick MacBride of the Glasgow-based McInnes, Gardner & Co., with additional input from Sir Hugh Casson, one of the Festival of Britain's co-ordinating architects who had recently undertaken the redecoration of apartments in Buckingham Palace.

HMY *Britannia* was launched on 16 April 1953 and delivered to the Royal Navy the following spring. The yacht was exceptionally well finished – the lustre of her dark blue hull and her immaculate decks thereafter being maintained in pristine condition by the navy's Royal Yachtsmen.

For nearly half-a-century, *Britannia* toured the world, regularly hosting the Royal Family and foreign dignitaries. Her stately three-masted silhouette and fairly substantial dimensions – resembling a 1950s channel packet liner – made her instantly recognizable and many regarded her as a successful ambassador for Britain abroad. In the latter 1990s, however, her age was beginning to show; her machinery tended to run hot during prolonged steaming at speed and the accommodation occupied by the Yachtsmen and Royal Marines band was incredibly cramped and far below the standards expected nowadays on modern warships. *Britannia* was withdrawn to become a popular visitor attraction in Leith Docks, Edinburgh. *BP*

**HMY** *Britannia* **at Portsmouth.** *Vanguard* **and** *Victory* **are visible in the background** *(photograph), Conway Picture Library*

# Compass Rose  Fictional Flower class corvette 1953

A fictional account, but based on his personal experience aboard the Flower class corvette HMS *Campanula* during Convoy OG 71 in 1941, Nicholas Monserrat's novel *The Cruel Sea* had been read by millions before it was adapted as a major film in 1953. The unglamorous struggle to protect Atlantic convoys from German U-boats is seen from the perspective of the inexperienced crew of the *Compass Rose*, commanded by Lieutenant-Commander George Ericson (Jack Hawkins), seen here on the corvette's bridge with his first officer, Lockhart (Donald Sinden). Eric Ambler's screenplay included the harrowing moment when Erikson has to depth-charge a U-boat in a patch of sea full of British seamen awaiting rescue, but avoided other distressing episodes of Monsarrat's novel.

*Compass Rose* was played by HMS *Coreopsis*, ex-Hellenic Navy ship *Kriezis*, and given the pennant K49 which had actually belonged to HMS *Crocus*. After

*Compass Rose* is sunk with the loss of many of her crew, Ericson and Lockhart are given the frigate HMS *Saltash Castle*, played by the Castle class corvette, *Porchester Castle*, in which they finish the war. Devoid of heroics, the film has been acclaimed for its honesty and accuracy.

Based on whale-catcher design, the first Flower class corvettes were ordered in 1939 as cheap, quick to build and easily operated anti-submarine warships. They were extremely seaworthy, but in bad weather they rolled to extremes, causing a great deal of sickness and making life wet and miserable for the crew, especially in winter. Success was hard won: 21 corvettes were lost to U-boats alone, and either single-handedly or in concert with aircraft and/or other warships the corvettes acounted for just over 50 enemy vessels. The only survivor of the class is HMCS *Sackville*, preserved at Halifax, Nova Scotia. *JH*

Actor Jack Hawkins on the bridge of his corvette in a scene from the film 'The Cruel Sea' *(film still), 1953, Hulton Archive / Getty Images*

[Typical data for class] 205ft x 33.2ft x 13.7ft (62.5m x 10.1m x 4.1m) • 1170 tons [D] • Hull steel • Armament 1 x 4in or 4in QF, 1 x 2 pdr pompom, 2 x 20mm Oerlikon, 40 depth charges (Hedgehog anti-submarine mortars later fitted) • Complement 85-109 • Built various yards in UK and Canada, 1939-45

# LV-112  Nantucket lightship 1954

The most perilous aspect of maritime travel remains that of safe navigation. Before modern construction techniques enabled lighthouses in treacherous seas and shallows, lightships were used as a means of warning vessels of impending dangers. Nantucket Shoals off Massachusetts was recognised early in the nineteenth-century as a station for lightships, which were typically light-draught, wooden-hulled platforms which used mushroom anchors to prevent dragging in silted, shifting seabeds and rough waters. Special signal lanterns and fog sirens served to alert approaching ships, and saved lives. Duty aboard these vessels was traditionally uncomfortable and hazardous.

Nantucket Lightship No. 112 (*LV-112*) was laid down in 1936 and incorporated into the US Coast Guard in 1939, which also absorbed the older Lighthouse Service. She was paid for by the British White Star Line, at a cost of $300,000, in compensation for the sinking of the previous Nantucket Lightship (*LV-117*) when she was struck by the RMS *Olympic* – sister-ship of the ill-fated *Titanic* – in 1934. As a result, *LV-112* was very strongly built, self-propelled, and lasted in service nearly fifty years. Today she is a designated US National Historic Landmark and under private restoration. *HF*

**The Nantucket lightship slowly moves toward Boston Harbor with the aid of the of CG Cutter *General Greene* (to starboard, not visible), having been torn from her mooring during Hurricane Edna** (photograph), 13 September 1954, Bettmann / Corbis

148.10ft x 32ft x 16.3ft (45.4m x 9.8m x 5m) • 1067 tons [D] • Hull steel • Armament (1942–1945) 1 x 3in (76mm) • Complement 11 • Built Pusey & Jones, Wilmington, Delaware, USA, 1936

# Nautilus  Nuclear submarine 1955

Completed in just over two years between 1953 and 1955, *Nautilus* was the world's first nuclear-powered submarine. Nuclear power had two major advantages over conventional diesel-electric machinery: the propulsion plant was completely air-independent, enabling the submarine to operate submerged for long periods; and using uranium as a fuel meant virtually unlimited high-speed endurance, making lengthy transits to a designated patrol area viable.

There were also disadvantages: a reactor small enough and light enough to be accommodated in a submarine needed to run on enriched uranium, and the reactor vessel and its coolant had to be isolated from the crew by heavy lead shielding. *Nautilus* was therefore significantly larger than the war-built US submarines, but her performance in the NATO exercise 'Rum Tub' in October 1957 was a revelation, and exposed the limitations of then-current anti-submarine warfare capabilities. In 1958 she undertook the first transit beneath the Polar ice-cap, starting out from Hawaii and ending up in Portland, Great Britain. Improved nuclear cores enriched by more than 40 per cent were subsequently developed, allowing a major increase in the intervals between refuelling. *Nautilus* served most of her active life as a test-bed, and was finally decommissioned in the early 1980s. She became a museum in 1982 in Connecticut, USA. *JJ*

**USS *Nautilus* approaches the dock to tie up at Groton, Connecticut, after an inspection cruise with Navy and Atomic Energy Commission personnel aboard** *(photograph), 28 November 1955, Bettmann / Corbis*

324ft x 28ft x 22ft (99m x 8.5m x 6.5m) • 3500 tons [D] • Hull steel • Armament 6 x 21in (533mm) torpedo tubes • Complement 105 • Built Electric Boat Corp., Groton, Connecticut, USA, 1954

# Andrea Doria  Italian ocean liner 1956

Had her tragic and well documented sinking not intervened in 1956, the Italian Line's *Andrea Doria* would have reigned as one of the truly iconic passenger ships of the twentieth century. To many she is still considered the most beautiful liner ever to see service with a refined exterior elegance and matchless modernist interiors.

The Second World War saw the loss of much of Italy's merchant fleet, including the liners *Rex* and *Conte di Savoia*, either to sinking or as reparations. Named after the great Italian sixteenth-century admiral, and with a sister-ship celebrating the other Genoese maritime hero, Christopher Columbus, *Andrea Doria* became the embodiment of post-war Italian national pride, hope and optimism in much the same way as Francis Gibbs's trailblazing SS *United States* was truly a 'ship of state' for the American super-power.

The Italian liner was the first to feature outdoor swimming pools and sought to combine luxury, functionality and beauty, thus echoing the comparable excellence that Italian designers have applied to cars, motorcycles and indeed buildings. She adopted the untainted 1950s modernist style for her interiors and her designers, including the celebrated Nino Zoncada and Giò Ponti, were strongly influenced by key American practitioners such as Florence Knoll, Charles Eames, Ludwig Mies Van Der Rohe and Eero Saarinen. The graceful and harmonious modernist style, rendered in new cutting edge materials including ceramics, glass and aluminium, was set off by more traditional artworks and sculptures inspired by earlier Italian art, crafts and culture. She was rightly termed the 'Renaissance Ship'. *JL*

**High angle view of SS *Andrea Doria*, New York City** *(photograph), date and photographer unknown, SuperStock*

701.5ft x 90.3ft (213.8m x 27.5m) • 29,083 tons [GRT] • Hull steel • Complement 563, passengers; 218 first class, 320 cabin class, 703 tourist class • Built Ansaldo Shipyards, Genoa, Italy, 1951

# Moshulu Barque 1956

The four-masted barque *Moshulu* was immortalized by Eric Newby in his books *The Last Grain Race* and *Learning the Ropes*, which record his time as a 19-year-old apprentice on the barque's voyage from Belfast to Australia and back to Glasgow in 1938–9, and include many fine photographs taken by him from aloft and on deck. *Moshulu*'s passage home with a cargo of wheat was completed in 91 days, beating the other 12 sailing ships also carrying grain.

She was built on the Clyde as the *Kurt* for German owners and was among the last few large sailing ships built in Britain. *Kurt* entered the nitrate trade from Chile to Europe until 1914, when she was interned in the USA. Then in 1917 she was seized by the USA when it entered the war, becoming the *Dreadnought*, although she was renamed *Moshulu* before her first voyage under the American flag. 'Moshulu' means 'fearless' (or 'dreadnought'; literally 'without dread') in the language of the Seneca tribe of Native Americans and the name was chosen by Mrs Woodrow Wilson, wife of the President.

*Moshulu* carried timber from the US west coast to Australia and South Africa between 1920 and 1928. In 1935 she was bought by Gustaf Erikson, who owned the last fleet of large sailing ships, and traded under the Finnish flag until 1940, when she was seized by Germany. After the war she was used as a floating grain warehouse and is now a floating restaurant at Philadelphia, USA. *PB*

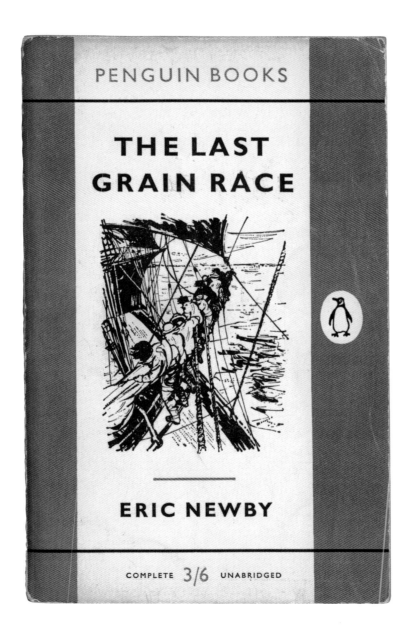

*The Last Grain Race* by Eric Newby, 1958 Penguin paperback edition *(photograph). Private Collection*

396ft x 46.9ft x 24.3ft (121m x 14.3m x 7.4 m) • 7000 tons [D] • Hull steel • Complement 33 • Built Alex. William Hamilton & Co., Glasgow, Scotland, 1904

# Granma  Revolutionary yacht 1956

Few 1940s cabin cruisers can claim to have had as great an impact on world history as the *Granma*, a leisure craft said to be named after the original American owner's grandmother. The 60ft yacht, designed to accommodate no more than 20 passengers, was acquired in October 1956 by the Cuban exile Fidel Castro, then in Mexico following the failure of his Moncada Garrison coup against the dictatorial Cuban regime of Fulgencio Batista in July 1953.

Late on 25 November 1956 Castro, together with some 82 rebels including his brother Raúl, Camilo Cienfuegos and Ernesto 'Ché' Guevara, boarded *Granma* and set sail from the Mexican port of Tuxpan. In a strategic and characteristically symbolic move, Castro made for the south eastern Cuban province of Oriente where support was strongest. The voyage emulated that of Cuban independence hero José Martí who landed in the same area fighting the Spanish in 1895.

The monstrously overloaded *Granma* was plagued with problems caused by a combination of rough seas and faulty machinery. After rescuing the yacht's navigator, who had fallen overboard, the rebels arrived two days late on the 2nd December, fifteen miles south of the designated spot. Castro's forces had to fight their way through the dense mangrove roots of the Playa de los Colorados and the swamp-like conditions meant they were unable to land their weapons. The rebels were split up and engaged in heavy fighting by the government forces. Only twelve were able to regroup high in the Sierra Maestra Mountains later in December and form their camp, from which grew the Cuban revolutionary movement that took power in January 1959.

*Granma* was brought to Havana and is now preserved, encased as a national monument, next to the Museum of the Revolution. A replica is often paraded through the capital while the official newspaper of the Cuban Communist Party is titled *Granma* as a tribute. *JL*

**A replica of the yacht *Granma* forms parts of the military parade in commemoration of the 50th anniversary of the Cuban revolution in Havana (photograph), 2 December 2006, Carlos Barria / Reuters / Corbis**

43ft (13.1m) • Hull composite • Complement 12-25 • Built USA, 1943

# Ranger  Forrestal class aircraft carrier 1957

After the Korean War the United States Navy began to rebuild the carrier fleet, replacing wartime ships with new super-carriers, the 65,000 ton Forrestal class. These were the first carriers designed from the keel up to operate jet aircraft and carry atomic bombs. With their angled decks, steam catapults and mirror deck-landing aids the new ships set a standard for naval aviation that would only be met and then exceeded by the USA. Able to operate up to 90 fighters, bombers and helicopters, with a crew of around 5000 and a suitably vast appetite for fuel, weapons and food; they were the central plank in the American surface fleet, the icon of sea power through most of the Cold War, and the standard response to every crisis within three hundred miles of open ocean. Completed in 1957, USS *Ranger* saw service in various wars and international crises; she was the first to take part in the Vietnam War, and was still up at the cutting edge in the First Gulf War of 1991. Successive rebuilds kept her up to date, able to operate successive generations of aircraft, from piston-engined Skyraiders to supersonic F14 Tomcats. *Ranger* finally paid off in 1993, but her descendants, the nuclear powered Nimitz class, are still the dominant surface-war fighting platform on the planet. *ADL*

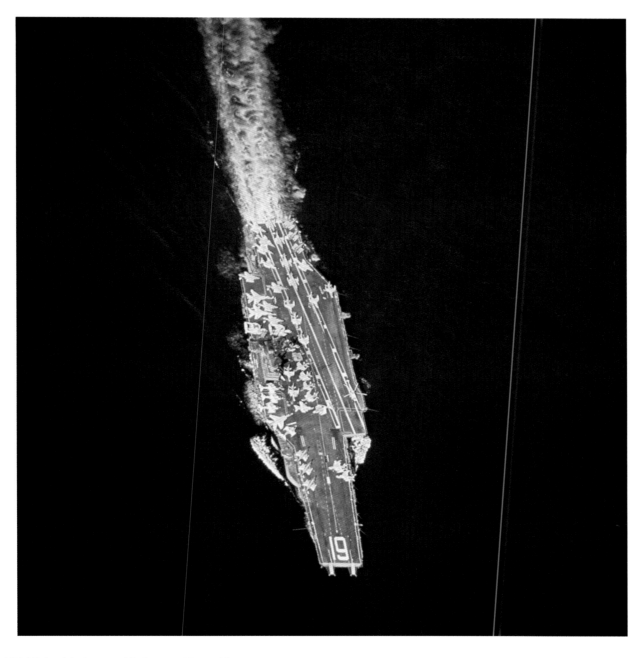

**USS *Ranger* (CV-61)** *(aerial photograph), Conway Picture Library*

769ft x 81.7ft x 19.7ft (234.4m x 24.9m x 6m) • 14.500 tons [D] • Hull steel • Armament 76 aircraft, 8 x 5in (later removed), NATO Sea Sparrow Phalanx CIWS • Complement 3826 • Built Newport News, Virginia, USA, 1956

# Rotterdam  Passenger ship 1959

On her launch, Holland-America line, the ship's owners, called her 'the ship of tomorrow … today!' It now seems, perhaps, a somewhat tired slogan, but in 1959 it captured the essence of a ship that really was like no other. In many respects, *Rotterdam* was groundbreaking, a vision of the future that acknowledged the approaching demise of transatlantic liner travel in favour of the leisure cruise.

Her Dutch designers created a two-class vessel, divided – uniquely – on a horizontal plane, a system of separation inspired by the ship's main stairway, in which two rectilinear staircases threaded through each other. First and tourist class spaces were separated, distinctly but not intrusively, through the ingenious principle of movable partitions. The novel design allowed for easy conversion from liner service to cruising, envisaging a ship whose primary function would not be one of transport but of pleasure.

*Rotterdam* was unique in numerous other ways, the most visible example of which was the two-thirds aft position of her machinery. This created a greater amount of passenger space in the ship's forward spaces but also meant that a conventional funnel seemed anachronistic. Instead, *Rotterdam* featured two tall, slim smokestacks, of aluminium-clad steel. These virtually eliminated the deposit of soot on the decks, a problem that had plagued earlier liners. It also allowed for broad sundecks and an outdoor swimming pool.

Original and elegant, *Rotterdam* was a considered response to the problems of passenger ship design. Detractors complained that she looked 'unfinished', but this was clearly a reactionary response, and the design proved to be highly influential. Ultimately, the fact that she served for over forty years, making an effortless transition from liner to cruise ship, while retaining most of her original features, is testament to the vision of those who created her. *MJ*

1947-2010

The promenade deck of the SS *Rotterdam*, showing the tourist class swimming pool (left) and the ship's tall twin exhausts in place of a funnel (photograph), 6 August 1959, Terry Disney / Central Press / Getty Images

748ft x 94ft x 29.5ft (228m x 28.7m x 9m) • 31,530 tons [D] • Hull steel • Complement 776, passengers 1456 • Built Rotterdam Drydock Company mij., Rotterdam, Netherlands, 1958

# George Washington  Polaris submarine 1959

*George Washington* was the world's first nuclear-powered ballistic missile submarine (SSBN). Previously, strategic nuclear weapons had been delivered either by long-range high-altitude bombers or by intercontinental ballistic missiles. However, sophisticated missile air defence systems posed a threat to the former, while the fixed silos of the latter could be targeted by increasingly accurate nuclear missiles in a preemptive first strike; a missile that could be fired underwater from a mobile platform which was difficult to locate was therefore an attractive, if expensive proposition.

Development of the Polaris missile by the USA took place simultaneously with the design of a new type of missile submarine which would need to stay submerged (for concealment) throughout its patrols. *George Washington* and her four sisters were converted from Skipjack class nuclear-powered attack submarines under construction by the insertion of a 130ft (39.6m) section housing 16 vertical missile tubes abaft the fin. The later US Navy SSBNs of the Ethan Allen and Lafayette classes were purpose-built, but had similar overall characteristics. The Polaris A-1 missile had a maximum range of 1000 nautical miles, and this was increased to 2500 miles in the A-3. However, the early SSBNs could not accommodate the more advanced C-3 Poseidon missile and were deactivated in 1980–81. *JJ*

**Launch of the USS** *George Washington* **at Groton, Connecticut** *(photograph), 9 June 1959, Mary Evans / Interfoto*

382ft x 33ft x 27ft (116m x 10.1m x 8.1m) • 5960 tons [D] • Hull steel • Armament 16 x A-1 Polaris SLBM launchers, 6 x 21in (533mm) torpedo tubes • Complement 112 • Built Electric Boat Corporation, Groton, Connecticut, USA, 1959

# Canberra Ocean liner 1960

At the time she made her debut, they called her 'The ship that shapes the future', and indeed in many regards *Canberra* was at least 10 years ahead of her time. She was conceived and created during a period of great progress throughout the shipping industry when the supertanker was coming of age, cargoes were being containerized and ordinary people were taking their own cars to and from the continent on board drive-on ferries. P&O's ultra-modern *Canberra* incorporated a number of the best ideas from these developments. Here machinery was located all the way aft, following the example of the modern tanker, and her twin side-by-side funnels were styled after those of P&O Trident tankers. Her entire centre body was thus freed of machinery, boiler uptakes and all other such functional parts, to be dedicated instead almost entirely to passenger services. *Canberra* was even fitted with two retracting lateral transporters to handle the loading, stowage and unloading of up to 80 passengers' cars through shell hatches in the hull's sides and with an airport-style automated conveyor system for handling baggage.

On board accommodation featured an innovative court arrangement, where, at the progressive widening of the secondary cabin alleyways towards the ship's sides, vertical ribbon windows were fitted to bring daylight to the inner rooms. There were also ingenious convertible tourist-class rooms featuring two Pullman-type fold-away bunks. These revealed concealed plumbing fixtures and a slide-out partition, effecting a quick change from four-berth emigrant occupancy without toilet facilities to a cosy two-berth cabin with en-suite for cruising.

Many of these ideas had appeared individually on earlier ships. It was the inspired fusion into a single, highly cohesive, attractive and functional design that made *Canberra* so successful. *PD*

**P&O flagship the liner SS** *Canberra* (photograph), date unknown, Conway Picture Library

818ft x 102ft x 32.7ft (249.9m x 31.2m x 10m) • 45,270 tons [GRT] • Hull steel • Complement 960, passengers; 548 First class, 1690 tourist class • Built Harland & Wolff, Belfast, Northern Ireland, 1960

# Vanguard  Battleship 1960

The tenth Royal Navy ship to carry the name, *Vanguard* was Britain's last battleship. She was completed too late to see action in the Second World War and, although developed from the King George V class, incorporated a number of modifications as a result of wartime experience. The initial impetus for her design was the availability of four twin 15in guns removed from the light battlecruisers *Courageous* and *Glorious* when they were converted to aircraft carriers during the 1920s. Although dated, the mountings were reliable, and in *Vanguard* they were allied to the most advanced fire control systems, with full remote power control (RPC) for the turrets and the Admiralty Fire Control Table Mk X. The secondary armament was similar to that of the King George V class, but a new sextuple 1.6in Mark VI Bofors mounting replaced the 2 pdr pompoms of the earlier ships. With her more powerful machinery and distinctive transom stern *Vanguard* was capable of 30 knots, and the bow section was given much greater flare and sheer, making her a better seaboat than her predecessors. Other innovations included cafeteria messing, which was initially unpopular but became a model for future warships. In service *Vanguard* became a flagship, then a training ship; the highlight of her career was a visit to South Africa in 1947 with the royal family on board. Her end was less glorious, grounding close to Portsmouth Harbour while en route to the breakers. *JJ*

**HMS *Vanguard* grounded at the Point, Old Portsmouth** *(photograph). August 1960. 'The News', Portsmouth*

814ft x 108ft x 31ft (248m x 32.9m x 10.6m) • 44.500 tons [D] • Hull steel • Armament 8 x 15in, 16 x 5.25in, 73 x 40mm Bofors AA • Complement 1893 • Built John Brown & Co., Clydebank, Scotland, 1944

1947-2010

# Enterprise Nuclear-powered aircraft carrier 1961

The most impressive warship of her time, USS *Enterprise* was the world's first nuclear-powered carrier. Although only slightly larger than her conventionally-powered contemporaries of the Kitty Hawk class, *Enterprise* benefited hugely from her nuclear propulsion plant. She was able to deploy at high speed anywhere around the globe without the need for refuelling – a series of nuclear-powered missile frigates were built to accompany her. Her internal layout was greatly simplified through not having to accommodate voluminous funnel uptake trunking, and she had a remarkably compact island superstructure of novel design, which could accommodate advanced new electronically-scanned planar radar arrays (the Terrier missile systems

originally projected were never installed). Finally, the oil fuel bunkers of conventionally-powered ships could be replaced by additional aviation fuel and ordnance stowage, which increased by around 25–30 per cent the number of consecutive days of strike operations she could sustain. *Enterprise* served off Vietnam during the 1960s, in the process proving the value of the CVAN concept. She was extensively modernized from 1979–81, when the original island was replaced and new radars with conventional rotating antennae were installed. As refitted she would serve as a template for a new generation of nuclear-powered carriers, the Nimitz class. *HF*

**USS *Enterprise* begins a shakedown cruise in the Atlantic** *(photograph, March 1963, Thomas J. Abercrombie/National Geographic/Getty Images*

1123ft x 255ft x 37ft (342m x 80m x 11.5m) • 75,000 tons [D] • Hull steel • Armament 90 aircraft, 3 x Sea Sparrow SAM launchers • Complement 5200 • Built Newport News, Virginia, USA, 1960

# Locarno Freighter 1961

The affluent resort of Rapallo lies sheltered in the Tigullio Gulf on Italy's northwest coast. On the afternoon of 3 January 1961 the inhabitants braved driving rain to go down to the palm-lined promenade after the Panamanian freighter *Locarno* went aground in heavy seas with her bows only 10 yards (9m) from the parapet while on a voyage from Genoa to Portiglione in ballast. The whole crew, apart from the master and engineer who remained aboard to oversee salvage operations, were safely taken off, and lights rigged up for firemen and frogmen to examine her.

Refloated on 28 January, she was declared a constructive total loss and later towed to La Spezia for breaking up.

Luck had finally run out for the old *Locarno* which was no stranger to accidents during a career of over 30 years. Built as the *Dunsley* in 1929 for the Whitby-based company Headlam & Sons, she was part of Convoy HX 90 when, on 2 December 1940 she was fired on by U-47 commanded by Günther Prien – less than two months after he had sunk HMS *Royal Oak* in Scapa Flow.

On 20 January 1946 she had run aground off Eastscar on the northeast coast of England and ended up on the beach at Stokesley Scar. Within a few weeks of being sold and renamed *Locarno* in 1954 she was towed into Gibraltar after running aground at Aguilas. *JH*

*Locarno* aground on rocks off the promenade at Rapallo, Italy *(photograph), 5 January 1961, Conway Picture Library*

360.2ft x 50.2ft x 22.6ft (109.8m x 15.3m x 6.9m) • 3899 tons [GRT] • Hull steel • Complement 22 • Builder R. Thompson and Sons Ltd., Sunderland, England, 1929

331

1947–2010

# Gorch Fock  Sail-training ship 1961

When sailing ships retired from the ocean trade routes some found employment as sail-training ships with various navies and mercantile marines. This tradition has continued, often leading to the construction of new vessels to replace their ageing forebears or to start off the practice in emerging maritime nations. The German *Gorch Fock* was completed in 1958 for the West German navy and is still operated by the German navy (Deutsche Marine) from her base in Kiel. She was built to the updated plans of the original *Gorch Fock* of 1933, which became the Russian *Tovarishch* ('Comrade') after the Second World War. The name honoured the popular

German writer of sea stories, Hans Kinau, who wrote under the pseudonym Gorch Fock. He was drafted into the German navy in 1916 and was lost in the same year with the cruiser *Weisbaden* in the Battle of Jutland.

*Gorch Fock* is a steel hulled three-masted barque (square-rigged on the fore and main masts, with fore-and-aft rig on the mizzen mast) and often participates in Tall Ships races. She also makes courtesy visits to ports worldwide and in 1987–8 circumnavigated the globe on a cruise that lasted 336 days. The illustration shows cadets unfurling sails while perched high in her rigging, as the ship prepares to sail from the Pool of London in 1961. *PB*

German naval cadets unfurl *Gorch Fock*'s main and topsails as she prepares to sail from the Pool of London, following a courtesy visit to the capital *(photograph), 13 September 1961, Conway Picture Library*

266.6ft x 39.2ft x 15.8ft (81.3m x 12m x 4.8m • 2002 tons [D] • Hull steel • Complement 66 + 140 cadets • Built Blohm & Voss, Hamburg, Germany. 1958

# Kynda  Kynda class missile cruiser 1962

The Rocket Cruisers (*Raketnyi Kreyser*) of the Kynda class, authorized in 1956, were the surface element of a Combined Arms force intended to contest the outer perimeter of the Soviet maritime defence zones in the Northern and Pacific Fleet areas and, in particular, to prevent incursions by NATO carrier task forces into Soviet waters.

The Kyndas, like their nuclear submarine counterparts of the Echo class, were equipped with 'over-the-horizon' anti-ship missiles which would be guided to the target by long-range reconnaissance bombers of the Tu 95 Bear D type. A powerful force of land-based bombers, also armed with anti-ship cruise missiles, constituted the third element of the anti-carrier force.

The Kynda made a considerable impression when she first appeared, as not only did it mark a clean break with post-war Soviet construction, but the ship design was quite unlike any ship in service with the Western powers. She was equipped with a full complement of new weapons and modern sensors. The prominent quadruple launchers for the 250 nautical miles (450km) SS-N-3 missile could be trained and elevated, and reloads were carried in the fore and after superstructures. There were also surface-to-air missiles and medium-calibre guns for self defence. Four ships were built (two for the Pacific, two for the Northern Fleet) before the Kynda was superseded by a new Rocket Cruiser, the Kresta I class. *JJ*

**Kynda** *(photograph), 1970, US Navy*

143m x 15.8m x 5.4 metres (469ft x 52ft x 17ft) • 4,400 tons • Machinery: two-shaft geared steam turbines, 100,000shp, 34 knots • Armament: 8 x SS-N-3 SSM launchers, 1 x SA-N-1 SAM launcher, 4 x 76mm (3in) • Complement 305 • Builder: Zhdanov Shipyard, Leningrad, Soviet Union, 1962

# France Ocean liner 1962

President De Gaulle's '*grand projet*' was to commission a luxurious transatlantic flagship liner to restore French maritime prestige following the tragic loss of the *Normandie* during the Second World War. Named *France*, the liner was built at St Nazaire and completed in 1961. Her hull design was similar to that of *Normandie* – but her funnels were of novel appearance, having wings on either side, through which smoke was emitted. While neither the world's fastest nor the largest liner, *France* had the distinction of being the longest – and also maintained the Compagnie Generale Transatlantique's tradition for exceptional cuisine and hospitality (her double-height Chambord first class dining saloon was reputedly the world's finest French restaurant.) While first-class passengers enjoyed a highly cultivated milieu amid the best of post-war French interior design, the CGT decided to replace tourist class with something new, which they called '*Rive Gauche*' – recreating at sea the stylish, informal and slightly bohemian atmosphere of Paris's Left Bank. This was a notable success – particularly with American students travelling to Europe.

Come the latter 1960s, the French Government decided to invest heavily in the supersonic airliner Concorde and in 1974 subsidies to maintain *France* were withdrawn, meaning that the CGT had no alternative but to lay the ship up in Le Havre. After five years in mothballs, she was purchased by Arab interests – but hastily resold to a Norwegian ship owner, Knut Kloster, for conversion into the world's biggest cruise ship, the *Norway*. After a complex rebuild *Norway* triumphantly re-entered service in 1980 as the flagship of Norwegian Caribbean Lines. For the next twenty years she was a highly successful and iconic cruise ship, sailing weekly from Miami. In 2003, alas, she suffered a boiler explosion and was withdrawn, being sold thereafter for scrap. The forepeak of her bow was rescued and returned to France, where it is now on public display in Le Havre. *BP*

1947-2010

**Tugboats welcome the liner SS *France* to New York by spraying water into the air** (*photograph*), *8 February 1962, Bettmann / Corbis*

1035ft x 110.6ft x 34ft (316.1m x 33.8m x 10.8m) • 66,343 tons [GT] • Hull steel • Complement, passengers; 407 first class, 1637 'Rive Gauche' class • Built Chantiers de l'Atlantique, St Nazaire, France, 1960

# Bremen  Steam turbine liner 1962

A 39ft (12m) scale model replica of North German Lloyd's fourth *Bremen* (foreground) recalls the 1929-built ship's sleek modern lines that made a clean and irrevocable break with traditional ship design. Below the waterline the hulls of *Bremen* and her near-identical sister-ship *Europa* were the first express liners to feature a bulbous forefoot to the bow that, like the head of a cod or salmon, both very fast swimmers, would in effect push a hole through the water, creating smoother flow lines for the hull to follow through. Above the waterline, in the public gaze, the sleek exterior, with its slender hull lines, low foredeck, rounded superstructure front, glass-enclosed promenade decks and low ovoid funnels were a foretelling of the future and the coming streamlined age of air travel and fast streamlined trains. *Bremen* and *Europa* also set the trends for other passenger ships, large and small, including the liners *Normandie*, *Queen Mary* and *Queen Elizabeth* and the smaller Lloyd Triestino *Victoria* and the Danish DFDS ferry *Kronprins Olav*.

In the background is the fifth *Bremen*, originally completed in 1939 as *Pasteur* for Compagnie de Navigation Sud-Atlantique's Bordeaux-to-Buenos Aires service and sold after a prolonged wartime and French Government service for extensive conversion as the eventual replacement for her North German Lloyd predecessor in 1959. The model of the earlier ship, which has a top speed of 12 to 14 knots, is being controlled by a pilot seated inside its hull who is provided with a small viewing port in the superstructure front beneath the navigating bridge. *PD*

A 39ft replica of the *Bremen* (1929) on the River Weser in Bremerhaven, with the new Norddeutsche Lloyd flagship *Bremen* (1957) moored behind (*photograph*), *June 1962, Conway Picture Library*

[Data refers to 1929 *Bremen*] 938.7ft x 101.7.6ft (286.1m x 31m) • 51,656 tons [GRT] • Hull steel • Complement 966, passengers; 811 first class, 500 second class, 300 tourist class, 617 third class • Built Deutsche Schiffe-und-Maschinenbau AG Weser, Bremen, Germany, 1928

# Michelangelo  Ocean liner 1962

Shimmering in the warm Mediterranean sun, proud and tall atop the shipyard's inclined building ways just before her 16 September 1962 launch, the smooth-sided and curvilinear hull looks like something from the design teams at Ferrari or perhaps Olivetti, or maybe even a *haute-couture* item from the fashion houses of Gucci or Armani. *Michelangelo* and her sister ship *Rafaello* were products of the glorious era of Sixties Italian design that so captivated the whole world's imagination. These ships boasted many advanced features such as drive-aboard side hatches and large on-board garages for carrying passenger automobiles. They were even designed with consideration for the possibility of conversion to nuclear power. Other thoughtful touches included such things as infra-red pool and lido area heating for added comfort in chilly weather.

Onboard, both liners were a veritable showcase of contemporary Italian design and craftsmanship. Although structurally identical, with their distinctive three-quarters-aft twin latticed funnels, spacious open decks, multiple lidos and pools (for passengers' enjoyment of the warmer, more southerly transatlantic crossing via the Straits of Gibraltar and the Mediterranean), their interior architecture, decoration and furnishings were radically different. Separate teams of architects, designers and artists had been engaged for each ship. Many of the first-class luxury cabins were individually designed and adorned with original works of contemporary art.

These were, however, among the last traditional liners built, and as such suffered the sad misfortune that their three classes of passenger accommodations were less easily adaptable for one-class cruising and that their machinery designed for 26.5-knot liner service was too costly to run at the lower cruising speeds. Unfortunately, these magnificent ships were withdrawn after only about ten years in service. Fortunately they disappeared quickly from the public gaze without their agonizing demise in Middle Eastern waters being widely witnessed. *PD*

***Michelangelo*** **on the slipway at Genoa shipyards, prior to her launch on 16 September 1962** *(photograph), Conway Picture Library*

904.9ft x 101.7ft (275.81m x 31.0m) • 45,911 tons [GRT] • Hull steel • Complement 720, passengers; 535 first class, 550 cabin class, 690 tourist class • Built Ansaldo, Sestri Ponente, Genoa, Italy, 1962

# Anosov  Soviet freighter 1962

If there is one point when the Cold War could really have turned hot, it was probably late October 1962. The world looked on as the two superpowers, the United States and the Soviet Union, played out a dangerous game of brinkmanship off the coast of Cuba – it appeared that mankind was on the brink of nuclear Armageddon.

The Cuban missile crisis was an attempt by the Soviet Union to covertly install R-12 Dvina theatre-range nuclear missiles on the island under the guise of shipping more conventional supplies to Fidel Castro's Cuban government. The USA was particularly sensitive to the Soviet Union's engagement with Cuba, and tension heightened when in August 1962 US spy planes appeared to show the construction of missile installation sites on the island. If fully completed and armed with missiles, the USA would have been under permanent threat – a rebalancing of power, the Soviets argued.

With the materiel coming into Cuba by sea, on 22 October 1962 President John F Kennedy implemented 'a strict quarantine on all offensive military equipment under shipment to Cuba', to be enforced by US armed forces. The escalating crisis was only brought to a peaceful conclusion by a US-Soviet agreement to remove the Cuban missiles in return for the removal of US nuclear missiles from sites in Italy and Turkey.

Key to winning the private psychological and subsequent public media battle was tangible proof of Soviet activity. While secret intelligence provided classified evidence to the US military and politicians as to what the Soviets were actually doing, it was only the release of images taken as the crisis began to subside, such as this photograph of the Soviet freighter *Anosov*, that not only proved to the world the accuracy of US claims but allowed President Kennedy to inform the population of the USA that the threat had passed. *MR*

**Close-up of the Soviet freighter *Anosov* en route from Cuba with missiles lashed to the deck for shipment back to Russia** *(aerial photograph),* *10 November 1962. Bettmann / Corbis*

No data available

# Empress of Canada  Ocean liner 1965

Lady passengers pillow-fight while straddling a greased pole over the ship's swimming pool as their shipmates look on. During the liner era, joyful amusement of this kind served to while away long warm days at sea on passages of anything from five days across the North Atlantic to upwards of four to six weeks from the British Isles to Australia, New Zealand and the Far East. This was an age when the shipping line provided an orchestra or band for evening dances, film shows in the cinema, afternoon Bingo, shipboard 'horse racing' and a daily tot on the ship's mileage, along with a well stocked library and an exercise room. In addition, passengers actively entertained themselves, with various deck games and competitions of one sort or another being a staple of daily activity. Bridge tournaments and whist drives were also a popular pastime. It was a gentler and more serene era, when hours would be whiled away in canvas deck chairs along deep shaded decks in the tropics or glassed-in promenades on the North Atlantic. These were times for socialising, exchanging shipboard gossip, or just dozing. Passengers strolled around the promenade deck to aid digestion and of course to inhale the wonderful fresh sea air. Back then there no casinos, cabaret or musical revue shows, no rock-climbing walls, no bungee jumping, surf simulators or glass bottomed whirlpools slung over the ship's side at dizzying heights fifteen decks up from the water. Nor were there the distractions of the Internet, iPods or iPhones. There was then no need for constant gratification; non-stop entertainment and organised activity virtually around the clock – people simply enjoyed the experience of shipboard living, relaxing and getting to know one another. *PD*

**1947-2010**

**Passenger entertainment: a 'greasy pole' competition aboard the *Empress of Canada** (photograph), c. 1935, Waterline Collection, National Maritime Museum, London (P85862)*

650ft x 86.5ft (198.1m x 26.4m) • 27,284 tons [GRT] • Hull steel • Complement 470, passengers; 192 first class, 856 tourist class • Built Vickers Armstrong, Newcastle, England, 1961

# Kungsholm Cruise ship 1966

The *Kungsholm* is one of the most beautiful and long-lived liners, but her construction proved disastrous for her builder, John Brown & Co. Anxious to maintain continuous employment for their workers pending the building of a new flagship liner for Cunard (the *Queen Elizabeth 2*), the shipbuilding firm tendered to build *Kungsholm* without a profit margin, neglecting to account for wage inflation, construction delays due to industrial unrest and rises in material costs. As a result, in 1966 Swedish American Line belatedly received an outstanding vessel, but John Brown & Co. lost over £3 million.

The *Kungsholm* was a motor ship, her twin Götaverken diesels being located towards the stern and exhausting through the aft funnel. Her forward funnel was a dummy whose main purpose was to balance the ship's profile. Painted in white, the liner was an exceptionally elegant flagship for 'The White Viking Fleet', as Swedish American was known.

Her interiors utilized the best of modern Swedish design and the craftsmanship of Clydebank's finishing trades. Although designed as a dual-purpose transatlantic liner and cruise ship, *Kungsholm* became best known in

the latter role – but Sweden too experienced significant wage inflation in the 1970s. Rather than employing a cheaper international crew in place of Swedes, Broström Ab, Swedish American's parent company, decided instead to close down the Swedish American Line altogether in 1974 and to sell their ships. The *Kungsholm* passed first to the Norwegian Oivind Lorentzen's Flagship Cruises, then in 1978 to P&O, for whom she was substantially rebuilt in Bremerhaven as the *Sea Princess*. Most controversially, her forward funnel was removed and the aft one extended, rather spoiling her hitherto immaculate appearance. P&O used *Sea Princess* in Australia, then on cruises from Southampton and, later still, from US West Coast ports. In 1995, she returned to Britain as the *Victoria*, but was sold in 2002 to a Greek cruise entrepreneur, Paris Katsoufis, becoming the *Mona Lisa* (a large copy of Da Vinci's painting was emblazoned on her funnel). Inboard, she remains much as built – one of the last 'classic' liners entirely finished in lustrous hard wood veneer. *BP*

The elegant MS *Kungsholm* in Swedish-American Line livery *(photograph)*, *Bruce Peter Collection*

660.6ft x 87.2ft x 28.1ft (201.3m x 26.6m x 8.6m) • 26,678 tons [GT] • Hull steel • Complement 417, passengers; 713 (transatlantic service), 450 (cruising), 782 (as of 2008) • Built John Brown & Co., Clydebank, Scotland, 1966

# Torrey Canyon  Supertanker 1967

Anyone born in the 1950s will have vivid memories of television and newspaper coverage of the *Torrey Canyon* disaster of 18 March 1967. Images of the huge oil tanker aground on Pollard's Rock, 7.5 miles (12km) off the Scilly Isles, with detergent being sprayed on the vast slick, were soon accompanied by shots of black beaches and thousands of dead seabirds. Ordinary people were confronted by this darker side of the world's reliance on oil, the lack of adequate contingency planning, and the impotence of governments to deal with the wreck of a tanker over which they had limited jurisdiction.

Registered in Liberia, owned by the Union Oil Company, California, chartered to British Petroleum and with an Italian crew, *Torrey Canyon* had loaded 119,000 tons of crude oil at Mena Al Ahmadi and was proceeding on auto-pilot to Milford Haven, under pressure to meet the narrow tidal window. A navigational error was realized too late, and the rocks soon holed the ship's bottom. An engine room explosion on the 22nd killed the Dutch salvage master, and hopes of refloating the tanker on the 26th failed. Two days later she broke in half, and the forepart in turn broke. Aircraft of the Royal Air Force and Fleet Air Arm dropped petrol and napalm, vainly hoping to set the cargo alight. Ultimately, the cleaning up was done by nature and the wreck is now a popular dive.

In the wake of the disaster came international regulations, covering safety and liability, notably MARPOL 1973, the International Convention for the Prevention of Pollution From Ships. Attention was also given to contingency planning, including the construction of tugs large enough to deal with the rapidly increasing size of the new leviathans. *JH*

The tanker *Torrey Canyon*, broken in two on Pollard's rock off the Isles of Scilly *(photograph), 18 March 1967, Conway Picture Library*

974.4ft x 125.4ft x 68.7ft (297m x 38.2m x 20.9m) • 120,000 tons [DWT] • Hull steel • Complement 36 • Built Newport News, Virginia, USA, 1959

# PBR Patrol boats, river c.1967

The instruments of sea power take many forms, from great battleships and carriers that fight for command of the open ocean, to smaller craft which turn that command into effect on land, where wars are decided. The US Navy has long been the pre-eminent 'blue water' fleet, spearheading vast carrier and nuclear submarine programmes. In every war from 1917 to 2010 these ships had to be complemented by new flotillas of gunboats, landing craft, minesweepers and other humble vessels.

The Vietnam War made peculiar demands on the Navy and Marine Corps, not least because the only naval action proved to be the cause of the conflict.

The need to operate in the Mekong River from the delta to the Cambodian border led to the construction of well over 400 PBR river patrol boats between 1966 and 1976. Armed with machine guns and grenade launchers the 6-ton PBR's patrolled the strategic waterway, and most remained in South Vietnam after the Americans withdrew. Years later the PBR achieved iconic status as the ship at the dark heart of Francis Ford Coppola's startling film *Apocalypse Now*. Some were brought into service for the First Gulf War in 1991, while the Iraq War of 2003 revived the river patrol mission, and new PBRs have been built accordingly. *ADL*

**US river patrol boats of Task Force 116 in Vietnam** *(photograph), date unknown, Conway Picture Library*

[Data for Mk I type] 31ft x 10.5ft x 2ft (9.4m x 3.2m x 0.6m) • 6 tons [D] • Hull fibreglass and aluminium • Armament twin 12.7mm machine guns, rear single .50 cal, 1 or 2 side-mounted M60 7.62mm machine gun, Mk 19 grenade launcher • Complement 4 • Built Uniflite, Bellingham, Washington, USA, 1966–71

# Gipsy Moth IV   Francis Chichester's ketch 1968

For a 64 year-old man to set out on a single-handed circumnavigation of the globe, with the aim of completing a non-stop first leg to Sydney, was unprecedented when Francis Chichester left Plymouth, England, in *Gipsy Moth IV* on 27 August 1966. His subsequent voyage made sailing history and inspired generations of single-handed circumnavigators. Chichester himself took inspiration from the Victorian clippers (such as *Cutty Sark*) which he had researched for his book *Along the Clipper Way*, and aimed to beat their average passage time of 123 days: in the event his non-stop 14,100 miles to Sydney took only 107 days. The non-stop second leg of 15,517 miles, around Cape Horn and home, lasted 119 days. Chichester arrived at Plymouth on 28 May 1967 to a rapturous welcome from more than 250,000 people on the Hoe, with millions more watching on television. He broke many records, including the fastest voyage around the world by any small vessel. *Gipsy Moth IV* went on display in a dry dock at Greenwich for nearly forty years (and is shown above arriving there on a transporter). She was then restored, re-launched on 20 June 2005, and started another circumnavigation on 25 September 2005 with a crew comprised of experienced yachtsmen and disadvantaged young adults. On completion of the voyage *Gipsy Moth IV* berthed in Plymouth on 28 May 2007, exactly forty years after the first remarkable homecoming. *PB*

*Gipsy Moth IV* **passes the** *Cutty Sark* **en route to Woolwich Arsenal from the Boat Show at Earl's Court** *(photograph), 22 January 1968, Conway Picture Library*

53ft x 10.5ft x 7.8ft (16.2m x 3.2m x 2.4m) • 11.5 tons [D] • Hull wood (mahogany) • Complement 1 • Built Camper and Nicholsons, Gosport, England, 1967

# Pen Duick IV   Aluminium trimaran racing yacht 1968

Éric Tabarly, the father of modern French yachting, stands in the bows of his new yacht *Pen Duick IV* prior to the start of the 1968 *Observer* Single-handed Trans-Atlantic Race (OSTAR). The former Marine Nationale officer has every reason to look confident – he won the 1964 OSTAR trophy in his 44ft ketch *Pen Duick II* in a time of 27 days, 3 hours and 56 minutes, despite the fact that his self-steering system had only worked for the first 8 days of the race. The victory had buoyed a troubled nation, and President De Gaulle had accordingly presented Tabarly with the Legion d'Honneur.

Tabarly returned for the next edition of the quadrennial OSTAR series with a brand new monster yacht; *Pen Duick IV*, a custom-built aluminium trimaran with rotating masts designed by André Allègre. Dubbed the 'giant octopus' and the 'floating tennis court', she was the largest yacht in the field of 35, and had captured the attention of the world's media.

*Pen Duick*'s radical design promised much, but she was largely untested and had been completed only a few weeks before the race. Preparations had also been disrupted by the May '68 strikes back in France. The problems with the yacht soon became apparent; the auto-pilot system was only reliable below speeds of 10 knots, and her boom braces broke en route from L'Orient to the starting point at Plymouth.

The race itself would be nothing short of disastrous for Tabarly, as the North Atlantic was swept by 60 knot gales. 17 competitors retired, including Tabarly after he collided with an anchored freighter at night not long after the start of the race. He had been standing watch but had ducked below to heat some coffee. Although *Pen Duick*'s inherent structural strength meant she survived the impact, she sustained a 4ft gash in one float, and her rig was damaged. Tabarly was forced to abandon the race and limp back to port. *MJ*

**Éric Tabarly stands on the prow of his trimaran yacht** *Pen Duick IV* **at Plymouth prior to the 1968 Atlantic Race** (photograph), 30 May 1968, Conway Picture Library

68.2ft x 35.1ft x 7.9ft (20.8m x 10.7m x 2.4m) • 8 tons [D] • Hull aluminium (duralinox) • Complement 1 • Built La Perrière shipyard, L'Orient, France, 1968

# Queen Elizabeth 2 Cunard ocean liner 1969

At the end of a shake-down cruise to the Canary Islands, during which her main turbines failed as the result of a design problem and she had to return to Britain at greatly reduced speed, *Queen Elizabeth 2* arrives at Southampton's Ocean Terminal on Thursday, 2 January 1969. This setback to the completed ship resulted in her maiden voyage being postponed until 22 April 1969 with an inaugural cruise to Las Palmas, Tenerife and Lisbon, before setting out from Southampton to New York on Friday 2 May.

Although *QE2* has since become one of the best-known and arguably most-loved ships of all times, she continued to be dogged by periodic technical problems until her machinery was completely replaced with a modern diesel electric installation as the major part of a six-month refit in Germany over the winter of 1986-7. During the nearly four decades of her service life much of the original élan of her 1960s styling was compromised to suit the tastes of a predominantly American cruising clientele through numerous reconfigurations, redesigns and refits of her passenger facilities. Various changes were also made to her exterior profile, including the replacement of her original slender modernist stack with a bigger traditional red-and-black funnel as part of the re-engining. Yet *QE2* has nonetheless retained a distinctive aura of originality, born of her unique design and singularity, and even seen at a distance her profile has remained unmistakeable. *PD*

*Queen Elizabeth 2*, **assisted by tugs, edges into the Ocean Terminal at Southampton on return from her trial cruise** (photograph), *2 January 1969,* Conway Picture Library

963ft x 105ft x 32ft (293.5m x 32m x 9.8m) • 48,923 tons [D] • Hull steel • Complement 1040, passengers 1892 (all berths) • Built John Brown and Co., Clydebank, Scotland, 1967

# Hamburg  Deutsche Atlantik ocean liner 1969

The post-war resurgence of Germany as Europe's leading industrial and economic power by the late 1960s is reflected in the design of the Deutsche Atlantik Linie's liner and cruise ship, *Hamburg*.

She was an impressive ship, with straight lines and a wine glass-shaped bow profile. The most distinguishing feature, however, was her funnel. Following wind tunnel testing, it was found that the most effective design was conical-shaped with a 'flying saucer' high above, supported by the boiler exhausts. This enabled a flow of air through the structure, preventing soot from being sucked down on the after decks.

Although measuring only 25,022 tons, the *Hamburg* gave the impression of being far larger than she actually was – thanks to large cabins and many public rooms of various sizes and functions. Her decor was by a Munich-based architect, George Manner, and represented the best of 1960s West Germany, with dark woodwork, abstract artworks and modern furniture throughout.

Despite being a magnificent ship she proved costly to operate as West German labour rates grew exponentially. Thus, in 1974, she was sold to the Soviet Union's Black Sea Steamship Company and registered in Odessa. Immediately prior to this sale, she was used as the setting for the film 'Juggernaut'. The Soviets re-named her *Maxim Gorkiy* and immediately chartered her back to a West German package tour operator. In December 1989, she was used for a crucial political summit between President Mikhail Gorbachev and US President George Bush in Malta, helping to bring about the end of the Cold War. During the break-up of the Soviet Union, her ownership passed to Russia's Sovcomflot and she continued to operate under charter to Germany's Phoenix Reisen until 2008. With oil prices at record levels, her steam turbines were too costly to fuel and so she was abruptly withdrawn and, still in pristine condition, scrapped at Alang in India. *BP*

The Deutsche Atlantik liner *Hamburg* (photograph). Bruce Peter Collection

642ft x 90ft (195m x 27m) • 23,500 tons [GRT] • Hull steel • Complement 340, passengers 790 • Built Howaldtswerke Deutsche Werft, Hamburg, Germany, 1968

# Suhaili  Racing sloop 1969

Robin Knox-Johnston was serving in India as a merchant navy officer with the British India Steam Navigation Company when he began to dream of his 32-foot ketch *Suhaili* ('southeast wind' in Arabic), which he promptly began building on a slipway in the Bombay Docks. When he became due for long leave, he sailed her the 12,000 miles (19,312km) back to London. His beloved *Suhaili* was based on early designs by William Atkins, influenced by Norwegian sailing lifeboats. She would prove up to the challenge of the Southern Ocean, some of the largest waves on earth.

Stocked with provisions, books, and a 'few essential bottles of whisky', Knox-Johnston left Falmouth in June 1968 in a bid to become the first man to sail solo and non-stop around the world. He had no electronic navigational equipment; in some respects, he had much the same gear as his great hero Captain Cook, relying on a sextant and chronometer and trusting in his experience as a master mariner. 'No one would call *Suhaili* a greyhound', he later said, 'but she was solid, strong and she needed to be!' She sailed into Falmouth Harbour on 22 April 1969 after 28,000 miles (45,062km) and 312 days at sea – entering the record books as the first ship ever to complete a circumnavigation without stopping. It was also the lengthiest voyage yet made.

*Suhaili* was briefly exhibited at Holborn and subsequently housed for some time as a museum exhibit in Greenwich, but the controlled atmosphere began to shrink her planking. Unwilling to see her 'die' in this way, Knox-Johnston removed her in 2002. Now re-fitted with her teak hull being re-fastened, *Suhaili* may soon return to the waves. *HLJ*

**British skipper Robin Knox-Johnston's yacht *Suhaili* is exhibited at Holborn Circus in London, 3 May 1969** *(photograph), AFP / Getty Images*

32ft x 11.5ft (9.75m x 3.5m) • 14 tons [D] • Hull wood • Complement 1 • Built Bombay, India, 1963

# Kiev   Russian Kiev class aircraft carrier 1972

*Kiev* was the first large air-capable ship built for the Soviet Navy. Designated a Large Anti-Submarine Cruiser, she is thought to have been designed to serve as the command ship for surface forces intended to protect the holding areas (or 'bastions') for Soviet SSBNs in the Northern and Pacific Fleet areas. The forecastle was dedicated exclusively to 'cruiser' weaponry; it was dominated by the large elevating launchers for the SS-N-12 anti-ship missiles, which could be reloaded from a capacious below-decks magazine located between them. The anti-submarine missile and rocket launchers were likewise mounted on the forecastle. The AA guns and missiles, which typified

the Soviet 'multi-layered' approach to air defence, were divided between the forecastle and the after end of the island superstructure, which also carried the main surveillance and fire control radars and housed all control spaces. The flight deck was angled to port, with a substantial deck park to starboard. Directly beneath it was a hangar served by two aircraft lifts. The designed air complement comprised 12 Yak-36 Forger VTOL strike fighters and 18 Ka-25 Hormone anti-submarine helicopters. Two further ships of the class, *Minsk* and *Novorossiysk*, were completed in 1978 and 1982 respectively, but the fourth ship, *Baku*, was rebuilt to a revised design. *JJ*

**Soviet aircraft carrier *Kiev*** (photograph), 1985, UK Ministry of Defence

895ft x 174ft x 31ft (273m x 53m x 9.5m) • 36,000 tons [D] • Hull steel • Armament 12 VTOL aircraft, 18 A/S helicopters, 8 x SS-N-12 SSM, 2 x SA-N-3 SAM, 2 x SA-N-4 SAM, 1 x SUW-N-1 A/S launchers, 4 x 76mm (3in) • Complement 1600 • Built Black Sea Shipyard, Mykolaiv, USSR (now Ukraine). 1972

# Alfa Class submarine   Nuclear-powered submarine 1974

The Alfa class submarine (Soviet Project 705 Lira) was a revolutionary design that had its origins in a series of projects initiated in 1956. The intention was to leapfrog early western nuclear boats by creating an advanced, deep-diving submarine with exceptionally high speed, capable of intercepting Western carrier task forces in the Northern Fleet area; later units were built for a similar missions in the Pacific. High speed was achieved by combining a small hull, in which hydrodynamic features were prioritized over internal volume, with a reactor that used liquid metal rather than water as a coolant. Using liquid metal meant reactor size and weight could be kept to a minimum, while the high power generated resulted in a maximum underwater speed estimated at 42 knots. However, the liquid metal had to be constantly maintained at a high temperature, even when alongside, and the prototype boat is reported to have been lost following a 'freeze' in the coolant. A diving depth of 700m (2296.6ft) was obtained by using titanium rather than steel for the pressure hull.

These submarines had a high level of automation; they were manned exclusively by officers and could not be maintained on patrol. They were also noisy at speed. Only six units were built, and the type was finally abandoned in favour of more conventional nuclear boats. *JJ*

1947-2010

**Soviet Alfa class submarine** *(photograph), 1987, UK Ministry of Defence*

267ft x 31ft x 23ft (81.4m x 9.5m x 7m) • 2900 tons [D] • Hull titanium and steel • Armament 6 x 533mm (21in) torpedo/missile tubes • Complement 45 • Built Sudomekh Shipyard, Leningrad, Soviet Union, 1974

# Finnjet Gas turbine cruiseferry 1977

The need for a ferry service from Helsinki and Travemünde resulted from the closure of Eastern Europe behind the Iron Curtain during the Cold War. As the Finnish and West German economies expanded and car ownership grew, by the mid-1960s, there was also a need to develop car ferry services. The 'first generation' of ferries all took two nights to make the lengthy Baltic crossing and so, in the early-1970s, Finnlines and the shipbuilder Wärtsilä investigated the possibility of a very large high-speed ferry to bring the voyage's duration down to 24 hours. The solution was to use Pratt & Whitney gas turbines to give a speed of over 30 knots, housed in a hull and superstructure of very innovative design.

The new ferry was the first example of 'large block principle' design, in which the hull and superstructure were conceived as a series of large blocks, each containing a particular part of the ferry's payload. The double-level vehicle deck formed a tunnel through the centre of the hull, with crew cabins on either side. The forward half of the superstructure was given over entirely to cabins of standardized dimensions, while public rooms were towards the stern. Beyond mere functionality, the ferry was conceived as a national flagship for Finland, intended to showcase technical and design know-how and so a range of leading Finnish architects were commissioned to design the interiors, which were notably modern and elegant.

Upon completion in 1977, *Finnjet* was the largest, fastest, longest, most capacious ferry in the world – the 'Top Trump' in all categories in the famous card game. Unfortunately, she was also very fuel-hungry, and was subsequently fitted with economical diesel electric engines for use during slacker periods. The end of the Cold War and the advent of budget airlines brought an end to her unique role and she spent her latter years making inexpensive booze cruises from Helsinki to Tallinn, before being withdrawn in 2005. Thereafter, she was chartered out for use as a hotel ship in New Orleans in the wake of Hurricane Katrina. After that, she was sold for conversion for cruising, but her new owner went bankrupt and so she was sold instead for scrap in India. The turbine-powered Finnjet remained unique – but while her machinery was too costly, her overall design pointed the way to developments in the 1980s and 90s and almost every large ferry built in her wake showed her influence. *BP*

GTS *Finnjet* in the approaches to Helsinki in conditions of -30 degrees celsius *(photograph), February 2005, Bruce Peter Collection*

698.8ft x 83.4ft x 22.7ft (213m x 25.4m x 6.9m) • 24,605 tons [GRT] • Hull steel • Complement 178, passengers 1781 • Built Wärtsilä Hietalahti shipyard, Helsinki, Finland, 1976

# Typhoon Nuclear-powered ballistic missile submarine 1981

The giant ballistic missile submarines of the Typhoon class (Soviet Project 941 Akula) were built for sustained operations under the Arctic pack ice. The 'Typhoon' was radically different in conception and design to earlier Soviet SSBNs and all western submarines of this type in that the launch silos for the 20 missiles were located forward of the fin. Within the outer hull casing there were no fewer than five separate (but interconnected) pressure hulls: two main pressure hulls running most of the length of the the submarine containing the machinery and the crew accommodation; a shorter cylinder forward for the torpedo tubes and reloads; a short cylinder amidships at the base of the fin housing the control centre; and a small cylinder aft for the steering gear. The propulsion machinery was divided into two independent units, each comprising a large OK-650 PWR reactor, geared steam turbines and the associated auxiliaries. The crew accommodation was exceptionally roomy, and included a sauna and even an aviary. Six submarines of this type were completed during the 1980s; a seventh was broken up while still under construction. One unit was damaged in 1991 following an accidental explosion during the loading of a missile; these submarines are now being dismantled with US assistance. *JJ*

**Typhoon class submarine, c. 1984** *(photograph), UK Ministry of Defence*

563ft x 75ft x 40ft (171.5m x 22.8m x 12.2m) • 18,500 tons [D] • Hull steel • Armament 20 x SS-N-20 SLBM launchers, 4 x 650mm (26in) torpedo/missile tubes • Complement 150 • Built Severodvinsk Shipyard, Arkhangelsk Oblast, USSR, 1980

# Ticonderoga   Aegis guided missile cruiser 1981

The advanced Aegis Combat System was developed to counter the saturation cruise missile attacks expected to form the basis of Soviet anti-carrier tactics. The system was originally to have been embarked in nuclear-powered missile frigates, but the enormous combined costs of Aegis and nuclear propulsion proved prohibitive, and it was decided instead to adapt the hull of the Spruance destroyer.

In the Aegis system four fixed, electronically scanned SPY-1 planar arrays are used to track multiple targets. Unlike earlier surface-to-air missiles, the Standard SM-2 requires target illumination only in the terminal phase of flight; in the mid-course phase the missile flies under auto-pilot to a predicted interception point, and is then guided to the target by one of the four Mk 99 illumination radars. This means that no fewer than 18 missiles can be kept in the air in addition to the four in the terminal phase. An elaborate Combat Information Centre, capable of accepting inputs from offboard sensors, monitors the air picture around the force.

A total of 27 ships of the Ticonderoga class were completed between 1983 and 1994 to provide two ships for each of the 12 USN carrier groups plus additional units for the amphibious forces. From the seventh ship onwards the Mk 26 twin-arm launchers (each 24 missiles) were replaced by the Mk 41 vertical launch system, which has a capacity of 122 missiles, including Asroc and Tomahawk. *JJ*

**US Navy sailors assigned to USS** *Ticonderoga* **(CG-47) depart the ship for the last time, during her decommissioning ceremony at Naval Station Pascagoula, Mississippi on 30 September 2004** *(photograph). Stacey Byington, US Navy / Public Domain*

563ft x 55ft x 31ft (172m x 17m x 9.5m) • 6560 tons [D] • Hull steel • Armament 2 x Mk 26 SAM launchers, 8 x Harpoon SSM launchers, 2 x 5in (127mm), 6 x 12.75in (324mm) torpedo tubes, 2 helicopters • Complement 345 • Built Litton Ingalls, Pascagoula, Mississippi, USA, 1981

# General Belgrano Cruiser 1982

Laid down in 1935 as the USS *Phoenix*, *General Belgrano* was one of two light cruisers of the Brooklyn class purchased by Argentina in 1951. Although refitted at the Philadelphia Navy Yard, *Belgrano* and her sister *Nueve de Julio* (ex-*Boise*) retained their original armament and remained virtually unmodified until the 1960s, when Dutch surveillance radars and the British Seacat short-range surface-to-air missile were fitted. At the same time the original reconnaissance floatplanes were replaced by helicopters, which were accommodated in the hangar beneath the quarterdeck.

In 1978 *Nueve de Julio* was retired, but *Belgrano* remained in service in the amphibious support and gunnery training roles. During the Falklands conflict

of 1982, *Belgrano* and two escorting ex-American destroyers armed with Exocet missiles were stationed to the southwest of the Falkland Islands, patrolling on a line just outside the 200 mile (321.9km) 'exclusion zone' declared by the British. Unknown to her, she was being stalked by the British submarine *Conqueror*, which, following a decision in Whitehall, despatched her with two elderly Mk 8 torpedoes. She sank in about 45 minutes with heavy loss of life. This provoked a subsequent controversy when it became clear that *Belgrano* was not only 20 miles (32.2km) outside the exclusion zone but was headed away from the islands and towards the mainland at the time of the torpedo attack. *JJ*

The Argentine cruiser *General Belgrano*; ex-USS *Phoenix* (photograph), 1982, AFP / Getty Images

608ft x 62ft x 23ft (185m x 19m x 7m) • 9,800 tons • Hull steel • Armament 15 x 6in, 8 x 5in, 2 x Seacat SAM launchers, 2 helicopters • Complement 930 • Built New York Navy Yard, New York, USA, 1938

# Antelope   Type 21 frigate 1982

Amphibious landings are among the most difficult military operations to implement successfully, not least because one of the many determinants for success is gaining effective control of local airspace. That was achieved in 1944 in Normandy; it was not in 1982 during the Falklands War. The resultant loss of HMS *Antelope* on 23 May 1982 provided one of the iconic images from that latter conflict.

The failure to invest in the range of capabilities required to project maritime power during the Cold War was epitomised by the 1981 Defence Review, commonly called the Nott Review after the then-Secretary of State for Defence John Nott. The Falklands was precisely the type of war that the Royal Navy would no longer have to fight, or so the politicians had said.

As a result, many of the frigates and destroyers tasked to provide air defence for the amphibious landings at San Carlos Bay in May 1982 had failed to receive upgrades to their air-defence systems, while in practice many systems did not work as envisaged. For example, it was found that the Sea Dart and Sea Wolf missiles often failed to lock on or track incoming hostile aircraft, especially at low altitude, leaving air defence to close-in weapons, which were not installed in sufficient numbers.

San Carlos became known as 'bomb alley', with HMS *Ardent*, HMS *Coventry* and HMS *Antelope* all lost and HMS *Argonaut* and HMS *Brilliant* damaged – indeed, if several Argentinian bombs had not failed to explode the results might have been catastrophic for the landings, which, despite the air-defence problems, went ahead. It was a close run thing. *Antelope* herself had been hit by two bombs that failed to detonate, but in attempting to defuse them a bomb disposal team accidently triggered one, which tore the ship open and created several major fires. After a successful evacuation, on the evening of 23 May *Antelope*'s missile magazines detonated in a series of explosions. *MR*

**The Royal Navy frigate HMS *Antelope* explodes in the bay of San Carlos off the East Falklands during the Falklands War** *(photograph), 23 May 1982. Martin Cleaver / Pool / Getty Images*

384ft x 41.9ft x 19.6ft (117m x 12.7m x 5.9m) • 3,250 tons [D] • Hull steel • Armament 1 x 4.5in Mk 8, 2 x 20mm Oerlikon, 1 x quadruple Sea Cat SAM, 2 x triple torpedo tubes, 1 x helicopter • Complement 177 • Built Vosper Thornycroft, Southampton, England, 1972

# Príncipe de Asturias  Aircraft carrier 1982

The *Príncipe de Asturias* was the first aircraft carrier built for the Spanish navy, and inspired similar small carriers built for Italy. The design, by the New York firm of Gibbs & Cox, is an adaptation of the Sea Control Ship (SCS) proposed for the US Navy during the mid-1970s but not funded by Congress. It features a 575ft (175m) flight deck with two lifts: one on the centre-line aft, the other offset to starboard just forward of the island to permit air operations to port. The propulsion system, which was designed for ease of maintenance, is identical to that of the U.S. Navy's Patrol Frigate (FFG-7 class), which was designed at the same time: it has two General Electric LM

2500 gas-turbines geared to a single shaft, with two small electrical propeller pods to get the ship home in an emergency.

Spain wanted a more capable ship than the original SCS, and *Príncipe de Asturias* was completed from the outset with a 12-degree 'ski-jump' at the forward end of the flight deck to enable the ship to operate a variant of the USMC Harrier V/STOL aircraft, the Matador II, and larger and more sophisticated command spaces. The only defensive systems fitted are the Spanish-designed 0.8in Meroka anti-missile gun and ECM jammers. Area defence against enemy air attack would be provided by missile frigates. *JJ*

**SNS *Príncipe de Asturias* (R11) steams through the Atlantic Ocean while participating in joint exercise Majestic Eagle 2004** *(photograph)*, US *Department of Defense / Public Domain*

643ft x 80ft x 31ft (195.5m x 24.3m x 9.4m) • 16,700 tons [D] • Hull steel • Armament 24 aircraft & helicopters, 4 x 20mm Meroka CIWS • Complement 650 • Built Bazán, Ferrol, Spain, 1982

# Rainbow Warrior Greenpeace ship 1985

The Greenpeace flagship *Rainbow Warrior* is seen lying on her side in Auckland harbour, New Zealand, on 10 July 1985. She was blown-up by French secret service agents during the night of 9 July 1985, as the ship lay docked while preparing for a protest expedition to the French nuclear test site on the Pacific atoll of Mururoa. At 11.49 p.m., an electric blue flash was seen in the water beside the ship, quickly followed by an explosion. Fernando Pereira, a Portuguese Greenpeace photographer, worried about his cameras, returned to his cabin just before the second blast went off, barely two minutes later. By 4.00 a.m., scuba divers recovered Pereira's body. He had drowned, trapped in his cabin, with the straps of his camera bag tangled around one leg. Pereira was the only victim of the explosion. Within days the embarrassed French Prime Minister, Laurent Fabius, admitted that French secret service agents, following orders, had attached explosives to the side of the *Rainbow Warrior*. The French minister of defence resigned.

The vessel had started life as the *Sir William Hardy* in the British Ministry of Agriculture, Fisheries and Food, and was acquired by Greenpeace in 1977 as their first ship. Two successive replacement Greenpeace vessels have also been named *Rainbow Warrior*. PB

The Greenpeace flagship *Rainbow Warrior* lies on her side in Auckland harbour *(photograph), 10 July 1985, AFP / Getty Images*

131.3ft x 27ft x 18.1 ft (40m x 8.2m x 5.5m) • 418 tons [GT] • Hull steel • Complement 12 • Built Hall, Russell & Co., Ltd, Aberdeen, Scotland, 1955

# Ekranoplan Ground effect vehicle 1987

The Ekranoplan ground effect vehicle (GEV) was an unusual aircraft designed by the Soviet engineer Rostislav Alexeev and used by the Soviet and Russian Navies from 1979 until the late 1980s. Ground effect craft use the extra lift of their large wings when in proximity to the earth's surface. The sole vessel of her class (Soviet Lun, NATO Utka), *MD-160* entered service with the Black Sea Fleet in 1987. Eight Kuznetsov NK-87 turbojets were mounted on canards forward of the main wings; these could be elevated to provide additional thrust on take-off. The craft normally flew at an altitude of 3.3–13.1ft (1–4m) above sea level, but could ascend to 9842.5ft (3000m). *MD-160* had a flying-boat-like fuselage with a large hinged deflecting plate to

provide a 'step' for take-off at the mid-point of the lower hull, and two smaller fixed steps close to the bow. It was fitted with six launchers for antiship cruise missiles, mounted in pairs on the dorsal surface of the fuselage, and advanced tracking systems mounted in the nose and tail.

A development of the Lun was planned for use as a mobile field hospital, one which could be rapidly deployed to any ocean or coastal location. However, serious corrosion problems were experienced with *MD-160* and similar craft built for amphibious operations, and the type was subsequently abandoned. *JJ*

**Soviet Ekranoplan A-90 Orlyonok; an open air exhibit at the Russian Navy Museum, Moscow** *(photograph), 31 May 2009, Sergey Rodovnichenko*

242ft x 144ft (73.8m x 44m) • 290 tons [D] • Hull steel • Armament 6 x SS-N-22 SSMs, 2 x 23mm • Complement 15 • Built Volga Zavod, Nizhniy Novgorod, USSR, 1979

# Herald of Free Enterprise RORO ferry 1987

Just before 7 a.m. on 6 March 1987, the RORO ferry *Herald of Free Enterprise* left the Belgian port of Zeebrugge bound for Dover. Within ninety seconds she had heeled over in shallow water, 91m (100yd) from the shore, and 193 people lost their lives in the ensuing scramble to safety. *Herald* and her sister-ships *Pride of Free Enterprise* and *Spirit of Free Enterprise* had been designed specifically for the competitive Dover–Calais crossing. Cars could be loaded from two decks simultaneously, thus speeding up loading and unloading time at both ports.

As with many maritime disasters, the ship's loss was caused not by a single error, but by a series of compounding factors. On the day of her capsize *Herald* was operating out of Zeebrugge, which was not her usual route and not a port for which she had been specifically designed. Zeebrugge had a different linkspan system that could only unload one deck at a time. The loading ramp could not reach the upper deck at high tide and so water had been pumped into the front ballast tanks to lower her bow. *Herald* left the port with her bow doors still open, which allowed water to enter and move freely on the car deck, making the ship unstable. New safety measures were subsequently brought into effect for this type of ship and passenger details now have to be recorded before a ship sails, so that harbour authorities know exactly who is on board. *AM*

1947-2010

**Herald of Free Enterprise lays on its side off the Belgian port of Zeebrugge surrounded by rescue boats** *(photograph), 7 March 1987, Boris Horvat / AFP / Getty Images*

432.9ft x 76.1ft x 18.9ft (131.9m x 23.2m x 5.7m) • 13,601 tons [GRT] • Hull steel • Complement 80, passengers 1300 (459 embarked at time of accident) • Built Schichau Unterweser, Bremerhaven, Germany, 1980

# Olympias  Athenian trireme replica 1987

Until the late nineteenth century everything that was known about this powerful Greek battlecruiser of the ancient world had been deduced from literature and artefacts. The excavation of the Zea trireme sheds and the discovery of the naval inventories at last provided concrete information as to a trireme's size and fixed the number of oars at 170 – 85 on each side in three stepped tiers. The 54 *thalamio* who rowed closest to the waterline pulled oars fitted with leather *askomata* that prevented  water entering the hull. Above them sat 54 *zygioi*, while the third rank of 62 *thranites* were stationed along an outrigger, the *parexeiresia*. All oarsmen were free citizens; even convict oarsmen were first given their freedom.

A sail set on the foremast and mainmast provided auxiliary propulsion on passage, but before a battle the masts were removed. From the bows protruded a bronze ram, designed to hole the enemy below the waterline.

In 1985 an Anglo-Greek team began work to build the *Olympias*, a replica of an Athenian trireme of the Salamis period. They used pine, a wood that would have been abundant in ancient Greece, and constructed a shallow-draught vessel, knowing that trireme crews usually ate and slept on shore. The two-year project greatly increased understanding of construction methods and performance.  Though crewed mainly by students, not top-class rowers, *Olympias* achieved over 9 knots, and could turn quickly in two-and-a-half times her own length. The results confirmed many of the claims made in classical Greek literature about the strength, speed and manoeuvrability of triremes.

Since carrying the Olympic torch in 2004, *Olympias* has been housed in drydock at Faliron, near Athens. *JH*

**Trireme *Olympias* at the Paleon Faliron Museum, Greece** *(photograph), April 2008, Public Domain*

121.1ft x 18ft x 4.10ft (36.9m x 5.5m x 1.3m) • 70 tons [D] • Hull wood (oak and pine) • Armament bronze ram • Complement 205 • Built Piraeus, Athens, Greece, 1987

# Eagle US Coast Guard sail training barque 1988

Originally launched as the Segelschulschiff *Horst Wessel* in June 1936 under the auspices of Adolf Hitler, this magnificent sailing barque remains today as an active training ship for US Coast Guard Academy cadets. Despite the advent of machine-propulsion in the nineteenth century, professional naval and maritime forces have recognized the need for school ships which teach modern sailors timeless aspects of the life at sea; namely teamwork, discipline and self-reliance under adversity. Following the Second World War, *Horst Wessel* was made a prize of the USA and recommissioned on 15 May, 1946 as the USCG cutter *Eagle*. At just over 1800 tons, the vessel represents one of the finest specimens of marine architecture; the culmination of hundreds of years of nautical experience and science. Steel-hulled, with a 1000hp diesel plant, *Eagle* boasts a spread of 22,000ft² of sail and has logged 19 knots solely under canvas. Three hundred tons of special keel ballast give her good righting ability even when heeled over at extreme angles. Internal watertight compartments have since been expanded. Three other ships still survive of her class, as designed by Blohm & Voss of Hamburg: *Gorch Fock* is a museum ship in Stralsund, Germany; *Sagres III* (formerly the *Albert Leo Schlageter*) was taken up by the Portuguese navy in 1961; and the *Mircea*, which was contracted for the Romanian navy in 1938. *HF*

**USCGC *Eagle* under sail** *(photograph). Conway Picture Library*

295 ft x 39.1ft x 17.6ft (90m x 11.9m x 5.3m) • 1813 tons [D] • Hull steel • Complement 19 officers, 56 crew, 175 cadets and instructors • Built Blohm & Voss, Hamburg, Germany, 1936

# Silja Serenade  Cruiseferry 1990

The Baltic ferry routes between Sweden and Finland are a unique phenomenon. Although these countries have only moderate populations, the vessels connecting Stockholm, Helsinki and Turku are amongst the largest of their kind in the world. The main reason is that alcohol has long been subject to high taxation and can only be sold in state-owned stores on terra firma. Thus, for Swedes and Finns, combining tax-free shopping with a mini-cruise by ferry is a big attraction and the vast majority of the populations of these countries make such trips several times a year. For much of the duration of these overnight voyages, the ferries navigate through beautiful archipelago scenery. The climate is extreme – with warm summer temperatures but perishing cold winters. Thus, all Baltic ferries require specially strengthened hulls to break ice.

The Finnish naval architect, Kai Levander, who specializes in cruise and ferry design, talks of 'ferry generations' – each responding to passenger expectations of different eras. Baltic ferries of the 1980s, built in the wake of Finnjet, were very large and featured restaurants and entertainment venues, but, by the 1990s, it was felt that the next generation would have to offer more to attract a younger and more demanding clientele, as well as keeping existing passengers entertained. There was stiff competition between two major operators, Silja Line and Viking Line, each seeking to outdo the other by building the biggest and most glamorous ships. For Silja Line, the solution was to design ferries resembling floating shopping malls, with very wide ranges of dining, retail and entertainment facilities.

The *Silja Serenade* was the first ferry to realize the concept of the floating mall – her superstructure being divided length-wise by a five-storey atrium, with cabins facing inboard as well as out to sea and retail facilities arranged along a teak-floored promenade at its base. Delivered in 1990, the ferry was an immediate success, becoming a blueprint for subsequent Caribbean-based cruise ships. After twenty years, *Silja Serenade* remains in front-line Baltic service, sailing nightly between Stockholm and Helsinki. *BP*

**Silja *Serenade* passing Kustaanmiekka, Suomenlinna, Helsinki, Finland** *(photograph). March 2007. Wolfgang Pöpken / Public Domain*

666.1ft x 103.3ft x 233ft (203.3m x 31.5m x 7.1m) • 58,376 tons [GRT] • Hull strengthened steel • Complement passengers 2852 • Built Masa-Yards Turku New Shipyard, Turku, Finland, 1989

# Kongo   Kongo class guided missile destroyer 1991

Navies are imposing visual statements of power and status and the guided missile destroyer *Kongo* certainly delivers such a statement. In 1986, when the US Congress authorized the sale of the sophisticated Aegis fire control system to Japan, the country's naval force became the first American partner to secure the procurement of this state-of-the-art combat system. Key to the Aegis is a set of phased arrays placed along the superstructure of the destroyer which eliminate the need for rotating antennas and offer the warship a constant monitoring of the surrounding battle space. This in turn enables the *Kongo* to engage simultaneously multiple incoming targets at a far greater distance than other traditional systems. Laid down at the Mitsubishi Heavy Industries shipyards in 1990 and commissioned in 1993, *Kongo* demonstrated Japan's effort to upgrade the anti-air warfare capability of its fleet as much as the country's commitment to both its national defence and the US-Japan security alliance. The volatile nature of the post-Cold War security environment in Northeast Asia brought the cutting edge technological features of *Kongo* to the attention of the wider Japanese audience, making this ship a true icon of the country's first line of defence. This destroyer, with her three sister-ships, are today the centrepieces of Japan's missile defence system which is currently being developed to shield the archipelago from ballistic missile attacks from North Korea. In December 2007, *Kongo* was selected to be the first Japanese ship to conduct a test of the SM-3 anti-ballistic interceptor system which was successfully completed shortly after. For these reasons, *Kongo* has not failed to enter popular culture, with a 2005 motion picture, a comic book series and a TV cartoon show all featuring a destroyer of her characteristics at the centre of the their storylines. *AP*

A Standard Missile-3 is launched from the Japanese Aegis Destroyer *Kongo* (DDG 173) during Japan's first Aegis missile test *(photograph)*. *17 December 2007, US Department of Defense / Public Domain*

528.2ft x 68.9ft x 20.3ft (161m x 21m x 6.2m) • 7250 tons [D] • Armament 1 x 5in, 2 x 20mm CIWS, 2 x triple torpedo tubes, 2 x Standard SAM/SSM/ASROC VLS (29 + 61 cells) • Complement 300 • Built Mitsubishi Nagasaki Shipyard, Japan, 1991

# Ulsan Class Frigates   Guided missile frigate 1992

With the USA having grown closer to China and the Nixon Doctrine threatening US troop commitments to the Korean peninsula, in 1974 the late President Park Chung-Hee launched the Yulgok project for military and defence industrial modernization. The purpose was to reduce South Korea's dependence on foreign military assistance. The programme for the Ulsan class frigates was one of the first Yulgok projects.

As indigenously designed ships to meet the Republic of Korea (ROK) Navy's strategic requirements, the 2000-ton frigates emerged as noticeably different compared to second-hand Second World War era US Navy destroyers in the ROK navy's inventory at the time. Nowhere in the world did a ship of such size pack such extraordinary firepower. The two 3in guns and four 1.2in guns were mounted to deal with the sheer number of North Korean vessels, whether they were swarms of patrol boats or anti-ship missiles. Due to the country's economic status at the time, only nine frigates were built, while scaled-down and more affordable versions of the Ulsan class

were pursued under two successive corvette programmes, the Pohang and the Donghae classes.

From an industrial standpoint, the Ulsan class frigates were the first-ever major surface combatants to be conceived, designed and built in South Korea. In addition to their heavy armament, the frigates were also the first South Korean ships to be equipped with an electronic combat management system. The achievements made with the Ulsan class would also mark the end of imported surface vessels. Since then, all ROK navy surface vessels have been designed and manufactured in South Korea.

Today's ROK navy possesses some of the world's most sophisticated naval vessels, as evidenced in their area air-defence destroyers and guided missile fast attack craft. Though their new designs are far sleeker and their weapons systems more sophisticated, every hull in the ROK navy, it could be said, slices through the waves with the indigenous spirit of the Ulsan embedded in their hulls. *MH*

**ROK *Kyong Buk*, during RIMPAC (Rim of the Pacific) Exercise, 1992, San Diego, California, USA** *(photograph), US Department of Defense / Public Domain*

(340.2ft x 41ft x 12.5ft (103.7m x 12.5m x 3.8m) • 2350 tons [D] • Hull steel • Armament 8 x Harpoon (2 quadruple launchers) ASM, 6 x 324 mm Mark 46 torpedo, 2 x Otobreda 76mm, 3 x Otobreda 40 mm compact CIWS, 2 x Super Barricade launchers • Complement 186 • Built Hyundai Heavy Industries Co., Ltd. and Daewoo Shipbuilding & Marine Engineering Co., Ltd, South Korea, 1992-2001

# Charles de Gaulle Nuclear-powered aircraft carrier 1994

*Charles de Gaulle* is the only aircraft carrier powered by nuclear reactors to be built outside the USA. She was authorized in 1986, but budgetary problems resulted in a construction period of 12 years. Each of the two reactors – the same K15 model which powers the SSBNs of the Le Triomphant class – is inside a protective confinement structure. The adoption of a two-shaft propulsion plant placed constraints on both maximum speed and overall size, so that despite being larger than earlier French carriers *Charles de Gaulle* can only just cope with modern fixed-wing aircraft. A broad US-style flight deck, with the two aircraft lifts on the deck edge to starboard, was adopted, but the two 250ft (75m) US C13-3 steam catapults intrude on to the angled deck, prohibiting simultaneous take-off and landing operations. The French-built Rafale fighter and Super-Etendard strike aircraft are smaller and less capable than their US counterparts, while the U.S. Navy's E-2C Hawkeye AEW aircraft has proved difficult to accommodate and to operate. Among the more advanced features of the *Charles de Gaulle* are the SATRAP active fin stabilization system and the Aster SAAM vertical launch missile air defence system. *JJ*

The British tall ship *Grand Turk* and the French aircraft carrier *Charles de Gaulle* in the Solent off Portsmouth during Trafalgar 200 *(photograph), 28 June 2005, Stephen Hird / Reuters / Corbis*

858ft x 211ft x 28ft (262m x 64.5m x 8.5m) • 36,500 tons [D] • Hull steel • Armament 40 aircraft, 4 x SAAM, 2 x SADRAL missile launchers • Complement 1750 • Built DCN, Brest, France, 1994

# Channel Ferry British Cross-Channel ferry 1998

Asked to create a vision of maritime Britain, the artist Humphrey Ocean avoided the obvious nostalgia of sailing ships, but instead turned his attention to mundane ferries plying their way across the English Channel. The National Maritime Museum in Greenwich commissioned the work, 'First of England', in 1998 and Ocean used sketches and photographs gathered on various ferries around Britain. He tried to evoke the isolation of everyday experience while also reflecting on the influence of the ship in modern life: no longer a golden age of beautiful sailing vessels but reduced to the unromantic, badly designed, metal box-like craft, the functional rather than aesthetic, a maritime nation as stale as the coffee in the painting's polystyrene cup. Ocean's work also acknowledged Ford Madox Brown's Pre-Raphaelite vision 'The Last of England', which showed a pair of stricken emigrants as they sail from home for ever – a famous work that underscored the social and national significance of sea travel during the 1850s.

'I imagine a fair proportion of Britons have at one time or another been on a ferry,' Ocean later commented, 'which is now an extension of the car as well as being a floating high street.' He also saw bleak 'parallels with eager day trippers being conveyed back to England from a shopping trip in France and descriptions of troops in the First World War' being shipped to battles on the Continent. In the shadow of the iconic Dover cliffs and 'oblivious to each other, they behave with characteristic British nonchalance. No one looks at the figure lying on the bench, not caring if he is drunk, dead or just asleep'. *HLJ*

**The First of England, 1998** *(oil on canvas), Humphrey Ocean, 1998, National Maritime Museum, London (D9948)*

# Kursk   Oscar II class nuclear cruise missile submarine 2000

Between 1986 and 1991, the Soviet navy commissioned 11 Antey 949A nuclear-powered submarines, which until 2007 remained the largest in the world. Capable of diving to around 1968ft (600m), the class is designed to carry cruise missiles with nuclear or conventional warheads that can travel some 600km (372 miles). These are housed between the outer and the pressure hull, while a formidable array of torpedoes and anti-submarine missiles are carried inside a forward torpedo compartment.

On 11 August 2000 at 11.30 a.m., during the Northern Fleet exercises in the Barents Sea, the seventh in the class, *Kursk*, attempted a simulated attack on the flagship using an old practice torpedo fuelled by paraffin and highly reactive hydrogen peroxide. A devastating fire and explosion in the torpedo room set off the other warheads and the cataclysmic blast tore through the next two compartments, sending the *Kursk* to the bottom.

Crew in the compartments further aft had survived, and the reactor was shut down. Twenty-three men took refuge in darkness in the partially flooded ninth compartment, where one of them compiled a list of names and wrote a farewell note to his wife.

Nobody can be certain how many hours or possibly even days they lasted, but the likelihood is that an oxygen replenishment cartridge was accidentally dropped into the water, causing a flash fire that used up their oxygen. The Russian Federation Navy was incapable of mounting a rescue effort and too concerned about pride and security to accept the offers of international assistance that came in when it became clear from seismic data and other sources that a submarine was in distress – though by then it must have been too late.

The remains of the submarine were raised in 2001. *JH*

The conning tower of the *Kursk* breaks the surface in the port of Roslyakovo, near Murmansk, 23 October 2001, after being raised from the seabed but prior to her examination in dry-dock by state investigators *(photograph). AFP / Getty Images*

505.2ft x 59.7ft (154m x 18.2m) • 24,000 tons [D] • Hull steel alloy • Armament 24 SS-N-19 Granit cruise missiles (various ordnance including nuclear capability), 4 x 21in (53cm) and 2 x 26in (65cm) torpedo tubes  • Complement 107 (118 at time of accident) • Built Sevmash Shipyard, Severodvinsk, Arkhangelsk, Russia, 1995

# Sea Cloud II   Sailing cruise ship 2001

The tough world of the merchant sailing ship has been replaced by the luxury of the sailing cruise ship, of which increasing numbers are putting to sea. The character of these sailing cruise ships is unlike that of huge cruise liners, and much more like that of a private yacht. They are relatively small vessels, able to use small harbours and hideaway anchorages. They rarely carry as many as 200 passengers, and though these are accommodated in considerable luxury, there is often much emphasis on watersports, wildlife, and seagoing – diving, sailing dinghies, beach landings in small Zodiac craft; and on the interest of sailing the ship itself. Some of them offer long ocean passages under sail, such

as crossing the Atlantic or the Indian Ocean. *Sea Cloud II* is a fine example. A modern barque, she can spread 29,600ft$^2$ of canvas on three masts, the fore and main being square-rigged and the mizzen fore-and-aft rigged. In the right conditions she can sail at 12 knots, and when there is no wind she can use her auxiliary engine. She is rated as five-star, with no more than 94 passengers attended by 58 crew. Unlike some other comparable ships, a special point of interest in *Sea Cloud II* is that the square sails are still handled in the traditional manner, the crew going aloft and out along the yards to furl or loose sail. *GH*

*Sea Cloud II* at Bequia *(oil on canvas), Geoff Hunt, 2002*

384ft x 52ft x 18ft (117m x 16m x 5.7m) • 3849 tons [D] • Hull steel • Complement 58, passengers 94 • Built Astilleros Gondan, Figueras, Spain, 2001

# Black Pearl   Captain Jack Sparrow's ship 2003

Part wood, part computer-generated image (CGI), the fictional vessel at the heart of the Disney film trilogy *Pirates of the Caribbean* was launched for the East India Trading Company during the first half of the eighteenth century as the *Wicked Wench*, and enjoyed an initial career as an East Indiaman. A disagreement with her captain, Jack Sparrow, led the company to set fire to the ship, but she was subsequently raised by Sparrow with the help of the legendary Davy Jones and registered at Isla de Muerta as the *Black Pearl*, marking the start of her adventurous career as a pirate ship with trademark black sails. With cannon mounted on two decks, she was capable of a delivering an effective broadside but was handicapped by the inexplicable lack of bow chasers to attack fleeing prey and stern chasers to hinder pursuit. Square rigged with a lateen mizzen sail, and oars as auxiliary propulsion, she

was the fastest ship in the Caribbean despite her tattered sails..

In the first film, 'The Curse of the Black Pearl' the eponymous ship, like HMS *Dauntless*, one of the Royal Navy vessels, existed as a construction mounted on a steel barge, capable of making only 2 knots and extremely unwieldy to manoeuvre into position. HMS *Interceptor*, however, was played by a real tall ship, *Lady Washington*. The two sequels used a much larger *Black Pearl* which had been built over an existing ship, the 109ft (33.2m) *Sunset*. The kraken episode in *Dead Man's Chest* was shot using models, live actors and CGI, and required a team of up to 80 compositors, with one scene alone taking two-and-a-half months to complete, and helping the film to a Best Visual Effects Oscar. *JH*

Johnny Depp and Geoffrey Rush as Captains Jack Sparrow and Barbossa in a scene from 2007 film 'Pirates of the Caribbean: At World's End' *(film still)*, 2007, Walt Disney/The Kobal Collection/Stephen Vaughan

No data available

# Queen Mary 2  Cunard flagship 2003

Cunard Line's *Queen Mary 2*, virtually the only true ocean liner now in service, departs from San Pedro Harbour, Los Angeles while in her alternative role as a cruise ship. Unlike the majority of today's large passenger ships, where an individual identity and character is in essence superimposed upon near identical structural and technological platforms of multiple sister-ships (such as Carnival's Vista Class or Royal Caribbean's Voyager series), *QM2* was designed and built as a singular entity for a special dual-role function. Conceived to ultimately replace Cunard's famed and much-loved *Queen Elizabeth 2*, the new *QM2* was planned to continue the express North Atlantic liner service inaugurated as far back as 1840 and maintained to this day, as well as for the cruise service for which *QE2* became perhaps best known during her career of nearly forty years.

From her outward appearance *QM2* is very much a deep-sea ocean liner, with the greater height of her hull's sides up to the open decks above, and extended length of her bow and stern decks forward and aft of the superstructure. She is in fact heavier and more robust than her predecessor *QE2*, at nearly twice the earlier ship's original size when completed in 1968. While her massive hull and powerful machinery have the stamina for

sustained North Atlantic service, this newest Cunard flagship also includes all of the features and services expected by today's luxury cruise clientele. These include a predominance of cabins with private verandas, multiple restaurants and a wide variety of entertainment facilities and leisure and sports activities, along with plenty of open deck spaces. *QM2* also boasts a number of unique features, notably the distinctive axial layout of her public rooms around a wide central promenade along the ship's centreline. She also boasts the world's only fully functional planetarium at sea. Her top-grade accommodations include eight two-storey duplex suites with spectacular views over the ship's stern from double-height panoramic windows and a further four single-level luxury suites forward that, with but the closing of a few doors and opening of others, can be combined into a single Royal Suite. In this guise the suite has its own curvilinear enclosed promenade space across the front of the ship two decks below the navigating bridge.

Although her size has already been eclipsed by others, *Queen Mary 2* remains a ship of singular identity and character befitting her status as the flagship of the world's longest-serving shipping line and today's only true North Atlantic express ocean liner. *PD*

1947-2010

*Queen Mary 2* **on her way out to sea in San Pedro harbor, Los Angeles, California** *(photograph), Stock Connection / SuperStock*

1132ft x 135ft x 33ft (345m x 41m x 10.1m) • 148,528 tons [GT] • Hull steel • Complement 1253, passengers 3056 • Built Chantiers de l'Atlantique, Saint-Nazaire, France, 2003

# B&Q Trimaran racing yacht 2004

Built by Boatspeed in Australia to a design by multihull expert Nigel Irens, the ocean-racing trimaran *B&Q* was launched with one objective – to set new solo speeds. In the hands of Ellen MacArthur she set a new record for a single-handed round-the-world voyage in 2005, crossing the finish line in 71 days, 14 hours, 18 minutes and 33 seconds, beating the previous time set by Francis Joyon.

Multihulls are inherently stable. They are much lighter than monohulls and therefore much faster in almost all wind conditions. However, they achieve this at a price. Unlike a monohull, if a multihull is flipped over or pitchpoles it cannot right itself. For Irens the challenge was to create a boat big enough

to give it longitudinal stability and lessen the risk of nose-diving while tackling the massive waves of the Southern Ocean and allowing the boat to maintain high speeds in rough conditions, but not so big that it compromised Ellen's ability to keep control of it. Her circumnavigation was a huge feat of endurance over 27,000 miles, during which she had to contend with technical problems, mountainous seas, icebergs and a near miss with a whale.

*B&Q* was subsequently bought by Oman Sail, renamed *Musandam*, and modified to accommodate a crew of five. In 2010 she was again put up for sale. Francis Joyon re-took his record in 2008 in another multihull designed by Nigel Irens. *AM*

**1947-2010**

**Ellen MacArthur on board the yacht *B&Q/Castorama* as she approaches the end of her non-stop solo circumnavigation attempt on 7 February 2005** (photograph). *Liot Vapillion / DPPI via Getty Images*

75.1ft x 53.5ft (22.9m x 16.3m) • 8.3 tons [D] • Hull carbon fibre composite • Complement 1 • Built Boatspeed, Australia, 2003

**369**

# Bulwark   Albion class LPD assault ship 2005

The strongest element of the Royal Navy's presence at the International Fleet Review in 2005 was the Amphibious Ready Group, consisting of the LPH *Ocean* and the two new LPDs, the sisters *Albion* and *Bulwark*. These ships, with their troop accommodation, landing craft and flight decks, provide a flexible response for any situations requiring land intervention from the sea, ranging from trouble hotspots to disaster relief. In 2006, for example, *Bulwark* evacuated 1300 people from Beirut at a time of impending conflict. *Bulwark*'s flight deck can accommodate two Sea King helicopters or a Chinook, while her four larger landing craft, capable of carrying main battle tanks, are launched from a floodable dock within the ship. An Assault Squadron of Royal Marines is permanently embarked. This type of ship was originally developed during the Second World War as the Landing Ship Dock, a type which proved so useful that it has been continuously developed and enlarged ever since. The illustration is a painting by Geoff Hunt, who was on board *Bulwark* on the occasion of the 2005 International Fleet Review. *GH*

**HMS *Bulwark* at the International Fleet Review, 28 June 2005** (oil on canvas), Geoff Hunt, 2005

579ft x 84ft x 20ft (176m x 25.6m x 6.1m) • 18,500 tons [D] • Hull steel • Armament 2 x CIWS, 2 x 20mm, four large and four small landing craft •
Complement 325 plus 300-700 troops • Built BAE Systems, Barrow-in-Furness, England, 2004

# Emma Mærsk   Container ship 2006

When delivered in 2006 from the Lindø shipyard near Odense in Denmark, the *Emma Mærsk* was the world's biggest container ship with a theoretical capacity of up to 14,500 TEU (Twenty-foot Equivalent Unit) containers. In practice, her capacity is limited to 11,000 because her owners calculate the average weight of a container at 14 tons. Capacity aside, the *Emma Mærsk* is a vessel of statistical superlatives – 397 metres long, 183 metres in beam and powered by a single mighty Wärtsilä-Sulzer diesel generating 109,000 horsepower (80,080 kW) to give a service speed of just over 25 knots. Notwithstanding her great capacity and power, thanks to sophisticated onboard technology, her crew numbers no more than 13. Such efficiency helps to make today's globalized economy possible, enabling consumer goods to be shipped en masse and at very low rates from the Far East to Europe. On the return leg of her maiden voyage from China, the *Emma Mærsk* made newspaper headlines as she was loaded to capacity with containers bringing Chinese-manufactured Christmas gifts for retailing across Northern Europe.

Container ships such as the *Emma Mærsk* play a vital – but usually hidden – part in an increasingly well-developed (and highly automated) global logistics system, involving vast container ports, motorways, railroads and distribution centres which, together, make our contemporary world of mass-manufacture and mass-consumerism possible. Indeed, her owner, the Copenhagen-headquartered A.P. Møller-Mærsk, claims to be the world's largest transport company, managing a global infrastructure consisting of 500 ships, nearly two million containers, several major container ports, an American railroad, a oil exploration division and retail outlets. *BP*

*1947-2010*

**Emma Mærsk** and the **Mærsk Malacca** arrive at the port of Bremerhaven, northern Germany *(photograph), 10 September 2006, Hero Lang / AFP / Getty Images*

1302ft x 184ft x 51ft (397m x 56m x 15.5m) • 170,974 tons [GT] • Hull steel • Complement 13 (with room for 30) • Built Odense Steel Shipyard Ltd, Denmark, 2006

# Freedom  Littoral combat ship 2006

The Littoral Combat Ship (LCS) is the first of a new family of surface ships for the US Navy. It is a fast, highly manoeuvrable, networked surface combat ship with a shallow draught, designed to operate in coastal waters to counter growing potential 'asymmetric' threats of coastal mines, quiet diesel submarines and small, fast armed boats carrying explosives and terrorists. It has a hangar large enough to accommodate two MH-60 Seahawk helicopters and a capacious flight deck, small boats can be launched and recovered from side doors or the stern ramp, and there is sufficient hull volume to deliver a small assault force with armoured vehicles to a roll-on, roll-off port facility. The LCS designs offer reduced air defence and surface-to-surface capabilities compared with a destroyer; instead the emphasis is on high speed and flexible mission module space. *Freedom* (LCS-1), unlike her General Dynamics trimiran competitor *Independence* (LCS-2), is a semi-planing steel monohull with an aluminium superstructure, powered by gas turbines and diesels driving four waterjets, which give the ship a top speed in excess of 45 knots. The core crew will normally be 40 seamen, usually joined by a mission package crew and an aviation detachment totalling some 75 men. Although the LCS programme has attracted criticism in Congress due to cost overruns, current plans are for 55 ships to be in service by 2020. *JJ*

**USS *Freedom* (LCS 1) conducts a replenishment at sea operation with the amphibious assault ship USS *Bonhomme Richard* (LHD 6)** *(photograph), 17 June 2010, US Navy/public domain*

378ft x 57.5ft x 12ft (115m x 17.5m x 3.7m) • 3000 tons [D] • Hull steel • Armament 1 x 57mm, 1 x RAM Surface-to-Air system, 2 x .50 cal machine guns, 2 helicopters • Complement 40 + 75 • Built Marinette Marine, Marinette, Wisconsin, USA, 2006

# Astute   Nuclear-powered attack submarine 2007

Built in the 176ft (51m) high Devonshire Dock Hall at BAE Systems Submarines, Barrow-in-Furness, HMS *Astute* is the first of up to six nuclear powered hunter-killer submarines replacing the Royal Navy's Trafalgar Class. Construction began in 2001, with completed sections being taken to the Dock Hall for assembly. Design problems and cost overrun have bedevilled the project and, despite innovative modular construction, *Astute* was launched four years late on 15 June 2007, a week after her naming ceremony.

Although smaller than the submarines of the USA and the Russian Federation, *Astute* is the largest and most powerful submarine ever built by the Royal Navy, displacing 7800 tons. She carries Tomahawk land attack cruise missiles with a range of more than 1000 nautical miles, and Spearfish heavyweight torpedoes for use against surface and submarine targets. Faster underwater than on the surface, she can reach any destination within 14 days, and her diving capability exceeds 984ft (300m). Optical periscopes have been superseded by two optronic masts that send data from thermal imaging cameras and television and video sensors back to console screens. The 2076 SONAR is the most advanced in the world, and the submarine's quietness and low magnetic signature make her extremely difficult to detect.

*Astute* is powered by a Rolls Royce PWR2 reactor with a 25-year life span that will never require refuelling. Coupled with the self-contained purification systems, this could theoretically allow the submarine to spend her entire career submerged. In practice, the need to replenish food stocks, dispose of waste, and rest the crew limits patrols to three months. *JH*

**HMS *Astute* sails up Gareloch on the Firth of Clyde to her new base at Faslane, in western Scotland** *(photograph), 20 November 20 2009, Andy Buchanan / AFP / Getty Images*

323ft x 37ft x 32.8ft (97m x 11.3m x 10m) • 7800 tons [D] • Hull steel • Armament 6 x 533mm (21in) torpedo tubes for 38 missiles; Tomahawk Cruise Missiles, Mk 24 Tigerfish, Mk 8 anti-ship torpedoes, Sub Harpoon anti-ship missiles; Mk 5 Stonefish or Mk 6 Sea Urchins, mines • Complement 98 • Built BAE Systems, Barrow-in-Furness, England, 2009

# Dragon  Type 45 destroyer 2008

HMS *Dragon* is one of the Royal Navy's latest Type 45 destroyers. This class has been designed as air defence ships, carrying missiles capable of destroying aircraft and other missiles 75 miles (120.7km) away, though they can undertake many other roles as well. The PAAMS surface to air missile system can engage eight targets simultaneously, while the advanced radar system is said to be capable of tracking all the aircraft landing or taking off at Heathrow, Orly and Brussels airports at once. Although classed as destroyers, these powerful ships are the size of Second World War cruisers. Despite this, modern design gives them stealth characteristics so that the ship's radar signature is that of a fishing trawler. The six ships of the class (*Daring*, *Dauntless*, *Diamond*, *Dragon*, *Defender* and *Duncan* ) have been constructed on the unit system, the complete front section at the Vosper Thornycroft yard in Portsmouth, the remaining 6 per cent by BAE Systems, Scotstoun. The picture is a painting by Geoff Hunt, completed entirely on location at the Vosper Thornycroft shipyard during two days in July 2007. Their entire shipbuilding complex is under cover and self-contained, forming a production-line process in which flat steel sheets are fed in at one end and completely fitted half-ships emerge at the other end. The front half-ship is transported by barge to be united with the rear half. *GH*

**Type 45 HMS *Dragon* building at VT, Portsmouth, 2007** *(oil on canvas), Geoff Hunt, 2007*

500ft x 70ft x 24ft (152.4m x 21.3m x  7.3m) • 8000 tons [D] • Hull steel • Armament 48 Aster 15/30 missiles, 1 x Mk 8 4.5in gun, 2 x 30mm Oerlikon, decoy systems, 1 x Westland Merlin helicopter • Complement 190 • Built BAE Systems, Portsmouth, England and Scotstoun, Clyde, Scotland, 2008

# Queen Elizabeth   Queen Elizabeth class aircraft carrier (CVF) 2010

Most naval commentators are approaching the subject of the Royal Navy's two new 65,000 ton Queen Elizabeth class aircraft carriers with a certain sense of déjà vu. Amidst the wrangling over cost and use which has taken place, the fact remains the last major attempt by Britain to build large American-style carriers ended in the 1966 Defence White Paper. As costs and tonnage spiralled they were cancelled, along with their escorts, to save money. Moreover, with the Royal Navy shaped to concentrate on anti-submarine warfare in the North Atlantic it was felt there would be little need for large carriers. Instead, the smaller Invincible class was procured.

Roll on a generation or two and, set against expensive military commitments in Afghanistan, the same criticisms are being laid against the Queen Elizabeth class. Such ire would seem somewhat blinkered and even misguided. At an estimated total cost of £5bn, when they enter service the new carriers will provide value for that investment over at least 30-40 years by contributing towards the achievement of British national strategic interests. As a maritime nation with maritime interests, Britain should possess a degree of maritime power in order to safeguard those interests – indeed, in today's globalised world, the majority of British imports and exports and vital fuel supplies are transported by sea.

In the past British interests were safeguarded by the ability to project credible and capable military assets across the globe and for much of the twentieth-century the western powers have benefitted from uncontested access to the world's shipping lanes. That cannot be guaranteed in the future with a resurgent Russian Navy, and the growing maritime capabilities and ambitions of China, India and Brazil. If Britain cannot safeguard her own interests is it worth taking the risk that other nations or even organisations like the EU do so?

During the past two decades the British political elite seem to have forgotten that Britain's interests are, and are increasingly so, maritime and global. The Queen Elizabeth class will play a key role in safeguarding them for future generations. *MR*

Artist's impression of the new Royal Navy aircraft carriers HMS *Queen Elizabeth* and HMS *Prince of Wales* (CGI), BAE Systems, 2010

931.8ft x 239.5ft x 36.1ft (284m x 73m x 11m) • 65,600 tons [D] • Hull steel • Armament 40 (50 full load) aircraft; 36 x F-35 Lightning II, 4 x Airborne Early Warning aircraft • Complement 600 (capacity 1450) • Built BAE Systems Surface Ships, Thales Group, Babcock Marine, England, 2008-2015

# Index of ships

A Conway Maritime book

First published in Great Britain in 2010 by Conway, an imprint of Anova Books Company Ltd.,
10 Southcombe Street, London, W14 0RA
www.anovabooks.com
www.conwaypublishing.com

© Conway Publishing, 2010
Introduction © Andrew Lambert, 2010

The authors and contributors have asserted their moral rights to be identified as the author(s) of this work.

ISBN 9781844860760

Distributed in the US and Canada by
Sterling Publishing Co., Inc
387 Park Avenue South
New York, NY 10016-8810

Cataloguing in Publication Data:
A CIP catalogue record of this book is available from the British Library.

Picture credits
Front cover: Hamburg-Amerika Line poster [detail], Henning Koeke, c. 1930 © Swim Ink 2, LLC/Corbis
Frontispiece: The first Battle of Schooneveld, 28 May 1673 (pen; grisaille on canvas), Willem van de Velde, the Elder, 1684 © National Maritime Museum, Greenwich, London (BHC0305)

Designed by John Heritage
Reproduction by Rival Colour Ltd.
Printed and bound by 1010 Printing International Ltd., China